The GREAT PARTNERSHIP

ALSO BY CHRISTIAN B. KELLER

Southern Strategies: Why the Confederacy Failed

Pennsylvania: A Military History
(with William A. Pencak and Barbara A. Gannon)

American Civil War: The Definitive Visual History
(with Wayne Hsieh, Robert Sandow, et. al.)

Chancellorsville and the Germans:
Nativism, Ethnicity, and Civil War Memory

Damn Dutch: Pennsylvania Germans at Gettysburg
(with David L. Valuska)

The GREAT PARTNERSHIP

Robert E. Lee, Stonewall Jackson, and the Fate of the Confederacy

CHRISTIAN B. KELLER

PEGASUS BOOKS
NEW YORK LONDON

THE GREAT PARTNERSHIP

Pegasus Books, Ltd.
148 West 37th Street, 13th Floor
New York, NY 10018

Copyright © 2019 Christian B. Keller

First Pegasus Books paperback edition May 2021
First Pegasus Books cloth edition July 2019

All maps by Hal Jespersen, www.cwmaps.com

Interior design by Maria Fernandez

All historical interpretations expressed in this book are solely the author's,
and do not officially reflect or represent those of the U.S. Army War College,
the U.S. Army, or the Department of Defense.

All rights reserved. No part of this book may be reproduced in whole or in part without
written permission from the publisher, except by reviewers who may quote brief excerpts
in connection with a review in a newspaper, magazine, or electronic publication; nor
may any part of this book be reproduced, stored in a retrieval system, or transmitted in
any form or by any means electronic, mechanical, photocopying, recording, or other,
without written permission from the publisher.

ISBN: 978-1-64313-604-2

10 9 8 7 6 5 4 3 2 1

Printed in the United States of America
Distributed by Simon & Schuster
www.pegasusbooks.com

For Kelley, and for Him

who guides my way

CONTENTS

INTRODUCTION

"A great national calamity has befallen us."

The late afternoon sun of May 10, 1863, was warm and pleasant, filtering through the young trees of the Virginia wilderness and creating a patchwork quilt of bright and dark spots on the forest floor. Here the light focused on a young fern, struggling to unfold itself into life, there it landed on a burned corpse or newly dug grave. Spring had come to central Virginia, but so had the war. Shattered rifles, shell fragments, broken canteens, and even the jagged remains of a drum littered the sides of the Richmond Stage Road, down which a small group of men were galloping full speed toward Fredericksburg. Those men had just been at the home of Thomas Coleman Chandler, who lived in a hamlet on the Richmond, Fredericksburg and Potomac Railroad called Guiney's Station. All that Sunday, they waited outside a small frame house on his estate and prayed for the man lying on the bed inside, offering supplications to the Almighty that he may be spared and return to duty. At 3:15 they found out that their prayers, and those of thousands more in the Army of Northern Virginia, had not been answered. General Thomas Jonathan "Stonewall" Jackson was dead. [1]

Just the day before, the ailing leader dispatched his friend and corps chaplain, the Reverend Beverly Tucker Lacy, from his bedside to army headquarters near Fredericksburg. His mission was to conduct Sunday morning worship for the troops, as usual. Lacy preferred to stay, but Jackson insisted: the spiritual welfare of the men was paramount, regardless of what happened to him. The chaplain dutifully complied, leading the service on the 10th to a flock of 1800 soldiers—and their army commander, Robert E. Lee. The great victory at Chancellorsville had been achieved primarily by Jackson's smashing flank attack on May 2, and now, at the height of his military success, Lee faced the possibility that his most trusted lieutenant and adviser might soon leave his side. Hearing of Jackson's worsening condition, Lee asked Lacy to express "my affectionate regards, and say to him: he has lost his left arm but I my right arm." That was three days ago, when Jackson, his amputated arm healing nicely, had first displayed the troubling signs of a secondary infection—pneumonia. Now, despite fervent prayer and the best medical care in the Confederacy, Lacy had to admit to the commanding general that the end was near. The normally stoic Lee was surprised and visibly shaken at the turn of events. "Surely General Jackson must recover," he told Lacy before the church service. "God will not take him from us, now that we need him so much." His faith in his subordinate's recovery seemingly strengthened by the chaplain's sermon, Lee approached Lacy afterward and said, "I trust you will find him better. When a suitable occasion offers, tell him that I prayed for him last night as I never prayed." These were brave words spoken by a brave man and devoted Christian, but Lacy saw through them. Lee could say no more in sight of the troops, and quickly "turned away in overpowering emotion."[2]

The riders, their horses fatigued at the long, hard run from Guiney's Station, reined in at Lee's headquarters about 5:00 and, hats in hand, approached the commanding general's tent. How exactly they conveyed their disturbing news, and what reaction Lee may have exhibited, is unknown, but the response from the soldiers in the ranks was immediate as the word spread. "The sounds of merriment died away as if the Angel of Death himself had flapped his muffled wings over the troops. A silence profound, mournful, stifling, and oppressive as a funeral pall" descended over the camps. Grizzled veterans of The Seven Days, Antietam, and Fredericksburg, some of whom had even fought with Jackson in the Valley, cried like babies. The shock to the living body of the army was palpable, according to this eyewitness. Another remembered, "that evening the news went abroad, and a great sob swept over the Army of Northern Virginia; it was the heartbreak of the Confederacy." Indeed it was. Lee managed to restrain his own immense sadness in a simple message to Richmond. "It becomes my melancholy duty to announce to you the death of General Jackson." He continued for a few brief sentences that described the transport of the body to the capital and then abruptly ended the wire. The next day, he issued General Orders No. 61 to the army in an attempt to assuage the grief hanging over it, but the message's tone left no doubt that Lee himself was still in shock: "The daring, skill, and energy of this great and good soldier, by decree of an all wise Providence, are now lost to us. But while we mourn his death, we feel that his spirit still lives, and will inspire the whole army with his indomitable courage and unbroken confidence in God as our hope and our strength. . . . Let officers and soldiers emulate his invincible determination to do everything in the defense of our beloved country." Having duly erected this bold public front for the benefit of others, privately the army commander could not check his emotions. When he attempted to speak about Jackson to General William N. Pendleton that same day, Lee broke down in tears and had to excuse himself. The strong religious faith that helped cement the bond between Lee and Jackson doubtless comforted Lee now in his moment of greatest despair, and he wished the entire army to know its palliative effects. Yet his prayers and those of countless others had not saved Jackson, and his death left a great void—one with strategic consequences for the cause Lee defended. Privately he confided to his son, Custis, "It is a terrible loss. I do not know how to replace him." On May 11, President Jefferson Davis probably reinforced Lee's dread with a simple telegram: "A great national calamity has befallen us." Faith would help Lee move forward personally, but the death of Jackson was a professionally mortal blow from which the Confederate chieftain, and the Confederacy, would never recover.[3]

The often discussed, over-romanticized, and well-explored relationship between Robert E. Lee and Stonewall Jackson may initially appear to be a subject of little interest today, especially in a world in which things Confederate have fallen out of vogue and social and cultural interpretations of the American Civil War attract the attention of most scholars. Although the last dual history of the generals was published several decades ago, one might ask why yet another book on rebel military leaders, about whom we apparently already know everything we could possibly want to understand, is necessary? It is a worthy question, but like good books written about Abraham Lincoln or Gettysburg, two subjects also seemingly exhausted but which inspire new publications every year, fresh interpretation based on new historical evidence and argumentation provide the answers. Certainly, immense popular interest remains in both Lee and Jackson—they still stand as the chief Confederate icons and as such will always attract attention, good and bad. Thus the more we know about them the better informed we will be when their names arise in private and public discourse. More important, though, the generals offer us today, in our 21st-century world of technological complexity, digital interconnectedness, and political and social uncertainty, an example of the lasting power and resonance of human relationships. People still make things happen in the world, just as they did in the 19th century. People rely on friends, colleagues, and even enemies to help them understand their environment. And leaders of people still make decisions that affect the happiness, careers, financial well-being, and existence of their followers. Relationships among leaders are therefore still the most important fundamental foundations for long term success, whether that be for armies, businesses, or nations. The relationship between Lee and Jackson, at a basic level, tells us about the significance of leader relationships, how they are created and ideally function, and how devastating it can be when they disintegrate.

Senior leaders—those at the very top of their organizations—are charged with nothing less than the survival of their enterprise. If they fail to make the right decisions at the right time, dire consequences tend to result, and the very continuation of their organization may be jeopardized. Also known as *strategic leaders*, these individuals must establish a consensus for their vision, grow and energize subordinates, and develop and exploit opportunities that finally resolve major problems. They cannot afford the luxury of mistakes and must work hard with others at their level to avoid them, proactively manage unsolvable conflicts, and achieve organizational goals in the short, medium, and long term. These are difficult tasks and can weigh heavy on leader relationships. More is generally needed to fortify them at the higher levels than simple professional competence and collegiality. Friendships based on common, immutable bonds often provide the glue that keep senior leader relationships intact, and thus ensure better decisions are made for the good of the country, company, or community.[4]

At the heart of this book are four historical theses: first, that the Lee-Jackson command team was professionally successful because it was rooted in personal friendship underpinned by trust and shared religious faith. Initially the personal relationship was weak, long-distance, and tentative, and was strained by Jackson's poor showing during the Seven Days battles around Richmond in June 1862. But by the end of the winter of 1863 it had grown into a powerful bond that cemented the already-strong professional relationship, even enhancing it. Second, that it was within this unique relationship that the most successful elements of Confederate strategy in the Eastern Theater first germinated, were operationally implemented, and, with Jackson's death, permanently stymied. Jackson, in essence, became Lee's chief strategic adviser as well as his preferred operational lieutenant. (Lee in turn was Jefferson Davis's primary source of strategic advice, a point well substantiated in secondary literature.) Third, Jackson was himself a strategic-level leader, a general who thought early in the war about how to win it for the Confederacy, offering numerous suggestions to Lee, the president, and others at ranks higher than his own, and even dabbled in policy making through his relationships with congressmen. And fourth, with Stonewall Jackson's death following the Chancellorsville Campaign in May 1863 the Confederacy suffered a strategic inflection point, a contingency that held momentous implications. Spanning all four historical arguments is a larger observation that has significance for political, military, and business leaders today and in the future: the command relationship between chief leader and chief adviser is supremely important, especially at the highest levels of responsibility, because it is within the boundaries of that association that the best strategic ideas—the ones that win wars and save failing corporations—are created. Every senior leader needs a trustworthy adviser or a group of trusted advocates. When that relationship is founded on personal friendship or religious faith, it is strengthened. When it is absent or broken, the implications can be grave.[5]

In war, whether it be modern or historical, there are theoretically several levels of command and leadership, each of which affects the others. Occasionally, events occur that witness a conflation of the levels of war—what is called a nexus point—whereby tactical actions, for instance, may determine operational outcomes, which in turn might strongly affect theater strategy or national strategy. The history of the Civil War demonstrates all these levels of war were at play just as they are today, and although its leading participants may not have used the same nomenclature as modern practitioners, they implicitly understood the different layers of command and control as they existed at the time and had at least a commonsense understanding of how they interacted. As in modern war, however, the Confederacy's senior commanders made mistakes, sometimes fusing the levels together accidentally or erroneously applying ideas and concepts workable at one level to another. This was due in part to the weak theoretical education they received at West Point in the antebellum years and to the state of military theory at the time, which was in substantial flux, with important works such as Carl von Clausewitz's *On War* not yet translated into English and Baron Antoine-Henri de Jomini's *The Art of War* taught only in watered-down form. We should not fault them for their foibles and errors, however; the leaders of the Union and the Confederacy both made the decisions they thought best based on what they then knew combined with their personal experiences, personalities, and command structures, much as we do today.[6]

Grand strategy—the careful integration of national diplomatic, informational, military, and economic strategies into a coherent, long term "super strategy" with grandiose, possibly world-altering designs—was unknown to them, but all the other levels were not only thought about, considered, and implemented at various times in diverse manners, but were also altered and adapted as the contextual realities of the war shifted. President Davis, assisted ostensibly but not consistently by the secretaries of war and the chairmen of the most powerful military-affiliated committees in Congress, operated and decided at the *policy* level, making national decisions such as fighting the war to achieve independence, creating geographic departments, instituting conscription, and ultimately submitting to defeat. At the *national military strategy* level, Davis, again along with the various war secretaries but often including Lee and other theater commanders, discussed and implemented major ideas that affected all three theaters of war, such as whether to fight the war primarily from a defensive or offensive approach or some combination in between (the latter organically developed by mid-1862), which branch of service would be allocated what percentage of scarce resources—the army obviously winning out over the fledgling Confederate navy—and which theater of war would take precedence over the others. Resources: men, money, materiel, and national transportation capabilities governed much at this level. *Theater strategy* referred to the concepts and ideas implemented broadly within a given theater of war, such as the Eastern or Western, and was generally determined by the major departmental or army commanders in that theater in concert both with the national command authority in Richmond and trusted operational-level subordinates, such as Jackson and General James Longstreet. Lee's primary strategic responsibility rested at this layer of war, but as Davis's official and de facto adviser he ascended to the national military strategic level and as army commander descended daily to the *operational* level. This theoretical space was where major campaigns were planned, altered, executed, or scuttled, such as Jackson's Valley Campaign, the Second Manassas or Sharpsburg campaigns, or Lee's attempt to trap General Pope's forces between the Rapidan and Rappahannock rivers in early August 1862. Operations were characterized by major maneuvers and actions of specific armies, and could witness one great battle or a series of battles before one ended and the next one began. How operations concluded often set the course for future theater and even national military strategy, sometimes very quickly, as in the case of the Seven Days and Gettysburg Campaign. The *tactical* level of war dealt with the planning and execution of specific battles within a given operation or campaign. It pertained, for instance, to where and when certain corps or divisions were sent in an engagement in pursuit of battlefield victory, such as Jackson's famous flank march at Chancellorsville or Longstreet's attack on August 30, 1862, at Second Manassas. Both Lee and Jackson by default had to dwell often at this level, but a dramatic tactical success offered operational, theater-strategic, and even national strategic possibilities. On a theoretical basis, that is why Lee and Jackson constantly pursued an aggressive method in most of their battles. Passively awaiting the enemy's blows on the defense not only mitigated against tactical victory, as Napoleon noted, but also made translating that success into an operational or higher-level victory less likely. Both men understood this on an intrinsic level, as did the great Federal military leaders, Grant, Sherman, and Sheridan.[7]

For a weaker nation at war, it is imperative to take one of two possible national military approaches: either adopt a patient, low-energy national military strategy that conserves available resources (also known as *means*) utilizing defensive theater strategies and operations (also known as *ways*) highlighting the use of small regular units, guerrillas and irregulars, and foreign aid to achieve policy and strategy objectives (also known as *ends*); or strike hard, fast, and decisively with all available conventional military means in powerful offensives designed to knock the stronger adversary off balance, convince its government that the war will be too costly, and achieve the ends in that manner. Practically all the historical war efforts of weaker powers over time have utilized one or the other approach. The Carthaginians adopted option #2 in the Second Punic War against the Romans and almost won it under Hannibal's leadership; Alexander tried it and defeated the Persian Empire but failed with it in India due to inadequate means; Frederick the Great won the First Silesian War of 1740–42 using a similar approach but almost lost his kingdom in subsequent wars incorporating it with insufficient means; Napoleon marched to victory against the Austrians, Russians, and Prussians in 1805 and 1806 with a comparable national military strategy; and Winfield Scott, with whom Lee served in the Mexican War, succeeded in his march on Mexico City employing an analogous theater strategy, albeit with a very small army.

On the other hand, Washington adopted option #1 in the Middle Colonies during the American Revolution, carefully choosing where he committed the understrength Continental Army and picking, from 1777–1780, smaller fights with isolated British units whenever possible, relying on irregulars and a small core of conventional units in the Southern Theater until 1781. Spain, its armies defeated repeatedly by Napoleon's marshals early on, also relied primarily on a guerrilla war strategy after 1808 in conjunction with a small regular force and Wellington's British army, ultimately expelling the French occupiers. Even the Confederacy's own Trans-Mississippi Theater, under the leadership of Major General Thomas

C. Hindman, tried a guerrilla-war theater strategy in 1862, but inadequate means, poor internal communications, and weak leadership doomed it to failure. In the East, Jackson immediately encouraged an offensive into the North using all available troops, with an eye toward not only demoralizing the northern population and government, but also wrecking its logistical and economic means, thus preventing it from making war. He never relented from this advocacy. Lee, resistant to such a "hard war" approach and more readily aware of rebel war-making limitations, nonetheless quickly came to realize that only an offensive theater strategy that attempted destruction of the principal enemy army, or at least repeatedly defeated it to the point the North gave up, would suffice to achieve Confederate ends. Wearing the heavy headdress of theater and army command simultaneously, he could not wantonly engage in Jackson's version of strategic radicalism and often found himself stymied by Union offensives he had to parry, but agreed that bringing the war north was necessary for final victory. Both generals understood that a national military strategy predicated solely on defense, employing irregulars to a large degree, and allowing the large Federal armies to penetrate the heart of the Confederacy, would simply not succeed in their theater and would lose the South the war in short order. As most historians now agree, Southern political, cultural, and societal institutions mitigated against it as well. [8]

Only option #2, modified as it was by the availability of troops, supplies, and other means and the actions of the enemy, was ever considered. Those caveats often made the theater strategy of the East under Lee's leadership appear as if it was primarily defensive, but Lee's intent, advised by Jackson, was always to attack the enemy, even if the seat of war remained in Virginia. To a large degree, President Davis agreed. Initially he responded to intense political pressure from state governors and national legislators in 1861 to early 1862 to preserve their states' territorial integrity, developing a national strategic approach called the "perimeter defense" that attempted to defend all Confederate soil from Union invasions. But military disasters borne of this strategy in the West coupled with a realization of dwindling Southern means impressed upon him by mid-1862 that offensive theater strategies, when possible, were preferable. Most of them would have to be employed while still fighting in the Southern states because of geographic and economic restraints and Union numerical superiority, but those realities did not detract from their offensive strategic essence.[9]

By the winter of 1862–1863 the Eastern Theater of operations, i.e., the states of the Confederacy east of the Appalachian Mountains, had become the most strategically critical theater for Confederate hopes for national independence. Scholars have fiercely debated the point, but most now argue that if the war was to be won, it needed to occur in that theater, and that meant the Union's principal field army, the Army of the Potomac, would have to be decisively defeated.[10] Robert E. Lee had tried, with Jackson's assistance, throughout the spring, summer, and fall of 1862 to effect that result, but several good opportunities eluded him. Civil War armies were notoriously difficult to destroy in the field, a reality that Lee and his command team, ultimately consisting of Jackson, Longstreet, and James Ewell Brown (J.E.B.) Stuart, painfully came to understand. Time and again, during the Seven Days, before and after Second Manassas, and at Fredericksburg and Chancellorsville, they had realized the challenges inherent in transforming tactical/operational victories into strategic ones. In each of these successful campaigns, Lee-Jackson discussions, both private and in consultation with other leaders, molded Confederate theater strategy attempting to remedy the problem.

Jackson's early strategic thoughts in late 1861 into the spring of 1862 about raiding the North and bringing a punishing war to the enemy were thought pragmatically impossible by most in the Confederate national command authority in Richmond. Yet they were not only worth Lee's consideration, who was then ensconced as Davis's military adviser and de facto general-in-chief, but also reflected the strategic realities contextually facing the Confederacy: the loss of much of Tennessee, the Mississippi River Valley, and northern Arkansas by mid-1862 meant that recovery in the Western and Trans-Mississippi theaters was unlikely. There, the Confederacy could only hope to delay the inevitable, but in the East the war could feasibly be brought to a successful conclusion. Northern, Southern, and European public opinion focused on the East and could be more strongly influenced by events on the battlefield there than in the West; Union civilian morale could be directly affected by damaging raids and thus endanger Abraham Lincoln's political base in future elections; and vital mining, transportation, and manufacturing centers in Pennsylvania could be disrupted, thereby undermining Federal logistical power. Jackson's correspondence with Lee before he left the Shenandoah Valley to join in the Peninsula Campaign in June 1862 revealed a strategically forward-thinking mind, one that quickly made its mark on the future commander of the Army of Northern Virginia and would continue to influence Lee's own strategic and operational thought for the remainder of the war. But Lee's personal preferences as a leader combined with the exigencies of the strategic-political arena he had to operate in—managing at once Davis's expectations and leading the Confederacy's primary eastern army—meant that he could not immediately and unconditionally accept Jackson's strategic thoughts. The Union army and the poor state of Confederate logistics also dictated many of his actions.

Deferential, loyal, and frank, Jackson first impressed Lee as a military professional who could effortlessly follow his intent and achieve operational objectives. Sometimes late but never failing, the Valley General earned Lee's respect through his performance in the Cedar Run, Second Manassas, and Sharpsburg campaigns, ensuring his lackluster performance in the Seven Days was viewed as an anomaly. Even then, however, he began to confer regularly with Lee and started the process of building personal trust. That trust was buoyed by a shared devotion to evangelical Protestantism. Although approaching their Christianity from different denominational perspectives, Jackson's unswerving adherence to God's laws and spreading of the gospel among his troops made a strong impression upon the deeply religious Lee, who, by the winter of 1862–1863, was attending worship services with Jackson. The Reverend Beverly Tucker Lacy, an old friend of Jackson's brought in by the general to serve as his corps chaplain, and the spiritual reforms they wrought, were instrumental to the development of this religious bond between Lee and his subordinate. This connection, in turn, strengthened what had become a strong personal friendship during the winter encampment outside of Fredericksburg.

By the time of the Chancellorsville Campaign, Jackson had superseded Longstreet as Lee's primary lieutenant, and along with Stuart, was integral in helping the commanding general achieve victory over the Federals against long odds. Yet fickle chance intervened in the woods on the night of

May 2, 1863, as it had so many times both for and against Lee in previous campaigns. Shot accidentally by his own men, Stonewall was dropped twice from the litter carrying him to the rear, and, surviving the amputation of his left arm, succumbed to pneumonia ten days later. It was a personally crushing blow for Lee, who lost not only a man who had become a close friend but also his chief strategic adviser and battlefield operator. The damage done to the Confederate war effort was perceived by nearly all in the Confederacy, from Jefferson Davis all the way down to common citizens in Texas and even little children. Regardless of biased postwar Confederates, some of whom like former Jackson staff officers R. L. Dabney and Henry Kyd Douglas attempted to use his death as a "Lost Cause" excuse for rebel defeat, Jackson's sudden demise was recognized by Southerners in 1863 as a strategic turning point in the war. This reality became startlingly clear in the ensuing Pennsylvania Campaign, when it was apparent that Jackson's absence left a gaping hole in Lee's command team and badly impaired its efficacy. A tragic cascade of secondary and third-order effects impacted the results of the operation and ensured the failure of Lee's new theater strategy. That, in turn, hastened the final defeat of the Confederacy.

Some final thoughts are in order before we return to 1862, a year pregnant with strategic contingency for the future of the young Confederate nation. Military theorists and practitioners, political and business executives, and leaders of any ilk looking for insights drawn from the Lee-Jackson relationship will profit from reading the appendix, where I summarize many of the key points elucidated in the text and offer "so what" takeaways for current and future senior leaders. Scholars interested in deeply exploring debates in the extant literature, the locations of primary sources, and recommendations for further reading, are kindly directed to the notes, which go into substantial detail about certain topics that many may find of interest. I purposefully left out of the text of this introduction a meticulous examination of key works on Confederate strategy, biographies of Lee and Jackson, and histories of the great campaigns to entice the interest of the educated layperson, someone who knows the basic parameters of the American Civil War and possibly even those of Lee's and Jackson's exploits in 1862–1863. In graduate school and even today when I read about this war and other historical conflicts, exhaustive analyses of historiographical arguments—some of which do matter, actually, for the accurate retelling of good history—nonetheless remind me of the old adage about cooked fish and houseguests. After about three days both need to be thrown out. I have always thought a parallel rule should apply to literature reviews embedded in greater historical narratives: after about three lines they need to be thrown into the notes. So there they are for anyone interested.

The book follows a chronological path forward with occasional flashbacks inserted to emphasize key themes in the Lee-Jackson relationship and reinforce the major theses. Some readers may wish certain historical incidents receive greater or lesser emphasis, and others may not like the admixture of narrative and analysis. I believed it important to include both as we trace the evolution of the generals' interactions, thoughts, and deeds. I took artistic license in a few isolated sections to better recreate the historical backdrop they operated in or illustrate how they would have appeared or behaved. In no way have I departed from the evidence contained in available primary and secondary sources; if, for example, I inserted some details we cannot be certain about at a specific point in time, like facial expressions, I derived my narrative from (especially) primary accounts documenting those particulars during an earlier historical episode. In most instances the factors behind such issues are addressed in the notes and most scholars should be satisfied with my explanations.

Regarding the source material itself, it is important for readers to understand that wartime letters, diaries, and newspaper editorials hold significantly greater interpretative value and reliability than post–Civil War letters, memoirs, articles, and books written by ex-Confederates. The latter category unfortunately is numerically larger than the former, and although I relied strongly on wartime archival and newspaper sources, the postwar material does comprise a greater number of readily accessible historical accounts. But in the sub-realm of Confederate history the historian must be cautious. What is known as the Lost Cause permeates many of these sources. First coined by Edward A. Pollard, editor of the influential *Richmond Examiner* in his 1866 book of the same name, the term was in common parlance throughout the last third of the 19th century to denote the fallen Confederacy, but has come to represent in modern times the overly reverent mythologizing of the Confederate leadership, the rebel soldier, loyal Southern women, dutiful slaves, and the valiant but doomed effort for independence against, as Lee himself put it in his farewell address at Appomattox, the "overwhelming numbers and resources" of the Union. These themes, along with the shunting aside of slavery as the underlying cause of the war, helped white Southerners come to grips with defeat but played fast and loose with history and are detectable in many (although not all) postwar accounts written by former rebels. The practice of unobjectively idolizing the saintly Lee or the flawless Jackson, or both, unfortunately contaminated a good number of the accounts describing the generals and their relationship, making the historical reality difficult to discern from postwar fantasy. Among the most blatantly worshipful were the generals' former staff officers, who sometimes vied with each other in their claims of greatness for their former chiefs. For many years there was even an acrimonious rivalry, evident in the historical record, between the acolytes of Lee and Jackson that, to our modern sensibilities, borders on the ridiculous. [11]

Nonetheless, the reality of the Lost Cause taint in many postwar accounts written by the generals' staff officers and others close to them—sources that necessarily had to be consulted for this book—means that most of their formal publications should be viewed with a grain of salt and their words prudently evaluated in the context in which they were written (i.e., the 1870s–1890s). Personal letters tended to be less overtly infected, and therefore I tried to consult them whenever possible, but even so the writer's partiality and foggy memory may have been factors that intervened in their historicity. Jackson's followers, for example, at times ascribed to him superhuman powers of generalship and intuition and Lee's closest associates defended his every action as perfect, while both groups denigrated Longstreet and blamed him for ultimate defeat. Armed as I was with a skeptical eye, throughout the text readers will notice occasional references to the reliability of certain individuals' accounts and should rest assured that in all cases I thought carefully about the likelihood of prevarication, overgeneralization, and personal bias in these source materials. Scholars interested in deeper evaluations should consult the notes. If they find no caveats or elaborations, I either believed the veracity of the source strong enough to stand on its own (for that particular section of the text) or, perhaps, made an error in interpretation. Doubtless, some will take issue with my judgment, claiming for instance I relied too heavily on the correspondence of Jedediah Hotchkiss and Hunter McGuire, Jackson's topographer and personal surgeon, or on other ex-Confederates, or on early secondary sources like the works of Douglas Southall Freeman that gleaned much from them. To such critics I confess neither perfection in professional historical discernment nor knowledge of all contextual factors that may have influenced the postwar sources. But I promise I did my utmost to evaluate all accounts, both primary and secondary, with a scrupulous eye.

Finally, this book is indisputably a work of military history focused on the historical realities of how Robert E. Lee and Stonewall Jackson thought about, planned, and executed military strategy, operations, and, occasionally, tactics. It focuses on the large questions attached to their relationship that deal with strategic theory, leadership, faith, and the fate of the Confederate nation. It does not attempt nor should be misconstrued as a commentary on the cause for which they fought. If I have done my job well, the reader will follow the narrative mindful that these men did indeed fight to dissolve the Union and preserve the antebellum Southern way of life, which included slavery, but will not judge them for that; instead, he/she will evaluate them as military decision-makers, people, and leaders of a team trying to achieve a common goal that proved elusive. Putting aside modern political sensitivities will allow him or her to realize how much we can yet learn from Lee and Jackson, two men who were, after all, human like us. But they were also leaders—generals who, together, created a partnership unique in the American Civil War and one that still offers much to those who aspire to lead.

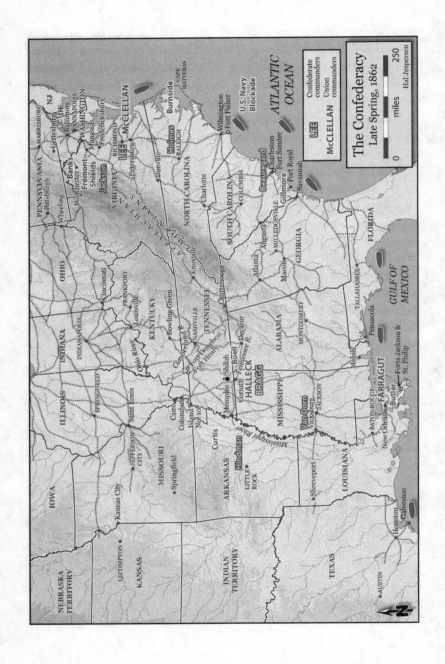

The Confederacy
Late Spring, 1862

LEE   Confederate commanders
McCLELLAN   Union commanders

0   miles   250

Hal Jespersen

ATLANTIC OCEAN

GULF OF MEXICO

U.S. Navy Blockade

CAPE HATTERAS

Burnside
Holmes
McClellan
LEE

Wilmington
Fort Fisher

RALEIGH
NORTH CAROLINA

Charlotte

SOUTH CAROLINA
COLUMBIA
Beauregard
Charleston
Fort Sumter
Gillmore
Port Royal
Savannah

Augusta
MILLEDGEVILLE
GEORGIA
Macon
Atlanta
MONTGOMERY
ALABAMA

FLORIDA
TALLAHASSEE

Pensacola
Mobile

Forts Jackson &
St. Philip
FARRAGUT
Butler
New Orleans
BATON ROUGE
JACKSON
VanDorn
MISSISSIPPI
Vicksburg

LOUISIANA
Shreveport

TEXAS

AUSTIN

Houston
Galveston

INDIAN TERRITORY

ARKANSAS
Hindman
LITTLE ROCK

Curtis

MISSOURI
Springfield
Saint Louis
JEFFERSON CITY

Kansas City

KANSAS
LECOMPTON

NEBRASKA TERRITORY

IOWA

ILLINOIS
SPRINGFIELD

Cairo
Columbus
Island No. 10
Memphis
Corinth   Shiloh
HALLECK
BRAGG
Tennessee R.
Decatur

TENNESSEE
NASHVILLE
Fort Donelson
Fort Henry
Buell
Cumberland R.

Chattanooga
Knoxville

APPALACHIAN MOUNTAINS

KENTUCKY
Bowling Green
FRANKFORT
Louisville
Ohio River

INDIANA
INDIANAPOLIS

OHIO
Cincinnati

Wheeling
VIRGINIA
Pittsburgh

PENNSYLVANIA
HARRISBURG
Gettysburg
Banks
Fremont
Shields
Jackson
Winchester

MD
DE
NJ
Baltimore
ANNAPOLIS
WASHINGTON
Manassas
Fredericksburg
RICHMOND
Petersburg
Danville

LEE   McCLELLAN

Mississippi River

N

ONE

"I am willing to follow him blindfolded."

LEE, JACKSON, AND CONFEDERATE STRATEGIC IMPERATIVES

It had been a long, dusty, tiring ride from Fredericks Hall, fourteen hours and fifty-two miles total, with a few stops at local plantations to exchange worn-out horses. Three aides came along, offering more in the way of moral support than companionship, because the general had that determined look about him, bent on completing his mission. There had been no time for pleasantries or lingering along the way, not even a cold biscuit, which on this hot, 84° day would have been most welcome. Time was of the essence. When, around 3:00 P.M., the small party from the Valley Army finally reached their destination, the Widow Dabbs house on the Nine Mile Road just a mile and half northeast of Richmond, his staff officers dismounted with the joy of anticipated rest. A comfortable yard with thick, green grass beckoned both man and beast, but before either could enjoy it, Stonewall Jackson was off his horse, bounding up the wooden steps to the two-story farmhouse. He was there to see Robert E. Lee, new commander of the Army of Northern Virginia.[1]

1

It was the first time the two would meet as Confederate generals. Both native-born Virginians and graduates of West Point in different years, they may have encountered each other in the early 1840s, when Jackson was a cadet and Lee a commissioned officer on the 1844 examination board. They crossed paths during the war with Mexico, the elder Lee once inspecting fortifications for a section of batteries in which the young Jackson was an officer, but neither man made a noticeable impression on the other. Both served in military colleges after the war, Lee as superintendent of the Military Academy and Jackson as a professor at the Virginia Military Institute, and they both witnessed the hanging of John Brown in 1859. As military professionals from the same state they certainly knew each other, but were only acquaintances, their lives and careers taking strongly divergent courses in the late 1850s, with Lee posted around the country at various army installations and Jackson settling in to his teaching routine at Lexington. Then came the election of 1860. The states of the Deep South united in fear regarding the intentions of president-elect Abraham Lincoln and his Republican Party, their leaders convinced they heard the croak of doom for the "peculiar institution" of slavery and the agricultural and caste-based Southern society that was dependent on it. One by one, in the fateful secession winter of 1860–1861, most of the southern half of the United States left the country and formed a new nation, the Confederate States of America. War appeared imminent. [2]

Lee and Jackson followed these monumental events with great concern, but it was not until the secession of their home state from the federal Union in April 1861, in response to Lincoln's appeal for 75,000 volunteers to suppress the rebellion, that they were dragged into the burgeoning conflict. Almost immediately Virginia called on her cadre of trained military officers to defend her and raise troops, and neither man failed to heed the summons, setting in motion centrifugal forces that would inexorably bring them together. The "blue light" Presbyterian commoner, born in the Appalachian hill country, and the blue-blood Episcopalian aristocrat, born in the Tidewater, shared a devotion to God and the Old Dominion that trumped loyalty to country, a spiritual and temporal allegiance that was foundational, unyielding, and unquestionable. In that they were no different from thousands of their future soldiers who followed their states into the

Confederacy, but unlike most of them, these two men were leaders, whose abilities destined them to command.[3]

It was not a foregone conclusion that either would rise so quickly. Providence had cleared the way, creating opportunities denied to others. Jackson, for instance, had been at the right place at the right time to make the decision to stand his brigade "like a stone wall" at First Manassas in July, thereby winning his first moment of national fame, a major generalship, and a nickname: "Stonewall." By virtue of his sterling prewar reputation and high rank in the U.S. Army, Lee was given command of all Virginia forces days after secession, a position that placed him near the top of the new Confederate command hierarchy after the national capital moved to Richmond, and helped recommend him to president Jefferson Davis, who appointed him his personal military adviser. True, the two had also suffered professional setbacks and discouragement, both ironically in the western mountains (Lee at Cheat Mountain and Jackson in the Romney Campaign), but in so doing they preserved the trust of policy makers who perceived their inherent qualities and retained their services. Now the events of the still-young American Civil War thrust the generals together, necessarily forcing a military partnership that would soon foster a deeper, profound friendship with vast strategic implications. June 23, 1862, therefore found them newly elevated, professionally recovered, and on the cusp of ventures their new nation required them jointly to pursue. Twelve months of official correspondence, some of it interspersed with compliments and well-wishes, had bred a congenial familiarity and mutual respect between them. "Old Jack," as his soldiers called him, had just concluded a remarkably successful campaign in the Shenandoah, perfectly aligning with Lee's strategic thinking.[4]

One of the commanding general's young staff officers, perhaps Charles Marshall or Walter Taylor, greeted Jackson at the door, and politely asked him to wait a few minutes until Lee could see him. Not sure what do with himself, he went back outside where exhaustion set in. "Leaning over the yard-paling," his sun-bleached kepi cap pulled down over his eyes and his head bent over, as if ready to sleep, Stonewall was barely recognizable in his simple, threadbare uniform when his brother-in-law, Major General Daniel Harvey (D. H.) Hill, rode into the yard. "He raised himself up as I dismounted," Hill recalled, and looked "dusty, travel-worn, and apparently very tired," but immediately greeted him with a warmth that belied his humorless, taciturn reputation. Hill was honestly surprised to see him here, believing as did many others North and South that Stonewall was still in the Valley, pursuing the defeated Union generals Nathaniel Banks and John C. Frémont, whom he had recently thrashed at Winchester and Cross Keys. So carefully had Lee arranged for the transfer of Jackson's 17,500-man army across Virginia and so secretly had Stonewall begun the movement that almost no one, even in Richmond, knew he was there. That was just as secretive Old Jack liked it; the less known about him and his men's whereabouts, the better.[5]

The two walked up the steps and into the house, where Lee shook their hands and welcomed them into his simple office. A table, a couple chairs, a desk, and a few furnishings accented the room, and other than some "refreshments, courteously tendered by General Lee" himself, there was little about the place bespeaking the impeccable lineage and decorum that characterized its occupant. For a moment, the man recently labeled "the King of Spades" for all the entrenchments he ordered dug around the capital, and the man termed "an enthusiastic fanatic" by one of his subordinates, exchanged glances. The fifty-five-year-old son of Revolutionary War hero Henry "Light Horse Harry" Lee bore the marks of a Virginia gentleman, with a high, receding hairline of curly, gray hair, white-gray beard, high cheekbones, and dark eyes that evinced at once a gentle demeanor and sharp intelligence. Solidly built, at 5 feet, 10 inches tall, his fitted uniform appeared "elegant" on his physique, and he carried himself with a poise only the high-born could master. Yet, Jackson must have noticed, there was not an ounce of pretension about this man, but instead an air of humility and normalcy that only made him appear more graceful, more impressive.[6]

Declining all other libations, Stonewall happily accepted a glass of milk, and if Lee thought any less of him because of his bedraggled appearance or simple tastes, there is no record of it. The new chief of the principal Confederate field army in the East was himself, at heart, a modest man. He knew full well how far Jackson had come to be here, and in an age of horse-borne transport (for train travel in the South could not always be relied upon for those with tight schedules), dust and grime after such a long journey were to be expected. On a normal day, Old Jack looked more like a teamster than a general in his faded, worn-out uniform and cap, over-sized boots, and large hands, with sun-bronzed face framed by a "receding forehead" and a bushy brown beard. On this day the thirty-eight-year-old looked especially unkempt, his "angular, strong" five foot, eleven inch–tall frame stooped over by fatigue. But if Lee had any doubt about his sincerity of purpose, acumen, or physical condition, all that was required was a glimpse of those "dark-blue, large, and piercing" eyes. They revealed the spirit of an indomitable will, the same one that had just earned his soldiers the sobriquet of "Jackson's foot cavalry" for their forced marches amounting to twenty-five miles a day or more. Followed up by four smashing victories in May and June, some of his men thought him mad for how hard he pushed them, but began to love him for delivering success afterward.[7]

So, too, had the people of the Confederacy, who had heard nothing but bad news since 1862 began. Stonewall's exploits in the Valley turned him into the first Confederate national icon, not only because he had beaten the enemy, but also because of *when* he beat him. In late May, the *Richmond Dispatch* declared him "THE HERO OF THE WAR." Up until then, South-erners had been desperate to hear anything, even a morsel, that could be verified as militarily positive. In February alone, Federal armies captured Roanoke Island on the Outer Banks of North Carolina, Forts Henry and Donelson in Tennessee with their 15,000 defenders, and Nashville, the Volunteer State's capital. In early March, Missouri and northwest Arkansas were permanently lost to the Confederacy at the Battle of Pea Ridge and Jackson himself had been repulsed at Kernstown, south of Winchester, Virginia. April depressed spirits even further with the fall of mighty New Orleans to the Union navy, the occupation of much of western Tennessee, and the disappointment of the bloody battle at Shiloh, which saw the main Southern army in the Western Theater defeated and its able general, Albert Sidney Johnston, killed, after a promising surprise attack. Then in May it appeared as if Richmond might be captured by the Union Army of the Potomac under Major General George B. McClellan, who had earlier started creeping his gigantic force up the Virginia peninsula southeast of the capital. Attempts to delay and deceive him about the weakness of rebel defenses had generally succeeded, and several small battles at Yorktown, Williamsburg, and Seven Pines had made him take pause, but slowly and

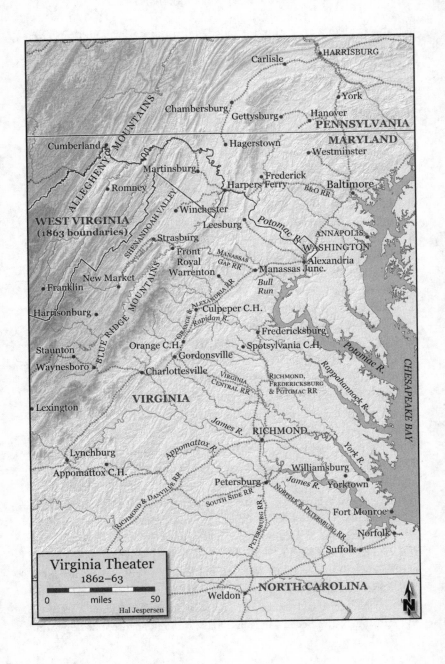

Virginia Theater
1862–63

0   miles   50

Hal Jespersen

methodically, like an elephant wading a deep river, he had inched ever closer. Now he was very close, near enough to launch a powerful assault on the city's incomplete eastern defenses. If something decisive was not done, and done quickly, Lee realized Richmond would probably fall. With it, he and President Davis surmised, would fall the Confederacy. The success of Jackson's Valley Campaign would be for naught.[8]

Davis had given Lee command of the principal Virginia army on June 1, the day after General Joseph E. Johnston, its previous commander, fell badly wounded at Seven Pines. In many respects, it was a lucky break for Lee, Davis, and the new Southern nation, as Johnston had displayed little fire in his belly for offensive operations against McClellan, instead preferring careful withdrawals. Seven Pines was an exception, but the Confederate attacks were poorly synchronized, and at the end of the day the enemy had only been bloodied and precious little room remained between the still-defiant Federals and the capital. Few other acceptable candidates beckoned as replacements for the fallen Johnston, so Lee definitely had proximity and timing on his side. But the president had also grown to trust Lee as his adviser through months of difficult discussions, decisions, and administrative work. Much of that trust was due to Lee's high emotional intelligence that enabled him to handle the often prickly Davis and his cabinet with aplomb. When coupled with a national perspective gained by months laboring at the president's side, a naturally logical mind, and extensive prewar military experience, Lee had evolved into an exceedingly good strategic and operational thinker. Despite the hiccup as a field commander in the Cheat Mountain Campaign in western Virginia in September 1861, after which he was quietly shuttled to the South-Atlantic states to oversee the construction of fortifications, he had otherwise impressed Davis, and was therefore the natural choice to succeed Johnston. Jackson unequivocally agreed. He once claimed "Lee is a phenomenon. I would follow him blindfold[ed]," and believed him "a better officer than General Scott," the revered former general-in-chief of US forces and victor of the Mexican War. Old Jack had trusted Lee's guidance from his earliest posting at Harpers Ferry in May 1861 up through his recent campaign, and witnessed firsthand how Lee, in turn, supported him from afar and trusted him to use his discretion to win victories. Now Stonewall had come in person to help Lee win a victory necessary for Southern national survival.[9]

Within minutes of taking his first sip of cool milk, Jackson turned around to the sound of heavy boots scuffling over the threshold of the Dabbs House doorway. Into the small office strode the last of Lee's two invitees, Major Generals James "Old Pete" Longstreet and Ambrose Powell (A. P.) Hill. Both had fought at Seven Pines, along with D. H. Hill, and the three men familiarly greeted each other and Lee with nods and handshakes. Then Longstreet and Hill turned to the newcomer, Jackson, who had little to say in response to their questions about his much-lauded successes in the Valley. They may have misconstrued his brief, abrupt answers for aloofness or impertinence, when in fact the introverted Stonewall was tired and often felt awkward in new social situations with people he did not know well. Walter Taylor, Lee's aide and one of Jackson's former students at VMI, described him as austere and quiet, but "once the outer shell was pierced he was always genially warm in manner and sympathetic at heart." Sometimes it took a while for that to occur, even with other devout Christians, and in professional settings, once an individual gained his respect and had proven his reliability, Jackson would slowly open up to them, but certainly not until some time had passed. He knew next to nothing about the forty-one-year-old, stocky Longstreet, with his dark hair and long beard and, as one observer put it, gray-blue "pig's eyes" that seemed to shrewdly take the measure of all and everything around him. Like Lee and Jackson, Old Pete was physically tall, and like Old Jack, a man of few words, especially since his family had been tragically reduced by the deaths of three children in the last half year. Once naturally droll and merry, his personality had begun to transform, his more negative traits, including a dour melancholy and opinionated stubbornness, increasingly dominant. But he was gifted with an inherent talent to command large bodies of men, a steadfast persistence, and an ability to discern the root of a military problem, qualities already evident at this juncture of the war, and ones that had earned him a place at this and prior meetings of the rebel high command. "Little Powell," as A. P. was fondly called by those who knew him well, was the youngest and most diminutive of the group, of slighter build, with brown hair worn long to his shoulders. Stonewall knew him as a classmate at West Point, and the two had not gotten along well. The highborn Hill, son of a prominent Virginia family, had then poked fun at the diffident Jackson from the backcountry, and still retained the impetuous dash and egotistical pride that his fellow cadet remembered him for. Yet Hill had already developed a reputation for personal bravery and a fierceness in combat on the Peninsula, characteristics that would soon make him an essential member of the army's leadership. [10]

After a few minutes of pleasantries and introductions, Lee closed his office door, announcing "he had determined to attack the Federal right wing" and, as D. H. Hill recounted, "selected our four commands to execute the movement." Other Southern divisions would hold Richmond's defenses and occupy the enemy's attention while the bulk of the rebel army swooped down on McClellan's northern flank and inflicted serious damage, threatened his supply depots, turned him out of his entrenchments facing the Confederate capital, and thereby eliminated the pressure on the city. Once that was achieved, Lee hoped to inflict more injury on the vast Union host as it fled back down the Peninsula. It was a bold operational design, one all the generals present except Jackson had previously mulled over to some degree. This was the first time Stonewall had heard of it. His mind, suddenly awake, grappled with the possibilities inherent in the plan as he listened intently to Lee's further explanation. The commanding general had sent a division toward the Valley to create the impression Jackson was being reinforced for a movement north that might threaten Washington, D.C., making sure the Richmond newspapers broadcast the fact, while instructing Stonewall to bring his army in secrecy to the city's environs to bolster Confederate numbers and participate in the assault on McClellan. The Union army was vulnerable, Lee had learned from his cavalry chief, J.E.B. (Jeb) Stuart, split by the Chickahominy, with approximately one-third of it north of the river and the rest below it. Jackson's triumphs in the Valley had arrested the march south of Federal reinforcements by way of Fredericksburg, and with its own ranks swelled by regiments and brigades recently arrived from the Deep South, the Army of Northern Virginia now had enough men to meet the Army of the Potomac in a fair fight. But timing was everything. Jackson had to bring his army, strung out along the Virginia Central railroad between forty and fifty miles westward, to Ashland, a town north of Richmond, and from there commence the strike on McClellan's right flank at Mechanicsville, while the other Confederate divisions, close by and rested, pushed due east just a few miles against that point. Everything depended on Stonewall's timely arrival and a precise ordering of divisional attacks. The assault had to begin quickly, within days, before word of Jackson's presence reached the enemy and they acted upon it.[11]

Old Jack had understood he and his army were to assist in the battles to save Richmond—sidelining his proposal, which he had already proffered twice, to raid into Pennsylvania—but the prospective magnitude of the results of Lee's plan, if successful, were apparent and exciting to him. As the Valley General had come to know over the past several months, Lee's mind, like his own, was not limited to the tactical or even the operational objectives in his immediate line of sight. The army commander thought more broadly, strategically, in ways that signified a clear understanding of what had to be done to win the war and achieve the policy goal of Southern independence. Thus, after careful thought, he had supported Jackson's earlier proposal to carry the Confederate banner into the North once the Shenandoah had been cleared of Federals and, as he told Davis, "change the character of the war." But the Union juggernaut's relentless, if languid movement up the Peninsula had forced Lee to prioritize, and seizing an opportunity to prevent the fall of the capital, he ordered Stonewall and his army to join him. As Lee finished describing his intent for the operation, Jackson faintly smiled even as he wondered how he would accomplish what was asked of him. It would be difficult, but his army had just overcome worse tests of endurance in the Valley. And he would not let the commanding general down. Behind the genteel manners and noble bearing of this gray-haired gentleman was a brain that contemplated nothing less than mauling the Army of the Potomac, snatching the strategic initiative in the Eastern Theater, and then . . . perhaps . . . moving onto the offensive.[12]

Such a course strongly suited Jackson's preferences. From the first days of his moniker "Stonewall," he yearned to take the war to the enemy's territory out of an innate strategic sense that the Confederacy could not win a long war and therefore needed to move swiftly, deliver heavy psychological and logistical blows that would stagger the waking Northern colossus, and win an early peace. The ancient wars of the Israelites, as described in the Old Testament of the Bible, and the *Maxims of Napoleon*, books that traveled in his knapsack, offered guidance. Whatever ways and means, however destructive, that accomplished the bold strokes he envisioned and led to independence were completely acceptable. Directly after First Manassas, as the Confederate army recovered from the shock of victory and tried to overcome its own disorganization, he supposedly urged his superiors to "give me ten thousand men, and I will be in Washington tonight." The veracity of that statement has been questioned, but not so others made over the next year. To General Gustavus W. Smith, who ranked third in command in the fall of 1861 when Jackson and his brigade lay in camp with the rest of the army near Centreville, Stonewall proposed to "invade their country now, and not wait for [the Federals] to make the necessary preparations to invade ours. If the President would reinforce this army by taking troops from other points not threatened, and let us make an active campaign of invasion before winter sets in, McClellan's raw recruits could not stand against us in the field." Smith, lying on his tent cot as Jackson spoke, was surprised by the specific details of the plan he then revealed. "Crossing the Upper Potomac, occupying Baltimore, and taking possession of Maryland," he claimed, "we could cut off the communications of Washington, force the Federal Government to abandon the capital," and, if the Army of the Potomac came out to meet the Confederates, it could be drawn into the open where it would be outmaneuvered and beaten. Thereafter, the rebels would "destroy industrial establishments wherever we found them, break up the lines of interior commercial intercourse, close the coal mines," destroy "the commerce of Philadelphia, and of other large cities within our reach . . . subsist mainly on the country we traverse, and making unrelenting war amidst their homes, force the people of the North to understand what it will cost them to hold the South in the Union at the bayonet's point."[13]

These were frightfully harsh ideas suggesting Jackson understood the strategic realities underpinning the "paradoxical trinity" of Carl von Clausewitz, the great Prussian philosopher of war, who posited that all war efforts were comprised of three fundamental nodes of power: reason, associated with the government; passion or violence, expressed by the people; and chance or friction, best managed by the military. Stonewall never read Clausewitz's book, *On War*, but he did travel in Europe, visited Waterloo, and thought deeply about history. His recommendation to Smith not only signified a comprehension that, as Clausewitz theorized, successful targeting of one or more nodes of the trinity could cripple an enemy's war effort, but also implied, in its emphasis on attacking northern commercial assets, an inherent grasp of the essentiality of strong economic and logistical power for successful war-making, a major part of what comprises the means of war. In this manner of thought he was unique among the leaders of the Confederacy; not even Lee thought so incisively about the critical dependence of the Union war machine on its coal mines (necessary for railroads and steamships), for instance, and it foretold the "hard war" Union generals such as Ulysses S. Grant and William T. Sherman would later prosecute against the rebels to great effect. But at that early point in the conflict, such designs were nothing short of revolutionary, especially for a Confederate government publicly on record as pursuing a defensive approach to the war. Smith pondered Jackson's words for a moment, studying him, and said nothing. Unable to contain himself, Stonewall asked if the general did not favor his views. "I will tell you a secret," Smith blurted, and then told Jackson some of those very ideas had already been discussed and dismissed in a recent war council with the president, Joseph E. Johnston, General P.G.T. Beauregard, and himself. "I am sorry, very sorry," Stonewall replied, and "went slowly out to his horse . . . mounted very deliberately, and rode sadly away."[14]

Jackson did not give up on his strategically aggressive views, instead refining and adapting them to the new contextual realities he faced when transferred to command in the Shenandoah Valley in November 1861. His thoughts for its defense, confronting multiple threats from different directions, were not confined purely to the operational and tactical level as most previous scholars have accepted, but also ranged well into the realm of strategy. He pursued to the utmost any local opportunity that presented a chance to go on the offensive into the North and accomplish even a portion of what he described to Smith, and, in keeping with his strict sense of military decorum, communicated this intent to Lee, who now oversaw his movements. Twice he sent Alexander R. Boteler, who was at once a member of his staff and a representative for the Winchester district in the Confederate House of Representatives, to the capital to confer with Davis and Lee about his proposals. On May 30, just days after his victory over Banks at Winchester, Jackson asked Boteler to go to Richmond and reason with the national command authority. "I must have reinforcements," he said. "You can explain to them down there what the situation is here," and "you may tell them, too, that if my command can be gotten up to 40,000 men a movement may be made beyond the Potomac, which will soon raise the siege of Richmond and transfer this campaign from the banks of the James to those of the Susquehanna." Just two days earlier Stonewall had received a telegram from Lee congratulating him on "your brilliant success," adding, "if you can make demonstrations on Maryland and Washington it will add to its great success." Doubtless, this sign of support from Lee encouraged Jackson, and Boteler must have succeeded in speaking to Lee, Davis, and probably also Secretary of War George W. Randolph, because in short order Jackson received a dispatch from Davis on June 4. It indicated that Boteler had failed to convince him of the need to send more men, but that the government placed its full confidence in Stonewall: "I return to you my congratulations for the brilliant campaign you have conducted . . . in the valley. . . . It is upon your skill and daring that reliance is to be placed." Unbeknownst to Jackson, the next day Lee wrote to Davis—perhaps influenced by Boteler and the messages he carried from Jackson—asking him to reconsider reinforcing Jackson, as it would truly "change the character of the war" by allowing him to "cross Maryland into Pennsylvania," which would recall "the enemy from our Southern coast & liberate those states" and, he insinuated, possibly alleviate the growing menace of McClellan, "who will make this a battle of posts." The new commanding general also contacted Randolph to discuss the reinforcements for Stonewall "you propose," implying the Secretary agreed with Lee. Together, they obliged Davis to agree to send a full division, approximately 7,500 men, to the Valley. [15]

Within days Lee and Davis received confirmation that Jackson was a leader worthy of their full support as news trickled in of his double victories at Cross Keys and Port Republic. On June 8 Lee lauded the Valley General, with whom he was now becoming well acquainted, "for your accustomed skill and boldness," but by then Lee had begun to appraise the deteriorating situation near Richmond and felt he must order Jackson to the East, a likelihood he first mentioned to him in the same letter. In a last-ditch attempt to stay that order, Jackson sent Boteler to Richmond again on June 13, the congressman meeting with Randolph, then Davis, and finally Lee. Old Jack told his friend to reiterate to them that with 40,000 men, "I will be in Harrisburg in two weeks: and this is the way to relieve Richmond." Davis liked the proposal very much, interestingly claiming "he always was in favor of an aggressive policy," but asked Boteler to check with Lee. The commanding general, reluctant to quash Jackson's valuable idea but concerned for the safety of the capital, told him, "No, Jackson must come here first & help me to drive these people away." Boteler pleaded with him to reconsider, handing him a letter from Jackson, claiming "that Jackson has been doing so well with an independent command that it seems a pity not to let him have his own way." Lee listened attentively, nodded, and then chuckled. "I see that you appreciate General Jackson as highly as I myself do, and it is because of my appreciation of him that I wish to have him here." The matter was closed, and a dejected Boteler returned to his chief. Expecting such a result, Stonewall replied positively to Lee's letter of the 8th, writing "You can halt the reenforcements [sic] coming here if you so desire," and immediately began plans to move his army eastward. On the 16th, Lee penned him again, asking him to keep the movement secret and emphasizing, "I should like to have the advantage of your views, and be able to confer with you. Will meet you at some point on your approach to the Chickahominy." The commanding general had begun to seek Jackson's advice.[16]

Beyond military strategy, Jackson also exhibited interest in Confederate military policy, especially as it affected his district and the overall prospects of the Southern war effort. Corresponding directly or through Boteler with chairman of the House Military Affairs Committee, William Porcher Miles, Stonewall urged Congressional action on topics as diverse as initiating a draft and eliminating poor officers from the armies. These were national-level reforms he sought, and he did not hold back his estimation of what was necessary to accomplish them. Some of his politicking bore fruit. On December 28, 1861, Jackson penned Miles from his camp in Centreville, recommending adoption of "a combination of the Prussian and French systems . . . a levy en masse of all within certain ages." Most of the conscripts raised would go into the army immediately, but "from that levy a selection of one third (illegible) should stay at Home, liable to selection [by draft] again, to fill up the ranks in the field as they are thinned by death or discharges, or disabling sicknesses or causes of any such so that the force in the field should always be kept up to the MAXIMUM STANDARD [original emphasis]." Continuing, he claimed he had drawn up "such a system as I have sketched above" for the state of Virginia, which he would send "in a day or two, to Colonel Kemper, Speaker of the House of Delegates." The plan "has the favor of Genls Johnston and Beauregard and of all volunteer officers and privates who have seen it. . . . I shall ask Kemper also to show you the Bill, and I trust you will have time to read and ponder it—with such a system what an army it will furnish!" This letter, never before published, must have had at least some influence on Miles, as his committee debated, revised, and met with its Senate counterpart on a bill of eerily similar ilk throughout the late winter of 1862 and into the early spring. The result was the April 16 passage of the Conscription Act, the first national draft in American history.

How much Jackson's voice mattered in this process is unknowable from the historical evidence, but another episode is more concrete. On March 3 Jackson wrote to Boteler, recommending Congress "pass a law that if any officer is reported for being ignorant of his duties, or for inefficiency, it shall be the duty of the commanding officer of the Department to order a Board of Officers to examine the officer," and if he is found guilty, cause him to "be dismissed the service." On March 5, Chairman Miles, probably after lobbying from his colleague Boteler, uncannily introduced a bill to the House "to purge the military service of ignorant and inefficient officers" that was immediately referred to his committee, and like the conscription bill before it, was debated and amended for several months. Jackson wrote Miles directly on March 15 to reinforce his case: "Inefficiency should be driven from our army. . . . Inefficient generals should be removed [more] than those of any other grade in as much as their commands are larger." Possibly prompted by the assignment to his command of some brigadiers he deemed problematic, Stonewall added, "Whilst I highly prize military education, yet something more is required to make a general." On the 24th, Miles read a letter to his committee from Lee, "favoring the passage of the bill," but it was "laid over until tomorrow." Events overtook the committee's deliberations and, unfortunately for Jackson, the bill died. [17]

How much of this recent personal experience coursed through Old Jack's brain as he stood quietly listening to Lee's campaign plan is open to conjecture. It is plausible he compared Lee's aggressive approach to his own, musing about the potential climactic results on the Peninsula if all went according to the commanding general's design. Perhaps he thought the war could be won here if God so willed it, that the combination of his smaller army with Lee's larger one was a divine appointment. Probably he felt certain, by the time Lee finished, that if anyone could lead the Confederates to independence, it was this man. Suddenly, the commanding general stopped and stood silent. Then he curiously "excused himself to attend to office business," exited the room, closed the door behind him, and left his subalterns to hammer out the details of the operation he just laid out in bold strokes. Although a bit odd, he may have done this because Longstreet and D. H. Hill had already discussed with him its major parameters, and he felt they could explain the particulars to the younger Hill and Jackson. The action was also in keeping with what would become a hallmark of Lee's generalship: setting forth the objectives of the greater mission and then allowing his lieutenants to execute the plan, figuring out the specific "how" to his "what." In this circumstance, however, it may have been unwise, because his subordinates (excepting Jackson) were still new to their level of responsibility, unacclimated to Lee's command style in the field, and unused to working out intricate maneuvers with one another.

For Stonewall, exhaustion was also beating on the door of his consciousness, exacerbating these issues and making his unfamiliarity with the local roads, streams, bridges, and crossroads a potential stumbling block. In the Valley he had capable staff officers like topographer Jedediah Hotchkiss and ordnance officer Alexander "Sandie" Pendleton, who, like him, understood the lay of the land and its peculiarities, but here in the Tidewater, with its strange, meandering roads, thick pine forests, and murky swamps, he was like a hunter lost in dense fog. When Longstreet asked him when he thought he would be in position to begin his march to the Federal right flank, "as your move is the key of the campaign," Jackson "promptly responded, 'The morning of the 25th'." Old Pete, noticeably unconvinced, wondered aloud if that might not be too ambitious, and Old Jack thought for a moment and reconsidered, suggesting the morning of June 26. The generals discussed a few other points, and then Lee came back in the office, listened to a summary of their proposed tactical maneuvers, and reiterated that the extra day was necessary for Jackson to be ready. Approving the final details of the operation and adjourning the meeting, Lee gave final "verbal instructions," which were "followed by written orders, embodying in minute detail the plan already given in general." The commanding general shook hands with his subordinates, saw them out the door of the Dabbs House, and went back to his paperwork. Marshall and Taylor, who had kept themselves busy with the other staff in an adjoining room while the generals conferred, exchanged knowing looks with each other and realized they, too, would soon be hard at work, writing out the orders.[18]

Jackson walked back outside, awoke his resting companions on the lawn, and rode all through the rainy night of the 23rd back to his command, the lead elements of which he met at Beaver Dam Station about 10:00 A.M. on the 24th. It was a miserable journey, made worse by Stonewall's growing anxiety at the state of the roads, which were quickly turning into quagmires. When he finally pulled up the reins to his horse and dismounted at the station depot, even more weary than before, a disappointing scene greeted him. Only the advance guard of his army was assembled there, far less than he had expected had a normal pace of march been followed in his absence. Some quick questions with available officers revealed the unhappy truth: the rest of his command remained spread out along the railroad for fifteen miles, and his chief of staff, Major Robert Lewis Dabney, a Presbyterian minister and professor at Union Theological Seminary, lay sick in bed. Based on his previous good record managing the staff and performing administrative duties in the Valley

Campaign, Jackson thought Dabney could easily oversee the continued progress of his columns, but that trust had clearly been misplaced. The task of managing the minute logistics, railroad timetables (the artillery, baggage, and some infantry traveled by train), and routes of march of a large army overwhelmed him, and the correspondingly heavier burden that fell on the rest of Stonewall's aides, especially quartermaster John A. Harman, had all but consumed them. When combined with the foul weather and the tired state of the Valley Army after weeks of unremitting fighting and marching, it became clear why his men were not where they should be. One of them wrote they kept tramping "until completely exhausted," the "suffering of this night excel[ing] anything I have ever experienced . . . completely drenched." Jackson could have jumped into action at that point, as he had so many times in the previous months, and ridden up and down his sluggish columns, shouting, "Press on, men, press on!," yet for reasons not entirely clear from the historical record, but probably because of his own fatigue, he accepted the reality that confronted him. Giving orders to his available staff to quicken the pace and hurry the advance, Old Jack found a nearby house, removed his wet uniform, read a novel for a bit, and fell fast asleep.[19]

This was not like Stonewall Jackson, but even a man with boundless vigor, a steadfast faith in God's providence, and "iron fortitude," as Dabney described him, was still a man, a physical being requiring more than prayer to sustain him. The general seemed to realize that limitation when he retired for those critical hours, but doubtless also recognized he was falling behind Lee's prescribed timetable. The next day, having regained some of his physical strength, Jackson redoubled his efforts, and moved his army to within five miles of his goal, Ashland. It was another energy-draining slog for his infantry, twenty miles in oppressive heat and humidity they were not used to, over ramshackle bridges damaged by swollen creeks, and on roads that seemed to be allies of the Yankees, pulling shoes off the men's feet in the thick mud. His soldiers had almost accomplished the impossible, again. But this time, unlike earlier in the Valley, "almost" would not be good enough. Jackson dispatched a brief note to Lee explaining he had fallen short, promising to have his soldiers marching by "early dawn" to make up the difference. To Stonewall's rising consternation, however, it did not happen, most of the brigades not on the road until 8:00 A.M. on the 26th. He had spent much of the night planning the next day's march and beseeching the Lord for mercy and guidance, but it became quickly evident that compiled fatigue, unfamiliarity with the local area, the heat, and delays caused by harassing Federal cavalry would ensure his army failed to be where and when Lee expected it to be. Although Old Jack now had good guides to help him navigate the roads, a deserter had informed McClellan that Jackson was nearing the Peninsula, and the Union general took appropriate action, canceling a planned attack on Lee but also ordering his horsemen to fell trees and burn bridges along Stonewall's likely route of advance. Jackson still possessed no reliable maps upon which he could depend—an oversight of the Confederate War Department and possibly of Lee—and had received a communication from the commanding general suggesting various routes of march that only exacerbated his cartographic confusion. Feeling compelled to move cautiously, he was running six hours late, and Old Jack was distraught. The entire battle plan for the day, indeed for the campaign, so meticulously detailed in the written orders sent by the commanding general two nights earlier, was now in jeopardy, and it was his fault.[20]

Jackson had experienced eight hours of sleep in the last three and a half days, and much of the exhaustion he was now enduring, and which had already manifested itself for his troops, was unavoidable based on previous exertions. The entire Valley Campaign had drained his last reserves, and the rides to and from Lee's headquarters had been inescapable. Yet he was part of the problem too. He could have easily allowed himself at least several hours of rest on the night of the 25th, but instead "under the stress of his great anxiety and heavy responsibilities . . . devoted the whole of it to the most energetic preparations and to prayer," his widow recounted. As one major chronicler of the ensuing Seven Days Campaign pithily concluded, "the single most important commodity that might have been applied to the Confederate cause in Virginia was a good night's sleep for Stonewall Jackson," but he deprived himself and his country of that opportunity.

Careful planning and thinking about contingencies and risks of upcoming operations is a sign of a good commander, and Jackson had previously demonstrated the fruits of such work. But his devotion to prayer, from which he drew abiding peace and strength, in this case worsened the situation by robbing him of much-needed rest. How long he spent specifically in prayer as opposed to planning that night is unknown, but one of his division commanders, Major General Richard S. Ewell, recalled returning to Jackson's tent to retrieve his sword, left behind after a meeting, and found his chief on his knees, deep in fervent supplication to God. Earlier impressed by Jackson's piety in the Valley, Ewell reportedly said, "If this is religion, I must have it," and so Stonewall succeeded in an unintentional, quiet witness that would eventually transform the profane, complaining Ewell into a new man. But Christian witness and evangelism, as highly as Jackson prized them, were not his priorities that night; his focus was on preparing himself and his command for the next day's demanding duties. In his heart, Old Jack certainly believed the large amount of time spent in prayer *was* a necessary part of his preparation (a fact substantiated throughout his Civil War career), and so the question boils down to the relative valuation of physical versus mental and spiritual strength for the individual military commander. Then as today, a balance must be struck. Clausewitz wrote, "Amongst the many things in war for which no tariff can be fixed, bodily effort may be specially reckoned." Only through "a great directing spirit," the Prussian continues, "can [we] expect the forces will be stretched to the utmost." But that willpower, which is supremely important for victorious leaders—and was a hallmark of Stonewall's success—comes at a price. It is derived partly from "the physical exertion of generals and of the chief commander." And therein lay the rub for Clausewitz: that "bodily effort" is, "like danger," one of the "fundamental causes of friction" in war. An exhausted leader can accomplish only a fraction of what he might otherwise achieve, and worse, might accidentally create difficulties in a greater plan he is supporting, spawning unintended consequences. Jackson made his decision to weigh spiritual empowerment over physical recovery, in true conformity with his steadfast faith, but in so doing produced even more friction than already existed from his tired state. The outcome of the Seven Days was probably affected as a result.[21]

It was also affected by misuse or mistakes in staff work, weak communications among the Confederate command team, poor utilization

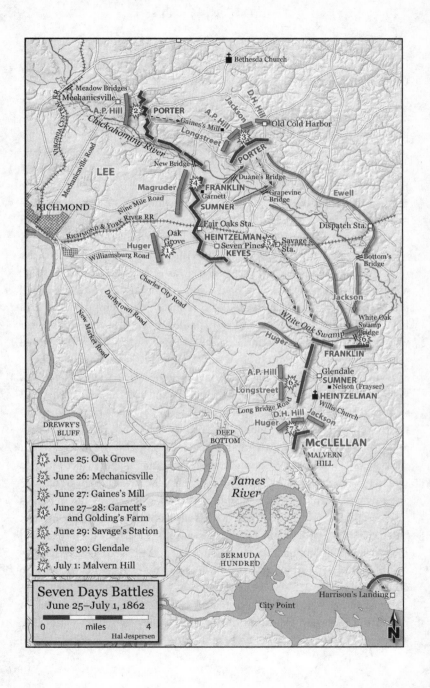

Bethesda Church

Meadow Bridges
Mechanicsville
A.P. Hill
Chickahominy River
PORTER
A.P. Hill
Jackson
D.H. Hill
Old Cold Harbor
Gaines's Mill
Longstreet
PORTER

New Bridge
Duane's Bridge
Ewell
FRANKLIN
Garnett
Grapevine
Bridge
Magruder
SUMNER
LEE
Nine Mile Road
RICHMOND
RICHMOND & YORK RIVER RR
Fair Oaks Sta.
Dispatch Sta.
HEINTZELMAN
Savage's
Sta.
Huger
Oak
Grove
Seven Pines
Bottom's
Bridge
Williamsburg Road
KEYES
Charles City Road
Jackson
Darbytown Road
White Oak Swamp
White Oak
Swamp
Bridge
Huger
FRANKLIN
New Market Road
Glendale
SUMNER
A.P. Hill
Nelson (Frayser)
Longstreet
HEINTZELMAN
Long Bridge Road
Willis Church
D.H. Hill
Jackson
DREWRY'S
BLUFF
Huger
McCLELLAN
DEEP
BOTTOM
MALVERN
HILL

*James
River*

BERMUDA
HUNDRED

Harrison's Landing
City Point

1	June 25: Oak Grove
2	June 26: Mechanicsville
3	June 27: Gaines's Mill
4	June 27–28: Garnett's and Golding's Farm
5	June 29: Savage's Station
6	June 30: Glendale
7	July 1: Malvern Hill

Seven Days Battles
June 25–July 1, 1862

0   miles   4

Hal Jespersen

N

of real-time, tactical intelligence, and the proximity and actions of the Union army. Jackson did arrive over six hours late to the Polegreen Church area, located above Beaver Dam Creek and the Federal position at Mechanicsville, but where he halted his command and where Lee *thought* he would stop were not the same, a mistake of about three miles based on an inaccurate map the commanding general used to design his battle plan. That discrepancy meant—Jackson's tardiness aside—that the Union wing commander, Major General Fitz John Porter, whose flank Stonewall was supposed to turn and who, Lee then predicted, would be obliged to retreat from his impressive earthworks behind the creek as a result, never felt threatened. About mid-morning Jackson made contact by courier with the commander of a brigade linking the Valley Army with Longstreet's and A. P. Hill's divisions, which according to the plan were to sweep forward once Porter was in retreat, but the message apparently never reached Lee or the other generals. Nor did Lee send out even one horseman in search of Stonewall, or attempt to find him himself, despite the fact several of his aides noted Lee was anxious for word from Jackson. Further, both the original orders Jackson received and the subsequent communiqué suggesting various march routes said nothing specifically about attacking the Federals, so when Old Jack reached his destination he stopped and waited for the rear end of his winding, five-mile column to close up. His soldiers were tired, worn-out from the previous weeks' labors but also by the removal of fallen trees and other obstacles thrown in their path by the Union cavalry. Their nerves, and those of their commander, were almost shot. According to Dabney, who tended to deify his former chief, Stonewall "appeared to me anxious and perplexed," a plausible observation based on the general's fatigue and the fact he had heard the sounds of battle to the southeast but received no orders. Vast forests separated him from the noise, and Lee's written orders had been explicit, not intent-based, as they usually would be in later campaigns. Jackson read them over and over again to doublecheck—yes, this was the spot.

Jeb Stuart, whose cavalry guarded his left flank, sent a series of reassuring messages from that direction, but they told Jackson nothing about what lay to his front and right. One author has also suggested that the Valley General may have not yet discerned how best to use Stuart, whom he had known and admired back at Harpers Ferry in 1861, to assist in making tactical decisions. He would soon remedy that problem if it existed, and, as with Lee, begin an unlikely friendship with the cavalryman that enhanced their professional relationship. The jovial, flamboyant Stuart, who loved to play the cavalier with his flowing cape, plumed hat, and jingling spurs, and the reticent, reserved Jackson in his simple, threadbare uniform were an odd couple, but gave proof to the adage that opposites attracted. Stuart's steadfast Christian faith, professionalism, and unshakeable sense of duty and loyalty to the Confederacy and to Lee were admirable to Stonewall. His "fondness for General J.E.B. Stuart was very great," recounted one of Jackson's staff officers, and Stuart came to see him as his closest friend in the army.[22]

Five and a half years later, during a postwar interview, Lee recalled, "he was disappointed in not finding J[ackson]" on June 26. "Uneasy for fear the enemy seeing his movement and the stripping of his Richmond lines, would push forward and reach the city," he continued, "he attacked at . . . Mechanicsville with what troops he had, and in spite of the formidable works, in order to occupy the enemy and prevent any counter movement." The enemy was very well-entrenched and the commanding general realized losses may be high, "but he was obliged to do *something*." [original emphasis] In reality, his hand was forced by A. P. Hill, who had been chomping at the bit all day and, true to his temperament, commenced a frontal assault against the Union defenders behind Beaver Dam Creek on his own volition late in the afternoon. Longstreet and D. H. Hill, assuming Little Powell had made contact with Jackson per Lee's original plan, albeit late, came to his support. Lee and his staff finally "rode forward from his headquarters" around 5:00 P.M., and accompanied by a curious President Davis, Secretary Randolph, and a small multitude of civilians, watched the last futile Confederate assaults charge the Federal position. Despite his misgivings, Lee allowed them to go forward. The rebel infantry, with their artillery support knocked out by the enemy, had to cross about four hundred yards of open meadows, followed by an abatis of felled trees and limbs and the creek itself, and then face the fortified slope of the enemy, bristling with cannon and musket barrels. Filled with a reckless heroism only green soldiers eager to conquer possess, the ranks of outnumbered Southerners were no match for the sheets of iron and lead flung at them, and melted away. By the end of that oppressively hot day Porter's men in blue had scored a lopsided victory over the rebels, whose dead carpeted the creek bottom "like flies in a bowl of sugar." A soldier in the 16th North Carolina wrote of the scene after the sun went down: "our surroundings were a solitary desert of horror. . . . Nothing could be heard in the black darkness of that night save the ghastly moans of the wounded and dying."[23]

Allowing his men to encamp at Hundley's Corner, where he had stopped that day, Jackson finally got a fitful night's rest, assured that Stuart's cavalry videttes protected his command from surprise by the Unionists. That was the last thing George McClellan had in mind, however, when he ordered Porter to abandon his position at Beaver Dam Creek and march southeast toward the Chickahominy, where he was to guard the crossings north of the river to allow the bulk of the Union army to shift south and west to a new supply base. Lee's operational plan was starting to work, the debacle of the previous day notwithstanding, and along with McClellan's vast overestimation of his opponent's numbers, Jackson's presence had been instrumental in convincing the Federals to withdraw. Now the question facing Lee was how best to strike Porter before he scurried out of reach, and thereafter, how to successfully engage the rest of the Army of the Potomac. Stonewall and his staff rose early on the 27th and, partially refreshed, ate a quick breakfast and had the men begin the march anew. Exhibiting some of the later insight that would characterize his professional relationship with Lee, on this morning Jackson heard cannon fire to the south, and, remembering his primary mission to outflank the enemy from Lee's orders, accordingly started Ewell's division down the road, the rest of the Valley Army swinging in behind it. At about 9:30 Jackson, riding at the front of his troops near the Walnut Grove Church intersection, encountered A. P. Hill, exchanged a few words and salutes, and started to feel he was no longer isolated and out of touch with the main army. Before Hill departed, a large contingent of horsemen approached from the north, in the direction of Mechanicsville. It was Lee, attempting to remedy the mistake of yesterday by personally riding to meet with his subordinate. Jackson watched him arrive, a superb horseman who rode his mount with ease and grace, his resplendent gray uniform a marked contrast with Stonewall's own dingy one. It was the first time in the war the two generals had met in the field. [24]

Lee and Jackson greeted each other, dismounted, and led their horses into the churchyard, where Lee found an old cedar stump and sat down. Stonewall remained standing, took off his cap, and listened as the commanding general outlined his plan for the day. Porter, he believed, would have to make a stand at Powhite Creek, about a mile to the southeast, and Jackson, given command of D. H. Hill's division and Stuart's cavalry, was to outflank that position by continuing his march generally southeastward, toward Cold Harbor. Once in position to the Federals' right and rear, Stonewall's position should once again oblige the enemy to retreat, and when that occurred, Lee would unleash Longstreet and A. P. Hill from the north, driving the discomfited Porter directly into the waiting jaws of Jackson. Possibly a third of the Union army could be destroyed. It was another bold, audacious plan, and Old Jack's eyes flashed at the audacity of it. Inflicting that much damage on the enemy would not only lock in victory in the campaign, but perhaps set up the conditions to wipe out much of the rest of McClellan's army. That could win Confederate independence. Observers watched him nod in agreement after Lee completed his instructions, the conference ended, and the two generals rode off in different directions. [25]

Unfortunately for the Confederates, Lee again made a mistake; his assumption that Porter had formed his defensive line behind Powhite Creek was incorrect. Instead, because McClellan had decided to abandon his supply depot on the York River and established a new one on the James, Porter need not cover the rest of the shifting Union army so far to the west and north. He selected another naturally strong defensive position just a few miles distant, anchored behind a swampy stream called Boatswain's Swamp near a mill operated by the Gaines family. Once again he enhanced the advantages of the local terrain with good fieldworks, and again Jackson was slow in reaching the field, this time due to a wrong turn at a crossroads. His local guide, a member of

Stuart's cavalry, led the general's force exactly where he asked it to go; the problem was that there were two villages named Cold Harbor, one "New" and one "Old," and Old Jack, unfamiliar with the area and unsure which one Lee meant, chose the wrong one. Exhibiting good military instinct as he had that morning, when the error was discovered Jackson countermarched to the sound of the growing battle, but oversights and blunders on the part of Dabney and possibly Quartermaster Harman caused confusion in his tactical deployment and delayed entrance of his brigades into what became the Battle of Gaines's Mill. Lee had been "waiting anxiously" for his lieutenant to arrive, and in the postwar interview claimed that by late afternoon "Jackson was still not up" and "now the two Hills &c. all being over the river he was forced to push forward and attack at Gaine's Mill [sic] with all his energy." If he had not, Lee feared the bulk of the Union army south of the Chickahominy would strike directly at Richmond. For his part, Jackson was "evidently disturbed" for most of the afternoon, "his usual quiet and cool manner now evinc[ing] restlessness and anxiety."

As Jackson's men came into line as they arrived, the two generals met one more time, along the Telegraph Road, amidst the cheering of nearby soldiers. "Ah, General, I am glad to see you!" Lee purportedly said. "I had hoped to be with you before!" Stonewall said something unintelligible in reply to the cloaked rebuke, and then sat on his horse tight-lipped, his bleached kepi cap pulled down low as usual, listening to Lee's new orders. By the time he had finished, Old Jack appeared to be a new man, the fire in his eyes and physical energy reignited. He barked terse, clipped commands to his staff, consulted briefly with Stuart, and ordered his brigades forward. It was a close-run event, but by the end of the day Lee managed to assault Porter's overstrained line with over 50,000 soldiers in the largest combined infantry attack his army would ever launch. Porter's defensive lines, though formidable, cracked under the unrelenting pressure and only nightfall saved him from disaster. A. P. Hill's and Longstreet's divisions had taken heavy casualties earlier in the day, however, and those generals began to resent Stonewall's tardiness for the second day in a row, even though the battle resulted in the first great victory for the Army of Northern Virginia.[26]

During the night the battered Porter escaped across the Chicka-hominy and the Seven Days continued. Savage's Station, White Oak Swamp and Glendale, and bloody Malvern Hill followed in succession, and the exhaustion that Jackson had temporarily staved off at Gaines's Mill returned with a vengeance. At White Oak Swamp on June 30 he appeared comatose when awake and then fell fast asleep for an hour as his artillery banged away at Union guns on the opposite bluffs, impossible to rouse. And contrary to his creative thinking and indomitable will in the Valley, he seemed cognitively challenged to find an alternative crossing route besides the destroyed bridge the enemy had left for him, even though subordinate officers offered various possibilities. According to a letter sent home the next week to his wife, Mary Anna, he may have been ill, "suffer[ing] from fever and debility." Debate has swirled about whether he truly understood Lee's intent for the battle at Glendale, which his command was to have joined that day, and if he could have actually found another way to get his men through the swamp and into the Union rear. Most of Major General William B. Franklin's Union Corps was posted advantageously all along the western side of the swamp, placed there purposefully to arrest Stonewall's movement. It is possible Old Jack could have broken through had he been "his very self," but the cost probably would have been high, and whether it would have been in time to initiate the chain of events resulting in McClellan's destruction, as Lee envisioned, is questionable. Yet Longstreet and his staff never quite forgave Jackson's perceived languor that day, as their command again paid in blood for the lack of coordination with the Valley Army and other divisions. E. Porter Alexander, an artillery officer whose account of the entire war remains one of the most reliable and insightful narratives of the conflict in the East, wrote later, "When one thinks of the great chances in General Lee's grasp that one summer afternoon, it is enough to make one cry to go over the story how they were all lost. And to think too that our *Stonewall Jackson* [original emphasis] lost them."[27]

But if that is true, Major Generals Benjamin Huger, John Magruder, and Theophilus Holmes were equally to blame for their enfeebled, non-existent, or poorly executed attacks, which, Lee civilly noted in his official report, left "Longstreet and Hill . . . without the expected support."

Jackson himself told his staff, who questioned his judgment at the Swamp a couple of weeks later, "If General Lee had wanted me, he could have sent for me." Lee never asked for him and chose not to ride over to Jackson's position to consult even though it was but a short distance away. Two prominent Jackson biographers also note that Lee may have given Old Jack mixed messages regarding his intent for that day, and that Stonewall followed his earlier written orders to the letter, interpreting a later meeting in person with Lee as not altering them. At Glendale Lee also contributed to the missed opportunity through continued unfamiliarity with most of his staff officers, their capabilities, and their proper use in the field. Douglas Southall Freeman, Lee's foremost biographer, appraised this problem (that afflicted the commanding general throughout the campaign) by claiming Lee "was scarcely more adept in handling a staff at this time than the officers were in serving him." As time wore on, the staff issue would largely dissipate, but when coupled with Jackson's lethargy and the absence of Stuart and his cavalry, which were inexplicably left on the east bank of the Chickahominy as the Confederate infantry divisions pressed west and south, the situation evolved into one, giant missed opportunity for the rebels. Indeed, it appears inconceivable that Stuart would not have helped keep Lee in touch with his disparate divisions, correct errors in the maps, and inform him better of the enemy's whereabouts.[28]

Whatever the causes of the failure to demolish McClellan, Glendale represented one of the first nexus moments of the war, where the tactical, operational, and strategic levels converged to provide a unique chance to permanently alter the course of the conflict. Also referred to as contingency or inflection points, such occasions are rare in any war and were especially scarce in the American Civil War, when armies were exceedingly hard to destroy in the field. At Glendale, and indeed throughout the Seven Days, Lee the field commander demonstrated the sophisticated tactical- and operational-level thinking necessary to maximize the likelihood such contingencies would occur in favor of the Confederacy and produce a strategic-level event: a victory strategic not only in its immediate effect on Federal military power, but also in the concomitant political damage done to the Lincoln administration by crushing northern home front morale. It would not be the last time he did this, and indeed the problems that combined, á la classic Clausewitzian friction, to deny him the strategic success he sought on the Peninsula were in many ways related to the newness of his command team (staffs included), a matter that could only resolve over time. Stonewall would increasingly play the leading role in that evolution, Lee relying on him to produce the nexus points required to achieve a potential strategic triumph. And both men had already exhibited strategic-level thinking about *how* to fight the war in the East—the character of campaigns needed, for example—in order to achieve the policy aim of independence, although they differed somewhat in the precise ways and means required. On the evening following the battle of Glendale, however, that future was in doubt. Jackson fell asleep at dinner, a biscuit still clenched in his teeth, symbolic of one of the key reasons the rebel victory in the Seven Days was not more complete.[29]

The day after the bloody repulse at Malvern Hill on July 1, where wave after disjointed wave of Confederate brigades assaulted yet another well-prepared Union defensive position, Lee and Jackson and some of their staffs met at the Poindexter House, on the margin of the battlefield. It was a good sign for the professional relationship of the two generals that, the bungles and errors of the past week notwithstanding, Lee still viewed Stonewall as a key subordinate and sought his advice, the commanding general perhaps realizing that he, too, was to blame for some of the disappointments. It was a dismally rainy day, reflecting Jackson's mood, disconsolate and apprehensive in the belief that precious time was ticking away as the enemy retreated. Dabney and Dr. Hunter McGuire, Stonewall's medical director—whose postwar observations, like Dabney's, were laced with pro-Jackson and Lost Cause motifs—both observed the conference, held in two rooms with "good fires" to shield the attendees from the damp. McGuire noticed the fretfulness in Jackson's body language. "He knew that McClellan was defeated, that he had left us with his dead and wounded, many cannon, and thousands of stands of small arms and every possible thing that a defeated army could leave in the grasp of its adversary." McGuire also claimed Stonewall urged upon Lee a rapid pursuit of the retreating enemy who could still be damaged before he reached the James and the safety of the Union navy's big guns. There were five good miles of opportunity, as the staff officers' joint recollections opined, but what they either did not know at the time or glossed over later was how disorganized the Confederate army had become after seven days of relentless marching and fighting and the resilient strength of McClellan's army. The roads had again turned to mud, Stuart was nowhere close to provide intelligence on the enemy's dispositions, and any pursuit, if Jackson indeed suggested it, would have been fraught with peril and the probability of failure. The Yankees had too much of a head start in their withdrawal.

Lee and Old Jack were examining maps on a table when Longstreet arrived to join the meeting, and stomping his feet to remove the wet and mud, immediately asked, "Gen., sending anyone to Richmond today?" Lee answered, "Yes, an orderly will set out soon; can we do anything for you?" Longstreet asked if his wife, then in Lynchburg, might be officially contacted to tell her "I am alive yet." Lee thought it would be better if the general wired her personally. Using the same skill that had aided him many times with the president, he replied, "Oh, Gen. Longstreet, will you not write yourself? Is it not due to your good lady after these tremendous events?" Old Pete, apparently convinced, "flopped down on a chair and scribbled a short note," rose back to his feet, and the meeting continued. What the three generals discussed thereafter is unknown, but after a short while the door to the dwelling opened again. To everyone's shock, President Davis and his nephew doffed their capes and hats and walked into the room. It was a surprise visit. Already on edge from his fatigue and anxious about losing time, desperate to convince Lee of his conviction, the president was probably the last person Old Jack wanted to see. Stonewall had forgiven him for initially backing up former Secretary of War Judah P. Benjamin's indictment of his Romney Campaign, his first independent operation conducted in the winter of 1861–1862, which succeeded in clearing the Federals out of three counties of northwest Virginia but also resulted in complaints sent by subordinates to Richmond. In protest, Jackson had temporarily resigned but was talked out of it by Joseph E. Johnston and Governor John Letcher. Shortly thereafter, Davis asked Benjamin to become Secretary of State and purposefully tried to win back Jackson's esteem by listening to Boteler on his visits, staying out of Valley affairs (which he left Lee to oversee), and then dispatching congratulations for his victories in the Valley. But damage had been done to the relationship.[30]

Jackson did not immediately recognize the president. McGuire purportedly whispered in his ear, and then he "stood bolt upright like a corporal on guard looking at Mr. Davis." Lee "greeted him very warmly," exclaiming, "Why, President, I am delighted to see you." Shaking hands, Davis turned to Longstreet, greeting him just as amiably. Then he glanced at Jackson, not knowing who he was. "Why, President, don't you know Stonewall Jackson? This is our Stonewall Jackson," Lee said. Davis started to walk toward him, hand extended, "but the appearance of Jackson stopped him, and when he got about a yard Mr. Davis halted and Jackson immediately brought his hand up to the side of his head in military salute." The president, realizing customary social graces were hopeless, bowed elegantly and turned back to Lee. Jackson relaxed, found a chair, and sat down. He remained a participant in the meeting, but became "silent, reserved, diffident, never volunteering any counsel or suggestion; but answering when questioned, in a brief, deferential way." The commanding general dominated the discussion, with Davis offering suggestions that, "in a polite way, Gen. Lee would receive . . . and reject." Dabney observed the entire meeting from his perch near the fire, later insisting "that Lee's intellect had already obtained a clear intellectual ascendancy over Davis." He and McGuire also studied their chief intently, claiming that what they saw indicated the military thinker in Jackson was in sheer agony. His "mind was uttering a mournful protest against their conclusions. He sat in his modest corner, withdrawn into himself," Dabney recalled, his face expressing "first surprise, then dissent, mortification, sorrow, anguish. As a true soldier he was too subordinate to say a word to his superiors" out of turn, but his mental torture was apparent. Whether or not the Valley army's chief of staff accurately remembered Jackson's facial expressions is questionable, and it seems unlikely Stonewall sat passively throughout the rest of the council. Dabney may also have wished to portray his former boss as possessing superior military acumen. But it makes sense that Jackson did not know Lee well enough yet to intrude his opinion, and he felt uncomfortable around Davis and Longstreet. He *was* the most experienced battlefield leader in the room, instinctively understanding that McClellan "was retreating, not maneuvering," and that the Union troops, despite holding their line at Malvern Hill, were crestfallen and demoralized. Often oblivious to human limitations and logistical realities, he would have dismissed reports from scouts that the mud was too thick for an effective pursuit, or that the enemy was too strong, knowing full well what his own soldiers had accomplished in the Valley (albeit at great cost). But his intelligence of the tactical situation was inferior to Lee's and the Peninsula was not the Valley. His former staff officers nonetheless claimed, "Jackson's mind reasoned if these invaders can trudge through mud and mire, to save their bacon, surely patriot heroes could do it to save their country and to reap the fruits of a great victory bought for us with so much precious blood." Dabney's and McGuire's partiality aside, the question of pursuit definitely arose in the meeting, and Stonewall weighed in. Some sources reveal the president asked Jackson's opinion of how to deal with the retiring enemy. Perhaps harkening back to how he handled Banks after Winchester, the general answered, "They have not all got away if we go immediately after them."[31]

Several days later, after the Army of Northern Virginia cautiously pursued the withdrawing Army of the Potomac and stopped to encamp, unable to assault McClellan in his final, well-fortified position, Jackson called Alexander Boteler, his itinerant aide and congressman, into his tent. "In a tone of considerable excitement," Stonewall declared, "Do you know that we are losing valuable time here?" Boteler shook his head. "How so?" We are repeating the error made after Manassas, Stonewall exclaimed, "allowing the enemy leisure to recover from his defeat and ourselves to suffer by inaction." Continuing his argument, Jackson asserted, "Yes, we are wasting precious time and energies in this malarious region that can be much better employed elsewhere." McClellan was beaten, would not make any more moves to threaten the capital, and could not go anywhere quickly. Now was the time to "carry the war across the Potomac," make the North feel the hardships of war, and "finish the riddance of Va." He wanted Boteler to ride to Richmond, talk to the president, and convince him, although "it was no desire to push himself forward." "What is the use of my going to Mr. Davis, as he'll probably refer me again to General Lee," the congressman asked. "Why don't you yourself speak to General Lee upon the subject?" Jackson thought for a moment, looked down at the ground, and answered, "I have already done so." Boteler pumped him to find out what Lee had said. Stonewall paused, looking at his subordinate. "He says nothing," gently adding, "Don't think I complain of his silence; he doubtless has good reasons for it." Boteler felt indignant for his general, blurting, "Then you don't think that General Lee is slow in making up his mind?" Jackson responded immediately, a new energy infusing his voice. "Slow! By no means, colonel; on the contrary, his perception is as quick and unerring as his judgment is infallible. But with the vast responsibilities now resting on him, he is perfectly right in withholding a hasty expression of his opinions and purposes." Old Jack paused, and then added, "So great is my confidence in General Lee that I am willing to follow him blindfolded. But I fear he is unable to give me a definite answer now because of influences at Richmond, where, perhaps, the matter has been mentioned by him and may be under consideration." If Boteler went to see the president now, Jackson thought, they might strike while the political iron was hot and finally take the war to the enemy. The next day the congressman-turned-colonel did go to see the president, and the conversation they had is lost to time, but within a week Jackson received orders to move his troops off the Peninsula and head north. The rest of the Army of Northern Virginia would soon follow them.[32]

By the end of the Seven Days string of battles, Lee had pushed the Federals halfway back down the Virginia Peninsula to Harrison's Landing, where the defeated Army of the Potomac sheltered under the heavy guns of Union warships in the James River. True, there were many lost opportunities along the way, but it was still a momentous strategic success for the new army commander, the Confederate government—which breathed a sigh of relief—and the Southern people, who sensed the seemingly unstoppable tide of Federal victories was now truly at an end. And Jackson, they believed, who had brought such precious hope earlier that spring in the Valley, had helped make it possible. Most enlisted men thought this, too, affording Old Jack an honored place in a brand-new pantheon of leadership that had marshaled Lee's triumphant host. A joke started to circulate through the camps explaining the "real" reason the Yankees lost: "First, they had to climb two damned steep *Hills*, then came a *Longstreet*, and next a *Stonewall*, which was impregnable." [original emphasis] The Confederate press crowed about Stonewall's achievements around Richmond as if the general of the Valley and the Jackson of the Peninsula were one and the same, and for the first time people started to pair the names of Lee and Jackson together. *The Southern Literary Messenger* declared, "In the blaze of Lee's deserved glory, Stonewall Jackson has not been forgotten. That go-ahead, really great fighter—the pride and joy of the people—still stands in clear relief before the public gaze. Can any man tell what Lee would have done on the Chickahominy but for the unparalleled Napoleonic campaign in the Valley? Shall we ever forget the work of Jackson in the battles before Richmond?" The Richmond *Dispatch* also credited Stonewall for much of the victory, claiming in one issue McClellan "was badly beaten, and his retreat by his rear was cut off by the operations of Stonewall Jackson," and in another, "Lee [had] carr[ied] all their batteries, and Jackson had completely turned their right flank and rear." For the Confederate public, and especially Virginians, Jackson's bumbles were never illuminated and his previous aura now combined with Lee's as a result of the overall success in driving back the enemy from the capital. Remarks about his weak performance from brother officers certainly never made print, and even within the Army itself most of those who witnessed Stonewall stumble (and fall asleep) confined their criticism to private letters. Their focus was on the future. The Seven Days cumulatively represented a turning point in the war that wrested the strategic initiative in the Eastern Theater away from the enemy and conferred it upon Lee and the Army of Northern Virginia. Bright horizons beckoned for those who wished to see them.[33]

Yet the Army of the Potomac, although punished with over 16,000 casualties, had not been devastated, despite numerous chances that had presented themselves, some of them preconceived and planned by Lee. Most historians of the campaign agree those plans were sometimes miscommunicated and contained flawed expectations of synchronization among the rebel division commanders that were unrealistic given the green nature of the army, and McClellan's relatively skillful retreat and stubborn stands made by his subalterns in the various battles ensured his losses were not greater. Confederate staff work was poor, good maps scarce, and Stuart's cavalry and the intelligence it wrought underutilized. Even more determinant in the final result, however, were failures on the part of Lee's lieutenants. More than once, Stonewall's name must have crossed the commanding general's mind along with those of Magruder, Huger, and Holmes, who had all failed spectacularly at Glendale and would soon be sent away. The Valley General was terribly late at Mechanicsville, stopped cold at the White Oak Swamp, and performed only marginally at Gaines's Mill and Malvern Hill. After that last climactic engagement, the old Jackson seemed to reassert himself, as if he had literally awakened from a bad dream, his military acumen supposedly returning at the Poindexter House war council. By then he had gotten some much-needed sleep (although he was not yet fully recovered) and allusions to his exhaustion disappear thereafter from the historical record. Lee must have noticed the reappearance of the man he had come to know through correspondence and deed in the Valley, and forgiven him, even allowing him independent command again—convinced by Davis after Boteler's visit?—as a new threat and a new army, under Union Major General John Pope, materialized south of Washington. It was a decision laden with risk, as Lee had no way to know which General Jackson would emerge in the coming campaign, but it was one weighted with more personal knowledge of the man, his gifts, and weaknesses. No other subordinate except Longstreet had yet demonstrated any ability to command more than one division of troops, so Stonewall may have also benefitted from the paucity of other acceptable candidates. Whatever his reasoning, Lee had to act swiftly, and on July 13 ordered Old Jack and Ewell to board their divisions and entrain for Gordonsville, commencing what would become the Second Manassas Campaign.[34]

"Under ordinary circumstances the Federal Army should have been destroyed," a crestfallen Lee later wrote in his official report of the Seven Days. In a classic understatement of polite generality, he informed his wife Mary, "our success has not been as great or as complete as I could have desired, but God knows what is best for us." For this incomplete triumph, the rebels suffered over 20,000 dead, wounded, and missing, a number beyond the South's limited means to replace quickly, and Richmond, not yet prepared for carnage on such a scale, was inundated as the unrelenting heat of a Tidewater summer began to take its toll on those recovering in crowded, understaffed infirmaries and private homes alike. "The whole city is a hospital and the very atmosphere is poisoned and loathsome," wrote one Georgia soldier. Yet the capital had been saved, the enemy beaten, "thousands of arms and forty pieces of superior artillery" were captured, and Lee, in his debut as commander of the Army of Northern Virginia, had scored a strategic victory. He did not take it for granted, and true to his demeanor was thankful: to his soldiers, officers, and to God. Like Jackson, Lee firmly believed that divine providence steered the actions and thoughts of believing Christians toward blessings, if they but yielded their own will to His, and by extension, good fortune would also come to an army and nation that penitently submitted to the Lord. That the survival of both depended on war, with all its horror, suffering, and destruction, antithetical in its very nature to the gospel of the New Testament, was a brutal irony not lost on Lee throughout the war, but if his conscience ached for what he had just done on the Peninsula, there is no evidence of it. In General Orders No. 75, a congratulatory message to the army, he announced, "The general commanding, profoundly grateful to the only Giver of all victory for the signal success with which He has blessed our arms, tenders his warmest thanks and congratulations to the army, by whose valor such splendid results have been achieved."

Possibly imbued with the spirit of this message, and after over half a year had passed, months during which he and Jackson grew much closer personally and won most of their great campaigns together, Lee wrote the official report of the 1862 Richmond campaign. He took great care not to censure Stonewall, giving him, in the words of one biographer, "the maximum benefit of every permissible doubt," and gracefully explained away in a few phrases Jackson's obvious lapses. Thus, Lee's report of the Seven Days was not a true reflection of how he felt about Stonewall directly after the smoke cleared the fields southeast of the capital. In mid-July 1862 the commanding general was actually "deeply, bitterly disappointed," according to Porter Alexander, even as he must have realized that Jackson, his other lieutenants, and their soldiers had just endured a necessary seasoning experience. Next time should be better, but "the chances of battle," as Baron Jomini put it, made all war a risk. Jackson retained Lee's professional respect, but just barely. He would have to prove himself anew to renew his reputation with his chief. To become a partner in command, he would not only need to spend more time with Lee in person, but also continue earning that respect by demonstrating again the natural genius Lee detected in the Valley. [35]

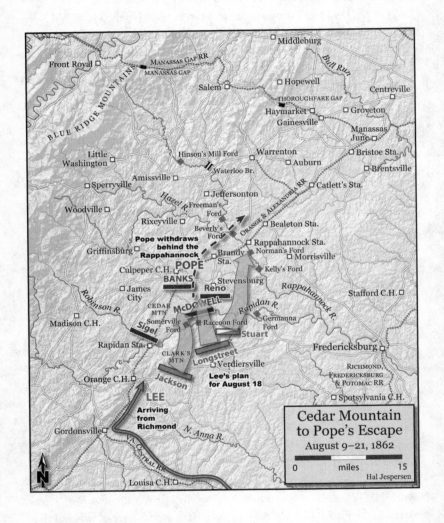

Cedar Mountain
to Pope's Escape
August 9–21, 1862

0   miles   15

Hal Jespersen

TWO

"God blessed our arms with another victory."

THE PARTNERSHIP CREATED

S unday, August 17, 1862 dawned warm but not too humid, a relief to the thousands of soldiers in gray and butternut under Stonewall Jackson's command encamped south of Clark's Mountain. Located about six miles northeast of Orange, Virginia, and just south of the Rapidan River, the "mountain" rose 1,100 feet above sea level, just tall enough to offer a splendid view on a clear day of the beautiful Piedmont countryside all the way up to Culpeper, but not so steep that parties of mounted men could not easily ascend its slopes to the lookout at its summit. There Jackson had placed a signal station, where observers from his army could keep a close watch on the Federals on the other side of the river. A trained eye using binoculars could discern tens of thousands of men in blue, soldiers of John Pope's newly formed Army of Virginia, by the white specks of their tents, which had sprouted up like mushrooms in the last several days. The Confederate signalmen watched their growth with apprehension, worried that nothing could stop so vast a host. Their commander, fresh from a camp church service in William Taliaferro's division and riding to meet Lee and Longstreet for a conference, held no such concerns. He saw a golden opportunity.[1]

So did Lee, and, although less enthusiastic, Longstreet. The three generals had met two days earlier in the genteel parlor of the Barbour House in Gordonsville, where Jackson, who had been operating independently in the area for almost a month, provided a brief review of the current situation. A good map prepared by Stonewall's topographical engineer, Jedediah Hotchkiss, lay on the table. The Valley General, now literally in view of the Blue Ridge that bordered his beloved valley, was animated as he described recent events, tracing points and routes with his finger as his colleagues looked on. Lee had sent him A. P. Hill's division in late July to bolster his numbers and assist in "suppressing" the "miscreant Pope," who had earned a loathsome reputation among Confederates for his bombastic proclamations, one of which determined to make war on Virginia's civilians. Watching and advising Jackson's operations from afar as he had in the Valley, Lee, who according to Jeb Stuart had at the time "rather a low estimate of Jackson's ability," once again found himself "relying upon [his] judgment, courage, and discretion, and trusting to the continued blessing of an ever-kind Providence." He sent him numerous letters both admonishing and bolstering him as July turned to August. Jackson replied quickly and eagerly, keeping communications strong and fully apprising his superior of developments. Slowly, through the course of this exchange of views, the commanding general began to notice the professional reemergence of Old Jack. Frustrated by poor cavalry support, annoyed by straggling in the ranks, and, as he informed his wife, "just overburdened with work," Stonewall had nonetheless substantially recovered from the exhaustion of the previous month and prayed that "In God's own time . . . he will send an army North and crown it with victory and make its fruits peace." Observing the Union army's approach from Culpeper in late July, Jackson waited for an opportunity to begin that process and assist the Almighty's purposes.

At Cedar Mountain on August 9 he found it, successfully attacking a wing of Pope's Army under the redoubtable Nathaniel Banks, who was determined to avenge the ignominy of Winchester. Conducted in scorching temperatures that saw men fall dead from heat exhaustion, it was another hard-fought rebel tactical victory, much like those Stonewall had won in the Valley, in which the general made some mistakes that cost lives. But like those battles, this one was unquestionably a success: Banks failed in his objective and retreated, Old Jack started to redeem his damaged reputation with Lee, and Pope was obliged to slow his advance toward the critical rail junction at Gordonsville. Lee, smiling when he received the news with Jackson's characteristic greeting, "God blessed our arms with another victory," wired back a sincere message of thanks that revealed at once some restoration of his confidence and a joint appreciation for the Lord's role in the success: "I congratulate you most heartily on the victory which God has granted you over our enemies at Cedar Run. The country owes to you and your brave officers and soldiers a deep debt of gratitude."[2]

Yet Jackson withdrew south of the Rapidan after his success because the rest of Pope's army had marched against him and tactically the battle almost miscarried, although that knowledge was not extant at the time. A. P. Hill's brigades had saved the day, despite the fact Stonewall had not heeded Lee's advice to "consult . . . and advise" with him, Ewell, or Sidney Winder, his other division commanders. Jackson's relations with Hill, already strained from the Seven Days, began to wither on the march to meet Banks, mimicking the condition of many soldiers, who suffered greatly in the heat. Hill complained of Jackson's secretiveness and lack of communication, whereas Old Jack thought Hill administratively careless and slow on the march. Both were right about the other. Winder, who commanded Jackson's old division and, despite his propensity for profanity, also his deep respect, was killed, affecting the Valley General deeply. "I can hardly think of the fall of Brigadier-General C. S. Winder without tearful eyes," he wrote Mary Anna. Yet he succored himself, as he had after earlier tragedies like the death of his first wife, with a complete trust in the Almighty and His divine will. "Let us all unite more earnestly in imploring God's aid in fighting our battles for us," he quickly added, secure in "the thought that there are so many of God's people praying His blessing upon the army," which "greatly strengthens and encourages me." Unbeknownst to all but a few who knew him well, Stonewall also enjoyed a good joke to help break the tension. The night before the battle, Hunter McGuire asked his chief if he thought they would fight the next day, and in complete calmness, Jackson answered, "Banks is in front of me, and he is always ready to fight." Then chuckling softly, he added, "and he generally gets whipped."[3]

The whipping of Banks rocked the boastful Pope back on his heels and obliged him to unify his army before continuing his campaign. He brought two divisions to Culpeper that had been threatening Fredericksburg and Lee's communications with Jackson, and joined with the rest of his army, increased his numbers to 50,000. More men would soon arrive. McClellan was still encamped defiantly at Harrison's Landing on the Peninsula, but had begun transporting elements of his army back up the Chesapeake. Lee, his headquarters returned to the Dabbs House after the Seven Days, had hesitated for weeks about leaving Richmond while the Army of the Potomac, although cowed, still threatened it. Now, thanks to captured northern newspapers like the *Philadelphia Inquirer* and his own local intelligence, he felt certain the Lincoln administration had ordered McClellan's embarkation. Taking a calculated risk and palliating Davis's concerns, Lee left a small force to guard the capital, sending Longstreet and the bulk of the Army of Northern Virginia westward to reinforce Jackson and concentrate on Pope. The commanding general sensed the same opportunity as Stonewall did, but framed it within the national strategic imperatives of the Confederacy: with McClellan en route to northern Virginia—the bulk of his army temporarily out of commission on naval transports—there existed a week, perhaps two, in which Pope might be struck a decisive blow before the first several corps of the Army of the Potomac reached him and swelled the combined Union army in Virginia to titanic proportions.[4]

Operationally and strategically Lee comprehended the key theoretical factors at work. First, the *timing* of the enemy's and his own movements determined everything. There was but a brief window during which he could assault Pope successfully, hopefully creating the chance for another inflection point like that which eluded him at Glendale, before the second factor came into play. And that one had been in the forefront of his mind since the outbreak of the war. Northern military and economic means, expressed in numbers of soldiers, cannon, and ships, and the financial and logistical apparatus that supported them, dwarfed those of the South, and combined with the geography of the Southern states, offered the Union an immense advantage *over time*. If Federal means were permitted to grow to their logical proportions and the Confederate leadership failed to arrest the process somehow, then, barring an act of divine intervention, the Confederacy's prospects for survival were slim. The rivers ran north to south in the Western Theater, greatly assisting Yankee incursions into the Mississippi River Valley, and most of the South's great cities were located on its coasts or along navigable rivers, where the Union navy could and already did convey a massive advantage to invading northern armies. Rebel generals had previously lost much in the West, Lee reasoned, making it unlikely a war-winning event would occur in that theater, and the coastal cities still in Southern hands, such as Charleston, could only hold out so long and tied up troops much needed by the field armies. If it was going to happen, the commanding general believed, the great stroke for independence would have to be executed in the East, and his army would have to achieve it soon. As Jackson explained in the meeting at Gordonsville, the local Virginia geography might assist him. Longstreet agreed, and the early morning of the 18th was set as the date to commence an offensive against the Federal Army of Virginia. On the 16th, the rebel infantry divisions of both lieutenants marched to the rear of Clark's Mountain to shield themselves from view and prepare for action.[5]

After Cedar Mountain, Pope condensed his corps in the triangle of land bordered by the Rapidan to the south, the Rappahannock to the north, and the Orange and Alexandria Railroad to the west. He had concentrated his army and now felt secure. The rivers could only be crossed at certain fords and bridges and were effective barriers—as they would continue to be throughout the war—between defenders and attackers. Once a riverine barrier was breached, however, the defender was at a disadvantage and had to either fight the assaulting force or flee. The railroad was Pope's only supply line back to Washington and represented a critical vulnerability that, if exploited properly by the Confederates, would not only jeopardize his campaign but also the survival of his command. His soldiers were already hungry, the supply trains held up by inefficiency. If the railroad bridge at Rappahannock Station could be burned simultaneously with a successful rebel crossing of the Rapidan, Pope would be in a very difficult situation. At the very least he would have to precipitously retreat, leaving behind huge quantities of stockpiled (non-edible) supplies, and possibly, just possibly, be forced to fight with Confederates behind and in front of him, setting the conditions for a Union catastrophe. Lee, Longstreet, and Jackson clearly realized these possibilities, but several difficulties stood in the way of enacting the previously agreed-to operational plan. The war council at the eastern base of Clark's Mountain that Sunday was called to work them out.[6]

In order to cut the Rappahannock Station bridge, sufficient and well-led cavalry was necessary. Brigadier General Beverly Robertson's brigade of horsemen, attached to Jackson's command since he arrived in the Gordonsville area had, in Stonewall's opinion, underperformed, and could not be relied upon. Congratulating Stuart on his "well earned promotion" to major general, Jackson sent him a note on July 31, informing him he had "suggested to [Lee] to have you assigned to the command of all the cavalry of the Department. I am desirous of seeing you along the front of my lines." Signing off, "very truly your friend, T. J. Jackson," the missive indicated the professional relationship rekindled on the Peninsula had evolved into a friendship between the two men, boding good things for the principal command team Lee was now settling upon. But Lee would not release Stuart to Jackson until he arrived in Gordonsville himself, still in need of the cavalryman's services around Richmond. Accordingly, Stuart had only recently arrived in the area before the 17th, and worse, he had had to leave half of his cavalry behind at Richmond as part of the force watching McClellan's departure. The other half, under Brigadier General Fitzhugh Lee, the commanding general's nephew, was still en route and farther behind than Stuart thought. Thus when he rode in to Lee's new mountainside camp that morning ahead of his colleagues and assured him he and Fitzhugh Lee's brigade would be ready at daybreak the next day at Raccoon Ford, the designated jump-off point, he created false expectations. He failed to mention that he did not impress upon the junior Lee the need for celerity, an omission that would shortly become important. Stuart left his chief almost as soon as he arrived, eager to meet Fitzhugh at Verdiersville, where the two would proceed together with their troopers to the ford. In short order, Jackson and Longstreet arrived, dismounted, and walked over to Lee's tent. Quickly it became evident there were problems to solve greater than absent cavalry.[7]

Longstreet sadly reported "his commissary supplies were so deficient, that it was impossible for his corps to move." His divisions had, in fact, left the Richmond area in haste and most brigades left their supply wagons behind, expecting them to catch up soon enough. Due to breaks in the Virginia Central Railroad line, however, and despite the herculean efforts of the company's workers to mend the tracks, the wagons still were not up and the troops were famished. Old Pete asked for a delay to the start of the operation, certain that by the end of the next day the wagons should arrive and his men would be able to march. Jackson could not believe his ears. Never had he worried about slow wagons. The quartermaster took care of that or faced charges. And soldiers followed their orders, regardless of the supply situation, and did their duty, or they and their officers were arrested. After the victory was won, they would forget their physical privations or take pride in them, as most of them had in the Valley. Astounded and dismayed, he glared at Longstreet, then looked at Lee. This time, unlike at Poindexter's, he would not hold back his opinion. No delay could be permitted, he argued, else Pope discover what lay in store for him and secrecy be compromised. The enemy had "most abundant supplies" at Brandy Station, just a "few hours march" away, which Longstreet's men "would undoubtedly capture by a rapid move." Even if it took longer to get there, "the intervening country had an abundance of green corn and green apples, both of which were relished by the soldiers." Here Jackson's assumptions, as recounted by a source unearthed by Dabney, were incorrect, as not all soldiers enjoyed these epicurean substitutes for army-issue rations, and Culpeper County had been picked clean by Pope's foraging parties. Moreover, Dabney joined the ranks of others after the war who relished any opportunity to boost their former chief at Longstreet's expense. But the exchanges in this brief meeting, if even partially accurate, reveal much about the three generals and their interactions.

Lee listened carefully to Stonewall, nodding in agreement, and seemed willing to order Longstreet to move when the latter reiterated his concerns. It just could not be done, he said. Interjecting, Jackson claimed he "had some surplus, and he would ride right back and send that down to Longstreet, if he would only consent to move" as previously decided. Lee hesitated, "with his courteous equilibrations of views," and pondered his options, aware of what was at stake. He rose from his camp chair, took a few steps, and peered into the woods. Stonewall, inspirited to loquaciousness by the threat the operation might be postponed, again spoke, "renew[ing] his entreaties with almost passionate eagerness," but it was too late. Lee had made his decision. The two wings of the army would now cross the Rapidan to the east of the mountain late tomorrow afternoon. In many ways, this was a compromise between Longstreet's wish for a longer delay and Jackson's desire to retain the original plan, and signified the commanding general's care in weighing advice from his subordinates. It also demonstrated a strong emotional intelligence, an ability to consider the feelings of others involved in making a decision, and ensuring their viewpoints were heard and their input valued. Lee had been gifted with this talent from his first years in the antebellum army and honed it in the pressure cooker of President Davis's office. Now he used it to resolve a dilemma as army commander, thinking hard about the chances that the postponement would create a possibility for Pope's escape. He deemed them unlikely. [8]

Jackson, utterly focused on winning the crushing victory, could not understand the compromise and walked dejectedly away to a nearby tree. His loyalty to Lee and adherence to military prerogatives was absolute, so once the commanding general made up his mind, Stonewall would not think of challenging the decision. Yet it was very clear he believed it unwise. Lying down on the ground, he "groaned most audibly," to the annoyance of Longstreet, who murmured to Lee such conduct "was not respectful to the council." If Old Jack heard the reproof there is no record of it, and in any case Lee must have forgiven him the outburst, as the next day Pope secretly began to prepare a withdrawal, proving the correctness of Jackson's instinct. As Longstreet oversaw the distribution of rations to his men, from the lookout post atop Clark's Mountain Lee and his staff peered through their binoculars and discerned the enemy in "fancied security," supposedly "in utter ignorance of the vicinity of a powerful foe," as one of Lee's aides remarked. But appearances belied reality. Pope had started to gather scraps of information from various scouts that the Confederates were up to something, and combined with a cautionary message from General-in-chief Henry Halleck in Washington suggesting retreat, he became nervous. His apprehension was confirmed when he obtained a copy of Lee's orders through the capture of one of Stuart's staffers earlier that morning, who, along with his chief, had been reposing at Verdiersville awaiting Fitzhugh Lee and his brigade when an itinerant probe of Yankee cavalry came storming down the road, having broken through an unguarded section of the Confederate line along the Rapidan. Stuart himself barely escaped capture, losing his famous ostrich-plumed hat and cape as he hastily jumped a backyard fence. Fitzhugh Lee was late, and Stuart blamed him for the misfortune, forgetting that he had earlier omitted to tell the young brigadier that speed was of the essence. The real reason behind the blunder was a disagreement between the infantry brigadier in charge of the breached picket line and Longstreet, which related to an earlier feud on the Peninsula. Yet combined with the Union army's own actions and Longstreet's plea for delay, these factors conspired in a vicious circle of friction reminiscent of the Seven Days to rob from the Army of Northern Virginia a resounding triumph in between the rivers. Even so, there was still a chance if the Confederates moved early on Tuesday the 19th they could catch the bluecoats in column as they withdrew. The younger Lee's extreme tardiness obliged his uncle to wait yet one more day before commencing the advance on Pope, and as Lee reported to Davis, "this [final] delay proved fatal to our success." When the commanding general and Longstreet ascended Clark's Mountain about noon on the 19th in response to reports from the signalmen that the Yankees were gone, all they saw were the receding dust clouds of Pope's army, which made good its escape across the Rappahannock.[9]

Characteristically stoic, Lee met the disappointment with determination and, aware he could not now deal Pope a heavy blow until north of the rivers, decided to allow his army the remainder of the day to rest. The men would need it; a week of long, hot marches lay before them as their commander tried to catch up to the Federals, get across the Rappahannock unimpeded, and land on the Yankees' operational right flank.

Early on the 20th the two wings of the rebel army, informally organized under Jackson on the left and Longstreet on the right, Stuart leading the way with the cavalry brigades, began splashing through the Rapidan in pursuit of the Unionists. Stuart, wearing a red bandana in place of his famous hat, endured jibes from both the gray infantrymen and his own troopers. Catcalls such as "Lookee, boys—Jeb's got a new hat!" or "Hi! Cavalry! Whar's yo' hat?" swarmed him from all sides. In a letter to his wife, he expressed no indignance, but swore revenge: "I lost my haversack, blanket, talma, cloak, & hat that had that palmetto star. Too bad, wasn't it? I intend to make the Yankees pay dearly for that hat." On August 22, as the infantry under Old Jack and Old Pete tramped northward in pursuit of Pope's retreating army and fought a sharp, bloody fight at Freeman's Ford on the Rappahannock, the cavalrymen received permission from Lee to commence a ride around the Federals. His mission was to burn bridges and hinder their progress while gathering information on the enemy. Stuart failed to burn the key bridge he encountered, but did obtain intelligence on Pope's dispositions and the proximity of McClellan's approaching corps. He also got his chance to avenge the captured hat. In a perfect example of Clausewitzian chance, as Stuart's troopers left Warrenton and approached the small hamlet of Catlett's Station, where they hoped to burn the railroad bridge over Cedar Run, an escaped slave wandered into their lines and freely told Stuart and his staff that Pope's headquarters lay just up the road. It was a very lucky break, both for the cavalry leader and his commanding general. In a drenching rainstorm that he called "the darkest night I ever knew," his men successfully attacked the encampment, capturing 300 prisoners, $20,000 in gold, Pope's dispatch book and other personal papers, and the general's dress uniform. The gold helped fund the Confederate war effort, the dispatch book and papers confirmed Lee's deductions about his adversary's plans and locations, and Stuart was able to write back to his wife, "I have had my revenge out of Pope." He proposed a "a fair exchange of the prisoners"—his hat and cape for Pope's coat—but Pope refused to reply, and the coat was soon on display in Richmond, a trophy of war.[10]

Returning from the raid and soon to be escorting Jackson's wing of the army, Stuart may have encountered Stonewall riding his horse, a diminutive, imperturbable little mare named Little Sorrel, at the front of his wing of the army. The cavalryman's leading biographer questions the veracity of the story, but supposedly Stuart rode up on his impressive charger, all smiles and bluster, his staff streaming behind him. "Hello, Jackson!" he called out. "I've got Pope's coat; if you don't believe it, there's his name." Holding up the dress uniform with its inscribed monogram for Stonewall to see, Stuart's smile grew wider by the second. Old Jack, peering upward from underneath his cap's visor, inspected the garment and blithely rejoined, "General Stuart, I would much rather you brought General Pope instead of his coat."[11]

If true, the episode was a rare moment of mirth in a period brimming with anxiety and expectation for Jackson. Both the 22nd and the 23rd were days of frustration, with less progress made on the march than he wished, and on the 23rd a near disaster had been averted. Brigadier General Jubal Early's brigade became isolated on the enemy-controlled east side of the Rappahannock the day before, thanks to fast-rising water from mountain storms. Stonewall had ordered them across at the ford at Warrenton Sulphur Springs in hopes of securing a bridgehead to begin flanking Pope. Expecting the already high water to subside, the river rose instead, threatening the loss of one of his best fighting units and generals. If the Yankees suddenly descended on the exposed Early no amount of artillery support from the west bank could save him. Old Jack watched helplessly from his side of the stream as the day wore on, his mood descending as rapidly as the water rose. By midafternoon it started to subside, and Jackson pitched in himself to help a work party build a makeshift bridge. By the early morning of the 24th Early had managed to extricate his brigade, but Stonewall's nerves had not yet recovered, and he slept fitfully. He knew the affair at the ford had held up the entire army's progress, and that bothered him. Then a note from Lee arrived. The commanding general desired a meeting and would come to his headquarters. By the afternoon of that day the Valley General had made camp at a little village called Jeffersonton, about twelve miles northeast of Culpeper, and prepared to receive Lee.[12]

Who decided the council would take place in the middle of a grassy field, with one table spread with maps and a couple folding camp chairs to accommodate the generals, is unknown. "It was a curious scene," an onlooker recalled, "not even a tree within hearing." Possibly the recent capture of Pope's dispatches, coupled with the earlier loss of Lee's own attack plan, instigated the decision for secrecy. No official records of the meeting exist, and none of the major participants ever wrote down any details of it in private correspondence. Two sources only, written after the war by officers in Stonewall's staff (Henry Kyd Douglas and McGuire) known for their bias toward Jackson, provide enough information to reconstruct this momentous gathering. That it was strategically of the greatest significance is unquestionable, because what the generals discussed in this "very brief" colloquy not only set up the conditions for the Second Battle of Manassas, which in turn influenced the decision to cross the Potomac a few days later, but also signified a major change in how Lee dealt with his subordinates and led his army. No more would only written instructions issue forth from the commanding general's tent, explicating in painstaking detail the dates, times, and march routes of a given operation. Instead, any written orders would *complement* verbal ones that had been given beforehand or clarify for those not present at key meetings what was expected. Going forward, Lee would allow his primary subalterns a wide berth of discretion to execute his general intent. Put simply, he would tell them what he wanted accomplished—often after careful consultation with them—and then leave it to their own devices to ensure those objectives were achieved. On a theoretical level, this represented a fundamental shift in command responsibility and bespoke Lee's ability as a leader to learn from mistakes (the Cheat Mountain and Seven Days campaigns come to mind), delegate proper authority to those deserving it, and *trust* his subordinates' judgment. Certainly, he had earlier demonstrated harbingers of all these traits, but the discussion and outcome of the Jeffersonton council marked a watershed moment for Lee and his command team. It spoke volumes not only about Lee's leadership skills but also those of the generals he trusted most. That shift in command and control represented a major step forward in the Lee-Jackson relationship, indicating that Lee now believed Stonewall fully capable again of independent command and able to use his good judgment to conceive successful ways to achieve Lee's ends. That those ends also tended to coincide with Old Jack's own strategic designs should not be surprising, especially considering the offensive predilections of both generals, their similar grasp of the strategic imperatives facing their country, and correspondence between them corroborating both. Longstreet and Stuart attended the meeting as well, which also made this cursory council of war the very first in the history of the Army of Northern Virginia where the triad of Lee's principal lieutenants met with the commanding general to decide the future of the Confederacy.[13]

Neither of the two accounts that describe what happened were written contemporaneously and neither McGuire nor Douglas heard any of the conversation except Jackson's very last words. They and the rest of Lee's and Jackson's staffs "were lounging on the grass of an adjacent knoll," enjoying the temporary respite from duty. The day must have been warm and blessed with sunshine after the heavy storms of the 22nd; if it were too hot or rainy the generals would have never met out in the open. The grass glimmered with the deep, luxurious green color of the late summer and one can imagine how much Little Sorrel and General Lee's favorite mount, a male grey named Traveller, must have relished grazing nearby. After the preliminary salutations Jackson started talking, according to McGuire, "very much excited," found a clear patch of dirt next to the table and began "drawing with the toe of his boot a map in the sand, and gesticulating in a much more earnest way than he was in the habit of doing." Unlike during the Seven Days, Stonewall had very good maps of the local area, thanks to the diligent work of Jedediah Hotchkiss, and would have known precisely the lay of the land before him. "Lee was simply listening," examining his colleague's boot sketch, and said nothing until "after Jackson had got through." Then "he nodded his head, as if acceding to some proposal." At some point during this demonstration, Longstreet and Stuart must have arrived and taken seats next to the commanding general, "Longstreet . . . on his right, General Stuart on his left," with Jackson remaining standing opposite Lee. Douglas noted the positions with such precision that, when combined with McGuire's account, it appears plausible Jackson may have dominated the discussion (a conclusion, of course, Douglas would have desired), but to extend that premise to assume the Valley General originated the bold plan to divide the army and outflank Pope with his smaller wing while Longstreet and Lee followed with theirs, is speculative. That that new approach to the operation against Pope was considered and agreed to at Jeffersonton is not. Stuart later told Hotchkiss in 1863 that "Gen. Jackson was entitled to all the credit for the movement around the enemy and Gen. Lee had, very reluctantly, consented to it," but no other source substantiates that entry in the mapmaker's journal. In all likelihood, Lee and Jackson developed the plan together, with input from the later-arriving Longstreet and Stuart, and the commanding general made the final decision after weighing the risks and the potential benefits. Such a probable division of the mental labor involved in devising the new operational plan makes sense based on Lee's evolving command style and the precedent of the earlier Clark's Mountain war council. Regardless of how it was precisely determined, the course the four generals set for their army was a daring one and laden with strategic contingency. At stake was nothing less than the transfer of the theater of war from the vicinity of Richmond to that of Washington, the fate of their army, and probably John Pope's as well. They could not have known—although some authors have hinted Lee and Jackson had it in mind—how the decision made at this table in the sunny meadow would create a string of events fulfilling Jackson's wish to bring the war north. As the meeting adjourned and the leaders bade their farewells, Old Jack called for Douglas, and as the aide approached, he heard Jackson tell Lee, "I will be moving within an hour."[14]

The troops did not exactly start moving in an hour, but Stonewall did, sending messages to Hill, Taliaferro, and Ewell, and providing specific orders for his staff. The men were to cook three days of rations and leave the baggage wagons behind, proof that fast and hard marching was imminent. Evidence that Lee handed Old Jack complete freedom of maneuver is derived from a note he gave his chief engineer, asking for the most efficient but "covered route to Manassas," which indicated also that Jackson intended to end up in that general vicinity. But letters from Lee to Davis provide insight into Confederate intentions for the campaign, which did not apparently include fighting a climactic battle on or near the site of First Manassas. Instead, Lee's primary objectives, at least initially, were to "change the theater of the war from James River to north of the

Rappahannock" to relieve the logistical pressure on central and southern Virginia and other points south and to keep forcing Pope's army to move farther north and east. If Jackson cut the Union general's supply line, which was still the Orange and Alexandria Railroad, it would almost certainly cause him to fall back toward Washington. Accomplishing that would temporarily keep his force from uniting fully with McClellan and possibly open other opportunities, such as striking elements of the moving enemy in detail or shifting operations to the west, perhaps to the northern Shenandoah Valley. From Pope's captured dispatches Lee understood the Army of the Potomac's leading corps had already landed east of Fredericksburg and were well on the way to joining with the Army of Virginia. From this intelligence he also correctly deduced he had only a few more days before the weight of Union numbers would grab the theater initiative away from him and hand it back to the Federals.

Preparing for that unhappy possibility even as he expected success from Stonewall, Lee almost demanded Davis send him "all available reinforcements," and then started ordering up individual units himself using his authority as department commander, bypassing the president and secretary of war. "Should you not agree with me in the propriety of this step please countermand the order & let me know," he wrote Davis on the morning of the 24th. The president was hardly going to do such a thing, and Lee knew it, revealing the general's political sagacity and emotional intelligence in dealing with the policymaker. He understood, in its intrinsic substance, where the line that separated civilian commander in chief and military chief commander lay in the relationship, and he pushed it to the limit on this occasion (and others) to the benefit of Confederate fortunes. Other rebel army commanders, such as Joseph E. Johnston, Braxton Bragg, and P.G.T. Beauregard, never discerned where that line was in their ill-starred relationships with Davis, did not possess the requisite personal skills to work around his admittedly difficult personality, or both. That reality by itself made Lee a precious commodity for the Confederacy.[15]

Jackson's wing of 23,500 began moving in the predawn hours of the 25th, and to Stonewall's satisfaction the men proceeded with alacrity and the artillery and ambulances kept up with the infantry. Only one lone

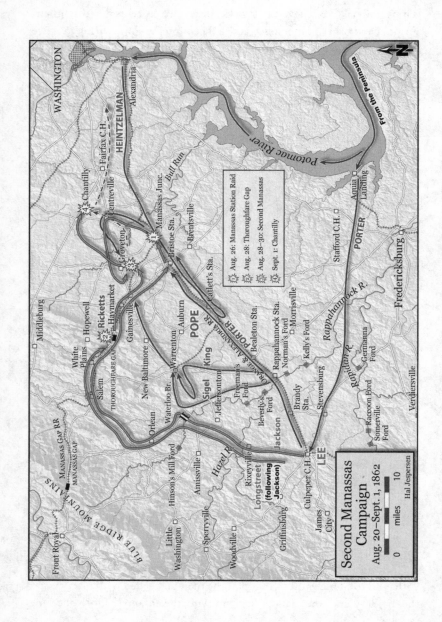

Second Manassas
Campaign
Aug. 20–Sept. 1, 1862

Hal Jespersen

0   miles   10

Aug. 26: Manassas Station Raid
Aug. 28: Thoroughfare Gap
Aug. 28–30: Second Manassas
Sept. 1: Chantilly

cavalry regiment, the 2nd Virginia under Colonel Thomas Munford, led the way, but for now it was enough. Stuart was under orders to join him soon and would meet him the next day at Gainesville with Robertson's and Fitzhugh Lee's brigades. From Jeffersonton to the equally tiny burg of Amissville, across the Rappahannock at Hinson's Mill, moving through another small village named Orleans up to Salem, marched the core of the old Valley Army plus A. P. Hill's "Light Division." Just outside Salem, their general stopped, dismounted Little Sorrel, and climbed a large stone by the roadway. His head in need of cooling, he doffed his worn-out kepi and watched bare-headed as the soldiers passed, receiving their cheers. Fearful enemy cavalry probes might hear, he motioned for them to be quiet and acknowledged their silent salutes as "the whole great column" marched past in packed ranks, each man with his own cap or hand waving in the air. The men's faces beamed as they watched the day's last light reflected in their commander's weathered face, "the splendid August sun . . . about to kiss the distant crest of the Blue Ridge" to their left. When the Stonewall Brigade hove into view, the soldiers could not restrain themselves and spontaneously broke into the rebel yell. "It is of no use," Jackson said with muted pride to a nearby staff officer. "You see I cannot stop them. Who could not conquer with such troops as these?" Still marching after darkness cloaked the wondrous landscape not yet despoiled by war, the entire army slept under the stars, collapsing on the side of the road and barely stacking arms before sleep overtook them. Most had tramped twenty-six miles, a mileage approaching Stonewall's records in the Valley. Characteristically understated, he simply reported it a "severe day's march."[16]

Napoleon would have been proud. His Ninth Maxim instructed, "The strength of an army, like the power in mechanics, is estimated by multiplying the mass by the rapidity; a rapid march augments the morale of an army, and increases its means of victory. Press on!" A student of the maxims, Jackson especially internalized this one and even adopted the emperor's last words as he encouraged his army onward the next day. The soldiers rose early, while the skies were still dark and only a hint of the glow of the morning sunrise could be seen in the East. Not long after they fell into ranks and started moving, their route turned toward the rising sun and soon the men found themselves crossing over Thoroughfare Gap in the Bull Run Mountains.

No enemy ambush greeted Munford's cavalry troopers in the front. Good, good, Stonewall thought, now they were getting close to their goal: Bristoe Station on the Orange and Alexandria. Once there, the tracks torn up and the depot burned, Stonewall could stop, having accomplished what Lee intended. His lead brigades, now protected by Stuart's cavalry on either flank, reached the place before dark without so much as a shot fired in anger. They captured the small Union garrison, tore up the tracks, wrecked two trains, and scared the daylights out of the engineers of two others that escaped. Learning that nearby Manassas Junction with its vast storehouse of Union supplies lay poorly defended just five miles distant, Jackson permitted Stuart's cavalry and Brigadier Isaac Trimble and two handpicked infantry regiments to storm it, which they did early the next morning. Jackson now had possession of Pope's major supply depot, stocked with all manner of commissary goods, a veritable heaven to the ragged, tired soldiers who would soon be allowed to plunder it. It had been another brutal day for the men in the ranks, but Jackson had more than accomplished his mission. Major G. Moxley Sorrel, Longstreet's chief of staff, later penned, "in swiftness, daring, and originality of execution," Stonewall's flank march against Pope was "almost extraordinary." But there had been some straggling on the second day, indicating the physical cost on his command had been high. A soldier in Hill's division remembered the two days of forced marches as an athletic endurance test with "no systematic halts" and "weary monotony," the "foot sore men, accoutered as they were" simply falling down on the ground at the end of the day "without so much as spreading a blanket." General William Dorsey Pender, a brigadier under Hill, said he did not like serving under Jackson, "for he forgets that one ever gets tired, hungry, or sleepy." Yet while most of the enlisted men were exhausted from becoming foot cavalry again, with fifty-six miles behind them in two days, they respected Old Jack for pushing them to the feat. "I do not think any man can take General Jackson's place in the confidence and love of his troops," a Virginia captain wrote. "I have learned to look up to him with implicit confidence." Other soldiers forgave him when they feasted on confiscated canned lobster, sardines, and champagne at Manassas Junction.[17]

While Jackson's men marched—and some later ate—their hearts out, Longstreet's wing of the army did its best to occupy the Federal leadership's attention and keep it focused on the Rappahannock line. Although the

Confederate flanking column was discovered mid-morning and reported to Pope, he misinterpreted the information and reasoned the rebels were headed to the Shenandoah and not to his rear. Confederate artillery duels with their Union counterparts across the river helped the Northern commander rationalize his estimate by impressing upon him the bulk of the Southern army still lay in his front (which it did, for a short time), and he even extended his line to the east downriver to better link up with elements of the Army of the Potomac. It was not until close to 8:00 P.M. that Pope realized his supply line had been cut and, combined with the small mountain of reports that had filtered in throughout the late afternoon and early evening, started to understand he was in trouble. How could this have happened? He asked himself: could Lee really be so mad as to divide his forces with my army in between, and McClellan on the way? Such a move, he perceived, defied any reasonable, orthodox military thinking of the day. One of Pope's subordinates coddled him by stating of the apparently partitioned Confederates, "Either of these operations seems to me too hazardous for him to undertake with us in his rear and flank." This was not helpful advice, and considering it came from the defeated Union general at First Manassas, Irvin McDowell, Pope should have been skeptical, especially considering his near-disaster in between the rivers just the week before. But the Union commander kept asking others for advice, dithering, allowing precious hours to tick away—time that Lee and Longstreet would need as they began their march to join Jackson on the 27th. A flurry of telegraphs back and forth with Halleck in Washington achieved little but false confirmation for Pope and exasperation for Halleck, who angrily told the field commander, "Just think of the immense amount of telegraphing I have to do, and then say whether I can be expected to give you any details as to movements of others, even when I know them." The Northern command and control system, centralized in Washington and in Pope's headquarters, had broken down in the face of a crisis. With nothing left to feed his army, the enemy seemingly everywhere at once, and no guarantees of assistance from McClellan beyond the divisions already close by, Pope decided to retreat northward. He puffed up the decision under the auspices of going to "bag Jackson."[18]

The decentralized Confederate command and control system, in contrast, was exhibiting marked improvement under Lee's new method. A score of carefully selected couriers kept Jackson and Lee in touch throughout most of the flank march and after Stonewall had taken up a defensive position at Groveton, adjoining the old First Manassas battlefield. Lee knew where his subordinate was and Jackson felt secure the commanding general would soon unite with him. Forced to withdraw his divisions to a safer, consolidated location on the 27th after small collisions with the enemy at Manassas Junction—now plundered and burned—convinced him the Unionists were both retreating in his direction and coming at him from Washington, Stonewall seemingly disappeared into the hilly woods behind a railroad cut and waited for Lee to reach him. Stuart, providing constant reports, guarded his flanks. In probable accordance with Lee, however, if opportunity beckoned to severely damage the enemy, he would take it. Anything that hurt the Yankees and attrited their ability to wage war was fair game to Jackson, whether that be Northern economic or military targets. On the late evening of the 28th, as Longstreet's wing marched hard following the same route Old Jack had just taken, an inviting military target would present itself in the form of the division of Brigadier General Rufus King of McDowell's corps, which was looking for Stonewall but would have severely interfered with Longstreet's approach were it not attacked. The sharp fight at Brawner's Farm ensued, a vicious affair that resulted in the wounding of Taliaferro and Ewell, both of whom would require months to recover and were temporarily lost to the service (Ewell losing a leg). But the Valley General had stopped King, alerted Pope to his location, and focused the Federal high command on him, allowing Longstreet and Lee to advance unimpeded. Thus began the second great battle on the same fields where Jackson had won his nickname over a year earlier. [19]

Stonewall was glad to have finally grappled with Pope. The previous month, prior to his departure for Gordonsville, his conviction that a hard, ruthless war would have to be waged against the North was confirmed and strengthened by the Union general's proclamations against Southern civilians. Jackson probably hated Pope personally and wanted him "suppressed" as much, if not more than Lee. In a confidential discussion with his brother-in-law, Captain Rufus Barringer of the 1st North Carolina Cavalry, Stonewall confessed his feelings privately in his tent one night: "I have myself cordially accepted the policy of our leaders. They are great and good men," he began, referencing the Confederate policy of waging war according to understood principles defined by Jomini in *The Art of War*, that, along with Napoleon's Maxims, had been distilled into lessons at West Point and to which all military men were supposed to adhere. "Possibly, too, as things then stood, no other policy was left open to us than the one pursued by President Davis and General Lee. But all this is now suddenly changed by the cruel and utterly barbarous orders of General Pope, who is not only subsisting his army on the people of Culpepper, [sic] and levying contributions upon them, but has laid whole communities under the pains and penalties of death or banishment; and in certain cases directed that houses shall be razed to the ground, and citizens shot without waiting civil process." Such a course defied accepted Jominian standards of conduct toward civilians and signaled an alternative way of war, brutal, terrible, and unrelenting. Indignant and clearly upset, Jackson, who knew Barringer only slightly before the war as Mary Anna's brother, confided what he had already done. "This new phase of the struggle is full upon us, and General Lee is in great perplexity how to meet it. I have just had a conference with him on this vital point. . . . I gave him frankly certain outlines of my own plan of waging the contest, which he considered favorably, and which he promised to lay before Mr. Davis, and try to secure his approval, in whole or in part." Stonewall then explained what he thought the new Confederate war "policy" should be, using the term in a manner consistent with what would today be termed a national military strategy. Cavalry would be important, he told Barringer, which was part of the reason he wanted him to hear his proposal.[20]

"As to a general policy," he said, "I think it unwise to attempt to defend the whole of our extended lines, especially our extended coast and water line. The enemy largely exceed us in men and material of war, especially in naval appliances, and our limited supply of both troops and munitions of war would ultimately be exhausted in a prolonged, gigantic struggle. To offset their palpable advantage in this respect, I would seek to utilize the special points in which the South clearly leads the North, and I would risk the whole issue on the development of these special characteristics, and the war policy based thereon." To all enemy combatants who dared to compromise "the safety of our Southern homes," Jackson offered the "black flag," a method that ostensibly inferred a no-quarter guideline for enemy soldiers caught pillaging civilians. To win independence, however, he advocated "giving up, as circumstances might seem to require, many exposed points and all untenable positions, and gradually concentrate our choicest fighting men and most valuable material at a few strong interior camps" from which, he maintained, the homeland might be better defended and communications upheld. So far, Jackson's thoughts, although a bit radical for that time in the war, illustrated the general military strategy of concentrating troops into larger armies, a process then underway throughout the Confederacy, and one that had replaced Davis's earlier misplaced "perimeter defense" national military strategy of attempting to defend all the frontiers. They also echoed the calls emanating from earnest Southern partisans in Congress, the statehouses, and newspaper offices that demanded punitive dealings with captured Yankee foragers.[21]

But a defensive approach to the war this was not. Jackson advocated that the "camps," which could be translated as small, highly mobile armies, would embark upon "ceaseless aggressions" upon the Northern states. "These counter-invasions would be the main feature of my policy," he averred, arriving at the startling details of his proposal, which were even harsher than what he shared with General Smith the previous year. "I would organize our whole available fighting force, so selected and located, into two, four, or more light moveable columns, specially armed and trained and equipped for sudden moves and for long and rapid marches. These light moveable columns I would hurl against the enemy as they entered our borders; but only when sure of victory, and when the loss of an army was impossible. But better, I would hurl these thunderbolts of war against the rich cities and teeming regions of our Federal friends. . . . I would subsist my troops, as far as possible, on the Northern people. I would lay heavy contributions in money on their cities," take no prisoners (paroling the enlisted men), but retain "noted leaders, held mainly as hostages for ransom or for retaliation. . . . All this just as Pope is doing in Northern Virginia." When one small army was returning to the South, another, "possibly hundreds of miles away" would move into the Union, thereby making it "hot for our friends at *their* [original emphasis] homes and firesides, all the way to Kansas . . . and doubly so for Ohio and Pennsylvania." Jackson admitted to Barringer that much Southern territory might be lost using such a military strategy, "but it would save the risk of losing whole armies by capture, disease, or death in battle. My whole policy would aim to husband our resources of men, money, and material." The people of the South, he claimed, would not have accepted this violent form of war earlier, but now "they begin to realize the scope and design of the Abolition element. Ben Butler, Frémont, and Pope are fast opening their eyes." After the loss of "whole armies at Donaldson [sic] and elsewhere" and the "great victories here at Richmond, our troops would now rejoice at the hope of an aggressive movement. . . . I would right now seize the golden moment to show the North what they may expect."[22]

Although it is probable Jackson's exact words were expanded and embellished by Barringer as he recollected the conversation several decades later, the overall theme of the discussion agreed with the Valley General's earlier strategic thinking as expressed to Smith, Boteler, and in letters to Lee. It also portrayed growth in that thinking as a result of recent events, which lends even greater credence to the likely veracity of Barringer's account. Most significantly, however, it displayed a mind that was unequivocally engaged with the truly *strategic* character of the Civil War as it was then evolving, and specifically the strategic problems facing the Confederacy. This was not merely the ill-considered rantings of a tactical-operational level leader, but rather one who continued to think deeply about war-winning and war-losing prospects. His proposals elucidated, in the context he then knew, the paradigms of ends, ways, means; risk acceptance; an understanding of political constraints and societal norms; geographic limitations; the theory of Jominian concentration in time and space; and a recognition that *warfare*—how wars are actually waged (methods, processes, tactics, technologies)—may change within a given military conflict. Clearly, Jackson now believed the time had come for his strategic way of war to be implemented. Yet the discussion with Barringer also denotes Stonewall's unquestioned loyalty to Lee and faith in his judgment. He would suggest, advise, and offer his opinion henceforth, but he would obey without flinching. That deferential quality in Jackson's personality was a key component of his professional relationship with Lee. That the commanding general respectfully considered his advice, and, perhaps, acted upon it, reinforced this predilection in Stonewall's behavior.[23]

Preparing his cot for a good night's sleep (which he relished after the fatigue of the Seven Days), the Valley General added, "But I well know that General Lee is not at liberty to choose his own policy now. In three hours I may be on the march—possibly to flank McClellan, but more likely to fight Pope. . . . General Lee has assented to a single phase of my policy, so far as to promise me the organization of at least one of these 'light moveable columns,' and with it I am to make the invasion, of course only at such point as may then seem open." Just before he fell asleep, he murmured, "All this may come to naught. If McClellan remains in command, such a policy could hardly be ventured upon. If Pope invites a battle and we beat him, the *whole* [original emphasis] army may have to pursue him. I should regret this; but the emergencies of war often leave us no discretion. And General Lee will do just what the situation requires." In retrospect of Lee's decisions to send Jackson to Gordonsville ahead of the main army; embark upon a new, decentralized, intent-based command style; dispatch Jackson and a sizeable "column" of almost 24,000 soldiers to Pope's flank and rear; the generals' shared antipathy for Pope; and the later decision to raid into Maryland after Second Manassas, Jackson's words, as transcribed by Barringer, ring prognostic.[24]

If, in less than two months' worth of time, between the end of the Seven Days and the Battle of Second Manassas, Robert E. Lee appeared to have become more in sync with Stonewall's aggressive strategic thoughts, there was more to it than outrage over John Pope's embarkation of hard war on Virginia civilians. Although Arlington House, located across the Potomac from Washington, was the home of his wife, Lee considered it his own, a place where his "affections & attachments are more strongly placed than at any other place in the world." Here he had raised his family and spent countless joyful hours, experiencing the satisfaction derived from domestic happiness. By the summer of 1862 the house and grounds had not only been occupied by the Union Army (which occurred in the spring of 1861), but countless personal effects not salvaged by Mary upon her departure in May 1861 had vanished, purloined by Federals interested in souvenirs, petty thievery, or personal revenge. Even George Washington's punch bowl and giant campaign tent, which had descended to Mary by inheritance, had been packed up and carted away. She was outraged. "Those cow thieves . . . will plunder & destroy everything," she wrote on March 8, 1862. As a career army officer, Lee was initially more reserved and reflective regarding the collateral damage caused by war, but devotion to his wife and to her home started to foment an intense bitterness in him that was spilling over by the summer of that year. As early as Christmas 1861, in a moment of candor, he wrote one of his daughters, "I should have preferred it to have been wiped from the earth, its beautiful hill sunk, and its sacred trees buried, rather than to have been degraded by the presence of those who revel in the ill they do for their own selfish purposes."[25]

Although his letters to Mary thereafter are silent regarding Arlington's fate, he was very well aware of the destruction of another Lee family estate, White House, on the Virginia Peninsula, burned by McClellan's retreating troops for apparently no good reason. Mary had sought refuge there after fleeing Arlington, and then found herself forced to leave a second home when the Federals began their advance on Richmond. She pinned a note on its door that read: "Northern soldiers who profess to reverence Washington, forbear to desecrate the house of his first married life [sic], the property of his wife, now owned by her descendants." She signed it, "A grand-daughter of Mrs. Washington." At first her request was honored, but in the chaos of the evacuation of the nearby Union supply depot after the Battle of Mechanicsville, the house was torched. It was a devastating blow to the entire Lee family, one the general doubtless knew almost immediately. His second son, Fitzhugh "Rooney" Lee (not be confused with his nephew Fitzhugh), rode with Jeb Stuart, who trotted past the smoking ruins the day after the burning. Stuart reported "an opportunity was here offered for observing the deceitfulness of the enemy's pretended reverence for everything associated with the name of Washington, for the dwelling-house was burned to the ground." The burning of White House piled on to the loss of Arlington, as one of Lee's recent biographers aptly noted, "radicalized [the Lees] with a power far beyond political rhetoric . . . It was an act of personal violation and as such invoked a personal vengeance." By the summer of 1862 those losses "and the destruction in Virginia had radicalized him" to the point "he disliked the idea of waiting passively to respond to Union attacks." For both strategic and personal reasons, then, Lee had come to believe the war must be brought northward. He had considered the idea previously during Stonewall's Valley Campaign, but now he was in earnest. He and Jackson were finally of the same mind, even if the ruthlessness intended by Old Jack was not in full accord with the commanding general's own personal preferences.[26]

Before any movement across the Potomac could even be contemplated, however, Pope had to be dispensed with. The Second Battle of Manassas, begun when Jackson struck King's division on the evening of August 28, continued for two more bloody days. On the 29th, the Federal general, certain he could destroy Stonewall before Longstreet appeared, launched a series of disjointed but powerful division-level assaults against Jackson's positions at Groveton. During the all-day battle, Old Jack's lines bent, but held, and nightfall witnessed Pope reinforced with more of McClellan's army but Jackson mightily relieved: Old Pete had arrived around noon and quietly filed his divisions into line roughly at a right angle to Stonewall's battered position. "We were all particularly anxious to bring on a battle . . . General Lee more so than the rest," Longstreet recounted, but Stuart provided intelligence that a large Yankee force was advancing from the east on a road that would outflank the Confederates to the south. Old Pete counseled caution, despite Lee's wish to attack immediately. Historians still debate who was right: had Longstreet launched his wing forward in the afternoon of the 29th, it may have crashed into Pope's exhausted forces as they were retiring from pounding Jackson, but it may also have been outflanked. Longstreet's advice prevailed, and in the evening he and Stuart dumbfounded and then checked their old Seven Days nemesis, Fitz John Porter, whose men comprised the Union flanking force, by creating the illusion that large numbers of rebels confronted him on his chosen route of approach. Preparations for the impending assault consumed most of the next day, but by 4:00 P.M. Old Jack held binoculars to his eyes and watched as almost 25,000 men in gray and butternut from Longstreet's wing surged forward simultaneously, battle flags fluttering and the rebel yell resounding across the plain, utterly smashing Pope's left flank. Jackson curiously held back much of his wing until it was too late to do much good; that, and bloody Union valor in a desperate rearguard action prevented the ensuing retreat from becoming a disastrous rout. He who had boasted he would "bag the whole [rebel] crowd" barely escaped bagging himself. Yet the Union catastrophe had not been completely unexpected. In a council of war on the morning of the 30th, some of Pope's generals advised extreme caution, as their scouts reported Longstreet ready to spring, but true to his character the Union commanding general waffled back and forth as the crisis grew and finally convinced himself of the wrong inference: Jackson was retreating. He then hurled Porter's hapless divisions against Stonewall's solid defense, thereby weakening himself just in time for Longstreet's grand assault.[27]

That Pope would be the one retreating had been in doubt for some time the day before, as only 20,000 Confederates under Jackson confronted over 70,000 Federals bent on their defeat. If the Union commander had better marshaled his forces or the rest of Lee's army had not arrived, Old Jack might have been forced to withdraw to the northwest, a contingency he had actually prepared for. But Stonewall had faith in Lee. Many years after the war, Hunter McGuire wrote to Hotchkiss, "Nothing saved us at the Second Manassas except Gen. Lee's being with Longstreet and prodding him along. You know he never left Longstreet, but kept close by his side and prodded him, as the keeper of a great elephant prods the great mass of flesh to make him move." Probably because Longstreet wrote some smallminded—and historically inaccurate—things about Jackson in the Sharpsburg Campaign in the decades after the war, Stonewall's surviving acolytes were quick to pillory him. But the issue of Old Pete's recalcitrant or unwitting slowness arose several times during the war, and even Lee himself wrote about it afterwards. William Blackford, one of Stuart's aides attached to Stonewall's staff, recalled, "We all felt . . . that we would like to hear that Longstreet was in supporting distance, for otherwise we would be tremendously outnumbered." The cavalryman continued, remembering "General Jackson rode about all day in a restless way. . . . The expression on his face was one of suppressed energy that reminded you of an explosive missile, an unlucky spark applied to which would blow you sky high." McGuire also had a strong impression of his chief's anxiety. Late on the 28th he and Jackson rode "a mile or two in the rear of our line of battle toward Thoroughfare Gap. I saw him get down off his horse and put his ear to the ground to listen if he could hear Longstreet's column advancing. I never shall forget the sad look of the man that night as he gazed toward Thoroughfare Gap, wishing for Longstreet to come." McGuire proceeded to tell him of the number of mutual friends from the Valley who had been killed at Brawner's Farm, men both officers had known for years. Taking off his hat and wiping his brow, the doctor said, almost under his breath, "We have only won this day by hard fighting." Stonewall looked up from the ground, turned around, and glanced directly at McGuire, his eyes blazing but "full of emotion." Slowly, softly, he replied, "No, sir, we have won this day by the blessing of Almighty God."[28]

Lee agreed with his colleague, closing his victory dispatch to President Davis with the heartfelt phrase, "our gratitude to almighty God for His mercies rises higher and higher each day." Yet the message, sent by telegraph at 10:00 P.M. on the 30th, also extended credit to earthly powers: "each wing under Genls Longstreet and Jackson" and "the valour of our troops." In this simple statement the difference between Jackson's and Lee's Christian faith was evident. Both men were ardent believers, evangelical Protestants who, although approaching their faith from different denominational perspectives, were unified in the solid, grounding conviction that Christ died for their sins, they were thus heaven-bound at some God-appointed time, and that, as His children, they could expect both personal blessings and a responsibility to live a praiseworthy life and spread the gospel to the unsaved. Both also struggled with the reality that they were, in fact, sinners, and thus undeserving of the Lord's grace. The difference lay in how each perceived the free will of man. Put simply, Jackson, hearkening back to Calvinist doctrine, felt the Christian was an instrument of God's will on earth, and the closer the believer came to living his faith in every daily action, the better the world would naturally become as it slowly approached the Almighty's perfect design. Man possessed free will to live his life as close to biblical precepts as humanly possible, he felt, and those who failed to do this were either innocently ignorant of the saving grace of God (and thus needed to be converted) or irredeemable. For Stonewall, conforming to the Lord's will through constant prayer, supplication, daily devotions, and strict adherence to His word as expressed in the Bible—such as keeping Sunday sacred—was the essence of Christianity. Yet he did sometimes march his command and fight on Sunday if necessary, exceptions that bothered him and technically qualified as sins, but which he rationalized as defensible in God's eyes. Also acceptable to him but probably not supportable in much of the New Testament was his devotion to killing the enemy; indeed, the very idea of bringing the terrors of war to the North, his prized dream, was antithetical to Christ's teachings. Still, he could say to McGuire during the Valley Campaign, "I have no fear whatever that I shall ever fall under the wrath of God. I am as certain of my acceptance & heavenly reward as that I am sitting here." One of his chaplains described him as "a man of deep-toned piety, who carried his religion into every affair of life," and a cadet at VMI noticed, "He laid every plan, purpose, and desire before his Great Master, implored his direction, and when assured what the will of God was, he never deviated one hair's breadth from the path of duty."[29]

Lee believed humans retained agency even as the Lord possessed omniscience. In a prewar letter to Mary, written from a remote cavalry camp in Texas, the future general all but summarized the major tenets of his faith: "I feel always as safe in the wilderness as in a crowded city. I know in whose powerful hands I am, & in them rely, & I feel that in all our life we are upheld & sustained by Divine Providence. But that Providence requires us to use the means he has put under our control. He deigns no blessing to idle & inactive wishes, & the only miracle he now exhibits to us, is the power he gives to truth & justice, to work their way in this wicked world." In other words, God's divine will could only be good, but He gave people the power either to use, misuse, or refuse to use the gifts he gave them. If they chose wicked ways, the world became worse for it, but in the end the Lord would make all right. When something good happened on earth, Lee thought, it was the result of people properly accepting or utilizing the blessings God granted them. When bad things occurred, however, it was a sign that man had sinned and either invoked temporary punishment from God to bring them back on the right path, or had not fully implemented the blessings bequeathed them. Jackson would have argued—and may well have, in quiet moments with Lee that were undocumented—that the devout Christian wished only to do the will of the Lord at all times, and thus nothing truly bad could happen to him, as whatever He allowed to occur was only for the increase of His kingdom on earth.[30]

These seemingly small but important differences in how the two generals practiced their faith spilled over into both their official, public correspondence and their private letters about family affairs, specific battles, and the course of the war overall. Jackson was more reluctant to single out individual officers or units for meritorious citation in his official reports than Lee, and never took credit for any of his own actions or decisions. God had decided to grant victory to his soldiers, brigades, and divisions, using perhaps Jackson's abilities as a conduit, yet Stonewall was but His humble servant. Lee, too, felt the Lord had guided events to occur in a certain way, but men had decided to act using their own volition, and that excellence or bravery deserved notation. Lee also humbly eschewed self-adulation in both public and private writings, and was loathe to criticize others (although he did occasionally indulge in accusations), as to do so was unchristian and ungentlemanly. Jackson was interestingly freer with his criticism, especially toward the undisciplined and careless in his command who risked the fulfillment of God's purposes by their mistakes. (A. P. Hill came to number among these souls.) Both agreed that all events occurred according to the wishes of Providence, however, and that a Christian army and Confederacy would be blessed. As the next eight months revealed, up and until Stonewall's death after Chancellorsville, the similarities in their faith far outweighed their differences and brought them closer together as men and as leaders in a command team increasingly indispensable for the hopes of Confederate independence. They would do all in their power to bring about that policy objective, but if the Southern people failed to submit themselves to the Lord's will, both feared all could be lost.[31]

No feeling of despair troubled the thoughts of either man on the morning of September 5, 1862, as they met together in the elegant parlor of Harrison Hall in Leesburg for a prayer service, the first documented occasion of such an event attended by both generals. Lee's hands were in splints thanks to a nasty fall, causing him to be fed breakfast by the lady of the house, but the slight physical pain and emotional embarrassment he felt was muted by a strong sense of gratitude to the Lord for His recent blessings on the army. Who conducted the service, and who else was present from the command team and their staffs is unknown, but the source recording the incident is plausible, and the import of it noteworthy. Not only did it demonstrate the two leaders believed it professionally acceptable to worship together, but also that they had developed enough of a personal rapport for each to respect and trust the other in such an intimate setting. Disparities in how they individually discerned their faith must have been subsumed by the greater commonality of their total trust in God and His will.

It is tempting to speculate how they may have jointly prayed for success in the venture immediately pending: crossing the boundary between the Confederacy and the United States and entering Maryland. It was a breathtakingly audacious proposal considering the deteriorated logistical support of the army, the thousands of ragged, footsore, and shoeless soldiers, and the proximity of a Union host behind the defenses of Washington numbering over four times their available manpower. "I am aware that the movement is attendant with much risk," Lee wrote Davis on September 3, but he was determined, now that Pope had finally been suppressed, to take full advantage of the strategic opportunity that presented itself. He believed it would take weeks for the Federals to reorganize from the "signal victory" scored against them at Second Manassas. The morale of his army was at an all-time high and he fully possessed the initiative in the Eastern theater. Most of all, he could now transfer the seat of the war beyond the national frontiers—a step he could have only hoped for just a month earlier—and subsist his army on the fat of the Maryland countryside for a while, buying time for Virginia farmers to gather in the fall harvest and Virginia railroad men to repair the tracks torn up in the recent campaigns. There was also some initial hope that Marylanders might flock to the rebel banners. Again, time was of the essence, as it had been along the Rapidan and the Rappahannock earlier. If he was to move, Lee needed to do it very soon. [32]

Jackson was delighted with the idea. Finally, here was a chance to bring the war to the enemy. Depending on where they crossed the river, Pennsylvania lay just a hard day's march north of the Potomac. On the 4th, Major John Pelham of Stuart's horse artillery wrote his parents, "We whipped General Pope last week at Manassas. Now General Lee is leading us into Northern territory. Tomorrow we'll cross the Potomac and enter Maryland. . . . I understand that General Jackson wants to invade Pennsylvania in order to strike the coal mines and railroads so as to cripple the enemy's industry and transportation. If all goes well I hope that the war will be over soon and then we can all be together again." It is probable Pelham, who was close to Stuart, received this information directly from him, who doubtless discussed the topic with his friend Jackson either privately or in war councils with Lee. Interestingly, that same day Lee composed another letter to the president, "more fully persuaded of the benefits" that would accrue from an immediate advance across the river. "Should the results of the expedition justify it, I propose to enter Pennsylvania, unless you should deem it unadvisable upon political or other grounds."[33]

As he had in his message of August 24, Lee took the measure of his commander in chief, and based on his familiarity with Davis's strategic preferences—which were at heart more offensive-minded than many scholars have admitted—also took the liberty of proposing an outright raid of the enemy's territory. Had Jackson's continual lobbying, through his own and Boteler's auspices, combined with Lee's own process of radicalization, finally borne fruit? Or was this simply sound military opportunism? Maryland was one thing, but Pennsylvania was another, and Lee's phraseology, although deferential, reveals his understanding of that political reality. Yet he knew full well that his men would be across the Potomac and he out of practicable communication with Davis before either the letters of the 3rd or the 4th could reach him and a reply sent. Hence, Lee based his decision-making entirely on his own and his lieutenants' counsel in a period of high strategic contingency, unable to receive official guidance from his civilian master. Moreover, his proclamation "To the People of Maryland," issued from his camp near Frederick on September 8, read like a political manifesto, providing all manner of justifications for the rebel army's presence in the Old Line State. Davis's dispatch regarding the same topic did not arrive in Lee's hands until well after the commanding general had already published his statement, and the next day Lee penned the president directly requesting a "proposal of peace" be issued to Lincoln and the Federal government while "it is in our power to inflict injury upon our adversary." "Such a proposition coming from us at this time," he suggested, "could in no way be regarded as suing for peace," but instead "would show conclusively to the world that our sole object is the establishment of our independence, and the attainment of an honorable peace." In the span of less than a week, Lee made a military decision of momentous impact on the fate of his country and, ultimately, the course of the entire conflict; issued a political decree; and strongly advocated for a diplomatic strategy that, had it somehow been accepted in the wake of a Confederate battlefield triumph, might have ended the Civil War. These were not the actions of a general thinking on the plane of military strategy only, but rather one who also clearly understood the fundamental truism of Clausewitz's famous dictum, "war is policy by other means." Lee understood it so well, in fact, that he blurred the line between civil and military authority, if he did not actually cross it.[34]

He did not do it oblivious of what else was occurring across the Confederacy, however, as some historians have averred, because his letter of the 3rd indicated knowledge of Braxton Bragg's offensive into Kentucky, which was then underway. And he certainly did not make these important decisions alone. Lee had consulted both Stonewall and Longstreet in several meetings since the end of the Second Manassas Campaign, continuing the process of thinking through operational and theater strategy with them, rather than unilaterally. The last of these discussions concluded just before the morning prayer service at the Harrison House on the 5th. Both subordinates heartily endorsed his thought to move north, eager to take the theater-strategic offensive and realizing as he did that no other good options presented themselves. Remaining in the picked-over counties directly west of Alexandria, watching the Federals in their capital's fortifications, was logistically impossible. Retreating back to the Culpeper area relinquished the hard-fought rewards of the recent victory, and staying in Loudoun County around Leesburg, where Lee had moved the army after the inconclusive battle at Chantilly on September 1, was only a temporary solution. In a postwar conversation, Lee recalled "Jackson . . . advised him to go up into the Valley and cross the Potomac at or above Harpers Ferry, clearing out the forces at Winchester &c," but this course was also imprudent because the Army of the Potomac would either not go into Maryland and free up Virginia's northern counties or would operationally outflank Lee and head directly south for Richmond. It had been disappointing to watch Pope escape after his drubbing on the plains of Manassas, the Confederates' attempt to block his safe passage to Washington failing in the mud, wet, heat, and exhaustion of the last several days, but much goodness could still result if the Army of Northern Virginia successfully moved the war north. "We cannot afford to be idle," Lee told the president, "and though weaker than our opponents in men and military equipments, must endeavor to harass, if we cannot destroy them." Lee wished to get the war out of Virginia for a season, if possible, but his aggressive instinct, like Jackson's, also sought a decisive victory.[35]

Had that occurred, the political damage for Lincoln and the Republicans might have been irrevocable; midterm elections in both the national legislature and in various northern statehouses were imminent that fall. Lee indicated knowledge of this when he wrote, "the proposal of peace would enable the people of the United States to determine at their coming elections whether they will support those who favor a prolongation of the war, or those who wish to bring it to a termination." Queen Victoria's cabinet in London also teetered precariously on the precipice of formally recognizing Confederate independence, a step Jefferson Davis had sought since the war began. At Second Manassas, the Unionists absorbed "a very complete smashing," according to Prime Minister Viscount Palmerston. More such defeats were likely, he wrote to the foreign secretary. "If this should happen, would it not be time for us to consider whether in such a state of things England and France might not address the contending parties and recommend an arrangement upon the basis of separation?" Such a diplomatic gesture was not a mere formality but symbolized real and valuable support for the Southern nation that could be translated into easier foreign loans, contracting and procurement of more and better state-of-the-art naval vessels, and official offers of mediation between the warring American states. The legality of the Union blockade of Southern ports, then starting to have a noticeable effect on the rebel economy, might have come into question. It was also not inconceivable that English or French military intervention would ensue should the Federal government prove intractable or bellicose in the wake of such an action. There is little to no evidence Lee was aware of the high diplomatic stakes then in play, but there is almost no doubt that one more shattering Confederate victory, especially in the East, coming in the wake of the Union disgrace of the Seven Days and the thrashing at Second Manassas, would have shifted the balance of power in the British cabinet toward recognition. Such an event, in turn, regardless of its potential economic and military effects on the war, would have reduced, or in the words of one recent chronicler, "buried" the political power of Lincoln's Emancipation Proclamation, which he had already written by this time and was holding back, in hopes of a Union victory to buttress its strategically transformative effect.[36]

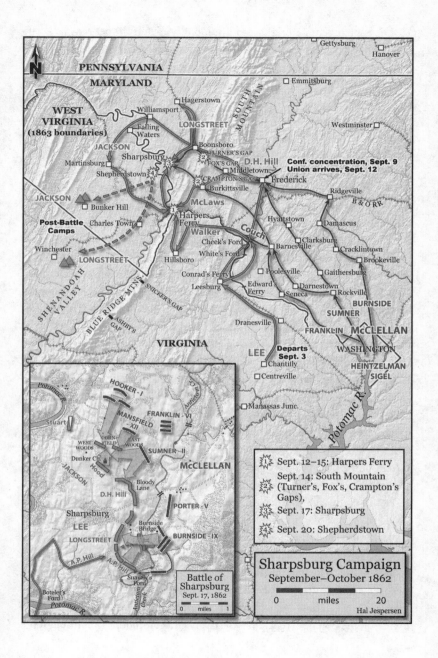

Battle of Sharpsburg
Sept. 17, 1862

Sept. 12–15: Harpers Ferry
Sept. 14: South Mountain (Turner's, Fox's, Crampton's Gaps),
Sept. 17: Sharpsburg
Sept. 20: Shepherdstown

Sharpsburg Campaign
September–October 1862

0   miles   20

Hal Jespersen

On September 5, a bright, beautiful, but hot late summer day, Jackson's wing of the Army of Northern Virginia waded across the Potomac at White's Ford, just north of Leesburg. To the accompaniment of military bands playing "Maryland, My Maryland" and cheers from thousands of throats, rebel soldiers' feet, some of them bare as they emerged from the water, tread for the first time on soil belonging to the United States. Most of the men were enthusiastic and excited. "Never in my life did I feel more proud than on this occasion that I was a Virginian," wrote John Riley of the 31st Virginia in his diary. Frederick, the largest town in Maryland west of Baltimore, lay just to the north and for several days Lee's united army would encamp in its vicinity, resting, gathering supplies and stragglers, and awaiting the approach of the enemy. Unbeknownst to the Confederates, Pope had been removed from command and the remnants of his army consolidated with the Army of the Potomac under McClellan. In a matter of days—record time for the methodical Union general and especially considering the demoralization of Pope's soldiers—the northern host began its careful march out of Washington in three great columns, pointed like daggers to the northwest. Stuart, his troopers posted at Urbana and other places the Federals would have to pass through to follow the Confederates, alerted Lee to their approach, although he misjudged their speed. The commanding general was somewhat surprised how quickly the Unionists had moved to intercept him, but not alarmed. He simply needed to adjust his campaign plan accordingly, and to that end called Jackson to his headquarters at Best's Grove on September 9. Stonewall was greeted by some of Lee's staff, probably Marshall and perhaps Colonel Robert Chilton, who would soon write out one of the most important orders in the history of the war. Walter Taylor had been sent to intercept President Davis, who could not contain his excitement at the prospect of the army's impending success in the enemy's country and had sent word he was coming to join it. Lee would have none of it, and politely sent a quick note and Taylor to accost him.[37]

Jackson entered Lee's tent and the commanding general closed the flap down to ensure a modicum of privacy. What he was considering needed to be kept secret as long as possible. Stonewall took a seat on the humble camp stool, and to his surprise, Lee asked him to recross the Potomac and attack Harpers Ferry, whose large garrison had not yet fled and remained poised to disrupt the potential rebel lines of supply and communication through the

Shenandoah Valley. With this, Lee revealed his intent to move further west, across the South Mountain spur of the Blue Ridge and ultimately into the fertile valley beyond, which was the Maryland extension of the Shenandoah. There he could gather more commissary and quartermaster goods for his army (the Frederick area was already showing signs of depletion), reap the rich fall harvest, and lure the Federal army far away from its base at Washington, creating greater opportunities to outmaneuver it, cut its long supply lines, and possibly defeat it in another Manassas-type engagement. Jackson had originally proposed advancing into this area directly from Virginia, with an eye toward then moving yet deeper into the North, but once the army had crossed the Potomac downstream he assumed Lee had set his course to remain east of the mountains.

Old Jack peered at his chief quizzically, his eyes a bit squinted, and gently shuffled his feet. The proposal certainly made sense from a logistical perspective, he must have thought, but with the Yankees drawing near faster than anticipated, it was risky. Could they not wait a few more days, discover what opportunities emerged as the enemy closed up, and then make a decision about the Ferry? Perhaps then they would no longer require the supply line through the Valley but could move into Pennsylvania and subsist off the land there. Stonewall "opposed the separation of our forces," urging "we should all be kept together" for the meantime. Lee shook his head and reiterated his reasoning. Jackson started to think about the possibilities. He knew every nook and cranny at Harpers Ferry, how hard it was to defend, how easy it would be to capture if he could gain control of the three ridgelines that frowned down upon the decisive point. It could be done. His foot cavalry would do it. He agreed with Lee that McClellan should, despite his recent alacrity, continue to advance relatively slowly, so if the rest of Lee's army placed the South Mountain between it and the Federals, that would probably buy enough time for him to complete the mission. The rewards of possibly capturing the Union stronghold would be tremendous, both logistically for the army and in terms of the blow it would give the enemy. Even if the Yankee garrison got away or partially escaped, it would still be a noteworthy Southern victory. Quietly, Stonewall nodded his assent.[38]

Just then they heard a familiar voice outside the canvas walls. It was Longstreet, who had ridden to army headquarters to discuss some minor issue. "I found the front of the general's tent closed and tied," he recalled decades later. "Upon inquiring of a member of the staff, I was told that he was inside with General Jackson." Old Pete must have felt a bit rebuffed, and "turned to go away" since he "had not been called," but Lee "recognized my voice, called me in." Longstreet immediately evinced that the decision had been made without him, a reality that doubtless irritated him, especially since Lee first broached the Harpers Ferry idea with him as they rode together from the Potomac to Frederick just days earlier. "I thought it a venture not worth the game," he wrote, and so advised the commanding general. Now Lee had changed his mind discussing it with Jackson, and without any further consultation with him. "Their minds were settled firmly upon the enterprise," Longstreet claimed, and he decided not to protest. Lee explained to him the major outlines of the new operational plan. Jackson's wing of the army would recross the Potomac above Harpers Ferry and descend on it from the western, or Virginia side, occupying Bolivar Heights. Major General Lafayette McLaws's independent division, followed at a distance by Major General R. H. Anderson's division, was to march to the Ferry via Crampton's Gap to Maryland Heights, sealing off that avenue of escape, and Brigadier General John G. Walker's division would recross the Potomac into Virginia via a nearby ford and move to Loudoun Heights. Meanwhile, Longstreet's remaining troops would march over the South Mountain to Hagerstown, with D. H. Hill moving behind him. Stuart was to watch and guard the mountain passes as well as "bring up all stragglers that may have been left behind." It was another daring, intrepid plan, even more complicated than that concocted against Pope. This time, because there were so many moving parts and so many different divisions marching in various directions, Lee wanted the specifics written down. Whether or not he ever thought twice about doing so is unknown, but it was a fateful decision. Clausewitzian chance, in what many chroniclers believe was its most impactful moment in the war, now inserted itself.[39]

Chilton wrote out General Orders #191 himself per Lee's dictation later on the 9th and then created copies that his chief designated for each of the commands involved in the fracturing of the army. The copy meant for D. H. Hill was mysteriously lost; how that exactly occurred has fed the imaginations of alternate history writers and professional historians alike and remains one of the great open questions of the Civil War, if not

American history. Hill, whose division technically fell under the purview of Jackson's wing of the army, received a copy of the order from Stonewall's headquarters, unaware that Lee had also sent him one. For the next several days, as the rebel divisions moved according to plan—Jackson falling behind schedule, however—there was no knowledge among the Confederates that anything was amiss. Then, in the late morning of September 13, Hill's missing copy was accidentally discovered by Corporal Barton W. Mitchell of the 27th Indiana Infantry, whose brigade was passing through a former rebel campground outside of Frederick. The precious piece of intelligence (forever known as the "Lost Orders") wrapped around three cigars ascended the chain of command all the way to George McClellan. In another piece of good fortune for the Federals, Chilton's signature at the bottom of the captured orders was recognized as legitimate by an aide to Brigadier General Alpheus Williams, a division commander in the newly formed Union 12th Corps. Had a soldier in another corps of the army picked up the missing orders instead, it is quite conceivable the document may have been construed as a ruse planted by the rebels and either discarded or delayed in verification. But all the stars aligned against Lee in this instance. Walter Taylor, who managed to return to Lee's side just in time for the ensuing battle at Sharpsburg, later wrote, "What an advantage did this fortuitous event give the Federal commander, whose heretofore snail-like movements were wonderfully accelerated . . . certainly the loss of this battle order constitutes one of the pivots on which turned the event of the war." Lee agreed. After the war he confidentially declared, "Had the Lost Dispatch not been lost, and had McClellan continued in his cautious policy for two or three days longer, I would have had all my troops reconcentrated on Md. side, stragglers up, men rested & I *intended then to attack McClellan* [original emphasis], hoping the best results from state of my troops & those of the enemy." Lee was confident of the chances of victory had that occurred. "It is probable that the loss of the dispatch changed the character of the campaign," he added, extolling in the same breath Jackson's fine performance despite all else that had gone wrong. [40]

Upon reading through the captured orders, McClellan was exultant, supposedly exclaiming, "Now I know what to do! Here is a paper with which, if I cannot whip Bobby Lee, I will be willing to go home." His words were, ironically, rather prophetic. True to form, the Union general took his time acting upon the unexpected windfall, and while not exactly "snail-like," his pursuit of the Confederates was slower than it should have been. It was not until late in the afternoon of the 13th that his army corps marched from Frederick to the foot of the South Mountain passes, where they encamped for the night. That was a precious gift of time for Lee, who read a dispatch from Stuart about 8:00 P.M. indicating the Yankees were moving uncharacteristically fast and were poised to attack the passes the next day; the message did not state that a copy of General Orders #191 had been captured by the enemy, but it is likely Stuart and Lee deduced something similar must have occurred. The difference between McClellan's actual response to the golden intelligence he received versus what he proclaimed was the first of several compensatory events that helped alleviate the grave damage done by the Lost Orders. It allowed Jackson's operation against Harpers Ferry to proceed unimpeded through the next day and gave Lee enough time to set up a defense, however rudimentary, of the three mountain gaps. The next morning the Federal commander, overestimating the Confederates' numbers proximate to Turner's, Fox's, and Crampton's Gaps to be close to 60,000, cautiously unleashed his army against them, and by the end of the day had won what became known as the Battle of South Mountain. D. H. Hill's brigades, reinforced toward nightfall by elements from Longstreet's command, were forced to abandon the mountain to the Unionists, but they had held up the enemy's advance long enough for a despairing Lee to receive welcome news from Jackson the next morning: "Through God's blessings the advance [on Harpers Ferry] which commenced this evening [the 14th], has been successful thus far, and I look to Him for complete success tomorrow. The advance has been directed to resume at dawn to-morrow morning."[41]

Lee had fallen to the pits of deepest despair over the prospects of his campaign the previous night. Stonewall's message retrieved both his spirits and the chances, however attenuated, that he could still prosecute the offensive. He ordered all units of his dispersed army to converge on the little town of Sharpsburg, just north of the Potomac. There, thanks to a good road network, they would coalesce again over the next two days, and there Lee would make a stand against the oncoming Federals. He had beaten McClellan on the Peninsula and may have reasoned he could defeat him again in Maryland.

Most modern authors agree that the decision to stay and fight was foolish from a purely military perspective, as Lee was outnumbered over two to one (85,000 vs. 40,000), was unaware how badly his army suffered from straggling, and had but one route of escape across the river in the event of defeat. Yet he was determined to salvage as much as he could from the considerable effort expended in the Maryland expedition. He was aware of many of the strategic contingencies at work during this time of the war, and if he could somehow squeak out a victory, the political benefits could be immense. To retreat now would hand a significant victory to the enemy, but to remain and try his luck offered a chance all could yet be well. He would not have been Robert E. Lee if he had not attempted it. [42]

On the 15th, Lee started to concentrate his scattered commands along the ridgelines to the north and east of Sharpsburg. McClellan advanced most of his corps through the mountain gaps and began to gather his army along the east side of Antietam Creek. He knew where Lee was and realized he had him backed up against the Potomac. Had he attacked the rebels on this day with the elements of his army on hand, he would have surely destroyed the rump of Lee's army before Jackson and the Harpers Ferry besiegers arrived, but he hesitated, falsely convinced he was still outnumbered. McClellan's chronic problem with operational intelligence about the enemy's strength amounted to an Achilles' heel for the Federal cause and may have represented the general's preoccupation with Jomini's admonition "to order movements only after obtaining perfect information of the enemy's proceedings." In that, he was no different from Lee, who also desired the most complete military intelligence on the enemy, but unlike his Confederate counterpart, McClellan utilized his cavalry poorly, relied on the independent and inaccurate Pinkerton agency for intelligence, and was reticent to risk a movement unless all available information strongly convinced him it would succeed. Lee, conversely, had a strong intelligence gatherer in Stuart (his mediocre performance in this campaign notwithstanding) and was disallowed the luxury of awaiting "perfect" intelligence, forced to take risky gambles throughout the war due to the paucity of means at his disposal. He had to take opportunities when they beckoned. When his leader's intuition combined with an intellect informed by *enough* intelligence Lee would jump at a reasonable chance to attack. Both Clausewitz and Jomini called this the coup d'oeil, the "glance of the eye," an ability only learned through rigorous experience, and it distinguished the best commanders from the average ones. Defined as "the rapid discovery of a truth which to the ordinary mind is either not visible at all or only becomes so after long examination and reflection," it enabled a general to cut through the fog of war. Lee definitely possessed it, as did Jackson. McClellan did not.[43]

That morning the literal fog rose at Harpers Ferry to a scene of utter discomfiture for the thousands of Union soldiers now caught in Stonewall's trap. Although he had fallen a good day and a half behind schedule, the Valley General's careful encirclement of the Federal garrison had witnessed the escape of only 1,200 cavalrymen. McLaws, now threatened in the rear by McClellan's advance, still occupied Maryland Heights, Walker was poised on Loudoun Heights with good artillery, and Jackson's own divisional artillery dominated Bolivar Heights, held by the enemy. Suddenly his guns, carefully positioned to bombard the hapless bluecoats in a deadly crossfire, opened up simultaneously. A New York soldier on the receiving end of these salvoes wrote, "The flash, the whistling shriek and explosion" of the rebel shells "came all at once." An Ohioan claimed "there was not a place you could lay the palm of your hand and say it was safe." A Virginian noted great "clouds of smoke . . . roll[ing] up to the tops of the various mountains, and the thunder of the guns reverberating among them, gave the idea of so many volcanoes." After only an hour the terrible barrage subsided and a blue rider carrying a flag of pale-colored tent canvas rode toward Jackson's lines. Old Jack met with the garrison commander shortly thereafter, demanding unconditional surrender of all personnel and equipment. It was the greatest single capture of United States troops until the fall of Corregidor in the Philippines in 1942, and it was all over by 8:00 A.M. Stonewall immediately scribbled a note to Lee and sent it off posthaste, its first line reading, "Through God's blessing, Harpers Ferry and its garrison are to be surrendered." A. P. Hill—whom Jackson had placed under arrest for insubordinate behavior on the march to Leesburg and then allowed to rejoin his command—would oversee the actual surrender, parole of prisoners, and confiscation of Federal property, which included over 12,000 soldiers and their small arms, 73 cannons, and tons of medical, commissary, and quartermaster stores. In one fell swoop, Jackson had secured many of Lee's objectives for the campaign. It was not the capture of Harrisburg, but it was a stunning victory nonetheless, accomplished after another long, hot, arduous march, which seemed to have become Jackson's prerequisite.[44]

The moment Lee received that message may have been the instant he and Jackson solidified their unbreakable professional bond. It was a little after noon on the 15th. The commanding general was immensely relieved and felt there would be at least this success to show for his efforts. Along with McClellan's inaction, the news of Harpers Ferry's complete capture, a possibility Lee had only dared hoped for (he was certain the Union garrison would flee—that they did not was due to conflict between McClellan and Halleck), became the second major mitigating event to the catastrophe of the Lost Orders. Lee's day was getting better, and with it his mood. "This is indeed good news!" he proclaimed to all within earshot. "Let it be announced to the troops." Within minutes riders emanated from Lee's headquarters to Longstreet's and D. H. Hill's divisions, and shortly thereafter the deep roar of cheers mingled with the shrill rebel yell, resounding through the woods and fields of the Maryland countryside. Taking pen in hand, the commanding general wrote a jubilant letter to the president, even as he stared down his Union enemy and prayed for more time. "This victory of the indomitable Jackson and his troops gives us renewed occasion for gratitude to Almighty God for His guidance and protection." Now all that remained was for Stonewall, McLaws, and Walker to arrive.[45]

Jackson and most of the Harpers Ferry expeditionary divisions arrived on the 16th. When he entered Sharpsburg that foggy morning, Stonewall headed straight for Lee's headquarters at Cemetery Hill. There he found the commanding general in conversation with Longstreet, and immediately the three conferred about the future of the campaign. McClellan was definitely preparing for battle but it appeared unlikely he would attack that day. McLaws and A. P. Hill were not up yet, and Lee wanted all the army concentrated before fighting the Federals. For now, until the entire army was unified, Longstreet and Jackson were to rest their men and prepare their positions. But Lee was already thinking about how to carry on the campaign and mentioned to his subordinates the possibility of sidling by the Federals' right flank on the Hagerstown Road and heading north. Old Jack must have been personally excited by the prospect, even as he well understood how many of his men had fallen out of ranks the past several days, unable to keep up the pace of march, and how tired those were who remained. After the war, Lee remembered, "When he came upon the field, having preceded his troops, and learned my reasons for offering battle, he emphatically concurred with me." Both generals wanted to fight.[46]

They would get the fight of their lives, one that almost cost the Army of Northern Virginia its own life. McClellan lost another good opportunity to obliterate Lee on the 16th as he gathered in the last of his corps and only initiated movement late in the day, but it was the beginning of a furious storm. Unleashing Major General "Fighting Joe" Hooker's I Corps in a swing across the Antietam to Lee's left, the Union general showed his cards that evening when Hooker's men clashed with Texans of Brigadier General John B. Hood's division in the East Woods. Lee now knew where the first blow, at least, was likely to fall the next day—in Jackson's sector of the line. McClellan developed a fine tactical plan for the 17th, with Hooker, supported by the XII and II Corps, plunging into Lee's left and Major General Ambrose Burnside's IX Corps pinning down, and if possible, punching in his right. Porter's V Corps and divisions of the VI Corps would be held in reserve with the entire cavalry either to drive in the center, á la Napoleon's masterpiece at Austerlitz, or rescue the attacking wings in case Lee's unseen hordes, hidden by the woods and hills, suddenly sprang upon them. In the third overall instance of compensation for the Lost Orders, chance again smiled on the rebels as McClellan, not unlike Lee during the Seven Days, bungled the synchronicity of his attacks all day long. About 6:00 A.M. Hooker went in alone against Jackson, and despite the ferocity of his assault was already spent when the XII Corps belatedly arrived in the famous Cornfield. It, too, was punished and pushed back. Then around 9:00 A.M. the II Corps attacked, and because of a mix-up in its command and control, one division barreled into a makeshift disaster in the West Woods while two others vectored away to the middle of the rebel line in Longstreet's sector. There they charged the Sunken Road three times, only cracking through after suffering atrocious casualties. Lee's line was finally broken and his army split in two.

But at that critical nexus point, another great moment of contingency in which the three levels of war converged, McClellan failed to exploit his success and ordered no reinforcements. As if the tragic restraint of the Union commander's generalship were not already enough to make strong men weep, Burnside's inability to puzzle through the conundrum of the lower, or Rohrbach Bridge across the Antietam all morning long allowed Lee to play fireman to Jackson's hard-pressed lines by shifting away one division after another to the north. When Burnside finally outflanked and simultaneously stormed the Confederate strongpoint at the bridge around 1:00 P.M., Lee faced another crisis but luckily it was not concomitant with any other further up his battle line. Still, it appeared all would yet be lost when a cloud of dust revealed the approach of a large column from the southwest. Lee's heart pounded. Jackson's command was totally spent. Longstreet had but one weak division between Burnside's huge corps and the town, which shielded Lee's only ford across the Potomac. The commanding general and his staff scrambled to find fragments of shattered brigades, divisions, and batteries in a forlorn hope to fight off Burnside's ponderous leviathan; they could not also meet this new threat now approaching. Unable to raise binoculars to his eyes due to his injured hands, Lee asked a passing officer to use his own and identify the oncoming mass. A frightful moment passed, and then the man said, "They are flying the Virginia and Confederate flags." Lee replied with visible relief, "It is A. P. Hill, from Harpers Ferry." Hill's brigades slammed into Burnside's flank about 4:00 P.M., killing one of his division commanders and sending his entire corps into disarray. McClellan had shot his last uncoordinated bolt, and the Army of Northern Virginia would survive the day.[47]

That night an impromptu council of war took place at Lee's new headquarters south of Sharpsburg. Generals wandered in by ones and twos, solemn, exhausted, and shocked from the day of wanton carnage. They did not know it, but their army had lost over 25% of its strength, well over 10,000 men. The Federals had also suffered, losing over 12,000, but at this point the "bloodiest day" of the war was not yet destined to be only one day. Lee summoned all the courtly manners he possessed and met each of his subordinates graciously. "General, how is it on your part of the line?" he asked repeatedly. After answering, each leader stood by, awaiting further guidance. "It is as bad as it could be," Longstreet responded, "apparently much depressed," when it was his turn. "My divisions have lost terribly and my lines barely held. There is little better than a good skirmish line along my front." Old Pete suggested an immediate retreat across the river. D. H. Hill cynically replied to Lee's query, "My division is cut to pieces . . . losses terrible . . . I had not enough troops to hold my line against the great odds against me." He, too, recommended withdrawal. Jackson stood with his arms folded, eyes shrouded by the fading light and the bill of his kepi, and listened. Lee turned to him next. Quietly, factually, he said, "I have had to contend with the greatest odds I have ever met. I have lost a good many generals killed" and many of his brigade and division commanders were casualties. "My losses in the different commands have been terrible." Probably to Lee's surprise, he also agreed retreat was a now a wise course. Hood came last, "display[ing] great emotion," and when asked where his "splendid division was," he choked out, "They are lying on the field where you sent them; but few have straggled. My division has been almost wiped out." Several moments of silence descended on the group, "an appalling stillness" that hung heavy in the odoriferous air. Lee seemed to gather his strength, and then announced, "Gentlemen, we will not cross the Potomac tonight. You will go to your respective commands, strengthen your lines." Send officers to the ford to collect stragglers, he advised, and bring them back. "If McClellan wants to fight in the morning, I will give him battle again. Go!" Lee's lieutenants turned away, some astonished, some dejected, but all taken aback.[48]

The next day, mercifully, McClellan decided not to renew the struggle. Civil War armies may have been hard to destroy, but they were easily worn-out and fought-out. So it was with the Army of the Potomac on September 18. The I, II, IX, and XII Corps, over two-thirds of the army, were temporarily shattered by their grapple with the rebels and their commanding general was emotionally exhausted. Although he put up a brave front and boasted to his wife about how "splendidly" he had fought the battle, the fight at Sharpsburg was a tactical defeat for him. Everywhere McClellan attacked he had been repulsed, lending credence to his delusion that he remained outnumbered by the Confederates. When asked by brother-in-law Barringer about the state of their own army the night of the 17th, Jackson admitted they had been hurt, but added, "Oh, how I'd like to see the Yankee camp right now!" Those in their own camps, however, were the lucky ones. Thousands of dead and dying soldiers lay in the fields where they fell, undergoing untold agonies as stretcher parties weaved back and forth with lanterns in the darkness, trying not to step on the bodies. It was a ghoulish, nightmarish scene.

On the 18th Lee stood defiant along his battle line, only slightly dented as a result of the previous day's slaughter. Although his army had been proportionately more damaged, Lee knew he had foiled the Union assaults, and remaining on the field one more day allowed him to legitimately claim a "non-defeat." Sending Colonel S. D. Lee of the artillery along with Jackson to scout out one last chance at flanking the Federals to the north, the commanding general was crestfallen when they returned and reported the Union right flank far too strong to turn. Reluctantly, Lee ordered his commands to prepare a withdrawal to Virginia. It was a wise decision. Tempting chance—which had been cruel to him with the Lost Orders but later so benevolent before and during the battle—one more day was pushing it too far, and he probably knew it, even with the 5,000-odd stragglers that arrived that day. That night, the Army of Northern Virginia successfully slipped away back to its namesake region, leaving its dead but barely a broken-down wagon behind. Jackson's dream of taking the war into Pennsylvania was forestalled. Lee's dream of reenacting Second Manassas and living off the enemy's country, then perhaps riding alongside Stonewall northward, faded away. McClellan's gleeful outburst at the discovery of the Lost Orders, however, soon came to haunt his dreams. He would indeed shortly be on his way "home," but not in the way he predicted: he was sacked by an exasperated President Lincoln who was tired of his excuses, his slowness, and his resistance to the Emancipation Proclamation, which was preliminarily released following what became known in the North as the Battle of Antietam. The Union now had a second war policy. [49]

After a sharp, brief fight at Shepherdstown on the 19th and 20th, in which McClellan half-heartedly probed Lee's temporary position across the river and received a punch in the face for his trouble, the two wings of Lee's army settled down in the Bunker Hill area, south of Martinsburg, for over a month of unexpected recuperation, reinforcement, and reoutfitting. The enemy did not follow them, providing the necessary breathing time and space for the Confederates to recover. The abundance of the nearby Shenandoah Valley harvest was a godsend while it lasted and everyone remarked on the unusual beauty of that fall, although the heat of the late summer persisted. The commanding general oversaw the return of thousands of stragglers, integrated new regiments and brigades into the army, bombarded Richmond with requests for shoes, blankets, tents, and horses, and requested his two primary subordinates be promoted to lieutenant general. It was time to formally divide his army into two large corps, and to do that properly, he required ranks for them requisite to the responsibilities they had been undertaking in a de facto sense since August. "My opinion of the merits of Genl. Jackson has been greatly enhanced during this expedition," Lee tellingly wrote Davis on October 2. "He is true, honest, and brave, has a single eye to the good of the service, and spares no exertion to accomplish his object." This was high praise indeed from Lee and represented both how far Jackson had risen in his personal estimation since the Seven Days and how professionally valuable Stonewall had become to his chief. Too, its wording indicated that Lee found his subordinate's personal qualities appealing, perhaps because they mirrored his own. Charles Minor Blackford, a staff officer who knew both generals well, wrote home about their interactions during the late summer and early fall. "I often think how these two men," he told his wife, "so utterly different in their characteristics and style should not only be such friends and have such confidence in each other, but should each seem to be the perfect military leader." He went on to describe the two as the quintessential odd couple, Old Jack the "Roundhead covenanter" and Lee the "Cavalier." The combination, although strange, worked well, he thought. Blackford's statement indicated that the strong bond between the two men was expanding past the boundaries of well-earned military respect and confidence. Lee and Jackson were forging a partnership based on several solid foundations, a development that boded well for the strategic future of a Confederacy now feeling the pinch of a hardening war.[50]

Stonewall was unquestionably pleased by the promotion and the adulation he received from the troops where ever he went that fall, but the Christian in him would not falter. He wrote to Mary Anna, "It is gratifying to be beloved and to have our conduct approved by our fellow men, but this is not worthy to be compared with the glory that is in reservation for us in the presence of our glorified Redeemer." Delighted to be back in his beloved Valley and no longer actively campaigning, Jackson turned his attention to many of the same duties confronting Lee, but also made time to fully support the chaplains and missionaries in his wing of the army, rejoicing in the first sparks of a religious revival as their spiritual work took root in some of his brigades. He was ordered to destroy the Baltimore and Ohio Railroad at Martinsburg, spent much time conferring with Lee at his headquarters, joked with Stuart—"Hello, Pennsylvania!" he greeted his friend when the cavalryman returned from a raid to Chambersburg—and also enjoyed the little pleasantries of camp life. One of them included the devoted attention of a new staff officer, Captain James Power Smith, who, like Sandie Pendleton, Jed Hotchkiss, and most of Stonewall's staff, happened to be a fellow Christian. Jackson often held prayer meetings for his officers, which helped solidify his own personal command team.[51]

Such unity would soon be necessary. After much prodding from Lincoln and Halleck, McClellan finally crossed the Army of the Potomac over its namesake river in late October and began marching toward the south and east. Lee reacted by splitting the two corps of his army and moving Longstreet south and parallel to the enemy, while once again granting Jackson independent command. For the better part of November, Jackson remained in the northern Valley, hovering on the Union army's western flank, waiting for an opportunity to destroy an isolated detachment. Major General Ambrose Burnside, since November 5 the new Federal commanding general, never gave him the chance, and quickly shifted to the southeast, temporarily surprising the Confederates. Lee and Jackson corresponded almost daily, trying to determine Burnside's intentions. It soon became clear he was headed for Fredericksburg, where, if he could force his way across the Rappahannock against Longstreet's outnumbered corps, he could advance directly on Richmond. On November 23, discerning this as a likely move, Lee wrote to Stonewall asking him to start marching toward him: "If therefore you see no way of making an impression on the enemy from where you are, and concur with me in the views I have expressed, I wish you would move east of the Blue Ridge and take such a position as you may find best." The latitude given to Jackson was clear and a remarkable testament to his ability. Lee trusted him completely but needed him nearby. Jackson began marching his divisions at once. He was now the "great and good" Stonewall, Lee's right arm.[52]

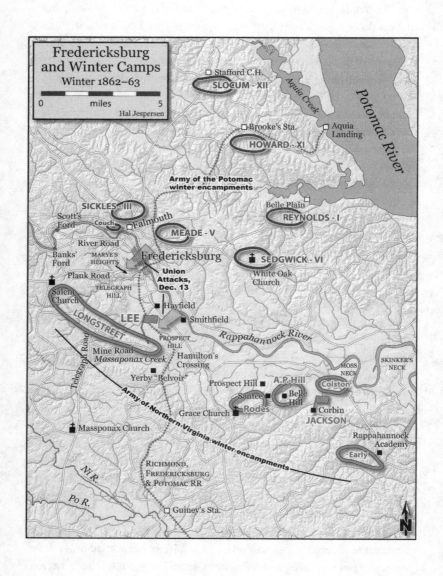

Fredericksburg and Winter Camps
Winter 1862–63

0 miles 5

Hal Jespersen

Stafford C.H.

SLOCUM - XII

Aquia Creek

Potomac River

Brooke's Sta.

HOWARD - XI

Aquia Landing

Army of the Potomac winter encampments

SICKLES - III

Belle Plain

REYNOLDS - I

Scott's Ford

Couch

Falmouth

MEADE - V

River Road

Banks' Ford

MARYE'S HEIGHTS

Fredericksburg

Union Attacks, Dec. 13

SEDGWICK - VI

White Oak Church

Plank Road

TELEGRAPH HILL

Salem Church

LONGSTREET

LEE

Hayfield

Smithfield

Rappahannock River

Mine Road

Massaponax Creek

PROSPECT HILL

Hamilton's Crossing

MOSS NECK

SKINKER'S NECK

Telegraph Road

Yerby "Belvoir"

Prospect Hill

A.P.Hill

Colston

Santee

Belle Hill

Rodes

Corbin

Grace Church

JACKSON

Masssponax Church

Army of Northern Virginia winter encampments

Rappahannock Academy

Early

RICHMOND, FREDERICKSBURG & POTOMAC RR

Ni R.

Po R.

Guiney's Sta.

N

THREE

"I trust that God is going to bless us with great success."

THE PARTNERSHIP PERFECTED

Christmas Day 1862 dawned sunny, unusually mild, and full of promise at Stonewall Jackson's new headquarters on the Corbin estate at Moss Neck, below Fredericksburg. Sandie Pendleton poked his head out of his tent and blinked in the early morning sunlight, the sleep of the night before chased away by the sudden brightness and a strange aroma triggering distant memories of holidays spent in more comfortable and commodious locations. Perhaps he thought of his college days at the University of Virginia or peaceful family gatherings in Lexington, and probably he thought most of answering the call of nature. But as he regained his bearings in the crisp air, the unmistakable, delicious odor of roasting turkey greeted his nostrils. As he made his way to the campfire in search of warmth and a cup of coffee, he noticed the slave Jim Lewis and J. P. Smith scurrying about the mess tent and camp stove, carrying all manner of baskets and bundles. It was Smith's turn to provide food for the staff, Pendleton remembered, and the general had announced two days ago he wished to host a Christmas banquet. Smiling to himself, Pendleton must have been glad to escape the duty even as his mouth watered in anticipation of the rare feast that would come later.[1]

For his part, Smith was satisfied with the progress he and Jim had made thus far, and even happier that the acquisition of all the victuals had cost him next to nothing. Making quiet inquiries at residences up down the Rappahannock the day before, he had succeeded in gathering two turkeys and "a bucket of oysters" and had been blessed with the timely arrival by post of a large box donated by a group of ladies in Staunton containing "another turkey, a splendid ham, a large cake, a bottle of wine, and the spaces filled with white biscuit and the best of pickles." Truly, this was a bounty that boded a repast worthy of the annals, a great rarity in such times as these, and especially in the famously spartan environs of 2nd Corps headquarters. Smith knew it would be a special event and determined to make it memorable. "It was a famous dinner," he recalled, reminding him and all present of happier, easier days.[2]

It was also a demonstration of the warmer, more convivial side of Jackson's personality that only his closest friends in the Army of Northern Virginia had yet witnessed. The mental and physical strains of operating as an independent army commander in the Valley and then serving as one of Robert E. Lee's principal lieutenants had all but suppressed that part of him, and now, with some of the burdens relieved, Stonewall felt more at ease with himself. It had been a grueling but immensely successful year since last Christmas, and with the retreat of the defeated foe from his threatening position on the other side of the river and the establishment of his own seasonal camp, it was time to relax a little. How better to do that than host a holiday dinner? The guest list would be short and exclusive, reflecting Jackson's limited inner circle. Lee was at the top of it. A deep professional respect for Lee had been complemented by a burgeoning friendship over the past year, and here was an opportunity to enhance the relationship. Their mutual friend, the clergyman and chief of the army's artillery, William Nelson Pendleton, should also be invited. He certainly relished a good meal and would offer an appropriate blessing. Last but not least, Jeb Stuart must come. Stuart, another brother-in-arms and of the cross, who could pull Stonewall's leg and make him laugh in spite of himself, would enliven everything with his good-natured "quips and cranks." Selected members of the generals' personal staffs would also be welcome, of course. There should be enough food for all, even with all the hungry young men.[3]

When the guests had arrived and found their places, General Pendleton opened the meal with a prayer. With one accord, the assembled officers repeated his "Amen" and then surveyed the wonder before them. Everyone was astounded at the groaning table: such culinary delicacies seemed totally misplaced in the midst of any Confederate camp, but especially Jackson's personal encampment. Even more striking was the appearance of Jim Lewis and John, the "dining room boy," both bedecked in white aprons, fastidiously attending to the serving of the food. Lee, in a jolly mood and amused by the irony, "declared we were only playing soldiers, and invited us to dine with him and see how a soldier ought to live," Smith later wrote. Jackson smiled, blushed, and said nothing to the jest, digging into his turkey. Then it was Stuart's turn to rib his friend. His merry eyes wandered about the tent and table, soaking up the scene. Surely, with such a proliferation of fair targets, there was something here worthy of a joke. First the white aprons and then the bottle of wine drew his playful fire; Stonewall had clearly changed his strict Presbyterian scruples! Next his gaze fell upon the butter. A well-intentioned lady from the neighboring estate of Hayfield had contributed a large pat of butter imprinted with the image of a rooster. A beautiful creation and a rare treat, "the servants . . . had chosen this to grace the centre of the board." Stuart drew in his breath, paused, and solemnly announced that yes, indeed, his host had either changed or had been hiding his true predilections all along. "See there, gentlemen!" he blurted, pointing at the offending design, "If there is not the crowning evidence of our host's sporting tastes. He even puts his favorite game-cock upon his butter!" The entire assemblage erupted in uproarious laughter, Jackson joining in the fun at his own expense. The dinner then commenced in earnest, and one of the lighter moments in the history of the Army of Northern Virginia passed into memory.[4]

That Christmas feast symbolized, in many ways, the state of Lee's army and the greater Confederacy as the Civil War limped toward the end of its second full year. Spirits were high among the rank and file in the primary field armies in both Virginia and Tennessee, and in Lee's army, at least, the command team had evolved into a symbiotically supportive system of opposites that could lay most differences aside and work successfully together. Like the wonder of the holiday meal itself, an air of abundant, almost carefree optimism wafted throughout the camps about the coming year and the chances for Southern independence. "Our army was never in such good health and condition since I have been attached to it," Lee wrote Mary on the 25th. Bureaucrats and politicians in Richmond as well as most civilians at home shared the army's enthusiasm and found sustenance in that spirit even as the privations of war closed in around them. A clerk in the capital recorded in his diary, "we have a merrier Christmas than the last one. . . . They have not men enough to subjugate us. . . . But turkeys are selling at $11 each! Shoes for $25 per pair." That reality—mirroring the realization among its attendees that the great Christmas dinner of 1862 was a marvelous epicurean anomaly—exposed a harsh truth that Lee and Jackson, despite their hopefulness, frankly acknowledged: the South was strategically losing the war through declining means that could never be replaced. The joy of the temporary feast paralleled the euphoria of the costly battlefield victories of 1862, bereft of enduring strategic permanency.[5]

The Seven Days, Second Manassas, Harper's Ferry, and most recently, Fredericksburg, fought on December 12–13, were all Confederate triumphs, but had frustratingly not ended the war. Even at Fredericksburg, where the casualty counts tallied up lopsidedly in favor of the defending rebels, the enemy still marshalled enough men to immediately make good their losses. Ambrose Burnside had flung his legions against Longstreet's carefully prepared defenses on Marye's Heights west of town and Jackson's stalwart veterans south of it, and excepting a temporary breakthrough in Stonewall's line caused by faulty deployment, they had been forced to recede like an angry wave on a rocky coast. It was a stupendous defensive victory for Lee's army and another example of his command team's excellence. The Unionists had suffered over 12,000 dead, wounded, and missing to Lee's 5,000. Yet the Army of Northern Virginia could land no killing blow, the enemy's batteries on Stafford

Heights across the Rappahannock securely protecting the withdrawal of his broken infantry divisions. Lee and Jackson had even begun preparations for a night attack, but it was discovered by the angry Yankee guns as soon as it commenced and had to be canceled. Like water's ability to erode stone over time, the Union Army of the Potomac replenished itself after each defeat, grew more experienced, and relentlessly came back again to wear down the rock that was its Confederate enemy. And that situation, unsustainable in the long term in the Eastern Theater, was the good news for the South.[6]

The strategic circumstances on the other side of the Appalachians were significantly worse. Union armies had penetrated deep into the supply-producing regions of the western Confederacy in the past year, sealing off nearly all of Kentucky, much of Tennessee, Missouri, and Arkansas, and even portions of Mississippi from future Confederate logistical support. Slaves were abandoning their plantations and farms by the thousands and running to Federal lines, jeopardizing national food production and civilian morale, and the Southern railroad network was rapidly proving unequal to the tasks demanded of it. The Northern naval blockade of Southern ports had grown much tighter and was strangulating commerce and contact with Europe, and, most ominously, pleas for reinforcements sent to the state governors increasingly provoked replies claiming no more men could be sent. The Confederate chieftains of the Army of Northern Virginia pondered these uncomfortable considerations as they settled down into their respective winter quarters, fondly remembering their time together at Christmas but alert to the dangers that lay ahead. For both Lee and Jackson, the winter of 1862–1863 would necessarily become one of strategic reflection and planning, spiritual renewal, physical hardship, and hope. Together, there was a fair chance they could decisively overcome the size and power of the Army of the Potomac in the spring and win the war in the East: the great blow had to happen then, though, or it might be too late. Both men knew the sands of time were draining the South's power while proportionately growing the North's, and they understood that military success was increasingly unlikely in the West. Only in the Eastern Theater could the Confederacy win by force of arms, yet due to the deterioration of strategic means across the seceded states, even there the odds grew longer. And everywhere, it seemed, expanding Federal military and economic power amplified the need for quick action.[7]

But it was winter time now, and the two leaders could not take the field. The weather and the condition of the "wretched, almost impassable" roads would not permit them, a fact that Burnside, who would try one more time to take the offensive, soon discovered. Instead, the colder months offered Lee and Jackson an opportunity to fortify their professional relationship and strengthen their new personal bond, their common faith in the Lord becoming the glue for that. Both turned to Him for succor, certain that His grace could easily support their own needs and those of their belea-guered nation, and both yearned for their countrymen to awaken to the truth. "Oh! That our Country was such a Christian, *God* (original italics) fearing people as it should be! Then might we very speedily look for peace," Jackson exclaimed to Mary Anna in a note written just before he greeted his guests on Christmas. Continuing his letter to Mary of the same day, Lee echoed a similar thought: "I have seen His hand in all the events of the war. Oh if our people would only recognize it and cease from their vain self-boasting and adulation, how strong would be my belief in final success and happiness to our country."[8]

The new year 1863 arrived bitterly cold, obliterating earlier, Christmas-time hopes for a milder winter and obliging both leaders and their troops to commence the necessary task of preparing more permanent seasonal quarters. Jackson contracted an earache by stubbornly resisting all calls to leave his Sibley tent on the lawn for the warmer confines of a room inside the Corbin manor house. Dr. McGuire finally prevailed upon him to make a move, but Jackson insisted on not disturbing the peace of the family, instead accepting as his new abode a small frame house on the grounds, formerly the estate's business office. There he would spend the next three months, within an easy ride of Lee's headquarters, "situated on the edge of an old pine field" along the Mine Road near Hamilton's Crossing. Lee vowed to reside in his "house tent" through the winter, refusing, like Jackson, the solicitous invitations of local homeowners. He, too, would fall ill from the continual exposure and in late March would relocate to the nearby Yerby house to recover. Both men wanted to share the hardships of their troops and set a good example during an unusually frigid and wet winter, but both grudgingly bowed to the limitations of their physical endurance. The older Lee was particularly feeling his age and frustrated by his infirmities, which would continue into the spring, putting a damper on his and Jackson's plans.[9]

The camps of the Confederates were spread out along the southern bank of the Rappahannock, stretching from Banks Ford in the northwest to Port Royal in the southeast, the divisions far enough away from each other that they would not cross-forage too much in the same, well-scoured area but close enough to unify quickly should the Federals decide to reopen hostilities. Two railroads brought just enough supplies to prevent wholesale, debilitating hunger: the proximate but over-utilized, one-track Richmond, Fredericksburg and Potomac Railroad and the larger but more distant and accident-prone Virginia Central Railroad. Even operating at full efficiency, both roads were insufficient to meet the needs of the army. Some soldiers joked that "General Starvation" outranked General Lee that winter. Others groused about "old rusty bacon and musty flour and not half enough," tattered clothing, and low pay, but many accepted their plight as typical for hard-fighting Confederates. Good-natured stoicism buoyed the majority during these lean months, but the failing, inadequate transportation network guaranteed that food was scarce for the troops and forage even scarcer for the horses. The men frequently subsisted without any rations one to two days each week and Lee was obliged to detach some of his cavalry and artillery to more distant pastures to prevent the deaths of the animals. With the army in such a physical condition, the commanding general despaired not only his ability to go on the offensive in the spring, a topic he and Jackson discussed repeatedly that winter, but also defend against any new Federal incursions across the river. "Our horses and mules are in that reduced state that the labor and exposure incident to an attack would result in their destruction, and leave us destitute of the means of transportation," he told President Davis. Despite this grim reality, Lee took solace in the impressive systems of breastworks and artillery lunettes that laced the countryside behind, below, and above Fredericksburg, guaranteeing any renewal of the December 13 assaults would result in an even worse Union disaster.[10]

The local plantations and farms had been largely spared the ugliness of war thus far except for the interlude of the late battle, but now, with almost 70,000 troops bivouacked for the winter in their midst, the landscape radically changed. "What a transformation of our quiet country home!" one of the Corbin girls wrote, "Thousands of soldiers around—the hills echoing with the sounds of army life. . . . In less than six weeks great forests were literally mowed down. Almost Phoenix like sprung into life settlements of little log huts dotted here and there with white tents. The smoke curled from hundreds of campfires!" The great country homes of the region, previously obscured from each other by the thick woods, now frowned at each other across vistas of stumps, log cabins, and canvas. In this environment the leadership of the Army of Northern Virginia hunkered down for the duration of the cold weather and attempted to recover a semblance of normalcy after a year of abnormal, if extraordinary exploits. Lee, Jackson, Longstreet, and Stuart caught up on long-delayed paperwork, pummeled Richmond with official requests, planned future strategy, and cemented friendships, all while battling snow, rain, mud, and wind. Soon Longstreet would be sent away with two of his divisions to the southeast, and Stuart would find himself frequently leading raids or parrying the probes of the enemy, leaving Lee and Stonewall mainly to themselves.[11]

Immediately pressing down on both men were the daily demands of command in the off-season, which varied significantly from those during the warmer, campaigning months. Late into the night Jackson tackled "great stacks of papers prepared by his own direction," the reduction of which demanded "all his capacity for organization," according to J. P. Smith. Continuing his penchant for direct correspondence with policymakers, the corps commander was in regular contact with the Secretary of War and committees of Congress about topics ranging from the tactical to the strategic level. To William Porcher Miles, chairman of the House Military Affairs Committee, he sent a letter in January "in relation to legislation on the subject of deserters from the army." Miles took action on his suggestions, introducing a bill "to provide for the arrest of soldiers absent from their commands without leave, and providing compensation for their capture." The bill made it to the House, where it became subsumed under other business, but may have helped inspire later legislation aimed at curbing desertion. [12]

More pressing even than his personal disdain for desertion, however, were Jackson's official reports of his past battles, none of which had been filed. It was an embarrassing situation, one that demanded attention, and to that end Stonewall brought in Charles Faulkner, a distinguished Martinsburg attorney, colleague of Alexander Boteler, and former U.S. congressman and ambassador to France. Appointing him as lieutenant colonel and titular chief of staff out of respect for his age created some grumbling among the younger staff officers, many of whom felt Sandie Pendleton had been slighted, but Jed Hotchkiss believed Faulkner was the right man for the job, "eminently fitted to collect and harmonize conflicting testimony." Faulkner proved a huge boon to Jackson—who had not written a single report of his operations since Kernstown—carefully composing most of the initial drafts after a conscientious and exhaustive search for accurate source material. But Stonewall personally and punctiliously edited each and every sentence before he approved it, removing flowery language he believed unnecessary and inserting his own little touches. This tedious work was not to the general's liking; yet, as with other duties that winter, he took to it with aplomb, creating an atmosphere in his corps of "energetic administration" that ensured "every bureau of the Richmond War Department was kept awake by Jackson's demands," even if after a long day Stonewall himself could sometimes be found asleep at his table, pen poised in mid-signature. Filling the ranks torn by deaths, wounds, illness, and desertion took on the aspects of a clerical crusade, as did the reestablishment of proper military discipline and drill. Pendleton, Smith, Hotchkiss, Harman, Faulkner—all spent countless hours coming in and out of that little office on the Corbin manor grounds, giving daily reports, presenting paperwork for approval, and ensuring "there was nothing of which he did not know and which did not receive his earnest attention." Courts martial that had been long delayed proceeded quickly, and the charges Jackson had pressed against A. P. Hill prior to Sharpsburg could finally be addressed. Most important to Stonewall—and fully supported by Lee—was the awakening (and reawakening) of Christian faith among the soldiers. His first desire, he claimed, was to command "a converted army." To achieve that result,

Jackson expended considerable time writing personal recruitment letters to qualified chaplain candidates, organized visits of famous ministers to preach to the men, and invited his friend the Reverend Beverly Tucker Lacy, pastor of a Presbyterian church in Kentucky, to become chief chaplain of his corps. This last clerical task Stonewall attacked with relish. It became one of his enduring legacies to the entire army as well as a pillar of his relationship with Lee.[13]

His lieutenant's daily responsibilities were daunting, but Lee's burdens were the more onerous, including not only oversight of supply and reinforcement for the entire army—duties that plagued him regardless of the day or week—but also management of countless administrative issues, such as routine promotions, leaves of absence, courts martial, and filling requests for transfers in and out of various units (including, incidentally, Hotchkiss's petition for official appointment as a topographical engineer in Jackson's corps). These seemingly minor concerns were dealt with on a priority basis throughout the year and individually required little attention, but after months of vigorous campaigning, those set aside had grown into a mountain of paperwork that could no longer be ignored. Lee's "known aversion to spending time over mundane official papers" notwithstanding, he insisted on keeping his personal staff small and delegated only very routine matters to them, persevering even in writing personal letters of thanks for small gifts sent to him from admiring civilians. Early in the morning or late at night, when the exigencies of professional duties had dwindled, the candlelight in his tent sketched his silhouette on the canvas, bent over his desk, diligently and carefully writing these missives, or notes of condolence to the loved ones of certain soldiers or officers who had fallen, or, most importantly, letters to Mary and his children. "I cannot tell you how I long to see you," he penned daughter Mildred on Christmas Day. "When a little quiet occurs and my thoughts revert to you, your sisters and mother, my heart aches for our reunion." Noting he had "little time for writing to my children," he assured her "that I am always thinking of you, always wishing to see you." Despite the unrelenting pressure of official correspondence, Lee still found time for his family.[14]

He also made time for constant communications with Richmond. Although no longer officially the president's chief military aide, the general continued de facto service as Davis's principal strategic adviser. Anticipating and responding to his requests, whether about the Virginia theater or affairs in the Carolinas and elsewhere, occupied much time and mental energy; additionally, Lee kept Secretary of War James Seddon in the loop on all matters related to the condition and operations of the army and sometimes schooled him, as he did Davis, in what he perceived to be necessary military policies and strategies for the entire Confederacy. Along with improving the agonizing supply situation, increasing available manpower was paramount among them. Universal conscription was not yet bearing enough fruit and the shortage of soldiers had become the South's great strategic challenge, much as Jackson had predicted the previous winter and was even then experiencing in his own corps. "More than once have most promising opportunities been lost for want of men to take advantage of them," Lee exhorted his civilian superiors, "and victory itself has been made to put on the appearance of defeat, because our diminished and exhausted troops have been unable to renew a successful struggle against fresh numbers of the enemy." Referring probably to the lost opportunity following the Fredericksburg battle, the commanding general offered a candid exposition of the disparity between Union and Confederate military means and the unsurprising results: "Losses in battle are rendered much heavier by reason of our being compelled to encounter the enemy with inferior numbers. . . . The great increase of the enemy's forces will augment the disparity of numbers to such a degree that victory, if attained, can only be achieved by a terrible expenditure of the most precious blood of the country." Urging an immediate and renewed effort "to fill and maintain the ranks of our armies, until God, in His mercy, shall bless us with the establishment of our independence," Lee ominously predicted that "blood will be on the hands of the thousands of able bodied men who remain at home in safety and ease." He fully comprehended that in a democratic republic at war, the will of the populace determined the success of national policies, adding that the "people of the Confederate States have it in their power" to ensure "every victory [will] bring us nearer to the great end which it is the object of this war to reach." Few generals on either side in the Civil War better understood the fundamental purpose of military victory, the means required to sustain it, and the relationships, as Clausewitz posited, between the people, the government, and the army.[15]

Richmond's inability to adequately address the manpower requirements and logistical difficulties facing the Army of Northern Virginia prompted Lee to send such urgent suggestions that bordered on political advice and often elevated him, whether he wished it or not, to the realm of policy. Yet this letter to the secretary of war, like those written specifically for the president, was carefully couched in obedient, factual language that avoided the taints of complaint, presumption, or obsequiousness, and was but one of many more dwelling clearly at the operational or theater-strategic level. Lengthy discussions about the problem of adequate provisions for the men and forage for the horses, which in turn converged with troubling news from southeast Virginia and eastern North Carolina, occupied center stage in many of Lee's correspondences during this time. Throughout the winter, Federal incursions in those regions threatened rich agricultural counties crucial to the already deficient sustenance of the army as well as the principal railroad that supplied the capital from points south. Lee realized, as do most good strategic thinkers, the interdependence of successful logistics and operations in the field, yet he resisted sending out troops from his own force in response to exaggerated rumors of impending doom further south. Until late January, when Burnside tried the hapless "Mud March" up the Rappahannock in an attempt to outflank the Confederates to the west, cross the river, and reignite the stalled Federal offensive, Lee was unsure if his enemy would go into permanent winter quarters or not, and was uneasy about releasing brigades from his army. To Secretary Seddon on January 5 Lee cautioned, "information should be obtained by our own scouts, men accustomed to see things as they are, and not liable to excitement or exaggeration." Although he had already put Robert Ransom's division on the march to Richmond as a palliative to the croaking Cassandras, he continued, "I hope it may not be necessary to advance him beyond Drewry's Bluff. I think it very hazardous now to divide this army. Much labor has been expended in its organization. It is now in excellent condition, physically and morally, and I wish to maintain it so if possible." Sending a dependable general to North Carolina would cost his army considerably less than any further troop detachments, reasoned Lee, so in the end the stolid D. H. Hill went home to command in his native state after requesting a transfer out of the Army of Northern Virginia. But Lee never got Ransom's division back, confirming his suspicion that acquiescing to requests to forward troops to other theaters equated with their permanent loss to his army. This reality haunted him up through the Gettysburg Campaign and contributed to his reticence in relinquishing Pickett's and Hood's divisions in mid-February. Losing *those* veterans, amounting to almost 16,000 men, and with them his other chief lieutenant James Longstreet, not only reinforced Lee's earlier-stated belief that numerical inferiority was a major strategic liability for the Confederacy, but importantly drew him closer to Jackson, on whom he would rely increasingly for counsel, and, as it turned out in the spring, victory. Longstreet's performance while on independent command also tarnished his image with Lee.[16]

The army commander initially agreed to detach Longstreet and half of his remaining corps to hedge against a large flotilla of Union transports and gunboats that steamed down the Potomac and landed the Union IX Corps at Hampton Roads, supplementing already sizeable Federal garrisons at Norfolk and Suffolk. Speculation about Federal intentions for this combined force, and reports that other large units from the Army of the Potomac had been withdrawn toward the docks at Aquia Creek above Falmouth, alarmed Davis and Seddon and obliged Lee to think about the safety of Richmond as well as the uninterrupted, if meager, supply network that sustained his army. First Pickett, then Hood, and finally Longstreet himself were dispatched toward the capital to safeguard against any potential Federal movements in that direction, southeastern Virginia, or North Carolina.

Why Lee sent Old Pete and not Jackson has never been adequately explained, as the historical record is frustratingly silent about the commanding general's motives in selecting Longstreet for the detached duty. In an officious-sounding letter to his subordinate on February 18, however, Lee described his intent for the transfer, clarified that this was not an independent command, and offered suggestions on seemingly menial, self-evident tasks that revealed much—and portended more—about their professional relationship. Could it have been the commanding general trusted Longstreet to complete his mission, but did not trust himself to counter a potential Union thrust along the Fredericksburg front without Jackson? Had Jackson become the more indispensable of his two corps commanders? Or did Lee believe Longstreet could better handle detached missions than Jackson? Certainly, Stonewall's record in the Valley and during the Second Manassas and Sharpsburg Campaigns belied such a notion. Regardless, the verbiage Lee selected in his initial orders to Longstreet disclosed a cautionary, redundant, less-discretionary tone that would have been unusual in orders to Jackson: "I desire you to join [your two divisions] and to place them in positions where their comfort will be secured and whence they can be readily moved. . . . I desire therefore you be prepared to receive them and to select encampments for their comfortable accommodation. You will be advised of their approach. . . . I need not remind you of the importance of selecting sheltered positions, where there is plenty of wood, and which may be convenient to supplies. . . . You will require at least two battalions of your artillery and probably one of your reserve corps. . . . The . . . horses might be transported by railroad, by which route all heavy baggage if possible should also be conveyed. . . . I wish you to inform me where I can communicate with you. To inform yourself of the movements of the enemy in your front, and to keep me advised."[17]

As the weeks passed and no Federal attack occurred, Longstreet, now given outright command of the Department of Southern Virginia and North Carolina by the War Department with oversight over three mini-departments and 40,000 men, flexed his muscles and attempted several small offensives in Eastern North Carolina that came to naught, partly because of acerbic and uncooperative subordinates and partly because of superior Union positions and numbers. Old Pete's star was drooping and he needed something to restore his diminishing reputation. As he sat in his office in Petersburg, twenty miles south of Richmond, listening to the hiss and clang of locomotives pulling in and out of the various terminals, he thought about a report his commissary general, Major Raphael Moses, had provided him. Moses discovered that the counties in northeastern North Carolina were bursting with hogs and corn and simply awaited proper requisitioning. Aware of the rampant hunger in the Army of Northern Virginia, Longstreet proposed what he believed to be a win-win operational strategy to Lee: invest Union-occupied Suffolk and nearby points with his divisions, pinning down the Federals, while Moses oversaw the gathering of provisions in the nearby counties, that, ostensibly, would be forwarded to Lee's army. If opportunity beckoned, Longstreet would retake Suffolk. [18]

A back-and-forth with Lee ensued, involving both Davis and Seddon, that did not paint Old Pete in a positive light and continued the nuanced caution and even micromanagement that the commanding general had exhibited toward him earlier. For his part, Lee worried that Major General Joseph Hooker, the new chief of the Army of the Potomac, would soon move against him with overwhelming numbers, and this anxiety certainly permeated his messages with Longstreet. Lee wanted his subordinate to remember where his primary responsibilities lay. On March 19, after a Federal cavalry probe across the Rappahannock had been repulsed, he admonished, "I need not remind you that it will be necessary to maintain great vigilance in your front as well as here, and to hold the troops at both points ready to cooperate whenever it is correctly ascertained where the attack of the enemy will fall. I hope you will be able to act on the suggestions contained in my letter from Richmond relative to obtaining all the supplies possible of forage and subsistence from North Carolina." Almost as if he had predicted this warning, Longstreet penned a letter to Lee the same day, claiming he could not work wonders: "I can, I think, get all of the supplies in that State if I can use my forces; but if the two divisions [Hood and Pickett] are to be held in readiness to join you, or even one of them, I can do nothing." Continuing, he ventured into the realm of theater strategic advice: "I am not prompted by any desire to do, or to attempt to do, great things. I only wish to do what I regard as my duty—give you the full benefit of my views. It seems to me to be a matter of prime necessity with us to keep the enemy out of North Carolina in order that we may draw out all the supplies there, and if we give ground at all it would be better to do so from the Rappahannock. It is right, as you say, to concentrate and crush him; but will it be better to concentrate upon his grand army rather than on his detachments and then make a grand concentration on the grand army?" [19]

Lee ignored his subordinate's concentration argument—which he doubtless interpreted as Longstreet's justification for continuing independent operations—and agreed fully with the need to obtain the North Carolina provisions. But he rebuked the insinuation that he could not collect them and also be ready to return to the main army, and later roundly dismissed the proposition of "giving ground." On the 21st, he coolly responded to Old Pete, "I have received your letter of the 19th instant. I had hoped that you would have been able with the troops in North Carolina to have accomplished the object proposed . . . and did not suppose that you would have required Pickett's and Hood's divisions. . . . . I still think if you can retain them in reserve, to be thrown on any point attacked or where a blow can be struck, it will be the best disposition of them." In a thinly veiled reproof that intoned some condescension, Lee concluded, "I am confident that at all times and in all places you will do all that can be done for the defence of the country and advancement of the service, and are ready to cooperate or act singly as circumstances dictate." A week later, he reinforced his intent and message. "You have about 40,000 effective men. The enemy can bring out no more. I feel assured that with equal numbers you can go where you choose." Retreat from the Rappahannock line was out of the question: "If this army is further weakened we must retire to the line of the Annas [rivers] and trust to a battle nearer Richmond. . . . It throws open a broad margin of our frontier and renders our railroad communications more hazardous and more difficult to secure." In a final gesture of concern about Longstreet, Lee closed, "Should you find it advisable to have a personal conference with me at any time I will be happy to see you here, or it may be that I could meet you in Richmond." Separately, to Seddon, Lee wrote dryly that "Genl Longstreet has been directed to employ the troops south of James river, when not required for military operations, to collect supplies in that quarter, and penetrate, if practicable, the district held by the enemy." To Lee, this correspondence clarified who was in overall charge, revealed Longstreet's difficulty with independent command and perhaps with himself, and stood in stark contrast with relations and discussions then occurring with Jackson. On the same day he expressed disappointment and disquiet with Longstreet, Lee sent Mary pictures of himself and Jackson created in England, perhaps cut out of a newspaper, and enclosed a note poking fun at his own appearance but complementing Stonewall's: "We are poor judges of ourselves," he wrote, "and I cannot therefore pronounce as to [the artist's] success. But I can say that in his portrait of Genl Jackson he has failed to give his fine candid and frank expression, so charming to see and so attractive to the beholder."[20]

This simple statement to his wife symbolized the affection Lee had slowly developed for Jackson over the past year, which, thanks to physical proximity for the first prolonged period since Stonewall left the Valley, had grown into bona fide friendship. The two leaders were together multiple times each week for reasons both personal and professional, their staffs intermingled constantly and fostered their own camaraderie, and as the snows of winter gave way to the winds and rain of early spring it was evident the two men not only shared a profound mutual respect but also genuinely enjoyed each other's company. In any given week "General Lee and staff sometimes called for a short interview," J. P. Smith recalled, and Jackson visited Lee's headquarters just as frequently. Of course, a good percentage of these occasions were devoted to military affairs, but the historical record reveals that more than a few were convivial, social events, or combinations of business and pleasure. For Stonewall, these times with his chief, like the Christmas dinner, were lighter, happier moments that ameliorated the drudgery of editing official reports, broke the tension of the ongoing legal controversy with A. P. Hill, and, like Lee himself, stalled, if but for a little while, the constant stream of necessary paperwork to and from Richmond.[21]

One of those notes concerned the possible designation of the Shenandoah Valley as a distinct military district and the permanent stationing of a large body of troops there. Naturally still concerned with the region's security and aware of how much Lee valued his advice, Jackson broached the topic with him after Burnside retreated back across the river. "I have repeatedly urged upon Genl. Lee the importance of protecting the Valley," he wrote Congressman Boteler on New Year's Eve, "and upon more than one occasion have apologized to him from a conviction that I was apparently forgetting my position and encroaching upon the prerogative of my Commanding General. He has always kindly received what I said." Yet he made it clear that he did not at all wish to leave Lee's side. "You must not think from what I have said to you at any time that I desire to be sent to the Valley, even if it should be made a Department. I would rather remain in a subordinate position as long as the war lasts; provided that my command is kept near my Commanding General. This is my real feeling." This frank letter is important in that it indicated Lee's interest in hearing what Jackson had to say, his receptiveness to that counsel—he once said he "wishe[d] he had a dozen Jacksons for his Lieutenants"—and in turn Jackson's personal devotion to Lee, even if it meant declining the prize of independent command in his cherished Valley. [22]

Later during the winter the Federals appeared to threaten a recrossing of the Rappahannock near Hayfield, an estate whose master, William P. Taylor, was one of Lee's relatives. The household had already had contact with Jackson's staff by donating some food to the great Christmas feast, but neither Mr. Taylor nor his wife were personally acquainted with the general himself. Lee requested Jackson, Stuart, Pendleton, and their staffs to accompany him on a reconnaissance of the area, and, satisfied the enemy was not preparing a movement, decided afterward to call on his kinsman. Greeted at the door by Mrs. Taylor, Lee, "with most distinguished manners," led the high command of the Army of Northern Virginia and their minions between the great white pillars and onto the front porch of the gleaming Georgian-style mansion. Many of the men had not been in such a grand house for a long time, if ever, and looked around as if they had arrived in another world. Received in the parlor by Mr. and Mrs. Taylor and other members of the family, it was standing room only for the staffs but the generals were comfortably seated. Jackson felt completely at ease, and Lee, for a moment, had returned to a more elegant place and time that evoked the playful-courtly side of his personality. He had "brought these great generals for the [ladies] to see," and, referring to Stonewall, continued, "You would scarce believe, my dear cousin, that amiable gentleman, who sits near you smiling so pleasantly, was one of the most cruel and inhuman men you ever saw." A small silence followed before Mrs. Taylor innocently replied she "had always heard that Gen. Jackson was a good, Christian man." A twinkle in his eye, Lee kept a straight face, explaining, "Why, Madam, the other day when he had the battle at Fredericksburg, it was as much as I could do to keep him from putting bayonets on the guns of all the men, and driving those people into the river." Aware now of the jest being played, Mrs. Taylor answered, "Well, General Lee, if those people ever cross on our place, I hope you won't do anything to keep Gen. Jackson from driving them into the river." Stonewall kept beaming throughout the entire exchange, fully enjoying the good-natured ribbing, and reportedly placed an order the next day for additional bayonets for his corps. [23]

When important visitors came to the army, they stopped at both Lee's and Stonewall's headquarters. Several members of the London press, a British nobleman, and the chairman of the Military Affairs Committee in Parliament arrived at the Confederate camps in late December 1862 and, after a few days of recovery in the company of Stuart's staff, proceeded to Jackson's camp at Moss Neck. "Old Stonewall so fascinated his English visitors by his kind and pleasant manners and the resources of his conversation that, quite against their previous intentions, they accepted his invitation to dinner," their escort observed, "and instead of a visit of twenty minutes, many hours were spent." Suddenly it dawned on the Englishmen that they had stood up Robert E. Lee, with whom they had prearranged a suppertime. Appearing quite late, sheepish and apologetic, at the commanding general's Hamilton's Crossing camp, they encountered an amused Lee who politely excused their tardiness when he learned where they had been. "Gentlemen, I hope Jackson has given you a good dinner," he exclaimed, "and if so, I am very glad things have turned out as they have, for I had given the invitation without knowing the poor state of my mess provisions, and should scarcely have been able to offer you anything." Other leaders might have been piqued that foreign guests had tarried too long with a subordinate, but this was not the case with Lee. He rejoiced that Stonewall could entertain them and had done so, especially when his own meager fare was insufficient. For his part, Jackson returned the favor a few weeks later by instantly forgiving Lee what might have become a serious misunderstanding among other command teams. The night before a blinding snowstorm, Lee sent his subordinate a note requesting him to come over "at his convenience." The message did not indicate what level of importance the visit would hold or its urgency, but Stonewall took it seriously, despite the weather. Early the next morning, J. P. Smith, awakened unexpectedly from a cozy slumber in his tent, was "soon in the saddle by his side without any breakfast, and a worse ride in the face of the storm for 12 or 14 miles I never had." Reaching Lee's headquarters, the commanding general, notified of their arrival, quickly came out of his tent, hatless, with a stern expression on his face. "You know I did not wish you to come in such a storm," he said, "it was a matter of little importance. I am so sorry that you have had this ride." Unreproached, Jackson blushed a little, smiled, and replied simply, "I received your note, General Lee."[24]

Another example from the realm of art offers an intimate view of the relationship. Just before the opening of the Chancellorsville Campaign at the end of April, photographer David T. Cowell of the famous Minnis and Cowell studio in Richmond arrived in Fredericksburg to take Jackson's picture. Lee was distressed he missed the occasion to have his own portrait taken, but in retrospect may have also been hoping for an opportunity to have a joint photographic portrait created. The timing was fateful. To Mary, he later lamented, "I told Mr. Cowle [sic] on his arrival here, that if he would notify me of the time and place of his taking Genl Jackson's likeness that I would attend, should nothing prevent—I heard nothing of him for two days. On the third [illegible] I recd [sic] a note from Genl J. written at the request of Mr. C—that he was at the house of Mr. Yerby for the purpose and that unless I was there by 11¾ that I need not come, as he would not have time to take my likeness—it was 11½ when I recd the note. My horses were out grazing on the hill and I was more than a mile distant. I thought it useless to attempt to reach him—It is all well as it is. You would not have liked his representation if made." Thirteen lines down in the same letter, dated May 11, Lee wrote, "You will see we have to mourn the loss of the good and great Jackson." Lee had lost his chance; Stonewall died the day before. Obviously, the incident in April disturbed him enough to devote considerable space about it in the same letter to his wife in which he announced Jackson's passing. Lee would not have so bemoaned missing a simple appointment with a photographer. It was the fact that he missed the opportunity to share it with his friend that bothered him, especially in light of his subsequent death.[25]

The personal tie between Jackson and Lee was strong, but another leader competed with the commanding general for Stonewall's fraternal affection and ensured the Army of Northern Virginia's command team was indelibly linked by powerful friendships. As one observer put it, despite obvious personality differences, "a strong bond of mutual admiration and confidence united them." Only Jeb Stuart, who once announced to a staff officer that "Jackson is a man of military genius," was possibly more welcome at the Moss Neck headquarters. On his first visit that winter, several members of Stonewall's staff witnessed a scene that revealed, if ever there was any doubt, the close relationship that had evolved between the cavalry leader and the corps commander, complementing that which had developed with Lee. Dismounting from his horse, spurs and sword jangling and resplendent in his new black-plumed hat, Stuart strode toward the humble office while Jackson, who knew instantly who had arrived, quickly stowed away loose papers and greeted him at the door with a big smile. Doffing his hat, Stuart stepped inside, his eyes adjusting to the darker lighting, and then immediately noticed the artwork bedecking the walls of his friend's temporary quarters. As was customary at the time, offices of the great Virginia plantations often were decorated with framed portraits of various animals, such as famous racehorses and hunting dogs. The Corbin office was no exception, and this offered Stuart, to the amusement of all, an irresistible temptation. Feigning "affected astonishment," and "pretend[ing] to believe that they were General Jackson's selections," he walked from one picture to the next, "and read aloud what was said about each noted race horse and each splendid bull." Over the modest fireplace hung a particularly explicit print of a terrier decimating a pack of rats. "With great solemnity," Stuart gazed at it, then glanced with raised eyebrows at Jackson, paused, stepped back, and declared that "he wished to express his astonishment and grief at the display of General Jackson's low tastes." Old ladies all over the Confederacy, he said, "who thought Jackson was a good man," would shudder at the thought that their hero had fallen into such disrepute. Stonewall pursed his lips, stifled a laugh, "with utter incapacity for response," and enjoyed the entire episode immensely. He "blushed like a girl, and hesitated, and said nothing," and then ordered Smith to ensure "a good dinner was prepared for General Stuart."[26]

Such episodes between Lee and Jackson or Jackson and Stuart, whether or not they were embellished by the passage of time, were important in revealing the strengthening ties of friendship that in turn fostered a deep trust among the Army of Northern Virginia's three most senior leaders. Especially with Longstreet's absence and Lee's concern over his performance, the triangle of trust among them that had sprouted and grown prior to Fredericksburg blossomed and matured during the winter of 1862–1863. That reality, in turn, enhanced already strong professional relationships that the strenuous campaigns of the past year had forged through blood and fire. Lee was certainly still the boss and commanded the utmost respect with both of his subordinates (especially the more junior Stuart) that could border on formality, particularly when in the presence of other generals. But in numerous other instances, Jackson and Lee displayed the hallmarks of a convivial, lighthearted friendship that underlay their military professionalism. That professional bond, so critical to the eastern Confederate army's success and indeed to the Southern nation's survival, was further undergirded by another major component: a joint, unswerving faith in the Lord and His will, both for themselves and for their country. During March and April 1863 that uniting faith grew substantially, both publicly and privately. [27]

Both Lee the Episcopalian and Jackson the "Blue Light" Presbyterian believed in the theological concept of divine providence, that, as Lee's religious biographer explains, provided a firm foundation for personal behavior, expectations of others, and comprehension of why events—whether good or bad—occurred. For them, an omniscient God created the world and watched over it and humanity, ordaining all events toward good according to His timetable and His will. His will could only be good, so when bad things happened it was because the wickedness of mankind, whether individuals or groups, temporarily triumphed and put themselves and their interests above the will of God. The Lord then disciplined the sinful, believers and nonbelievers alike, to bring them back to Him. People thus had enough free will to make a choice, even on a daily basis, regarding how they would use their God-given gifts and blessings: either to glorify Him by making the world better, or by choosing selfishness and sin. Both generals felt the Lord bestowed more blessings on those who resigned themselves to His will and husbanded His blessings for good, whereas He withheld them from the sinful. A person or a country could, therefore, gauge to some degree where they stood with the Almighty based on the blessings they received, but complete acceptance of His will, whatever occurred, was paramount. To his soldiers, Lee pronounced on a national day of prayer and fasting (March 23), "He has preserved your lives amidst countless dangers; He has been with you in all your trials; He has given you fortitude under hardships and courage in the shock of battle. . . . Devoutly thankful for His signal mercies, let us bow before the Lord of Hosts, and join our hearts with millions in our land in prayer." To Mary, Lee wrote on March 27, "I know you will unite with me in fervent prayers for His manifold individual and national blessings. I wish I could be sufficiently thankful for all He has done for us, and felt that we deserved a continuance of the protection and guidance He has heretofore vouchsafed to us. I know that in Him is our only salvation. He alone can give us peace and freedom and I humbly submit to His holy will." On April 10, Jackson composed a very similar letter to Mary Anna, emphasizing the national aspect of God's providence: "I trust that God is going to bless us with great success, and in such a manner as to show that it is all His gift; and I trust and pray that it will lead our country to acknowledge Him, and to live in accordance with His will as revealed in the Bible."[28]

This understanding of divine providence was not unique to the Confederate leaders, and indeed governed the spiritual life of most American Protestants at the time, regardless of denomination. It was rooted in the evolution of Christian thought dating back to St. Augustine, through the reformationists Ulrich Zwingli and John Calvin, and evinced influences from Arminianism, Enlightenment thinkers like Isaac Newton, and even deism. Growing naturally through the period of the Revolution and the Early Republic, the Baptists and the Methodists, the largest and fastest-growing antebellum denominations, wholeheartedly embraced it and the idea was evident in Presbyterian thought as well. The Second Great Awakening mightily affected how all Protestants perceived providence, injecting the spirit of evangelicalism directly into the heart of the concept, and thus into the mainstream of American spiritual identity and practice. Even the Episcopalians, among the most staid and formalistic of Protestants, came to embrace that salvation could come from either liturgically rooted baptism and confirmation *or* a personal conversion experience that embraced Jesus Christ as one's personal savior. Lee demonstrated this understanding when he wrote, "I know that in Him is our only salvation," and supported Jackson's herculean efforts to secure chaplains for his corps—a spiritual campaign that could only result in the expansion of God's kingdom and increased piety in the army. Lee approved of both potential results. For his part, Stonewall, even more rooted in evangelical belief than his chief, was decidedly convinced that a converted, Christian army would not only assure the salvation of thousands of souls but also increase the chances of military success. He knew personally from his own experience that a converted soul instilled a calm, brave spirit that could surmount whatever earthly troubles were thrust against it. Such faith, he asserted, was even more necessary for military leadership: "In the commander of an army at the critical hour, it calms his perplexities, moderates his anxieties, steadies the scales of judgement, and thus preserves him from exaggerated and rash conclusions."

One night in his office at Moss Neck, the light from his simple desk lamp illuminating his face, Jackson passionately expounded to Reverend Lacy that he "was assured of the love of Christ to his soul; he felt not the faintest dread that he should ever fall under the wrath of God, although a great sinner; he was forever reconciled by the righteousness of Christ, and that love for God and Christ was now the practical spring of all his penitence." Continuing, he exclaimed, "nothing earthly can mar my happiness." Nor could very much rattle the prayerful Jackson in war, including exposure to enemy fire, as he realized "that heaven is in store for me; and I should rejoice in the prospect of going there tomorrow." Although he represented one end of a broad societal spectrum, Stonewall was not way out of line compared to other providential evangelicals of his day and did not at all alarm Lee with his beliefs. The commanding general, perhaps more reserved about private matters, shared them with his lieutenant. Most chroniclers of Civil War–era religion agree that an evangelical interpretation of providence, probably a bit less strident than Jackson's, dominated the spiritual thinking of most Protestants and thus many Americans, including several prominent leaders of both sides. Lee and

Jackson joined the likes of Oliver Otis Howard, Abraham Lincoln, and Salmon P. Chase, therefore, in how they thought of God and viewed the unfolding events of the war.[29]

The Union president and his treasury secretary were not, however, in charge of the Confederacy's most successful field army and did not determine the hopes and fears of the Southern nation. Lee and Jackson did. By the spring of 1863, people across the South, and especially in the East, had come to identify the Army of Northern Virginia and its command team as the guarantor of eventual independence and the symbol of national resistance.[30] What the Confederate chieftains did was supremely significant, their decisions and actions of equal or, in most cases, greater importance in the perceptions of Southern civilians as those enacted by policymakers in Richmond or by generals in other theaters of war. What influenced the thinking of Lee and Jackson, then, mattered. For both men, the workings of divine providence controlled everything and determined their own personal fate, that of the army, and of the Confederacy. They fully accepted the Lord's will, but concurrently worried that God's benevolence, heretofore so richly bestowed, might be wearing thin. Both generals had written to their wives on Christmas Day about this very topic and it continued to gnaw at them throughout the winter. Jackson was especially troubled, speaking passionately of "the connection between national prosperity and obedience of the people to God, especially in sabb. [sic] observance," telling Lacy the "only thing which gives me any apprehension of [my] country's cause was sin of the army and people." Although the historical record is silent, it is likely he expounded on the theme during March and April in private conversations with Lee, who, based on many previous and subsequent statements, almost certainly agreed with him. Sick in bed at the Thomas Yerby House with a bad cold and acute pericarditis for some of these months, Lee fretted over his inactivity, lamented recent Union pillaging of Southern civilians, and wondered when the Almighty would act, whether in favor of the Confederacy or not. Perhaps consoling himself as much as his wife, he reminded Mary that "there is a just God in Heaven, who will make all things right in time. To Him we must trust and for that we must wait." Lee would have been upheld in that belief by a newspaper he doubtless had at his bedside, the *Southern Churchman*. He and Jackson both subscribed to this leading Southern evangelical weekly and read it regularly, the latter even allowing his personal statements and appeals for chaplains to be printed in it (minus his name). Aware that they shared the same religious convictions, were viewed as exemplars for the entire country, and that their decisions during that winter and spring of the new year would have momentous consequences, the two generals' common faith enhanced their confidence in each other, consolidating an already robust professional trust supported by friendship. [31]

Reverend Lacy was a common denominator for the Lee-Jackson religious connection. Immediately liked and trusted by Stonewall on their first meeting, the clergyman took up his permanent post at Jackson's headquarters in February 1863 and became one of Stonewall's closest associates, who regarded him as "a Christian brother" and treated him with "personal kindness tender beyond expression." Lacy served as the general's private chaplain as well as his de facto corps chaplain general, joining him in daily prayers and leading his staff in weekly prayer meetings. Jackson enthusiastically supported all his efforts, as did Lee, whose "aid was sought," according to J. P. Smith, "with all Jackson's influence at his back." Unifying all the Second Corps clerics under one governing body, providing chaplains for regiments currently bereft of spiritual officers, and serving as a conduit between the army and national denominational leaders were his primary duties besides preaching, but Lacy also spent much time ministering to those in the hospitals and counseling soldiers on heavenly matters. Amiable with a sense of humor, fond of good food, and presenting a fine appearance, the former Kentuckian quickly established a reputation among the troops as both a shepherd and a gifted preacher who consistently delivered meaningful messages of eternal hope, heavenly grace, and salvation. Samuel Firebaugh of the 10th Virginia described his sermons as "powerful" and wished "we could have him preach every Sabbath." Lacy himself advised his fellow chaplains, whom he formally organized into a Second Corps Chaplains Association, that their "words be few and well chosen. This is the principle: What are the few sentences that will save his soul if I never speak again? . . . Long sermons weary and injure your usefulness. Be short and sharp; brief, but brimful of the Gospel." [32]

Lacy started small, preaching primarily to the Stonewall Brigade in March 1863 in a simple chapel in the woods, but the impact of his services on the men who attended ensured that word spread and the congregations multiplied. One officer recalled, "the crowded house, the flickering lights, the smoke that dimmed the light, the earnest preaching, the breathless attention, broken only by sobs of prayers (with Gen. Jackson sitting among the men), made an occasion never to be forgotten." Soon Lacy found himself conducting worship for portions of multiple brigades simultaneously in a large outdoor space near Hamilton's Crossing, very close to Lee's command post and Jackson's new headquarters at the John Pratt Yerby Farm, to which Stonewall had moved in late March to be closer to Lee. This open-air church included large tents for the pulpit and high-ranking officers and visitors, while rough-hewn log seats accommodated several hundred enlisted men, with standing room for several thousand more on adjacent meadows. To most eyewitnesses these larger services were nothing less than awe-inspiring. On Sunday, April 5, Lacy preached to over 1,000 officers and men who had tramped through six inches of freshly fallen snow, some with only rags on their feet, to hear him speak on Romans 8:28. The soldiers filed into their places, reverent and silent, and as they did the day took on an aura of "singular beauty," the gentle sunlight warming the multitude and causing the ice crystals in the snow to sparkle. Gathering his energy to project his voice to all listeners, the reverend explained how "all things work together for good to them that love God, to them who are the called according to his purpose." Hardened faces that had seen the horrors of Second Manassas and Antietam softened and became moist with tears, and voices that had coarsely screamed the rebel yell in hatred now sweetly harmonized together "in the songs of Zion." Affected by the scene, Lacy observed, "I have seldom addressed so interesting and imposing an audience, and never one more respectful, solemn and tender. It was a noble sight to see there those, who led our armies to victory, and upon whom the eyes of the nation were turned with admiration and gratitude, melted in tears at the story of the cross and the exhibition of the love of God to the repenting and returning sinner. . . . Jackson and staff, and many brigade and regimental officers were present." Jed Hotchkiss, a devoted Christian and not one easily impressed, recorded in his diary that it was "a good sermon. Mr. L. is a very sensible man and one well qualified for a general missionary to the army."[33]

Every subsequent Sunday up to the onset of the Chancellorsville Campaign, Lacy conducted a similar outdoor service in the clearing near Jackson's new headquarters. Stonewall and his staff were always present, along with nearly all officers in the Stonewall Brigade; many from other brigades in the Second Corps, as well as enlisted men in the thousands, also attended. The spring of 1863 had become, to Jackson's and Lacy's gratification, "a great season of revivals" in the Army of Northern Virginia, and the chaplain's efforts stood at the center of it all. Jeb Stuart, when he could return from his new cavalry camp near Culpeper, was a worshipper along with most of his aides, and, most importantly, so was Robert E. Lee and many of his staff officers. Lee had missed the April 5 service due to his illnesses but hoped to be well enough to come the next Sunday. To his frustration, he was not, although he had already left his bed for occasional rides and excursions. "The Reverend Mr. Lacy held service within a mile of me today, but I was unable to attend," he wrote, "fearing to stand out in the open air, though the day was mild and bright." He did not neglect his devotions, however, conducting "solitary prayers in my own room" and digesting a sermon sent to him by none other than erstwhile Jackson staffer (and early biographer), the Reverend Robert L. Dabney, who had returned to his position at Hampden-Sydney College. Still a bit shaky but tolerably recovered, Lee, determined not to be absent again, came to the April 19 service and sat next to a glowing Jackson, who greeted him warmly but was clearly preoccupied. The night before Stonewall had received word that his wife and baby girl were finally in Richmond, having heeded his advice to come and visit him in camp before the spring campaign commenced. How Lee and Jackson interacted during the church service is unknown, but a newspaper reporter who later attended evening prayers at the latter's headquarters observed that the new father "offer[ed] up one of the most eloquent and thrilling prayers" he had ever heard. Perhaps Stonewall saw the hand of providence in the recovery of Lee, about whom he had solicited great concern the last few weeks, coupled with the impending happy arrival of his family.[34]

Lost Cause writers after the war wished to convey the impression of a saintly rebel army led by Christian believers and fighting for biblical principles, but a careful corroboration of (wartime) primary and postwar secondary sources indicates there was, in fact, much—if not comprehensive—religious unity. Lacy's April 26 church service, according to an eyewitness "one of the most brilliant and noble assemblies of military men ever brought together," demonstrated the Christian concord of Lee, Jackson, and much of the Army of Northern Virginia's high command. Mrs. Jackson was there, seated next to her husband under a large tent with their newly baptized daughter, Julia. Seated nearby were Generals Lee, Jubal Early, and Joseph Kershaw, "most of the *elite* [original emphasis] of Jackson's corps," and 1,500–2,000 soldiers, who sat on the log benches or "spread out in dense masses" in the grassy open places. The day dawned "bright and propitious," warm, "with a fresh breeze" that initially offered "some difficulty to the speaker," but as an observant chaplain noticed, "Brother Lacy was able, by the power of his full and strong voice, to overcome this; and he seemed to be listened to with profound attention." Preaching on the parable of the rich man and Lazarus, the reverend guaranteed his congregation that those who accepted Christ as their savior would see the miseries of this world exchanged for the joys of the next. Mrs. Jackson looked around in amazement at the vast multitude, hanging on Lacy's every word, a microcosm of the army unified in worship of their God. Her husband was smiling, almost "in triumph," and Lee sat perfectly composed, "reverent and impressive" in his dress uniform. Looking back years later, perhaps with a wistful memory, she remembered, "the preaching was earnest and edifying, the singing one grand volume of song, and the attention and good behavior of the assembly remarkable." Later that day, Lee, eager to formally meet his lieutenant's spouse, personally called on her at the nearby Yerby House. Jackson had secured a room for his wife there that coincidentally was the same one where his chief had lately convalesced. "General Lee and his staff [have] called to see Mrs. Jackson," a member of the household informed her, and as a "somewhat awe-struck" Mary Anna walked down the staircase she prepared herself for a rigorous interview. Instead, as befitting a man meeting his friend's spouse for the first time, in the parlor she "was met by a face so kind and *fatherly* [original emphasis], and a greeting so cordial, that I was at once reassured and put at ease. The formidable 'staff' consisted of only two or three nice-looking, courteous gentlemen."[35]

Lee's reception of Mrs. Jackson was emblematic of the personal relationship that had deepened between him and Stonewall during the winter and spring of 1862–1863, strengthened by proximity and Longstreet's absence, but most importantly by a shared providential, evangelical Christian faith. The religious awakening of the Army of Northern Virginia, sparked after the bloodbath at Sharpsburg, caught fire during these months, and both generals strongly supported the revival. Beverly Tucker Lacy was instrumental with his mass Sunday services, which themselves symbolized the unity of faith of the generals and the army writ large, but so were dozens of other chaplains who spread the gospel among the troops. "The good work extended out into the neighboring brigades," one of them wrote, "and went graciously on—only temporarily interrupted by the battle of Chancellorsville—until we took up the line of march for Gettysburg. Indeed, it did not cease even on that active campaign, but culminated in the great revival along the Rapidan in August 1863, which reached nearly the whole army. . ."

As the last days of April ticked away and signs of Federal activity across the river multiplied, Lee and Jackson, personally unified in friendship and faith, looked on their army with pride and confidence. "There never were such men in an army before," Lee would later tell General John B. Hood. To Lacy, speaking "with intense fire and energy" of the coming campaign, Jackson exclaimed, "we must make it an exceedingly active one. Only thus can a weaker country cope with a stronger." The Confederacy, he continued, "must make up in activity what it lacks in strength. A defensive campaign can only be made successfully by taking the aggressive. Napoleon never waited for his enemy to become fully prepared, but struck him the first blow." Both Jomini and Clausewitz would have agreed with Stonewall's strategic thinking.[36]

Lee harbored such thoughts as well. Neither he nor his subordinate desired a defensive campaign that spring and both wished to strike the Federals first. True, Longstreet's absence with his two seasoned divisions at Suffolk and insufficient provisions for underfed men and starving horses at Fredericksburg were problematic, but perhaps those issues could be overcome in time, before the enemy moved. Solidified by a heartfelt personal bond, in agreement about the nature of what needed to be done, their already formidable professional relationship ensured Lee and Jackson would plan effectively together throughout the winter. A simple endorsement Lee wrote on a letter from Stonewall to the Adjutant General in Richmond spoke volumes: "I have great confidence in the recomm[endations] of General Jackson." And Old Jack did not hold back in his suggestions, whether large or small. Promotions of various officers, capital punishment for deserters, courts martial, supply issues—the two leaders collaborated on all these routine matters, as well as in the great evangelical initiative Stonewall so strongly championed. But one idea still burned brightly in Jackson's mind that had war-winning consequences, one he had never abandoned and that could indeed make the spring campaign "an exceedingly active one": taking the war to the enemy in a deep and strategically damaging offensive.

He and Congressman Boteler corresponded about this several times during the winter. On March 7 Stonewall agreed with his former staffer, "I am cordially with you in favor of carrying the war North of the Potomac." To his current staff, he proclaimed one cold day, "We must do more than defeat their armies; we must destroy them." If that failed to convince the Northern people to accede to Confederate independence, then physical damage to their homes and industries would also be necessary. These were hard, ruthless thoughts in line with his earlier conversations with General Smith and brother-in-law Barringer, and not perfectly aligned with Lee's evolving strategic ideas. The commanding general did wish to take the war north again, but a destructive war on the *scale* Jackson had doubtless spoken to him about was not his preference, and probably unfeasible considering currently available rebel means. Lee now gravitated more toward decisive victories for political effect and supply acquisition. If Jackson was disappointed in this, there is no trace of it, and regardless, he knew his place and respected and admired his chief too much to usurp the protocols of military rank. Sliding comfortably into the role of Lee's adviser, deferentially but confidently offering ideas and proposals as he had earlier in the war and in December regarding the Valley District, would be his method. As in most professional partnerships, all was not perfect: the two cordially disagreed about artillery apportionment and promotions in February, and Jackson's ongoing feud with A. P. Hill and Lee's early spring maladies created headaches and delays. Yet by the end of the winter the two chieftains had decided what, specifically, they wanted to do. The war could only be won by going north, again, wrecking Federal logistical infrastructure if possible, obtaining critical provisions, and winning a great battle beyond the Potomac, perhaps in Pennsylvania.[37]

Incontrovertible evidence confirming this joint decision is elusive, but the proverbial smoke from the historical record still roils and twists thickly around an as-yet-unrevealed gun. Some scholars may find the source material unpersuasive, but there is just enough documentation to make a viable case. Jed Hotchkiss was among those who knew Stonewall the best during this period and spent countless hours with him, Stuart, Stuart's staff, and Lee's staff, and thus was privy to a vast amount of confidential information at the highest levels. His skills as a topographer, as well as his congenial personality and high intelligence, made him a confidant of sorts to the army's leadership. Jackson particularly relied on him. On February 23 he wrote in his diary, "I got secret orders from the General to prepare a map of the Valley of Va. Extended to Harrisburg, Pa., and then on to Philadelphia;—wishing the preparation to be kept a profound secret. So I went to reducing a map of Cumberland Co., Pa." Having spent a year in the Lykens Valley of Pennsylvania as a teacher before the war, Hotchkiss walked the roads and byways of the south-central part of the state and had personal knowledge of the area. Stonewall doubtless knew this when he ordered the map. For the next two weeks, as the fields south of Fredericksburg experienced a late winter thaw—"it was quite pleasant; frogs and birds singing . . . turtles crawling out in the sun"—Hotchkiss prioritized the creation of Jackson's secret map, seeking supplemental maps and other materials from Lee's and Stuart's headquarters. He spoke many times with the cavalryman and his staff during this period, perhaps picking their brains about Franklin County and Chambersburg, where they had raided the previous autumn, and gleaning personal information about how much Lee regarded Jackson and his abilities. Finally, on March 10, the mapmaker proudly presented his creation to his chief, who pondered it in his office at Moss

Neck. Two days later, Jackson and Lee spent the morning together in conference in Lee's tent at Hamilton's Crossing. Stonewall came back the next day and the planning continued. Then Lee took a train to Richmond to confer with the president. He remained in the capital until the 18th, where he picked up the cold that, along with the angina, knocked him off his feet by the end of the month.[38]

No record survives specifically outlining what Lee, President Davis, and the Confederate cabinet discussed during this long sojourn, but it is probable, as Hotchkiss's biographer states, that they weighed strategic options for the spring campaigning season across the Confederacy, including another attempt at a movement northward in the East. Postmaster General John H. Reagan, who was against the idea, wrote in his memoirs, "Early in the year 1863 the question of the invasion by our army of the country north of the Potomac was being discussed by the Cabinet and General Lee." Many historians have interpreted that imprecise statement as a reference to the later, more famous conference held in mid-May after Chancellorsville, but the month of May is not—and was not then—typically understood to be "early" in a given calendar year. Perhaps Reagan, whose inexactness regarding dates is legendary, was referring to a series of strategic discussions, commencing in the early spring and continuing onward, or maybe he was describing the theme of the March conference. Regardless, Lee, the president, and the cabinet did meet in that month and debated the opportunities and threats facing their new nation. Besides the proposal to move north, it was clear to all something had to be done to ameliorate the deteriorating situation along the Mississippi and take pressure off Bragg's outnumbered army in Tennessee, facts that Lee the strategist clearly recognized. Shortly after the conference, Davis wrote to Joseph E. Johnston, then in overall command of the Western Theater, that "General Lee concurred with me in an anxious desire to send you re-enforcements . . . but the prospect . . . is now less promising than at the date of my [initial] telegram." Too, Lee probably made a fervent case for improving the supply and transportation quandary besetting his own army, a prerequisite for any movement anywhere, and which in turn touched upon Longstreet's new mission in southside Virginia and northeastern North Carolina. Accordingly, Lee wrote to Longstreet while in Richmond on March 17 about his subordinate's mandate, the same letter that inspired Old Pete to venture that the Army of Northern Virginia should abandon the Rappahannock Line to allow him to retain the divisions of Pickett and Hood and accomplish his logistical objective.[39]

The difference between this enervated reply and Jackson's likely bold proposals, proffered in person the previous week, could not have been lost on the commanding general. Hotchkiss hinted at what those proposals may have been: "Jackson, in the Corbin Lodge at Moss Neck, although busy all the time strengthening his corps and putting it in a high state of efficiency by drill and inspection . . . was also thinking about his favorite design for a campaign into Pennsylvania, to break up the mining operations in the anthracite coalfield, and so seriously cripple the enemy by cutting off fuel supplies for his manufacturing establishments, his railways, and his numerous steamships." This was a reprise of Stonewall's earlier strategic vision for victory through destruction of essential Union means (i.e., coal), and indicates he had not given up on it. Certainly, the fact he ordered the map of southern Pennsylvania drawn up in February, well in advance of any possible campaign, points in that direction. The long, private talks in Lee's tent right after the map was finished and just before Lee left for the Richmond conference could not have been coincidental and almost certainly included discussion of such a plan, which would have been in Lee's head as he boarded the train for the capital. This thesis cannot be unequivocally proven, but the clues in the historical record make it eminently plausible. What *is* indisputable is that both Jackson and Lee preferred the offensive to the defensive and believed a final triumph—Southern independence—could only be achieved by a new offensive strategy in the Eastern Theater. As Lee declared to his son, Custis, "Nothing now can arrest during the present administration the most desolating war that was ever practiced, except a revolution among their people. Nothing can produce a revolution except systematic success on our part." But if disaster befell any of the western armies before the Army of Northern Virginia could strike a decisive blow, all could still be lost. Logistical and numerical issues remained a consistent challenge regardless of what happened, and the Army of the Potomac, and its boastful new commander, Joseph Hooker, were not likely to remain idle for long.[40]

Lee and Jackson predicted the enemy would advance sometime in April, as soon as the roads were dry enough to move large numbers of men, horses, and wagons. "If Genl Hooker is going to do anything we shall hear from him soon," Lee informed Mary from his sickbed on April 3. "He is reported to be all ready and only waiting upon the weather. I wish I could say the same for ourselves." If they were to pre-empt him and take the offensive first, much work had to be done in a short period. Late March and early April were therefore the witching time, but Lee's illnesses, bad weather, and the chronic problem of inadequate sustenance conspired mightily against Confederate prospects. On March 21, Lee nonetheless issued General Orders No. 43, which jump-started the army into readiness for "a resumption of active operations by the 1st of April." All extra baggage was sent to Richmond, leaves of absence canceled, and excess wagons were to be jettisoned. "The commanding general regrets the necessity for curtailing the comforts of an army which has evinced so much self-denial . . . but feels satisfied that ready acquiescence will be shown in all measures tending to secure success and the more speedy conclusion of the war." The army would be forced to move quickly and all wagons brought along were needed "for [the] transportation of subsistence when the army shall be removed from the vicinity of railroads."

This order reveals much about Lee's intentions. Despite the herculean obstacles still in his way, he clearly planned to move away from his logistical supply network. Moving *south*, retreating to the North Anna River or other points closer to Richmond, would bring him closer to supplying railroads, not farther away. Moving *north*, on the other hand, would certainly make the depots more distant. Speed would be of the essence, as would acquisition of provisions in counties currently occupied or sealed off by the enemy, and, ultimately in areas north of the Potomac. The secretary of war promised to help alleviate the current logistical problems in a letter on March 31, and tellingly added, "Meantime, I look with hope to the result of successful expeditions into the enemy's country for supplies." Lee wrote to Davis on April 2 explaining his belief that an advance by the Army of the Potomac was not imminent, and once "the roads permit of our moving, unless, in the meantime, General Hooker takes the aggressive, I propose to make a blow at [Union General Robert

H.] Milroy, which I think will draw General Hooker out, or at least prevent further re-enforcements being sent to the west."[41]

"At this juncture," explains Douglas Southall Freeman, "the fates that had so often conspired against the Confederacy at critical hours again intervened on the side of the Union." Lee's physical afflictions worsened as March turned to April, reflecting the deteriorating meteorological conditions, and it was all he could do to conduct routine army business, papers spread about his bedsheets and on the nightstands in his room in the Yerby House. Doctors came and went and "tapp[ed] him all over like an old steam boiler." His aides, Chilton and Taylor, visited frequently to receive dictations for orders, and the host family did all they could to make the general comfortable, bringing him the best food from their own table. Planning for the preemptive strike northward seemed to have been put on hold. Jackson was doubtless frustrated, but he found solace in the burgeoning religious revival and turned his attention temporarily to it and the efforts of his chaplains. By the beginning of the second week of April, however, the commanding general insisted on taking Traveller and his other horses for brisk rides over the estate grounds and getting some fresh air. He claimed to daughter Agnes, "I am much better . . . and now that the weather has become good, I hope I shall recover my strength." Precious time had been lost, but perhaps, just perhaps, the Army of Northern Virginia could still get the jump on Hooker and seize the initiative. [42]

Over the next week, Lee sent a flurry of letters to Davis, Seddon, and other authorities in Richmond in an attempt to retrieve his and Jackson's theater strategy. The president and secretary were still very concerned about the West and had politely inquired if Lee could spare troops for a transfer. To Seddon on April 9 he wrote, "Should Genl Hooker's army assume the defensive, the readiest method of relieving the pressure upon Genl Johnston and Genl Beauregard [commanding at Charleston, S.C.] would be for this army to cross into Maryland." The roads were not quite ready yet and food and fodder for man and beast remained insufficient, "but this is what I would recommend if practicable." Anticipating several large river crossings, on April 11 he penned Colonel Jeremy F. Gilmer, chief of Engineers, about a pontoon train that was on its way to him, and requested it be accompanied by an officer "who is acquainted with the business, and who could lay the bridge with rapidity." An immediate response was necessary on this topic, Lee continued, and asked to "keep the matter as quiet as practicable." Gilmer honored the general's request and sent a suitable officer, but the pontoons had only reached as far as Gordonsville by the 19th. Three days earlier, in a dispatch to Adjutant General Samuel Cooper, Lee calculated the numbers facing him and concluded, "I had expected to recall Genl Longstreet as soon as he had secured all the subsistence which could be obtained . . . to hold Genl Hooker in check, while Milroy could be driven out of the Valley." To reinforce the case for his strategic plan, the commanding general composed a carefully crafted letter to the president the same day, arguing that the best remedy for the woes of the western Confederacy and its understrength armies would still be to go on the offensive in the East. "I think it all important that we should assume the aggressive by the first of May. . . . If we could be placed in a condition to make a vigorous advance at that time I think the Valley could be swept of Milroy and the army opposite me be thrown north of the Potomac." But if Longstreet could not obtain enough supplies and return with them and his divisions in time, Lee could not commence the movement due to the "present immobility of the army, owing to the condition of our horses and the scarcity of forage and provisions." The fact that the national command authority in Richmond did not order away any more of Lee's army or the detachment under Longstreet was a tacit acceptance of his theater strategy, with which Jackson heartily concurred. [43]

Stonewall was excited by the renewed chance to embark on the offensive and sprang into action. The easier, more gentlemanly demeanor of the early winter and spring gave way to his normal abrupt and direct military bearing. He could sense the pending decisive action and it energized him. In his letter to Mary Anna on April 10, barely containing his enthusiasm, he ventured, "I trust that God is going to bless us with great success, and in such a manner as to show that it is all His gift." He redoubled his efforts to prepare his soldiers, following up Lee's General Orders No. 43 with his own, corps-specific order on April 13 that spelled out exactly how the march north was to proceed: "Each division will move precisely at the time indicated in the order of march, and if a division or brigade is not ready to move at that time, the next will proceed and take its place, even if a division should be separated thereby. On the march, the troops are to have a rest of ten minutes each hour. The rate of march is not to exceed one mile in twenty-five minutes, unless otherwise specially ordered. . . . When any part of a battery or train is disabled on a march, the officer in charge must have it removed immediately from the road, so that no part of the command be impeded upon its march." The order continued, providing specifics on establishing campsites during the movement, ambulance protocols, and care for the wounded. These were very detailed instructions, written to ensure his men consistently marched many miles each day. Not meant for troops likely to remain on the defensive, they were reminiscent in their tenor and intent of the actual deeds performed by his "foot cavalry" in the Valley the previous spring or during the Second Manassas and Sharpsburg Campaigns. Per Jackson's military personality, nothing was left to chance, even if the Lord's divine will would determine success or failure. Flushed with renewed anticipation as he watched the roads dry out, confident in his corps' abilities, and happy to allow camp rumor to work to his advantage, he was completely content. "My trust is in God," he told a staff member.

His friend and chief, more hopeful than ever that their strategy might work, optimistically wrote Mary on April 19, "If we can baffle them in their various designs this year . . . I think our success will be certain." Adequate supplies still dogged him, but "if successful this year, next fall there will be a great change in public opinion at the North. The Republicans will be destroyed and I think the friends of peace will become so strong as that the next administration will go in on that basis." The confident hope displayed by Lee and Jackson trickled down the ranks. Lieutenant Ham Chamberlayne, an artillerist, exulted, "we are anxiously expecting Lee's order for us to move, then the machine goes to work which never failed yet and we look forward to Maryland, my Maryland." Most everyone in the Army of Northern Virginia, it seemed, despite their physical hardships, expected decisive victory to result from the coming campaign. On the same day his commanding general wrote his spouse, General William Dorsey Pender told his own wife, "You say you hope we will not go into Md. I hope we will pass through it into Penn. And I believe the large majority of the

Army would like to. Our people have suffered from the depredations of the Yankees, but if we ever get into their country they will find out what it is to have an invading army amongst them. . . . They have gone systematically to work to starve us out and destroy all we have, to make the country a desert. I say let us play at the same game if we get the chance."[44]

Jackson could hardly have agreed more.

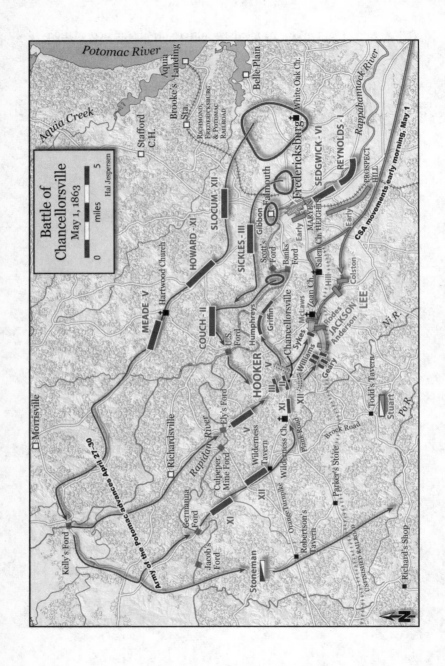

Battle of
Chancellorsville
May 1, 1863

0   miles   5

Hal Jespersen

FOUR

"Well General, you may try it."

CHANCELLORSVILLE

Lieutenant J. P. Smith reined in his horse abruptly and dismounted in one, dexterous movement, landing squarely on a patch of bright green grass, almost chewed down to the roots by other horses that had been brought to a stop at the exact same place. As he strode quickly toward Robert E. Lee's "house tent" among the cluster of canvas comprising the army's headquarters at Hamilton's Crossing, he scarcely attracted the attention of Charles Marshall and Walter Taylor, who were huddled around a campfire, cooking breakfast in the wet, morning mist. Fellow brothers-in-arms, staff officers, and commiserators, the three had spent a lot of time together over the past few months and knew each other well. Everyone also understood why Smith was there. Greeting him politely, Lee's associates offered some johnnycake and coffee and explained that the General was still asleep. Smith was about to accept their meager fare when Colonel Charles Venable appeared, suggested they should wake the "Old Man," and walked with Smith to Lee's tent flap and gently roused the commanding general. He was already half-awake. Quickly "turning his feet out of his cot, he sat upon its side," and listened intently to Smith's report. The Federals had finally acted, establishing powerful bridgeheads on the southern shore of the Rappahannock at Deep Run, almost precisely where Union General William Franklin's Grand Division had crossed in December, and not much more than a mile away. Lee was not surprised by the news and, as the lieutenant finished, broke into a slight grin. "Well, I thought I heard firing, and was beginning to think it was time some of you young fellows were coming to tell me what it was all about," he quipped. "Tell your good general that I am sure he knows what to do. I will meet him at the front very soon." So opened Wednesday, April 29, 1863, the beginning of the final phase of the Army of Northern Virginia's great partnership.[1]

Jackson had detected the enemy movement in his sector almost immediately thanks to the watchful eyes of his subordinate, Jubal Early, who sent a courier to wake him in his warm bed at the Yerby House, where he was staying with the recently arrived Mary Anna and Julia. Stonewall hurriedly dressed in his brand new uniform, pulled the kepi cap down low over his forehead, and embraced his wife and child one last time before scurrying down the stairs to prepare his corps for battle. His mind immediately went into action, prioritizing the sequence of events that must occur. After an initial reconnaissance of his battle line revealed Early had posted his brigades well, Jackson likely dispatched a messenger to Robert Rodes, senior brigadier in D. H. Hill's old division, ordering him to assume command and move up to reinforce Early. Next, he summoned Smith and told him to alert General Lee. As Smith mounted his horse and sped off, Jackson's thoughts turned to another priority: arranging for the safe transport of his loved ones away from danger. Reverend Lacy cheerfully accepted the duty, carrying a personal letter from the general to his wife explaining what must be done and invoking God's grace upon their travel. Within the span of a couple of hours the chaplain would fulfill his mission, having escorted the small little family to Guiney's Station where they boarded the cars for Richmond and safety. Jackson could breathe easier now, even as his anticipation grew. So the Yankees had finally started the ball, he must have thought. So be it. The Lord's will be done. Too bad we did not move first.[2]

Old Jack did not wait for Lee to meet him at the front, instead intercepting his chief before he left Hamilton's Crossing. Among the blooming "anemone, sanguinaria, and Houstonia" that graced the borders of that clearing, the two generals conferred about how they should react to Hooker's incursion. Lee believed it was a large-scale feint, meant to draw the Confederates' attention to their flank south of Fredericksburg while the main effort occurred elsewhere, perhaps upriver on his extreme left. Jackson was not so certain, but both men realized they needed more information. Jeb Stuart's cavalry was out there, guarding the fords upstream and watching the Federals from various positions north of both the Rappahannock and the Rapidan. Soon, they hoped, he would report. In the meantime, Jackson returned to his lines, called up Raleigh Colston's and A. P. Hill's divisions to bolster Early and Rodes, and oversaw the placement of batteries and digging of entrenchments. If the Unionists attacked him now, they would experience an even bloodier reprise of their experience in December. Lee ordered General Pendleton to bring up all the artillery horses and the reserve guns from their pastures to the south, and dashed off a flurry of telegrams to Richmond, informing his civilian superiors that the enemy had taken the initiative and begun active operations. All available supplies—food, fodder, ammunition—needed to be forwarded as soon as possible. Could D. H. Hill spare troops from North Carolina? If so, they should detrain at Gordonsville, as the character of the impending campaign was not yet known. Most importantly, Longstreet needed to come back immediately with his two divisions. Their absence had been a major hindrance to the advent of a Confederate spring offensive, yet their mission in gathering badly needed supplies had temporarily trumped Lee's desire to move first. The commanding general had permitted Longstreet's lethargic siege of Suffolk to continue the last two weeks, betting that he could push his luck vis-à-vis the Federals just a bit longer, recall Longstreet in time, and, strengthened both by his divisions and his supplies, launch the northern movement. He had even ordered the rebuilding of a bridge at Germanna Ford, on the Rapidan, in anticipation of winning that bet. Now it was clear Lee had lost the wager, and would have to face the grim consequences of fighting a defensive campaign without a quarter of his army and his other principal lieutenant at his side. Longstreet would not begin marching to Lee's aid until May 3, claiming it would take time to disengage properly from the siege and recall all the foraging parties. "I cannot move unless the entire force is moved," he telegraphed Adjutant General Cooper.[3]

Before noon the reports from Stuart started arriving. Oliver Otis Howard's XI Corps had crossed the Rappahannock at Kelly's Ford and it appeared George Stoneman, commanding the Federal cavalry, had brought his troopers across nearby. Lee reasoned both might be headed for Gordonsville and his fragile lifeline to Richmond, but another telegram in the afternoon dispelled that concern, replacing it with a more ominous likelihood: Stuart had captured prisoners from the Union XI, V, and XII Corps and stated that all three Federal corps were making for Germanna and Ely's Fords on the Rapidan. That intelligence was critical. It obliged Lee to think, for the first time, that a Northern adversary had actually stolen a march on him and was attempting to force him out of his prepared position at Fredericksburg. "Their intention, I presume," he told the president, "is to turn our left, and probably to get into our rear." Dispatches in the early evening confirmed Stuart's afternoon message. Hooker had committed a large percentage of his numerically superior army to an operational flanking movement, expecting the Southerners to retreat south or fight him at a disadvantage. The only question that remained was how much he had apportioned to the flanking column and how much to the one that had massed in Lee's front that morning. The Federal commander had bragged earlier that "my plans are perfect," and that Lee would require the mercy of God, "for I will have none." How Lee—and his adviser and friend Jackson—reacted now to Hooker's plan might well foretell the fate of the Confederacy.[4]

That night Lee ordered Richard H. Anderson's division, one of Longstreet's erstwhile commands, to leave its positions guarding the fords nearer Fredericksburg and move west down the Orange Turnpike toward the crossroads at Chancellorsville. The enemy had to go through there if he wished to catch Lee between his flanking force and the one positioned below the town, facing Jackson's corps. It was a miserable march, conducted in a pounding rain, and it was not completed until midnight. But Lee had begun to secure his flank. Far from yielding the field as Hooker expected, the Confederates had boldly hedged against the most likely contingencies. Anderson, ordered to entrench, would delay any enemy advance from the west, and in so doing firm up intelligence on the Federals' strength and intentions. Lafayette McLaws, in charge of the other division Old Pete had left behind, was told to have rations cooked and be ready to move early the next day to support Anderson. Jackson stayed where he was for the moment, improving his defenses against what was now identified as John Sedgwick's VI Corps, plus another major force, probably John Reynolds's I Corps.[5]

The next morning Stonewall arose early and inspected the enemy's line as best he could through the "drizzly and cool . . . misty and foggy" conditions. It was difficult to see, but it appeared the Federals had dug in themselves, perhaps inviting attack. Interesting. How many guns did they have on the other side of the river, on Stafford Heights? That was a gnawing question. His own line was as ready as it could be, and he had greater numbers than in December. Sedgwick could not possibly have more men than Stonewall had at his disposal. Here was an opportunity, he mused, depending on the Unionists' artillery support, to attempt what he could not accomplish the evening of the Fredericksburg battle. If we could demolish this wing of Hooker's army the results could alter the course of the war. . . . Hastily mounting Little Sorrel, excited by the prospect, Jackson rode to see Lee, who had had a slower morning in camp due to a slight recurrence of his angina. Lee was glad for the opportunity to get up and about, and invited Jackson to join him on a reconnaissance to ascertain if, indeed, a blow could be struck in this sector before necessity dictated turning to Hooker's flanking corps. On their way to a ridge that offered a good overlook of the Union position, the generals were noticed by some South Carolinians, who were "ready to yell on the least provocation. 'Old Jack' and Lee caught it mercilessly this morning while making the rounds," a lieutenant informed his mother.

Acknowledging the cheers, the generals rode onward and reached their observation point. The morning fog was clearing and through their binoculars they could see the well-prepared artillery and infantry of the enemy. Lee did not like the view. Only a night attack, he said, could be successful against those people; otherwise they would have "to move off and attack Hooker at C[hancellorsville]." Jackson listened carefully to his chief but remained sanguine, proposing an immediate assault by his corps before noon. For a moment, Lee weighed the option, thinking deeply about his partner's idea, attracted by its aggressiveness and portents of a powerful victory. Then he thought better of it. "I fear it is impracticable," he said, just as it had been at the first battle of Fredericksburg. Turning in his saddle to face his friend, he continued, "It will be hard to get at the enemy and harder still to get away if we dr[ive] him into the river." Jackson replied that he was certain he could do it. The fruits of such a victory would outweigh the cost in blood. Lee again considered his lieutenant's daring proposal. It was operationally and strategically tempting—if successful, it could change not just the character of the current campaign, but also the prospects for the Eastern Theater, and possibly the war. "If you think it can be done, I will give orders for it." Responding to his chief's spirit of trust and open-mindedness, Stonewall immediately returned the favor. He asked for some time to conduct further investigation of the propriety of the assault before committing to it. Lee agreed.[6]

This episode demonstrated the superb level of professional trust that had developed between the two Confederate chieftains, its functionality in a crisis situation, and the high regard Lee held for Jackson's counsel and opinions. With imperfect knowledge of the size of the large Union force bearing down on him from the direction of Chancellorsville and not knowing how long Anderson, and, conceivably, McLaws could hold it back, Lee was perfectly willing to commit the lion's share of his army—Jackson's entire corps—to an assault on the rest of the Federal army that was fortifying its position by the hour and enjoyed the support of strong artillery, impregnable in its position across the Rappahannock. Stonewall, for his part, well understood his position as Lee's second-in-command and his role as adviser and chief operator. If his friend did not believe the proposal was practicable, he would not consent to it, and further, if a judicious reconnaissance revealed the attack would be too costly or even fail, Jackson implied by his suggestion to conduct such an investigation that he would be the first to recommend its cancellation. This meeting, in many ways, foreshadowed another one that would occur the following night, exemplifying the power of their collaboration.

His artillery engaged in a desultory fire on Sedgwick's lines, Jackson spent the first half of the afternoon conducting a thorough analysis of every possible factor involved in mounting his proposed assault. He pored over maps, rode up and down his own line, ventured forward as far as he dared toward the enemy positions, inspected them and the guns on Stafford Heights through his glass, and studied every report he could find. This was a hallmark of good generalship, as time put in now would save countless lives. It was doubtless difficult, too, for Stonewall had to have grasped that precious time was slipping away. Time would simply have to be taken, however; a reckless decision now could be irreparable, and Old Jack knew it. His rubber overcoat shielded him from the rain, which had returned for a couple hours, but by the end of his careful evaluation, as he sat on his horse with the water dripping down, it became clear his corps would suffer too many casualties from the Federal artillery. Then the clouds cleared away and a bright sun broke forth among patches of light blue sky, and Stonewall rode to Lee's headquarters, probably disappointed but grateful he conducted his assessment. "It would be inexpedient to attack here," he simply stated to Lee, who fully accepted his friend's verdict, and likely appreciated him even more for having reached the hard—yet militarily wise—conclusion.[7]

But the commanding general did not despair the closure of that aperture. Both he and Jackson realized that regardless of the hypothetical damage they might inflict on Sedgwick and the military and political effect achieved thereby, the main threat was coming at them from the west, and it was approaching fast. Hooker simply had too many men, between his two wings well over 130,000 to the Confederates' 62,000, and he was in a good position to deal the Southerners a mortal blow. If he moved quickly, he would emerge out of the dense, second-growth forest known as the Wilderness that surrounded the river crossings and Chancellorsville and break into the open, rolling country just to the west of Fredericksburg. There his heavy battalions and powerful field artillery would be almost unstoppable, and Lee, with his back to Sedgwick, would be in a very tough spot. Even if the Confederates could somehow dispense with Sedgwick first, the brutal arithmetic and a cursory topographical review revealed that the Federals could absorb a disaster south of Fredericksburg and still potentially defeat the Army of Northern Virginia with the rest of their army. Lee was unaware of the precise numbers of the enemy, which probably lent him more boldness than he would have otherwise had, but he was painfully aware of the great numerical disparity and concluded that only audacity, at the right moment, could salvage the deteriorating operational situation. The plan he devised was rational but just as aggressive as Stonewall's earlier proposition: Jackson with three of his four divisions would march down the Turnpike to reinforce Anderson and McLaws (the latter had received orders to move early the next the morning), while the other division, Jubal Early's, would remain behind and watch Sedgwick, who would supposedly remain inactive. Jackson would have tactical command once he reached Anderson. Lee told him to "make arrangements to repulse the enemy," an order Old Jack correctly understood to mean "attack." Hopefully, a chance to defeat Hooker's flanking corps would present itself, and Lee the innovative opportunist, with Stonewall at his side, would jump on it. [8]

Returning after dark to his headquarters, Jackson pondered how best to implement Lee's orders. He was pleased they would march forth to meet Hooker, but worried that leaving at first light, as Lee directed, might be too late for Anderson, whom he knew would face the bulk of the Federal flanking force the next morning. Although entrenched, and soon to be joined by McLaws, Stonewall feared for Anderson and his division. How could he follow his chief's intent while ensuring his brother officer's safety? Reaching the familiar lights of his encampment, deep in thought, he dismounted and walked briskly toward his tent. Chaplain Lacy saw him coming and intercepted him, his normally cheerful face drawn tight with concern. "Falling back has been talked of. I'm depressed," he blurted. Taken aback, Jackson looked at him incredulously. "Who said that? No sir. We have not a thought of retreat. We will attack them." Without further discussion, he left Lacy standing by himself, opened his tent flap, and disappeared inside. But "after a little while" Stonewall reemerged and asked Lacy to join him. Knowing the reverend had family in the area and once ministered to a local congregation, he asked him about his knowledge of the roads toward Chancellorsville and potential guides. Lacy suggested the younger Yerby boy as a good candidate, and Jackson agreed. The two set out immediately for the nearby estate that had only recently served as the general's home away from home with Mary Anna and the place of Lee's convalescence. But when they arrived they found that the family had settled in for an early night's sleep, and Stonewall refused to have them awakened.

As they rode the short distance back to camp, Jackson confided in his friend and admitted his concern for Anderson and the success of the campaign. "The enemy is in force at Chancellorsville, and General Anderson is up there at Tabernacle Church about three miles in front of them," he said. Lacy asked, "Is the enemy likely to attack Anderson?" "Yes," Jackson tersely replied, and added that he could not be certain they would attack in the morning, but "they might do so at any time." Thinking through the conundrum, the chaplain responded, "Why not march up tonight? The moon is bright." Surprised for the second time that night by Lacy, Stonewall mused, "As a general thing, I make it a rule not to march troops at night, but the reason you suggest is weighty." The two fell silent for a while; the only sound that could be heard was the night breeze blowing through the small, young leaves of the trees on either side of their path, accompanied by the steady plodding of their horses' hooves in the dirt. Then Jackson asked Lacy "if he could find guides, who could take the troops up there by moonlight." The chaplain said yes, and spent the next several hours rounding them up. Old Jack, now "cheerful and lively compared with his usual quiet demeanor," returned to his tent, summoned Colston, Rodes, and Hill, and told them to have the men cook two days' rations and be ready to move at three the next morning. An energy, an "elation," as one of Stonewall's staff officers put it, spread throughout the Second Corps. Lee's principal adviser had himself taken good advice. [9]

When he returned to Jackson's headquarters early the next morning, Lacy was greeted by bustling activity. Soldiers hurried back and forth in front of the campfires, breaking down tents, leading horses, and carrying weapons, their dark silhouettes flitting about like black ghosts across the flames. He was informed he would personally guide Rodes's division, which would be in the lead, onto the Plank Road while his handpicked guides assisted the other two divisions. There was little sleep in the offing for the general, his chaplain, or his soldiers, but shrouded first by the darkness and then by a thick fog at dawn, Jackson's entire corps, minus Early's division, extracted from its trenches facing Sedgwick and marched in secret the ten miles to Anderson's position near the Tabernacle Church. Stonewall, in the vanguard, arrived about 8:30, his troops filing in behind him. By

11:00 on May 1, a warm, sunny, "proper May Day," they were all there. McLaws had come up with his division earlier that morning as Lee ordered and positioned his brigades to the north and right of Anderson, while Jackson's columns fell in behind the South Carolinian, a bit tired, but ready for action. Old Jack surveyed the fields and woods in front of him, and aided by some freshly drawn maps just delivered by Jed Hotchkiss, told McLaws and Anderson to stop entrenching and prepare to advance. Adapting to the situation he faced, Stonewall knew it was now time to transition from defense to offense. Five full Confederate divisions were coiled, primed to spring on their enemy.

The Federals were none the wiser. At first light, Hooker still believed he was facing only one rebel division, perhaps two. A 5:30 A.M. dispatch from his chief of staff, Daniel Butterfield, at army headquarters in Falmouth "confirmed" that a deserter rounded up by Sedgwick indicated "Jackson's whole corps is opposite Franklin's Crossing," exactly where the Union leadership hoped it was still located. If enemy dispositions changed, Hooker was confident his airborne observers in Professor Thaddeus Lowe's balloons, tethered at Banks Ford, would inform him. About 9:00 they did their job, spotting through the thinning fog the last of Jackson's long lines approaching from the east, but the telegraph line between them and the commanding general failed. Hooker wanted more information, and waited on ordering his three corps forward. That delay was critical for Jackson's divisions to finish their march. Lacy wrote, "By the time the morning fog had lifted sufficiently for the enemy's balloons to see them, they were plunged into the woody country toward Chancellorsville."[10]

Despite a paucity of intelligence on his enemy, Hooker expected imminent victory that day. The commanders of his flanking corps had easy objectives for May 1, would advance within supporting distance of each other, and after only a couple hours march unite the two wings of his army. The night before, he issued a proclamation to his troops, to be read aloud in every regiment to bolster morale, that, thanks to the near bloodless passage of the rivers, was already soaring. "It is with heartfelt satisfaction," the message began, "the commanding general announces to the army that the operations of the last three days have determined that our enemy must either ingloriously fly, or come out from his defenses and give us battle on our own ground, where certain destruction awaits him." The Union general was definitely right about one thing in this bombastic broadcast—the enemy had come out from his defenses and was about to offer battle. That was the extent of accuracy in Hooker's prediction.[11]

A courier bearing the yellow facings of the cavalry reined in his lathering horse in front of Jackson shortly before he ordered Anderson and McLaws to deploy their skirmishers. It was a note from Stuart. Stonewall visibly released some tension in his face and posture as he read its welcome lines. His friend had extricated himself and his horsemen from the other (western) side of Hooker's flanking corps, where they had retreated after the Federals crossed the Rapidan. He now had the cavalry massed to the south of Chancellorsville, just to the west of Jackson, and was endeavoring to make contact with Stonewall's lead brigades. "I will close in on the flank and help all I can when the ball opens. . . . May God grant us victory." Using the stub of a "badly pointed lead pencil," Jackson wrote on the back of the dispatch, "I trust that God will grant us a great victory. Stay closed on Chancellorsville," and sent the messenger back with it. He was doubly reassured: Stuart would cover his southern flank, and the Almighty would cover them all with his providential grace. Alone in his tent the day before, he had prayed that God would bless his efforts, and by all accounts, it appeared that prayer was being answered.[12]

The Confederate skirmishers advanced, and within a few minutes ran into the videttes of one of the few Union cavalry regiments Hooker retained with his infantry, the 8th Pennsylvania. The cavalrymen with their carbines fought a gallant delaying action, giving way before the weight of the Confederate infantry, and soon disappeared behind a line of Federal infantry skirmishers from George Sykes's Division of George Meade's V Corps. Hooker, still unsure of what he was facing, had sent his corps forward almost at the same time as Jackson, and now, like two half-blind giants in a wrestling match, they began pushing against each other, probing for weaknesses and discovering the other's strength. Jackson, however, was faster in comprehending what lay in front of him and uncannily pressed his enemy just where it would do the most harm to Hooker's confidence—in his center. Recalling Stonewall's performance on May 1, the normally critical E. Porter Alexander, who commanded some of his artillery that day, observed, "as a fighter and a leader he was all that it can ever be given to a man to be." Old Jack was totally absorbed with the task at hand, completely focused on the emerging battle when his ear discerned a noise different from the sporadic, staccato rifle shots of the skirmishers' fight. From the rear he heard a rolling series of cheers, emanating from his own troops, and moving closer to him. Turning in his saddle, he recognized the familiar sight of his chief and partner, Lee, moving toward him along the Plank Road with his staff. As the commanding general's party "pass[ed] each brigade they would raise a terrible cheer," one artillerist noted, which elicited from Lee a simple, respectful raising of his hat in acknowledgment. Greeting his friend as he brought Traveller to a stop beside Little Sorrel, Lee raised his binoculars to inspect the progress of the meeting engagement. The two generals spoke for a while and likely agreed to continue pressing the attack. Then, presaging another bold reconnaissance the next night, "Jackson left Gen. Lee and rode forward into the woods toward the enemy's lines which were in those woods. His staff followed." Stonewall, as he was wont to do, wished to inspect the Union dispositions personally. Lee did as well, riding north to the Turnpike to examine the enemy facing McLaws. [13]

The commanding general probably witnessed his division commander send forward his brigades in a simultaneous attack against Sykes. As his men encountered the enemy line, McLaws discovered he had numerical superiority and could overlap the Unionists on both flanks. Informing Stonewall of the situation, he proceeded to do just that, and reinforced with artillery Jackson dispatched to him, started putting heavy pressure on his adversary. Sykes, a career soldier commanding the Federal army's U.S. Regulars, some of the North's most stalwart fighters, became alarmed. His leisurely advance of the morning came to a dead halt, his skirmishers driven in by the solid ranks of butternut and gray approaching them. A vicious engagement commenced, and men began dropping in droves. "Now we had a fair, square, stand-up, open field fight," Virginian Westwood Todd remembered. Sykes's lead regiments were understrength, and while the blue lines held fast, stubbornly resisting at every scrub pine and grassy knoll, their general realized that without prompt reinforcements he would be forced to retreat. "I was completely isolated from the rest of the army," Sykes wrote. He knew he was far out in front of Henry

Slocum's XII Corps, which was supposed to be covering his southern flank along the Plank Road, and out of touch with the rest of his own V corps, which was marching under Meade's personal direction on the River Road, almost three miles to the north. Meade was under orders from Hooker to reach Banks Ford on the Rappahannock, where he would effectively reunite Sedgwick's wing with the three flanking corps. Such a juncture would have placed Lee in precisely the precarious position the Federal commander had planned for. Indeed, he might have had no choice but to "ingloriously fly."[14]

It was not to be, however. Hooker, now headquartered at Chancellorsville, received word of Sykes's predicament concurrently with several other pieces of surprisingly bad news. All of it hit him, like a body blow to the stomach, about 1:30 P.M. His grand plan was suddenly falling apart. Slocum was nowhere near his objective for the day, having fully deployed his divisions in the thick underbrush once they bumped into Anderson's skirmishers. Their progress was slow, thanks both to the terrain and to Stonewall's aggressiveness, who ordered Anderson into a full-blown advance, supported by the lead brigades of Rodes's division. Slocum thus could not come to Sykes's support, nor could Meade, who was too far to the north and east. The roads that could have brought one or both of Meade's other two divisions to Sykes's aid had been overrun by the rebels by this point. Certainly, Meade could have marched to the sound of the guns and abandoned his initial objective of Banks Ford, but the dense forest to his south would have posed difficulties, and more importantly, due to a lack of communication with Hooker, he had no reason to believe his southernmost division was in trouble. The Federal XI Corps, the last of the three flanking corps, and the II Corps, which Hooker had ordered transferred to him from Sedgwick's command, were too far in the rear to assist Sykes in a timely manner. The Union commander also received a series of signal corps dispatches from Butterfield, two of them badly delayed from the morning, indicating that heavy columns of Confederate infantry were marching toward Tabernacle Church and that Lee had apparently detached thousands of troops from Sedgwick's front. And worst of all, Sedgwick, whom Hooker had ordered "to threaten an attack in full force" that morning against the enemy facing him, had done nothing. In yet another example of the continuing folly that was Federal communications in this campaign, Butterfield did not receive his commander's order to transmit to Sedgwick until almost 5:00 P.M., far too late to serve its purpose of fixing Lee at Fredericksburg.[15]

Considering the avalanche of negative reports and the reality that the Confederates were exactly where they should not have been and worse, were belligerently assailing his advance, Hooker made a fateful decision. "From character of information have suspended attack. The enemy may attack me—I will try it. Tell Sedgwick to keep a sharp lookout, and attack if he can succeed," he wired Butterfield at 2:00 P.M. He sent out a flurry of couriers recalling an incredulous Slocum, Meade, and Sykes, ordering them to withdraw all the way back to the Chancellorsville crossroads, deep in the wilderness. There, they would prepare defensive positions in expectation of an attack from the south or east, concentrate their numbers on ground reasonably familiar to them, and await reinforcements—and a diversionary attack against Lee—from Sedgwick. Hooker, criticized almost immediately after the battle by most of his subordinates and by generations of historians for giving up on his own campaign, later wrote that he dismissed such criticism as emanating from "authors [who] have never seen the ground and kn[e]w nothing of my surroundings." Based on the intelligence he then had, the Union commander claimed, "I was hazarding too much to continue the movement." Perhaps that was true, but his analysis omitted one critical factor: Lee and Jackson might not act as expected. Indeed, in this and previous campaigns, they had already displayed an adaptive flexibility to deal with problems. Conceding the operational initiative to them brimmed with risk.[16]

Hooker made the decision to withdraw, but much credit should go to the Confederate command team for prompting him. Stuart had proffered integral intelligence just in time. Based on that knowledge, Lee correctly ascertained that boldly meeting the Federal flanking columns while leaving a scant holding force at Fredericksburg to face Sedgwick was the best way to possibly extricate the Army of Northern Virginia from the quandary their enemy had concocted. It was hazardous to divide his army, but also innovative and well calculated. Lee also rightly gave Jackson tactical command of the meeting engagement on May 1, providing him only the vaguest instructions about how to proceed, trusting fully in his friend's ability to carry out his intent. Jackson, for his part, thought carefully about the timing of his divisions' arrival at the Tabernacle Church, aware that much depended on *when* they arrived. He accepted the advice of a subordinate, Chaplain Lacy, and fully utilized the local intelligence he could provide. Then, assisted by some good luck in the form of literal fog and Federal communicative friction, Stonewall was able to order McLaws and Anderson forward with the full support of his own three divisions about the same time Hooker moved. The ensuing clash, completely unexpected by the Union commander at a time and place he had not foreseen, was rattling enough. But when combined with the aggressiveness of the Confederate advance—classic Jackson—and bad news from his generals (some of which Old Jack had created with his combative posture), it rocked Hooker back on his psychological heels. "Fighting Joe" suddenly and uncharacteristically became cautious and careful, withdrawing back into the gloom of the thick woods, relinquishing the chance to fight the Confederates in the more open country to the east. Now the rebel chieftains, recipients of fortune created by their collaboration, found themselves in a new sort of dilemma: how to exploit the initiative handed to them by their enemy before it was too late.

As the Federal troops dejectedly obeyed their commander's order to withdraw, the Confederate infantry vigorously pursued them, aided by timely bursts of Southern artillery fire. Jackson, near the front, sensed a tactical opportunity that could bloom into operational victory. It was clear the enemy was pulling back; this offered an opening. Perhaps remembering how he had routed the retreating General Banks almost a year earlier in the Valley, he realized if he could somehow split the disjointed and separated Union corps from each other before they coalesced, there was chance they could be destroyed in detail. Stuart's scouts started reporting the likely destination of the retracting northerners to be the Chancellorsville clearing. A rebel division or two in that location before the enemy arrived, Old Jack reasoned, could set Hooker up for a mighty fall. To that end, about 2:30 he ordered Brigadier General Henry Heth of Hill's division to lead three brigades directly toward Chancellorsville from the Plank Road, and told McLaws he was "pressing on up the Plank Road," urging him to "press on up the Turnpike, as the enemy is falling back. Keep your skirmishers and flank parties well out, to guard against ambuscade."

As the Confederate advance escalated, however, so did the Federal resistance. Slocum and Sykes executed a well-ordered, fighting withdrawal throughout the end of the afternoon, and combined with powerful, massed Union artillery on the clearings of Hazel Grove and Fairview, just to the southwest of Chancellorsville, denied Stonewall his opportunity. Still, ever alert for a chance to damage the enemy, at 5:30 Jackson pushed a brigade of Georgians toward Catharine Furnace, south of Hazel Grove, attempting to discover if the Yankees' southern flank might be turned. He galloped to the iron furnace himself to determine the prospects, and there met Jeb Stuart for the first time in days. Their meeting must have been heartfelt but likely overshadowed by the exigency at hand. Stuart told his friend the Unionists had entrenched around the clearings to the north and that the density of the woods would make any infantry advance in that direction difficult. Some of Stuart's horse artillery arrived and opened fire through a narrow avenue cut in the forest that led from the furnace up to Hazel Grove, and for a time the hopes of the generals rose as they watched through their binoculars the scampering of Federal soldiers amongst the shell bursts. Quickly, however, as if vindicating Stuart's report, Federal guns appeared out of nowhere, unlimbered and multiplied, and commenced to rain down an accurate and damaging fire on the rebel gunners. One of them recalled, "I do not think that men have been often under a hotter fire than that to which we were here exposed." Major Channing Price, Stuart's adjutant, was struck in the leg by a shell fragment and soon died from loss of blood. "General Jackson," the cavalry leader yelled over the explosions, "we must move from here." Old Jack, more oblivious to the enemy fire than his colleague, assented, and soon their two parties disappeared from the furnace clearing into the safety of the forest-enshrouded road.[17]

During most of the afternoon Robert E. Lee and his staff had been reconnoitering north of the Turnpike and even above McLaws's advancing lines, trying to determine the location and strength of the Union army's northern flank. Like his subordinate probing for the southern flank, Lee was searching for an opportunity to strike a telling blow that could not only alter the character of the campaign, but also the course of the war. And not unlike Stonewall but dissimilar to Hooker, who was worried about Confederate intentions and made assumptions based on them, Lee was focused on what he would do to his enemy rather than what his enemy might do to him. Confident Jackson had immediate affairs well in hand, the commanding general concentrated on the next move. As the Federals fell back toward Chancellorsville, however, his heart sank; it became increasingly clear that their northern flank would be well anchored against the Rappahannock and nigh unassailable. Especially rough terrain in the sector north and just to the east of the crossroads also mitigated against a major assault there, and Jackson sent word that his advance along the Plank Road had finally been checked. Disappointed but resolved to develop a favorable course of action now that he had pushed back the Unionists, Lee rode down to the intersection of the Plank and Furnace Roads and waited for Jackson, looking through his glass and chatting with his staff. Here was a good, central location to remain in touch with all his division commanders as the long shadows of night began to creep through the saplings and brambles of the wilderness. Here Jackson would easily find him, and the two could decide together how to make good use of the gift Joe Hooker had bequeathed them. [18]

About 7:00 P.M. Stonewall and his staff came trotting down the Furnace Road, a bit shell-shocked, having thoroughly digested the tactical situation near the furnace. Nothing more could be done this day to the Federals, and after carefully reviewing the sequence of events that had occurred, Jackson came to believe the bluecoats might well pick up and leave that night. He found Lee, mounted on Traveller, in the middle of the crossroads and after a warm greeting the two dismounted and spoke quietly together. It had been a successful day's work, but much more remained to be done. Suddenly bullets started spattering the dust around them. A hidden sniper, attracted by the large target of a nearby battery, had found the range of the Confederate generals. Someone suggested they retire to a rise of ground, shielded by cedar trees, on the northwestern corner of the intersection. Finding a comfortable log, the generals sat down and continued talking about the day's events. Various staff members—J. G. Morrison, Sandy Pendleton, Hotchkiss, James Boswell, T.M.R. Talcott,

Marshall, and Colonel A. L. Long, among others—hovered around nearby, hearing only bits and pieces of the earnest conversation as they set about establishing a temporary headquarters. Some of them, exhausted by their rigors and having risen in the wee hours of the morning, simply fell asleep on the ground. Darkness was falling fast and the moon was already up as the whippoorwills began calling to each other. "Thicker here than katydids up north," a Union officer wrote, they hooted and whistled "as if there was nothing but peace on earth, and save the occasional crack of the rifle away off . . . there was a solemn stillness that was almost oppressive." The air started to cool, but no one lit a fire, for fear it might draw unwanted enemy attention.[19]

Jackson looked his chief in the eye in the fading light and reiterated how easily he had pushed the Yankees back until evening. He had seen their entrenchment lines through his binoculars earlier, and was convinced they were preparing defenses to screen a withdrawal. Hooker had been spooked and would soon be gone. Gesturing with his hands, he asserted, "by tomorrow there will not be any of them this side of the river." Lee listened politely and expressed his hope that Stonewall was right, but it was clear he disagreed. He recounted his personal reconnaissance north of the Turnpike and explained how well-anchored the Federal line was against the river. He, too, had observed their defensive preparations and learned from Jeb Stuart that almost a third of the flanking force had not even been engaged. Hooker had expended far too much energy in an operational strategy that had almost succeeded and still possessed too many unused corps only to give up and go home. Also, Lee may have pondered Hooker's previous performance as an adversary, albeit at a lower level of command, especially at Sharpsburg. There he displayed a pugilistic aggressiveness that came close to shattering Jackson's defensive lines and endangering the Southern army's very existence. No, the Unionists would still be there tomorrow, and probably in greater numbers. Lee did not have the luxury to think otherwise. The responsibility for the survival of the Army of Northern Virginia, and by extension, the Confederate nation, in the end rested with him.[20]

If the right posed no opportunity, what about the center of the Union line, located no more than a half mile from where they then sat? Jackson listened intently, and concurred with Lee that there was a chance the center was not now, and would not be tomorrow, as well fortified as the right or as well posted with artillery as he had experienced on the left. More information was necessary. The moon was bright and offered enough light for those of younger years and keener senses to make a reliable judgment. Lee called for Major Talcott, his chief engineer, and Jackson summoned Captain Boswell, his staff equivalent. Instructed to ride toward the Federal center and ascertain the strength and disposition of enemy defenses there, the two aides immediately left on their assignment. The generals continued thinking and talking about how to proceed the next day, and theorized about what to do depending on the news their scouts brought back. An effort on the left, although at first glance discouraging based on Stonewall's personal observations, might be possible, but the roads in that sector beyond the furnace were not well-known, nor were the Union numbers and positions. Again, further information was critical. An exchange of clear-minded views . . . a back-and-forth of ideas, honestly conceived and respectfully spoken . . . a nod, a smile, a shuffling of boots in the dirt . . . the outline only of the other's facial features visible in the moonlight. The conversation proceeded slowly, carefully. Much was at stake, and both men knew it.

Then, out of nowhere, Jeb Stuart rode up, the jangling of his sword and spurs piercing the stillness of the scene like a thunderclap. Dismounting, he strode up to Lee and Jackson, barely able to contain himself. As if a prayer had been answered, he announced that Fitzhugh Lee had discovered the Federal right hanging "in the air." It was not tied down to any natural feature nor fortified at all. No cavalry guarded it, either, as Hooker had sent nearly all his mounted arm away on Stoneman's raid well to the south. As in previous campaigns, Stuart had brought key intelligence at the key moment. This new reality electrified both the commanding general and his lieutenant. They looked incredulously at the cavalryman, then at each other, Jackson probably smiling both at his friend's delight in sharing the news and at the prospects it uncovered. Lee started asking rapid questions: how did "Fitz" find this out? What roads did he use? Was there a good route infantry could use to get at the enemy right, one neither too close to the enemy picket lines nor so distant that it would fatigue the men before they fought? Stuart confessed he had no answers, but promised to deliver them quickly. He saluted, remounted his horse and rode off into the darkness to the west. Within a matter of minutes the entire episode, which immediately focused Lee's and Jackson's thinking, was over.[21]

Both men probably began voicing their thoughts aloud to the other, as they had done numerous times before. A new choice had just opened up to them. An assault on the enemy center was still an option, but the left—the Union right—dangled like a ripe plum. Could it be plucked? As they delved into consideration of this new proposal, Talcott and Boswell returned, close to 10:00 P.M., and reported the Federal center, as suspected, too well fortified to be overcome with a direct attack. The enemy infantry had been very busy, felling vast numbers of trees and creating a natural abatis, backed up by earthworks for both riflemen and artillery. They were ensuring clean fields of fire against any attack from the south and were still working as they spoke. Thanking and dismissing the two young men, Lee looked at Jackson in the darkness. The final piece of intelligence they needed was at hand. In an instant, the commanding general decided how to proceed. "We must attack on the left as soon as practicable," he declared. Someone, probably a staff officer but perhaps Lee himself, produced a map of the area, and a candle was fetched to provide sufficient illumination that would not attract unwanted interest from enemy pickets. Leaning over and contemplating the map spread on the ground, Lee asked, "How can we get at those people?" Unsure if the question was rhetorical or directed at him, Stonewall replied, "You know best. Show me what to do and we will try to do it." Peering "thoughtfully at the woods" around them for a moment, Lee, "encouraged by the counsel and confidence of General Jackson," looked down again at the map and ruminated for a minute, his eyes moving from one side to the other. He knew exactly what he wanted to do, but the question was how, exactly, it would be done. Then he started tracing with his finger a general route from east to west, starting with the Furnace Road, and ending up at the Orange Turnpike on the other side of the reported Union flank. Old Jack, silent, watched with intense anticipation, "his face lighted up," certain of Lee's intent. His friend likely said a few words about the thickness of the woods and the remaining uncertainty of the roads, and then added simply, as if it were an afterthought, "General

Stuart will cover your movement with his cavalry." For the moment, nothing more needed to be discussed about the new operational plan. Both men knew it carried risk, but it was the only viable option, and foretold of possible victory—perhaps even strategic victory. Both men realized that potential and completely trusted the other's judgment. Lee was audacious enough to envision it and Jackson perfectly suited to execute it. The great partnership, which had triumphed on previous fields employing this combination, stood in total, harmonious agreement. Jackson rose with a broad grin, saluted, and exclaimed, "My troops will move at four o'clock." Lee rose with him, returned the salute, kindly reminded him of the need for speed and secrecy, and sat back down on the log. [22]

Charles Marshall, who along with Talcott had overheard some of the conversation, parked himself where Jackson had just been, paper and pen ready for dictation. Lee asked him to write a note, to be wired to President Davis the next day, to inform him of the new operational situation and the momentous decision just made. In due recognition of civil-military prerogatives, the commanding general informed his commander in chief of the exigencies and risks at hand. If something went wrong on the morrow, the president was entitled to as much knowledge of its preamble as possible. "I find the enemy in a strong position at Chancellorsville and in large force," Lee began, adding that he expected Hooker to stay and fight and that he already divided his outnumbered army once, by leaving Early at Fredericksburg. "It is plain that if the enemy is too strong for me here, I shall have to fall back, and Fredericksburg must be abandoned," but if victorious, the city would be "saved and our communications retained. I may be forced back to the Orange and Alexandria or the Virginia Central road, but in either case I will be in position to contest the enemy's advance upon Richmond." Nothing was to be expected of "any re-enforcements from Longstreet or North Carolina," yet "we succeeded yesterday in driving the enemy from in front of our position at Tabernacle Church, on all the roads back to Chancellorsville, where he concentrated in a position remarkably favorable for him." Tellingly, Lee revealed, "We were unable last evening to dislodge him. I am now swinging around to my left to come up in his rear." But that hopeful phrase, referring to what would become Jackson's flank march of the next day, was diminished by a hard-nosed, realistic appraisal of the operational situation. "If I had with me all my command, and could keep it supplied with provisions and forage, I should feel easy, but, as far as I can judge, the advantage of numbers and position is greatly in favor of the enemy." Lee closed by including a few other remarks about prisoners taken and reports from other Virginia commands. Marshall, whose pen had been furiously scratching the paper, looked up, asked if that was all, and the postscript to the first of two meetings between the commanding general and his chief lieutenant promptly ended.[23]

The dispatch to Davis was the epitome of a realistic appraisal, divulging much of Lee's true thinking at the end of the first day of the battle of Chancellorsville, and directly after his consultation with Jackson. Although checked, Hooker was far from defeated, and his numbers worried the Confederate leader. The decision to attack his right would ideally result in an opportunity to strike his rear, presumably cutting the Federals off from the fords across the Rappahannock, but the Union position was "remarkably" strong and might successfully resist the assault. If that tactic failed, Lee was still sanguine about his ability to fall back in a manner that would "contest" any Federal thrust toward Richmond. Certainly, territory would be given up and Fredericksburg fall again to the enemy, but the railroads further south might offer faster supply than Lee now enjoyed, and all would certainly not be lost. Thus, he did not believe he was gambling too much by sending away Stonewall and the bulk of his army to the west in a bid to win a victory. It was a risk, to be sure, but one worth taking, and carefully considered from both a personal and an operational perspective. Success would likely be hard-won if it came, but in Lee's mind failure did not equate with the destruction of his army or the capture of the capital; he did not believe strategic disaster a prospect, whereas strategic triumph beckoned as a possibility. True, he was uneasy about the paucity of Confederate troops and provisions, and barely veiled a barb at Longstreet and D. H. Hill for failing to reinforce him, but the commanding general of the Army of Northern Virginia appeared to believe he had more than a fighting chance. That chance was upheld and bolstered by an implicit trust in Jackson's abilities, and in providence, which Lee and his lieutenant both believed would allow God's grace to intercede on their behalf, just as it had before. Lee need not worry about the details or contingencies of the operation because Stonewall, buttressed by their common faith, would properly attend to them. Lee knew his friend well—his absolute trust in the Almighty, his innate aggressiveness as a leader, his ability to oversee large movements quickly and secretly, and his omnipresent desire to strike the enemy decisively. If the movement was intercepted or the flank attack repulsed, Old Jack would handle it effectively. He had no worries about Jackson. The question was what Hooker would do, but Lee refused to allow his decision-making to be dictated by what the enemy *might* decide. [24]

After their meeting on the log Stonewall left Lee and sought a place in a nearby pine thicket to lie down. His mind was awake, pondering the possibilities and likelihoods of the movement he was about to oversee, but his body was tired and needed sleep. The physical temporarily overcame the mental, and finding his headquarters wagon nowhere in the vicinity, Old Jack unbuckled his sword, propped it against a tree, and resolved simply to lay out on the ground. Sandie Pendleton, observing the plight of his chief, offered his overcoat and was politely rebuffed, but in the end prevailed in covering the general with the cape of the coat. Jackson found a place next to Jed Hotchkiss, who had propped his saddle up against a tree, spread out his blanket, and invited the general to join him. There they slept for several hours, "with our saddles for our pillows," the bivouac around them suddenly silent and cold. The temperature had fallen considerably, and save a few lingering whippoorwill calls from the woods, all was quiet. Lee and his staff had united with Stonewall and his officers under the boughs of the pines, finding that the layer of fallen pine needles, when combined with a saddle blanket, made a tolerable makeshift pallet. They had all experienced far worse conditions than this, and many gratefully accepted the improvised accommodations. Hotchkiss remembered "having slept very soundly." [25]

He would not enjoy his repose for long. Jackson awoke early, probably between 2:00 and 3:00 A.M., his brain doubtless wrestling with the details of the coming day's work. And 4:00 A.M. was coming on quickly. How would I reach the enemy's flank, and in time to deal him the heavy blow required? What roads would I use? Whose division would lead? How much artillery should I bring? There were still too many specifics to figure out.

It was time to rise and hammer them out. The moon was yet bright, and combined with the dim light of a small fire a few paces off, the general discerned the familiar outlines of his sleeping staff. Ah, there was Pendleton. He looked cold, and no wonder, since he had given up his cape. Jackson gently lay it down over his slumbering subordinate and walked to the fire, probably lit by recent couriers. He eagerly embraced its meager warmth, as he felt chilled and noticed the first touches of a head cold coming on. A little heat and, hopefully, some coffee would help. A discarded Yankee cracker box offered itself as a seat. Good, good, he thought.[26]

Chaplain Lacy, who had grown used to Jackson's daily rhythms in the previous months, may have awakened at his stirrings. He was tired from the previous day's duties, but noticed the general alone, shivering by the fire. At the very least, he could offer the warmth of companionship at this early hour and, perhaps, he might again prove himself militarily useful. The night before, at Jeb Stuart's urging, Lee had asked him a few questions about the local roads to the west of the intersection to confirm the feasibility of the proposed passage of troops to the left. Jackson, already retired by that point, had missed the discussion, but might well also require the same information. Shaking off the last wisps of sleep, Lacy walked over to Stonewall and the two exchanged a friendly greeting. Looking up at his friend, the general asked him to sit down, but Lacy remained standing, unsure of where to sit since Old Jack occupied most of the cracker box. "Sit down. I want to talk to you," he insisted, and moved off to one side of the narrow wooden box, opening up just enough space for the reverend. "The enemy [are] in great force at Chancellorsville in a commanding position and to dislodge them by a front attack [will] cost a fearful loss," Jackson said as he stared into the fire. "Do you know of any way by which to flank either their right or left?" Lacy quickly answered, "Yes, there [is] a blind road leading from the furnace, nearly parallel to Plank Road, which [falls] into a road running northwards, which again [will] lead into the Plank Road 3½ to 4 miles above Chancellors." Stonewall's eyes brightened and he sprung into movement. "Take this map," he blurted, as he fumbled for and withdrew the document from his pocket, "and lay it down." Lacy traced the routes he mentioned with a pencil, Old Jack leaning over him, watching closely. When he was finished, the general, a bit crestfallen, protested the prospective march route was "too near: it will go within the line of the enemy's pickets. Do you know of another?" Lacy replied "that he *presumed* [original emphasis] the furnace road would intersect the other road leading back above Chancellorsville but he had never rode [sic] it himself." Jackson reflected on the new information, and the gleam returned to his face. This sounded promising, but he must be certain. There was no room for error; unequivocal intelligence would be necessary. "Go with Hotchkiss to [the] furnace. Ascertain whether those roads meet, and are practicable for artillery." Thinking on the timing and logistics of it, Stonewall looked Lacy straight in the eye and added with feeling, "Send Hotchkiss back with the information, and you get me a guide."[27]

The general strode over to the sleeping Hotchkiss and woke him, and within minutes the minister and the mapmaker were on their way to Catharine Furnace and Colonel Charles Wellford, its owner. Wellford, a veteran of the Mexican War, restarted his enterprise to supply iron for the Confederacy and had cut numerous rough roads through the Wilderness to bring logs to the greedy fires of his forge. Lacy knew him from his earlier days as a preacher in the area, and if anyone could supply the required missing information, the ironmaster was that person. He was also an ardent patriot, and after rubbing the sleep from his eyes, answered the aides' insistent knocks on the door. He recognized Lacy and bade them enter. Hotchkiss got right to the point and explained their mission. "Having spread my map of the country upon a table," he later wrote, "by the light of a candle [Wellford] indicated the location of a new road that he had recently cut across toward the Brock Road for the purpose of getting cord wood and iron ore for his furnace." Hotchkiss and Lacy must have sighed with relief. However coarse, this new route would fit the bill—not too close to the enemy's lines and not so distant that the soldiers in the flanking column would arrive exhausted. With a pencil, Hotchkiss carefully drew in the new road on the map and then asked Wellford if he would serve as a guide for the troops. The old colonel heartily agreed (he ultimately supplied his son, Charles Beverly, and another man), and the mapmaker, fully satisfied with the results of the visit, thanked him and hastily rode back to his general. Lacy stayed with Wellford a bit longer, perhaps to finalize the particulars of the guides.[28]

Hotchkiss galloped in to the bivouac at the intersection about 3:30, dismounted in a rush, and like Stuart before him, raced to the fire eager to report, barely avoiding stepping on some of his sleeping fellow officers. He found Jackson still seated on the cracker box by the fire, "with his back against a tree while opposite to him Gen. Lee sat on another box with his back against a tree. They were engaged in conversation." The commanding general had been up for about a half hour now, rising early after a late night interruption by J. P. Smith, whom Lee had sent to Anderson and McLaws in search of further information about the Union positions in their front. Smith, a favorite of Lee's and often personally detailed by him with Jackson's concurrence, came back after midnight with the requested information, woke the general, and offered his report. "Ah, captain, you have returned, have you?" Lee groggily inquired. "Come here and tell me what you have learned on the right." Propped up on one elbow, Lee "drew me down by his side," Smith wrote, "and, passing his arm around my shoulder, drew me near to him in a fatherly way that told of his warm and kindly heart." The captain remembered how relaxed and jovial the general appeared, even jesting at his expense, and roaring in laughter after Smith tried to break away from his grip, having had enough excitement for one day. Lee's reaction to the staff officer indicated his conscience was not too heavily burdened with the weighty decisions he had just made. Smith "was soon wrapped in the heavy slumber of a wearied soldier" while his commanding general quickly fell back asleep.[29]

Another officer, Colonel Long of Lee's personal staff, had also risen early and could be seen scuttling back and forth between the quiet headquarters camp and some nearby campfires, where cooks had just begun preparing breakfast. Long may have been awakened by Jackson's earlier talk with Lacy and decided to get on with the day's duties. Lee and everyone else was still asleep, but there, sitting by himself desperate to get warm by the little fire, Long noticed Stonewall, deep in thought and obviously cold. The colonel walked over to the cooks, fetched a cup of coffee, and handed it to the grateful general, who thanked him for his kindness, and the two had just begun to converse when Jackson's sword, which he had left resting against the tree, fell to the ground with a loud, metallic clatter. Long retrieved it and brought it back to Stonewall, who promptly buckled it on his belt without further thought. Years later, Long recalled thinking at the time that the fall of the sword bode inauspicious tidings, but if such a thought crossed his mind then, he said nothing of it to Jackson. It may have been the noise from the sword, however, that awakened Lee and initiated the second of the two conferences between himself and Old Jack that night. When Hotchkiss found them, they had already been talking for a while, doubtless wondering what news he and Lacy would bring them about the specifics of the roads to the left. It was clear the 4:00 starting time would not transpire. [30]

"I am ready to report," the topographer announced as the two generals identified his face emerging from the dark gloom around them. "Please do so at once," Jackson replied. Grabbing two other cracker boxes lying in the woods, Hotchkiss shoved one like a table in between the two leaders and sitting on the other, "spread out the map and showed the location of the road that Col. W. had opened." Both men bent over, studying the map intently, and asked him a couple questions to determine the final details of the route. Hotchkiss explained that the Furnace Road would empty onto the Brock Road, and that a left turn there would lead the column to the entrance of Wellford's new road about 600 yards south. Turn right there—the guides would show the way—and continue west until it rejoined the Brock Road just south of the Orange Turnpike. A mile, at most, of northward marching would bring Jackson to the pike and the right flank of the Union army. The final route encompassed twelve miles all together, hard miles that would not be easy to traverse, but the way was clear. Time was of the essence; the march would need to begin immediately to capitalize on daylight and maximize secrecy. The generals leaned back against their respective trees, cogitating on what they had just learned, and grew quiet, their minds pregnant with thought. Only a crackle from the campfire and a small breeze interrupted their reverie as the smoke from the fire twisted upward into the pine branches. Hotchkiss lingered to hear the fateful discussion that ensued. [31]

Lee broke the rapturous silence. "General Jackson," he asked, "what do you propose to do?" Staring at the map, Stonewall pointed at the route his mapmaker had just identified and answered, "Go around here."

Unsurprised, as this had been agreed upon in the previous meeting, Lee followed up with the big question that yet remained to be asked. "What do you propose to make this movement with?" Having meditated deeply on that very topic, and quite positive about it, Jackson responded immediately, "With my whole corps." He glanced up at his friend with complete sincerity, hopeful he would agree, but not absolutely certain. It was another risk piled on top of the already hazardous—but necessary—plan to split the army again and outflank the numerically superior enemy. Lee was definitely taken aback. He had not expected him to take all his troops. This was boldness personified, a daring proposition bordering on recklessness. For a few moments he pondered the possibilities and probabilities as any good general would: numbers, locations, names of divisions and corps flit through his brain. So did visions of what might occur, both good and bad. Already knowing the answer to his next query, he asked it anyway. "What will you leave me?" Stonewall again was quick to reply. "The divisions of Anderson and McLaws." Lee paused, considering the entire proposal. Undoubtedly, his friend had thought long and hard about the probabilities himself and was confident of success. He had not failed him at Second Manassas or Harpers Ferry, operations that also demanded a perilous separation of the army. Hooker should remain quiescent for a while longer, Lee mused, which left the Fredericksburg front as the likely problem. If Sedgwick attacked Early and broke through. . . . Much depended on timing, as always. But Jackson was a fast marcher. And with such power behind him as he now requested, the Federals could suffer a devastating blow. Perhaps this was the time and place to end it. Perhaps the Lord would cover this enterprise with His protecting grace, and, against all odds, finish the game here. Beyond stopping Hooker's offensive, an opportunity now beckoned to crush him. Lee was too much like Jackson to let it go untried. He pursed his lips into a slight grin, looked down at his feet for a moment, and then gazed directly at his collaborator: "Well General, you may try it." Jackson, with "an eager smile upon his face," nodded, and the two commenced a dialogue on the final details. Stonewall had already decided most of them, and around 5:00 A.M., their discussion over, he rose to his feet, offered a crisp salute, and declared, "My troops will move at once."[32]

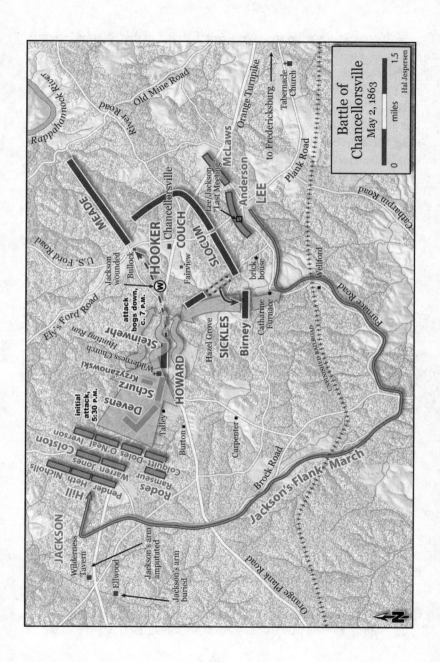

Battle of
Chancellorsville
May 2, 1863

0   miles   1.5

Hal Jespersen

They could not be up and on the march as fast as that, despite Jackson's best efforts to impel them. Lee realized this all too well. To start three large divisions, replete with ordinance, ambulances, and ammunition wagons, on a major maneuver along narrow wilderness roads would take time, but Jackson would push them. Stuart's cavalry would screen the movement well. And Old Jack knew precisely how he wanted to proceed—Rodes would lead, escorted by Fitzhugh Lee's brigade of cavalry (with Chaplain Lacy's guides leading them), followed by Colston and Hill. He and his staff rode briskly among the various commands encamped along the Plank Road, rousing them into action, explaining the route of march, and ensuring the officers would comply with the prescription for movement elaborated in his earlier General Orders No. 26, issued back in April. Delays and straggling could not be tolerated, the mandated ten-minute rest per hour would have to be foregone, and each regimental commander was instructed to detail a group of men to march at the rear of their column with bayonets fixed. This, Stonewall believed, should discourage those who considered falling out of ranks. It was an unnecessary precaution, however, as the spirit of his soldiers was at its zenith. Some had briefly driven the enemy yesterday and all were rested from the long winter's break. They were aching for a fight with the Yankees and were psychologically ready for it, even if their meager breakfast fare that early morning betrayed the greater logistical peril that beleaguered their army. By 7:30 A.M., the morning sunrise diffusing its brilliant, golden rays through the gaps in the trees, the first Confederate infantry passed by Lee's field headquarters on their way west toward Catharine Furnace. Lee walked to the side of the road to watch them, rubbing his arms for warmth. He felt the lingering chill of the night before, but the day promised to be mild and sunny. Spying their commanding general the enlisted men sensed something big was afoot, but were not yet certain was that might be. They yearned to break into a yell, but "cheering was forbidden, and all noises suppressed as far as possible." Any clamor might alert the Federals and spoil secrecy, which was essential to preserve the element of surprise. The only sound, according to one staff officer, was "the rhythmic click of the canteens."[33]

Close to 8:00 Jackson and his party, striving to reach the head of the column, trotted past the crossroads. Noticing Lee, now mounted on

Traveller, Jackson reined in Little Sorrel and joined his friend for a few brief moments. Unlike their recent conferences in the adjoining pine woods that had devised the very maneuver now underway, no one overheard their conversation this time, but many observed it. It was the last meeting the two leaders would ever have. Taking but an instant, it is likely Lee offered some final instructions for the march, an encouraging comment, perhaps even a quick word of prayer. Jackson said something in reply and Lee nodded. Then Stonewall started off, "pointing in the direction his troops were moving," his "face a little flushed," his gleaming eyes very noticeable underneath the pulled-down visor of his kepi cap. Lee watched him go, entrusting him and the Almighty with the fate of this day, unaware he would never see him again. It was simultaneously the apogee and the denouement of their partnership. But even had he the ability to foretell the future, the commanding general, like many great captains before him during times of decision, was disallowed the luxury of contemplating the moment. The press of immediate command demanded his attention. He quickly turned away and began issuing orders to McLaws, Anderson, and Early. Couriers went speeding away from the crossroads, carrying vital messages that stipulated actions short of general engagement—active skirmishing, demonstrative cannonades, and aggressive posturing—that would give Jackson as strong a chance of surprise as possible. It was Lee's job to keep the Unionists fixed on him while his lieutenant prosecuted the march and launched the subsequent assault. The success of each depended on the other's leadership and judgment, a symbiosis that could not function effectively as a whole without the unique contributions of its constituents. As it had been in planning, so it would be in generalship. How one performed today directly affected the fate of the other. Accordingly, Lee would risk the fact that his smaller wing of the army, comprising barely 15,000 men, would have to space its soldiers as much as six feet apart to maintain its battle line. If the enemy stayed focused on him (without attacking) and Jackson accomplished his mission, all would be well. Everything depended on the two leaders doing what they agreed to do within the time allotted, both wagering that Joe Hooker would do nothing.[34]

The ten mile long file of butternut and gray, twisting along twelve miles of the roundabout flank march route, required nearly all day to reach its objective, which lay a bit more than a mile due west of the extreme right flank of the Union army. Stonewall had taken almost 2/3 of the army, 28,000 troops, and was grimly determined that every one of them achieve that goal. "Press forward, press forward," he encouraged the officers. "See that the column is kept closed and that there is no straggling." There was no time to waste, and Old Jack knew it. "Press on, press on," he repeatedly said. E. P. Alexander, who rode with Jackson and his party near the very front, remembered that "the extraordinary consumption of time was due largely, not to the *badness* [original emphasis] of the road, but to its narrowness." The men could only march four abreast, and those in Alfred Colquitt's brigade of Rodes's division, which led the infantry directly behind Fitzhugh Lee's cavalry troopers, frequently had to stop and clear away brush or even pull out stumps. Necessary tasks to ensure the passage of the following rolling stock, such delays created a "halt and start, and halt and start, in the most heartbreaking way," generating an accordion-like quality to the movement that obliged the soldiers near the rear of the column, in Hill's Division, to move as slowly as 1½ miles per hour in between occasional bursts as fast as three miles per hour. "I thought that [Jackson] would kill all of us before we would get to the enemy," a Virginia private wrote his uncle of the ordeal. Mercifully, the ground was yet damp from the recent rains so there was no dust to clog their throats or noses (or signal the movement to the Federals), but water along the way was scarce and the canteens soon ran dry. By mid-afternoon the temperature had reached the eighties, which might have exacerbated the water shortage, but the trees shielded the soldiers both from the enemy's prying eyes and from the worst effects of the sun, the woods thick on either side of them. "For hours at a time," one of them noted, "we neither saw nor heard anything" but the backs of the ranks directly in their front and the muffled clunking and jostling of their own accoutrements. Yet "every man in the ranks knew that we were engaged in some great flank movement," Hunter McGuire recalled, "and they eagerly responded and pressed on at a rapid gait." A lucky few caught a glimpse of Old Jack as he moved back and forth along the column, urging speed and surveying its progress. B. B. Carr of the 20th North Carolina remembered a "courier . . . riding from the rear saying Gen. Jackson is coming but no cheering." No sooner had his regiment stepped to the side of the road than "along came Gen. Jackson on his long, gaunt sorrel horse in a long gallop with his hat raised and each soldier with his hat raised, but not a word spoken. We knew then something of importance was on hand."[35]

By late morning Hooker had also figured that out, but what, specifically, the Confederate movement signified remained unclear to him. As early as 8:00 A.M. soldiers from Daniel Sickles's Third Corps, situated at Hazel Grove, had first reported seeing the Confederate movement near Catharine Furnace through the gap in the forest that furnace owner Wellford had cut to connect the two locations. The reports filtered their way up to army headquarters at Chancellorsville, where they lay unread for an hour and a half; Hooker had gone for an inspection tour of his defensive line, which he deemed "secure." Reinforcing that perception was his belief that John Reynolds's First Corps, ordered at 1:55 that morning to leave Sedgwick and join him, would soon arrive to anchor the right flank against the river. A few brigades of cavalry Stoneman had left behind were also expected to reach the main army that afternoon and would be posted to the right. Yet when the Federal commanding general returned to the Chancellor mansion and read the messages from Hazel Grove, he began to have second thoughts about his security. This was truly either an attempt to flank him or a retreat, and if the former, there was a small chance the rebels might attack before Reynolds was in position. He took adequate precautions in case it was an aggressive maneuver, sending two succinct dispatches to Eleventh Corps commander Oliver Otis Howard, whose half-German corps held the flank. "We have good reason to suppose that the enemy is moving to our right," he advised, ordering him to have reserves "well in hand to meet this contingency," and to "please advance your pickets for purposes of observation as far as may be safe in order to obtain timely information of their approach." Hooker hoped it was a retreat, and through the opening in the trees at the furnace, along a small brook called Lewis Run, the ceaseless rebel line appeared to vector southward, giving credence to what he wished for. But if this was, indeed, one of the enemy's famous flank marches, further preparations were necessary. The second note to Howard included a chastisement that should have made the commanding general's intent crystal clear: "The right of your line does not appear to be strong enough. No artificial defenses worth naming have been thrown up, and there appears to be a scarcity of troops at that point, and not . . . favorably posted as might be." Howard ignored the spirit of the dispatches, deploying only two regiments and two cannon to face west and digging a shallow line of breastworks beyond the Wilderness Church. He believed nothing could possibly pass through the tangled undergrowth of the wilderness. It was simply too thick to be traversed.[36]

One of Sickles's batteries at Hazel Grove had opened fire on the rebels that morning, using the narrow tunnel through the woods as a natural alleyway for their case shot and shell. The Confederates reacted. Jackson ordered the infantry to march double-time through the clearing and redirected the baggage and commissary train to take another, rough-cut wilderness path that peeled off the Furnace Road just prior to the forge. Daniel Sickles himself, watching the graycoats through his binoculars and sensing an opportunity, repeatedly begged Hooker to be unleashed for a pursuit. The commanding general demurred until close to noon, when he finally allowed the Third Corps commander "to advance cautiously" and "harass the movement." Sickles eagerly launched one, and then two entire divisions, escorted by the crack Berdan's Sharpshooters, but the delay proved critical. It was now past 1:00 P.M. and all of Stonewall's infantry and nearly all the artillery had crossed through the precarious point of exposure. Sickles's men encountered only a rearguard, the hapless 23rd Georgia, whose soldiers ably performed their designated duty before being captured. That, and a few wild shots at distant wagons moving off to the south, was all Sickles could claim for his effort. Approaching the furnace with his staff, the Union general gained a new perspective, however, that altered both his and Hooker's thoughts about the Confederate movement. "The enemy column is still moving south," he told the army commander, and "for the past five or ten minutes only their wagon train is in sight." As a modern chronicler aptly put it, "then Dan Sickles leaped to a conclusion." He continued in his note, "I think it is a retreat." These were words that Hooker, despite his reservations and precautions, *wanted* to hear, as well as Howard, who was copied on the report. For the second time in the campaign, cognitive dissonance crept into the Union command team's decision-making. The Federals could now stop watching their flanks and begin thinking again about the offensive because the rebels had begun to "ingloriously fly."

Sickles requested troops from Howard to assist in pursuing the fleeing foe, but Howard refused. Then an order arrived at Dowdall's Tavern, the Eleventh Corps headquarters, demanding he provide support. Signed by Hooker, General Howard was obliged to obey, and so he dispatched his only reserve, Francis Barlow's brigade, and not wishing to miss the excitement rode south with it to reinforce Sickles. It was shortly after 3:00. [37]

By that time the vanguard of Jackson's column had reached the Brock Road and was about to turn north to the assembly position astride the Orange Turnpike. The general, having just glimpsed with Fitzhugh Lee the unpreparedness of the Union Eleventh Corps from a small hill, was excited, "his eyes burn[ing] with a brilliant glow, lighting up a sad face." Fitz Lee later remembered he seemed "radiant at the success of his flank movement," and may have quietly given thanks to the Lord as he peered through his glass at Federal soldiers going about normal camp routines, with no inkling of their impending danger. Stonewall had been unusually quiet during the march—even for him—and presented a "grave and silent" demeanor to those in his cavalcade, but now a new energy animated him, "a perceptible increase of eagerness," much as it had after Lee decided to meet Hooker head-on at Chancellorsville. Riding back through the woods to his entourage, he dismounted, sat on a stump by the roadside, and composed a hasty note to his friend. "The enemy has made a stand at Chancellor's which is about 2 miles from Chancellorsville. I hope as soon as practicable to attack." Completely confident in his shared faith with Lee, he added, "I trust that an Ever Kind Providence will bless us with great success." A postscript on the current positions of his three divisions completed the brief missive, which he immediately entrusted to a courier to bring to his chief. Lee would be anxious to hear of his progress, especially since their last exchange of reports had occurred in the late morning and early afternoon respectively, delayed by the time it took for horse-borne messengers to weave their way back and forth through the closely packed files of marching men. But Jackson was now very confident the plan he and the commanding general had created would succeed in its object. He had listened carefully for signs that his movement had been intercepted, and probably discerned the muffled thuds of cannon fire from the Catharine Furnace fight, but if he evinced any concern, no one noted it, and in any case Sickles's foray was checked almost as soon as it began by fast-reacting reinforcements sent by Lee and some of A. P. Hill's rearward brigades, which responded on their own volition. The interruption, so late in coming, was over quickly and failed to stop Old Jack's momentum. He had learned from Jeb Stuart, who had come and gone throughout the day, that Stoneman and the bulk of the Union cavalry was beginning to make mischief farther south, but that news held no import for his immediate mission. And it was about to succeed. He was focused solely on it, possessed by the certainty of it. [38]

From 3:00 to 5:00 P.M., "with daylight worth a million dollars a minute," as one Confederate officer recounted, Jackson's divisions filed into a 1½ mile–long line that straddled the Orange Turnpike about a mile west of Howard's flank, where only the 153rd Pennsylvania and 54th New York infantries and two lone field pieces faced west. Eleventh Corps scouts, some of them German immigrants and not fluent in English, had bumped into the rebels as they formed up, and, afraid and astonished, raced back to Howard's and Hooker's headquarters with their reports. There they were labeled "excitable Dutchmen" and rebuffed by Anglo-American staff officers who disdained their wild-eyed, grammatically incorrect admonitions of impending doom. Returning to their camps spread out along the Turnpike, they regaled their comrades about what they saw. Some regiments, particularly in Carl Schurz's division near the Wilderness Church, heeded the warnings and changed their dispositions to meet an attack from the west. Most did not. The enemy was retreating, they believed, as proven by the action at Catharine Furnace and General Sickles's statements. The Union soldiers resumed cooking their beef dinners, smoking, joking, playing cards and otherwise enjoying the end of an uneventful day. Not so far away, other men, Stonewall's men, would have loved such a respite, but most were tense and anxious, like racehorses constrained in their starting blocks, standing in ranks in the deep woods. They were ready, after their long march, to be unleashed. In contrast, their commander had seemingly conquered his earlier bout of nervous energy and, according to Heros von Borcke, was perfectly at ease while his brigades and regiments moved into their carefully assigned positions, guided by members of Jackson's staff: "I found [Stuart], with Jackson . . . stretched out along the grass beneath a gigantic oak, and tranquilly discussing their plans for the impending battle, which both seemed confidently to regard as likely to end in a great and important victory for our arms." Doubtless the two friends enjoyed these moments, not only anticipating the likely success to which they had both contributed, but also recounting earlier events that had witnessed their amiable collaboration. Neither man could have known it was their last time together.[39]

Not all of Stonewall's 28,000 troops were situated where he wanted them. Over half of Hill's division was still marching to the assembly area when Sandie Pendleton rode up to Jackson and Stuart and announced that all the brigades in Rodes's and Colston's divisions were properly prepared. Daylight was fading, and as he and Lee had anticipated in their meetings the night before, Jackson understood time was of the essence. He mounted Little Sorrel, rode to a nearby clearing accompanied by his staff, and there pulled out his pocket watch, holding it in his hand. Time would not allow him to wait any longer. He may have repeated what he uttered many times that afternoon: "Under no circumstances [is] there to be any pause in the advance." General Rodes appeared, along with Major Eugene Blackford, whom Rodes had put in charge of the skirmishers in front of his main battle line. Colston and other officers were close by; Stuart and his staff had moved to the Turnpike, where the horse artillery could have some effect. Everyone knew their tactical role and their immediate objectives. Beyond Dowdall's Tavern, adaptation and improvisation would be required, but Jackson was certain they would surmount any challenges. It was now 5:15, and all eyes were upon Stonewall, his "visor low over his eyes and lips compressed." An eyewitness studied the general intently. "As calm as if sitting upon the seashore a thousand miles from a battle field," he wrote, "not a muscle quivered on his face . . . It was as still as a village graveyard." A warm breeze gently stirred the small, young leaves in the adjacent bushes and saplings while a horse pawed the ground with his hoof. Abruptly, Jackson turned and asked, "Are you ready, General Rodes?" His subordinate, who was more than ready, replied with an enthusiastic "Yes, sir!" Then, almost as if it were an afterthought, Jackson quietly said, "You can go forward then."[40]

Rodes nodded to Blackford, who must have signaled a bugler. A lone blast of brassy music, and then another, and another, echoing up and down the line in the woods, and the skirmishers started advancing. One hundred-fifty yards behind them, stepping off with one accord, came the solid mass of Rodes's first rank, followed by the next. Now Colston's men began to move, steady, still perfectly aligned, like a great ripple of gray and brown coursing through the bright spring green of the forest. All told, 21,500 Confederates plunged eastward into the snarled and jumbled undergrowth of the wilderness. Briars tore at their clothing and skin and some tripped over hidden vines and rocks, but onward they pushed, driven by adrenalin and faith—some in their cause, many in God, but all in General Jackson.[41]

The first wave to assault the Federal Eleventh Corps consisted of four-legged and winged creatures, driven from their woodland realm by "a perfectly solid mass of men." Rabbits, squirrels, quail, turkey, and deer suddenly scampered out of the forest and into the camps of Charles Devens's Division, whose regiments had been refused permission to come to arms in expectation of the coming attack. Devens, who may have been drunk that afternoon, would not accept the reports of massing rebels to the west. His men, nervous from camp rumors spread by their pickets during the afternoon, found release in the antics of the frightened animals that suddenly appeared and for a brief moment had some fun chasing them around. Then they stopped and stood still, their ears perceiving an eerie, spine-tingling sound emanating from three sides around them. The rebel yell, the clarion call of fear for those who had heard it before, started off low and sporadic but quickly attained a shrill, overpowering crescendo as thousands of throats joined in the chorus. Major Blackford remembered, "we moved on about a ¼ of a mile in silence and then suddenly came upon the Dutchmen cooking in the woods. . . . With a yell we reached in." A devastating volley, and then a second one, rocked the 54th New York and 153rd Pennsylvania, which, despite their shock, had miraculously managed to form a ragged battle line. The leaves came "fluttering down upon us as though a thunder storm had broken loose," one Keystoner wrote, and "here and there a soldier dropped." The two regiments got off a couple incomplete, hurried volleys, and then ran for the rear. One North Carolinian wryly penned, "They did run and make no mistake about it—but I will never blame them. I would have done the same thing and so would you and I reckon the Devil himself would have run with Jackson in his rear." Other regiments and partial brigades in Devens's command attempted to make a stand against the onslaught, but "there was no stemming such a tide," and they too broke in confusion. Hopelessly outnumbered, they were simply too near the fateful point of impact with Stonewall's legions, had no time to react, and no space to maneuver properly in the thick underbrush. As this first Union division disintegrated, Jackson's battle persona reignited, his face flushed again, and the old glow in his eyes returned. He kept near the front, riding up and down the advancing line, shouting "Press On! Press On!"[42]

Rodes and Colston did press onward, their tight organization beginning to unravel, but still controllable. Officers dressed the ranks as best they could and followed Stonewall's prime directive to keep moving. About 5:45 they slammed into Schurz's Division, comprised almost exclusively of German immigrant troops. Unlike Devens, Schurz not only permitted but ordered the realignment of several of his regiments to face west, in defiance of Howard's earlier refusal to allow it. The German-born political general had been among the first convinced that the rebels were coming and did what he could to prepare, yet as one Confederate artillerist declared, "the shock was too great. . . . The resistance offered was speedily beaten down." Quickly defeated by any normal standard, yes, but any delay this late in the day—especially this day—with night fast approaching, could be fatal to Jackson's and Lee's grand vision to seriously cripple the Union army and change the character of the war. First along a makeshift line in front of the Wilderness Church, and then next to Dowdall's Tavern, where they joined a stolid brigade of Adolph von Steinwehr's Division behind shallow rifle pits, Schurz's boys put up a brave fight, delaying Jackson's advance about forty precious minutes. Colonel Friedrich Hecker of the 82nd Illinois, wounded and lying in the field, observed the action. Writing to a German-language newspaper after the battle, he was proud of the behavior of his corps: "[We] fought as long as possible against superior numbers that would have snuffed out resistance from any other troops." Accounts differ regarding Howard's behavior, who returned from Sickles's wild goose chase in between these two defensive stands, and reportedly tried to rally the broken regiments personally. Had Hooker not ordered away Barlow's brigade, his reserve, the corps commander would have been present when Stonewall first launched the attack and may have retarded Confederate progress even more with the extra manpower. Then again, the extra bluecoats may not have mattered much. Jackson's bigger enemy that evening was time. [43]

After overcoming Schurz, the rebel assault began to falter. Brigade and regimental cohesion collapsed near the front, many soldiers charging forward in disorganized clumps hailing from multiple organizations. Colquitt, whose brigade had led the flank march, suddenly decided to halt, which created a cascade effect south of the Turnpike and deprived Jackson of a quarter of his strike force. Most troubling, the shadows in the wilderness on the other side of the Dowdall's Tavern clearing grew long and black, with nightfall only minutes away. Already it was hard to see in the woods, but the men were still moving forward, yelling, scooping up prisoners, and full of vigor. And their general was ecstatic. Captain Robert Wilbourn, Stonewall's signal officer, noticed "[he] had never seen Gen. Jackson so pleased with his success as that evening. He was in unusually fine spirits and every time he heard the cheering of ourselves which was the signal of victory he raised his right hand a few seconds as if in acknowledgment of the blessing and to return thanks to God for the victory." The Yankees had run, and Jackson knew the road to U.S. Ford, one of Hooker's escape routes across the Rappahannock, lay just ahead, with his headquarters at Chancellorsville nearby. It was a race against darkness. Despite the numerical odds facing him and the difficult terrain, Stonewall believed the victory already won could be yet greater, much greater. He trotted down the Turnpike with the artillery, veering off into the trees from time to time to sustain the momentum of the assault by force of will. To one unit he thundered, "Men, get into line!" and to another demanded, "Whose regiment is this? Colonel get your men instantly in line!" The sun, big and red like the triumphant Confederate battle flags, was setting on a dark day for the Union—but one that could have been much worse. [44]

Old Jack probably perceived the last of the light with immense frustration. His heart yearned to keep pressing the attack, but his head warned him to stop it, reform his lines, and bring up Hill's Division. And so he ordered a halt. The men in gray and butternut, euphoric but exhausted, responded when the bugles sounded the recall, and officers set about the difficult task of identifying whose men were theirs and how far their

The famous 1863 photo of Lee in full dress uniform, by the Richmond studio of Minnis and Cowell. It is possible this image was taken in April 1863 in the field, just before the Chancellorsville Campaign, almost simultaneous with Jackson's well-known portrait. *Photo by Minnis & Cowell, 1863. Courtesy of the Virginia Historical Society.*

Jackson as photographed by Minnis and Cowell, late April 1863, Hamilton's Crossing. Known colloquially as the "Chancellorsville Jackson," this image captures the general's appearance mere days before his fateful wounding. Mary Anna Jackson thought the likeness too stern and resolute. *From the Collections of the Confederate Memorial Literary Society managed by the Virginia Historical Society by agreement of January 1, 2014.*

Circa 1866 print depicting Jackson and principal staff officers, 1862–1863, reproducing wartime photographs. Nearly all of these staff officers left vivid accounts of the general's wartime experiences and his interactions with Lee. *From the Collections of the Confederate Memorial Literary Society managed by the Virginia Historical Society by agreement of January 1, 2014.*

ABOVE LEFT: A wartime photo of Lee's aide, Walter Taylor, whose period letters and postwar publications lamented the effect of Jackson's death on Lee. *Courtesy of the Virginia Historical Society.* ABOVE RIGHT: A wartime photo of James Longstreet, Jackson's successor as Lee's chief advisor. *Courtesy of the Library of Congress.* BELOW LEFT: A wartime photo of Ambrose Powell (A.P.) Hill. *Courtesy of the Library of Congress.* BELOW RIGHT: Richard S. Ewell, a postwar print derived from a wartime photograph. *Courtesy of the Library of Congress.*

RIGHT: Wartime photograph of Jeb Stuart, probably taken in Richmond c. 1862–1863. The heartfelt relationship between Jackson and Stuart rivaled that between Jackson and Lee. *Courtesy of the Library of Congress.* BELOW: A wartime photograph of the White Oak Swamp, site of one of Jackson's weaker performances in the Seven Days. *Courtesy of the Library of Congress.*

ABOVE: The Poindexter House, Malvern Hill Battlefield, where Lee, Jackson, Longstreet, and Davis met following the Seven Days Campaign. *Courtesy of the Library of Congress.*
BELOW: An Alfred Waud wartime sketch illustrating Longstreet's powerful attack against Pope on August 30, 1862, at Second Manassas. Union troops retreat in the foreground. The Confederate victory was the combined result of Lee's revised command style, Jackson's flank maneuver, Longstreet's assault, and Pope's mistakes. *Courtesy of the Library of Congress.*

ABOVE: Alfred Waud's wartime sketch of the Army of Northern Virginia crossing the Potomac prior to the Maryland Campaign, with Union scouts in the foreground. *Courtesy of the Library of Congress.* BELOW: An Alexander Gardner 1861 photo of Harpers Ferry, Virginia. Jackson's successful capture of this decisive point at the last possible moment temporarily salvaged Lee's Maryland Campaign. *Courtesy of the Library of Congress.*

ABOVE: Alexander Gardner wartime photo of Union soldiers looking at dead Confederates in the Cornfield at Sharpsburg, with the West Woods—and Jackson's battle line—in the background. *Courtesy of the Library of Congress.* BELOW: The iconic Gardner photo of Confederate dead in front of the Dunker Church at Sharpsburg, taken days after the battle. *Courtesy of the Library of Congress.*

George B. McClellan   Fitz John Porter   John Pope

Ambrose Burnside   Joseph Hooker   Oliver O. Howard

The Union opponents of Lee and Jackson: George B. McClellan, Fitz John Porter, John Pope, Ambrose Burnside, Joseph Hooker, and Oliver O. Howard. *All images courtesy of the Library of Congress.*

ABOVE: An 1866 print depicting prayer at Jackson's headquarter's camp, c. 1862–1863. Like other providential evangelicals of his time, Jackson believed God directed his own and the Confederacy's destiny. *Courtesy of the Library of Congress.* BELOW: Moss Neck Manor, a modern-day view. Jackson selected the plantation's business office as his winter headquarters in 1862–1863. *Photo by Dave Ellis/The Free Lance-Star.*

ABOVE: The Yerby House (Belvoir), in a postwar photograph. Here Lee recovered from his winter illnesses in the early spring of 1863, Jackson hosted Mary Anna and Julia, and Ewell received a memorable welcome banquet upon his return to the army. *Courtesy of the Fredericksburg and Spotsylvania National Military Park.* BELOW: A postwar photograph of the intersection of the Plank and Furnace Roads, where the two meetings collectively termed the "Last Meeting" between Lee and Jackson occurred, May 1–2, 1863. *Courtesy of the Albert Kern Collection in the Montgomery County, Ohio, Historical Society.*

ABOVE: A postwar sketch (c. 1880s) depicting one of the conferences between Lee and Jackson on the night of May 1–2, 1863. From *Battles and Leaders of the Civil War*. BELOW: The famous but apocryphal 1869 Everett B.D. Julio print depicting the Last Meeting of Lee and Jackson at Chancellorsville on May 2, 1863. *Courtesy of the Library of Congress.*

ABOVE: An Alfred Waud wartime sketch of portions of the Union 11th Corps forming up near Dowdall's Tavern attempting to stem Jackson's flank attack, May 2, 1863. Stands such as this delayed the progress of the attack and bought time for Joseph Hooker to react. *Courtesy of the Library of Congress.* BELOW: An 1868 print depicting the defeat of the Union 11th Corps at Chancellorsville, May 2, 1863. The success of Jackson's flank attack against this organization was short-lived due to nightfall, Hooker's reaction, and Stonewall's accidental wounding in the dark woods. *Courtesy of the Library of Congress.*

ABOVE: Jackson probably glanced at this pocket watch before launching his flank attack at Chancellorsville. *Courtesy of the Virginia Historical Society.* BELOW: A postwar print depicting Lee entering the Chancellorsville clearing, May 3, 1863. Shortly after this moment, he received Jackson's note congratulating him on the victory. *Courtesy of the Library of Congress.*

ABOVE: The Chandler plantation office, Guiney's Station, where Jackson died on May 10, 1863. From a wartime photograph. *Courtesy of the Library of Congress.* BELOW: Jed Hotchkiss's 1863 map highlighting southern Pennsylvania, Maryland, and northern Virginia. Hotchkiss's maps proved integral to Lee's and Jackson's plans to take the war north. Original located at the Handley Library, Winchester, VA. This copy owned by Library of Congress. *Courtesy of the Library of Congress.*

ABOVE: Lee's Gettysburg headquarters. Near here on the evening of July 1, 1863, the general stood with A.P. Hill and pondered what to do about Cemetery and Culp's Hills. *Courtesy of the Library of Congress.* BELOW: An imaginative 1869 print depicting Lee at Jackson's grave in Lexington. *Courtesy of the Library of Congress.*

commands extended. For Jackson, there was no question he would continue to prosecute the attack that night. The moon, bright and full again,
shed just enough light, and although unorthodox and risky, the rewards
of resuming the assault would be worth it. Hill was obstreperous and hot-
tempered, to be sure, which is why he and Jackson constantly feuded, but
he was a superb fighting general. Stonewall had faith in him as a battlefield
leader. Hill would finish the job. Couriers were sent racing to the rear to
find him and bring his brigades forward. One of them, James Lane's, was
already up and in position. In the meantime, Jackson and his staff rode
back and forth through the dark forest, discovering how mixed-up Rodes
and Colston had become, restoring a semblance of order. There was much
work still to be done. At one point, the general ventured forward a bit too
far, spooking Sandie Pendleton. "General, don't you think this is the wrong
place for you?" Unconcerned for himself, perhaps because he trusted completely in God's divine will or because his focus on destroying the enemy
was so complete, Stonewall replied, "The danger is over. The enemy is
routed! Go back and tell A. P. Hill to press right on!" Pendleton departed
to locate the division commander.[45]

Hill and his party joined Jackson close to 9:00 P.M., and impatient to
learn where the enemy's lines were located, Stonewall decided to conduct
a personal reconnaissance. He realized Hooker had reacted to his flank
attack and sent fresh units into the woods west of Chancellorsville. Some
of them were ensconced behind hastily felled trees and rough fieldworks,
he had learned, but his knowledge of what lay ahead for Hill's men was
limited. As he had on every prior field, Old Jack wanted to glean as much
intelligence as possible for himself. Stuart, alas, was guarding the northern
flank, discharging an important duty there. He could not be recalled. It
was up to Jackson to find out what he could. He and eight staff officers and
guides rode forward on the Turnpike, entered the woods on its northern
side, and soon found a small, local trail called the Mountain Road that
paralleled the larger thoroughfare for several hundred yards. This would
be a safer route toward the front than the open, debris-strewn pike.
Accompanied by the mournful calls of countless whippoorwills, they
walked their horses cautiously up the Mountain Road until they were just
behind the outermost Confederate skirmish-line, manned by members of

the 33rd North Carolina of Lane's Brigade. There Stonewall lingered for several moments, listening and thinking. He probably heard Union axes chopping trees and branches deeper in the forest and occasional northern voices calling out orders for their placement. It was pitch black where the trunks and limbs of the larger trees blocked the moonlight, interspersed with bright patches where the heavenly glow penetrated to the ground. The enemy was closer than expected, Jackson noticed, and in greater strength. The plan may have to be altered. . . . Turning around and pondering what his senses had revealed, the general and his staff were wending their way back to Lane's main battle line when suddenly shots rang out south of the Turnpike. They were coming from Southern muskets. A ripple of discharges, then a ragged volley followed, moving northward and jumping the pike. Little Sorrel bolted at the abrupt noise and galloped to the north through the woods, Jackson barely holding on to the reins as low branches and saplings smacked his face. J. G. Morrison, whose horse had been killed, lay momentarily stunned on the ground but quickly regained his senses and ran toward the line of the 18th North Carolina, the regiment directly in front of the party. "Cease firing!" he screamed at the top of his lungs. "You are firing into your own men!" Seeing only the moving shadows of horsemen, the Carolinians could not be sure they were not Federal cavalry, which had just been reported in the area. An angry voice rang out from them: "Who gave that order? It's a lie! Pour it into them, boys!" [46]

Stonewall Jackson was struck three times, twice in the left arm and once in the right hand. Amazingly, Little Sorrel escaped unscathed. The general managed to stay on his horse until surviving members of the staff reached him and gently lay him on the ground against a tree. "All my wounds are by my own men," he murmured in painful surprise. The firing miraculously ceased, and Hill, whose cavalcade had also been grievously hit by the last volley, rushed to his chief's side. With obvious regret, not sure what to say, he blurted, "General Jackson, I am sorry to see you wounded and hope you are not hurt much." Stonewall could only reply, "my arm is broken." Hill immediately started helping Wilbourn and Morrison administer first aid to their stricken leader, reportedly even cradling his head in his lap. Assured there was little more he could do, Hill then assumed command of the corps, only to be wounded himself by an enemy shell fragment moments later.

Jackson, brought off the field in a stretcher, was dropped twice and fell on his wounded arm, exacerbating his serious condition. The second time he groaned in agony and lost much blood, yet grew silent in prayer. After an arduous journey in which several individuals recognized him—something he wished to avoid to preserve morale—the general was finally brought to a hospital tent near the Wilderness Tavern, where Dr. McGuire amputated his arm. Reverend Lacy, who joined him following the amputation, witnessed the power of his Christian faith firsthand and recorded their conversation. After all that had occurred, Jackson remained steadfast, perhaps even spiritually strengthened: "I thought, after I fell from the litter," he said, "that I would die upon the field: and I gave myself up into the hands of my heavenly father without a fear." But true to his belief, he confessed "I was in the possession of perfect peace. It has been a valuable and precious experience to me that I was brought face to face with death, and found all was well." He had absorbed, in that instant, a lesson he supposed greater than all the military experience in the world. "I learned . . . that one who had been the subject of converting grace, and was the child of God, could, in the midst of the severest suffering, fix the thoughts upon God and heavenly things, and derive great comfort and peace." In a later discussion, Jackson even revealed that he thought the loss of his arm "providential," and that, since it was God's will to take it, he would never wish to alter events had he the power to do so. In his darkest hour, Stonewall drew strength from his unswerving faith. At no other point in the war did it empower him so noticeably. Yet, as focused as he was on spiritual matters, he did not fail to continue discharging his duty as a subordinate partner in command. At some point later that night, before he fell into unconsciousness, Jackson dictated a small note of congratulations to Robert E. Lee for the victory, assuming none for himself.[47]

His friend and chief probably turned to prayer that night as well, but for Lee the overriding sentiment was sadness. Stonewall's staff members, Hotchkiss and Wilbourn, after doing all they could to assist their chief, rode to brief the commanding general. They found him at "his old camp" at the intersection of the Plank and Furnace Roads in the early morning of May 3. Wilbourn got there first and awakened the general, describing the extent of the victory so far and Jackson's wounds. Propping himself up on his elbow, Lee initially received the news of his friend's injuries with grace. "Thank God it is no worse," he told the aide, "God be praised he is yet alive." But after a moment of thought and a brief review of the fighting, he added, "Capt. any victory is dearly bought that deprives us of the services of Jackson even temporarily." When Hotchkiss arrived about an hour later, Lee's reaction was more despondent. Hearing more detail about the severity of Stonewall's wounds, he "was much distressed and said he would rather a thousand times it had been himself." Overcome with "profound grief," and "strugg[ling] to suppress his emotions," he told the mapmaker "he did not wish to converse about it." Lee then turned away, composed himself, and buried his mind in the problem at hand: securing the victory that the fallen Jackson had inaugurated. His sacrifice must not be in vain. Jeb Stuart had been given command of his corps after Hill's wounding, and Lee, in complete agreement with that decision, immediately sent a series of dispatches to Stuart prioritizing tactical objectives and providing guidance. "Those people shall be pressed immediately," Lee exclaimed to his staff, and to Stuart he wrote, "they must be pressed, so that we can unite the two wings of the army."

Throughout the morning of the 3rd the cavalryman-turned-infantry-commander skillfully led Jackson's divisions to a stunning consummation of the previous day's success, pushing back both the Union 3rd and 12th Corps beyond the Chancellorsville clearing, where, at around 10:00 A.M., Stuart's tattered brigades united with Anderson's and McLaws's veterans. It was probably the finest one day's worth of fighting the Army of Northern Virginia accomplished in its four-year existence. The artillery enjoyed special success, driving its Federal counterpart from one position after the other. E. P. Alexander wrote, "There has rarely been a more gratuitous gift of a battle-field." The victory, made possible by Stuart's personal leadership, the ferocity of the Southern attacks, some Federal tactical missteps, and Hooker's temporary incapacitation, was dearly bought but represented a vindication of the decision-making of Lee and Jackson two nights earlier. The flank march and assault had paid off, transforming the character of the campaign yet again, and though the Union army was far from destroyed as they had hoped, it was badly damaged and might be injured further. Lee decided to meet his troops and witness the moment.[48]

Charles Marshall rode at Lee's side as the general entered the clearing, the burning mansion and woods serving as a fitting backdrop. "One long, unbroken cheer" greeted him, "in which the feeble cry of those who lay helpless on the earth blended with the strong voices of those who still fought," and rising "above the roar of battle . . . hailed the presence of the victorious chief." At that moment, Marshall wrote, "[Lee] sat in the full realization of all that soldiers dream of—triumph; and as I looked upon him . . . I thought that it must have been from such a scene that men in ancient days rose to the dignity of gods." Yet minutes after receiving the thunderous acclamation from his troops—the apex of his military career—Lee received something else. It was Jackson's note. Marshall read it to him, shouting to be heard over the din. "I shall never forget the look of pain and anguish that passed over his face as he listened," he recalled, and "with a voice broken with emotion," he "bade me say to General Jackson that the victory was his." Despite all that remained to be done, including dealing with Sedgwick (who had finally broken through Early's defenses at Fredericksburg), Lee took the time to dispatch a message shortly thereafter that reached his friend, now bereft of his left arm, later that morning. J. P. Smith, who had been at Jackson's side most of the night, read it aloud. "I have just received your note informing me that you were wounded," Lee began, and "I cannot express my regret at the occurrence. Could I have directed events, I should have chosen for the good of the country to have been disabled in your stead. I congratulate you upon the victory which is due to your skill and energy." Jackson, listening to Smith's every word, was deeply moved. Turning his face away to hide his reaction, he stated, "General Lee is very kind, but he should give the praise to God."[49]

In General Orders No. 59, Lee did just that, commending his troops' valor and sacrifice in the Chancellorsville Campaign and calling upon all "to return our grateful thanks to the only Giver of victory, for the signal deliverance he has wrought." He also "earnestly recommended" all soldiers "unite on Sunday next in ascribing to the Lord of Hosts the glory due unto His Name." But by that time, Stonewall, who had temporarily rallied and appeared to be recuperating, had taken a serious turn for the worse. On the same day many of the troops heeded their commanding general's request to give thanks in worship—something Jackson had done so much to foster—Lee's partner and friend ironically labored for every breath. He had contracted pneumonia, probably resulting from complications caused by his falls from the litter combined with the cold he had caught. Mary Anna, baby Julia, Jim Lewis, and medical staff were by his bedside at the Chandler plantation office, Guiney's Station, where Lee had ordered him sent for recovery. His staff lingered outside, barely able to control their grief. When Dr. McGuire pronounced that he would not survive the day, Mary Anna broke down in tears, then recomposed herself, and asked her near-delirious husband if he was ready to go to heaven. His lips barely quivering, he responded, "I prefer it." A brief sleep ensued, and when he awoke, the general could see the blurry image of his adjutant, Sandie Pendleton. He asked where Lacy was, forgetting he had specifically ordered the chaplain to leave him and preach to the men. Pendleton, holding back tears, told him, "The whole army is praying for you, General." Jackson whispered, "Thank God. They are very kind." He paused, and added, "It is the Lord's Day. My wish is fulfilled. I have always desired to die on Sunday."[50]

And so he did. Stonewall Jackson passed away at 3:15 P.M. on May 10, 1863. The deliverance that Lee so fervently thanked God for only applied to his army, for Jackson, his friend and partner, the leader with whom he had won his greatest victories, was gone. Joseph Hooker and the Army of the Potomac had been decisively defeated, to be sure, and the theater-strategic initiative passed again to the Army of Northern Virginia. But the Union army did not suffer a devastating blow, as Lee and Stonewall had planned, and would soon reconstitute its losses. The rebels would experience much greater difficulty replacing theirs, and in a strategic sense the Confederate operational victory at Chancellorsville, the result of the apogee of the Lee-Jackson collaboration, was catastrophically hollow. In 1877, looking back to the recent past of shattered dreams, the historically reliable Walter Taylor, one of Lee's closest aides, offered his view: "Glorious as was the result of this battle to the Confederate arms, it was accompanied by a calamity, the contemplation of which . . . must ever be regarded as a supreme disaster. The star of Confederate destiny reached its zenith on the 2d day of May, when Jackson fell," shot by his own men at the pinnacle of his career, but "it began to set on the 10th of May, when Jackson was no more." Forty-six years later, just five years after another terrible war ended, former British Prime Minister David Lloyd George, who obviously had no stake in the Lost Cause movement, arrived at the same conclusion. He visited the modest frame structure where Stonewall died, walking around it and taking in an impression of the area. It was a haunting moment for him. The building was in decay, its condition emblematic of the fate of the Southern nation. Feeling the weight of history heavy in the air, George, who had a keen sense for historical moments and places, suddenly exclaimed to his companions, "That old house witnessed the downfall of the Southern Confederacy." Before the Civil War ended, most Confederates reached the same prophetic conclusion.[51]

FIVE

"Who can fill his place I do not know."

THE PARTNERSHIP BROKEN

"Something of strength, of hope, of life, appeared to be removed from every heart." [1]

T he reality of Jackson's death struck like a thunderbolt into the heart of the Confederate psyche. It was a strategic-level inflection point, a war-changing event, and Confederates widely interpreted it as such in private letters and diaries and in newspaper editorials. All across the South, men and women, soldiers and statesmen received the news with shock, pain, anguish, and dread. A great hero had fallen, they perceived, and with him fell the chances of independence. All was certainly not lost—Chancellorsville had been a miraculous victory and great captains aplenty still led the stalwart rebel armies—but the cause had suffered a grievous blow. In North Carolina, a female diarist, the wife of a planter, was paralyzed with abject grief, unable to go about her daily routine, while two hundred miles northward soldiers in the Stonewall Brigade, in prayer at Reverend Lacy's services, openly wept at the loss of their beloved leader. Others, such as a young girl in Lexington, Virginia, and even President

Jefferson Davis himself in Richmond were terrorized by the tyranny of fear; they realized, perhaps for the first time, that the South might lose the war. A few stoics, most of them in the army and accustomed to the caprice of death, reacted more calmly, or hoped that the general could be replaced by the rising of another leader. Among the latter group were not a few officers at the senior level, including—depending on the time and his correspondent—Robert E. Lee, who had shared the bond of Christian brotherhood with Jackson. These men knew fully well that Stonewall's loss was, as one of them put it, "a dreadful blow" and bore ill omens, yet they comforted themselves in their shared faith in God's divine providence; in effect, they resolved to achieve Southern independence despite Jackson's absence and inspired by his Christian example. Surely the Lord would not have called him home at this juncture of the war if He did not ultimately intend for the Confederacy to join the family of nations.[2]

Doubt and worry, those cancers that eat away at hope, nonetheless crept stealthily into the recesses of patriotic Southern brains even as the strong in faith declared that all would be well. By the end of 1863, the infection had become widespread, and many traced its beginnings to that dark May night in the Virginia wilderness. John Esten Cooke, a member of Jeb Stuart's staff and Jackson's first biographer, may have most eloquently expressed this feeling in the first edition of his book, published in Richmond mere months after Chancellorsville: "His name has been a tower of strength to all, and when this mighty bulwark of the Southern cause was overthrown, Heaven seemed to frown upon us, and to punish us. . . . Men looked up to him, as of old the Greeks did to the wise Ulysses or the thoughtful Nestor—as to one who was competent to hear and decide, as well as to act, in every emergency." A novelist by profession and a confessed romantic, Cooke, for all his flowery language, was a keen observer of human behavior and accurately painted a word picture of how the Confederacy overall reacted to Jackson's passing. "There was something childlike in the sentiment with which the whole nation mourned his death," he reported. "They listened to the announcement with a hush of awe, with that silence which salutes a great and irreparable public calamity. Strong men wept for him, with a sense of loss and desolation. . . . His veterans mourned as men do rarely—dumb and still before this terrible fatality." As for Lee, "who knew his incomparable value more than all other men," Cooke simply described him as having "tears in his eyes."[3]

The writer-turned-cavalryman, who had had personal and regular access to Lee, Jackson, Stuart, and their staffs, understated the effect of Jackson's death on Lee. The blow fell extremely hard on him, harder than on anyone else besides, perhaps, Sandie Pendleton and Jedediah Hotchkiss. Pendleton and Hotchkiss, their merits as staff officers and genuine grief notwithstanding, did not, however, lead the South's principal field army and advise Jefferson Davis. Barely recovered from the fit of angina and that early spring cold and worn out from the late campaign, Lee was staggered by the emotional body blow of losing his lieutenant. Troubling thoughts fluttered in and out of his mind as he grasped at the meaning behind the loss. How could he possibly replace him? What did this portend for his ability to command the army? What would be the effect on the country? Still in shock the day after Stonewall died, Lee could not afford the luxury of paralysis. Now, even more than before, his men and his nation required his leadership. All would look to him for words of solace and reassurance, even as he grieved himself. He must set the standard. With a sigh and perhaps a heavenly supplication, Lee resignedly sat down in his tent, pulled out some writing paper, and began dispensing the sad duty of telling those who needed to know. Family would come first, and then mutual friends and members of the high command. He penned his wife Mary, "you will see we have to mourn the loss of the good and great Jackson. Any victory would be dear at such a price." He then contacted Stuart, whom he must have known would be crushed by the news. But the cavalryman deserved to know right away, for multiple reasons. "I regret to inform you the great and good Jackson is no more," he wrote, adding that their friend died "calm, serene and happy." Aware that Stuart was also a Christian, he included a phrase that would be shortly echoed in numerous letters: "May his spirit pervade our whole army; our country will then be secure."[4]

Lee the general as well as Lee the man had been gravely wounded. "Such an executive officer the sun never shone on," he supposedly said later of Jackson's military abilities. "I had such implicit confidence in Jackson's skill and energy that I never troubled myself to give him detailed instructions. The most general suggestions were all that he needed," he told one of his staff. But the chief had lost much more than his operational "right arm," a blow that by any standard handicapped his ability to duplicate the great victories of the past year. He had also suffered the death of his primary military adviser, and, perhaps most importantly, a friend. Lee had few true friends within the leadership of the Army of Northern Virginia, and while admirers and fawning subordinates abounded, the fact that he was the boss at the top always provided—as it does yet today—a layer of separation between himself and all others. Jackson had respected that barrier as a professional, but as a friend and fellow Christian he felt at liberty to pierce it, and Lee reciprocated, especially during the winter and spring of 1862–63. That friendship, altogether absent at first, and only tentative later, had grown to be very significant for Lee by the spring of 1863, undergirding and empowering an already strong professional relationship that had won spectacular victories, most recently at Chancellorsville. Now it was utterly shattered. "Who can fill his place I do not know," a devastated Lee lamented to his brother. The commanding general mourned for himself, his army, and his country. [5]

Reticent to share his feelings openly as a rule, a surprising number of Lee's letters and personal interviews in the weeks and months following Chancellorsville revealed the jagged hole Jackson's death had created in the army commander's heart and head. Many of them also contained religious references, doubtless included to salve the pain on both ends of the exchange, but also referring reverently to the departed Jackson's faith—a steadfast belief in God's will that represented one of his greatest attributes, and indeed a necessary asset to a commander, an army, and a nation grieving the fallen hero and seeking to replace him. To General John B. Hood, commanding his division near Suffolk, Lee displayed both his personal sadness and his belief in Jackson's legacy on May 21: "I grieve much over the death of General Jackson. For our sakes not for his. He is happy and at peace. But his spirit lives with us. I hope it will raise up many Jacksons in our ranks. We must endeavor to follow the unselfish, devoted, intrepid Cause he pursued, and we shall be strengthened rather than be weakened by his loss." On the same day, Lee wrote to Virginia Congressman William C. Rives using almost identical language. "Since it has pleased Almighty God to take from us the good and great Jackson, may

He inspire our commanders with his unselfish, devoted, intrepid spirit, and diffuse his indomitable energy through our ranks. Then indeed we shall be invincible and our country safe." Three days later, in the letter to his brother, Lee repeated the same sentiments. "I unite with you in mourning at the death of Gen'l Jackson—any victory would be dear to us at such a price, still I am grateful to Almighty God for having given us such a man, whose example is left us, and whose spirit I trust will be diffused over the whole Confederacy and will raise in the Army many to supply his place." In his official report of the Chancellorsville Campaign, filed with the Adjutant General in late September 1863, Lee echoed in more officious prose what he had earlier written privately: "I do not propose here to speak of the character of this illustrious man, since removed from the scene of his eminent usefulness by the hand of an inscrutable but all wise Providence. I nevertheless desire to pay the tribute of my admiration to the matchless energy and skill that marked this last act of his life, forming as it did, a worthy conclusion of that long series of splendid achievements which won for him the lasting love and gratitude of his country."[6]

A major general, a congressman, his own brother, and the Confederate Adjutant General—to each Lee conveyed very similar thoughts about the loss of Stonewall Jackson. These messages mirrored, in somewhat more detail, the earlier letters to his wife and Jeb Stuart. They also strongly reflected the formal statement issued to the troops on May 11 in General Orders No. 61 announcing the "decree of an all-wise Providence" that deprived the Army "of this great and good soldier." Yet, the order continued, "while we mourn his death, we feel that his spirit still lives, and will inspire the whole army with his indomitable courage and unshaken confidence in God as our hope and our strength." The similarity among the phrases, nouns, verbs, and adverbs in all these communications is striking and elicited Lee's deep emotional and professional wound as well as his unswerving faith in his and Jackson's God; the Lord would infuse the Army with Stonewall's passionate faith and "energy," making it "invincible" and spawning righteous successors.

Did Lee actually believe these words or were they simply brave declarations to assuage other grieving souls? Certainly, his affirmations of personal loss came from the heart and were genuine expressions of how he felt.

There is no other way to interpret them. As a providential evangelical of the period and one who had devoutly attended church services with Jackson and thousands of his officers and men in the previous months, these utterances also reflected a steadfast *hope*, nurtured through his close affiliation with the departed, that God would, indeed, make good Jackson's loss. It would be tough going, he assured Carter Lee, "our labor rendered more severe, more onerous by his departure," but a faithful trust by all in the Lord's will *could* result in ultimate victory. In essence, Jackson's death, as crippling a blow as it was by earthly standards, shed light on the power that a true Christian spirit imbued in its possessors. That was Jackson's lasting legacy, both to Lee and to the Army of Northern Virginia. How to translate that spirit into battlefield victories that would win Southern independence was another matter, though, and one left for the pragmatic side of Lee to ponder. Hope could stir the soul, offer succor, and allow one to carry on during difficult times. It could not, however, guarantee military success.[7]

Lee's personal reaction to Jackson's passing did not go unnoticed at the time. Those close to the commander remarked on his deep and lasting sense of loss, despite his faith and heartfelt proclamations of hope to others. This was not Lost Cause–inspired postwar rhetoric, but instead truthful appraisals of what Lee had suffered in his lieutenant's death. Hardly had Jackson's body been removed from Richmond after it lay in state at the Confederate House of Representatives than Lee arrived in the city, on May 14. He was there to confer with President Davis and his cabinet about national strategy, in a meeting that would last three long days and result in the fateful decision to invade Pennsylvania—ironically, the dead Stonewall's favorite strategic option. Chancellorsville, despite its grievous casualties, had given the initiative in the Eastern Theater back to the Confederacy and Lee intended to capitalize upon it, making good on the plans he and Jackson had developed before the battle. William Preston Johnston, son of the late General Albert Sydney Johnston and Davis's personal aide, received Lee as he waited for the president. "We had a brief conversation," Johnston remembered. Congratulating Lee on his recent triumph, he paused and somberly added, "You have met a terrible loss, General, in the death of General Jackson." Lee was taken aback by the kindness of the remark, and emotion welled up in his voice. Gazing intently at Johnston,

Lee answered, "An irreparable loss, Colonel; a loss like a man's right arm. Why sir, there is nobody who moves like him." Continuing, he stated, "I ordered General ———— [original omission] to move at 3 o'clock in the morning with a division, and General Jackson at 7 with his corps, and at 9 o'clock Jackson was ahead of him." At that moment, Davis asked for Lee to enter his office, the interview with Johnston concluded, and Robert E. Lee started the laborious process of winning over the Confederate political leadership to the theater strategy he and Jackson had discussed in the months before the latter's death.[8]

Returning to his camp near Fredericksburg after the grueling Richmond conference, Lee began preparations for the movement north and consulted frequently with his remaining subordinates. Longstreet would be principal among them, and gaining his support and input was critical. Old Pete had actually come back from his adventure at Suffolk on May 9, his two divisions en route behind him, and shared a meal with his commander as they discussed the future. Writing years later in his memoirs, Longstreet recalled finding Lee "in sadness over the severe wounding of his great lieutenant, General Thomas Jonathan Jackson. With a brave heart, however, General Lee was getting his ranks together, and putting them in condition for other useful work." Beyond that, Longstreet termed Jackson's death a "great misfortune," and believed now "we seemed to face a future bereft of much of its hopefulness." That is nearly all the historical record reveals about how he felt about Jackson's wounding and subsequent death at the time. Possibly he quietly celebrated the removal of his colleague and rival, predicting that he, Longstreet, would now be Lee's primary adviser and operator, or perhaps, as his words forty years later insinuate, he recognized the blow that befell his commander and the Confederacy. In all likelihood it was probably some of both, but it seems that Lee did not confide much in him about the pain he felt with Jackson's death.[9]

Although recognized throughout the army (and by Lee himself) as marginally competent, General William Nelson Pendleton, Sandie Pendleton's father, was probably Lee's closest personal friend during this period as well as his Chief of Artillery. The senior Pendleton, who also happened to be an ordained Episcopal minister and had been close to Jackson, offered Lee a confidant to whom he could pour out his heart and with whom he could share his grief. The gray-haired artillerist, omnipresent at Lee's headquarters camp throughout the war, was in a unique position to comment on the effect of Stonewall's death on the commanding general. Writing his wife on June 1, Pendleton reported, "had last week a long and <u>feeling</u> [original emphasis] talk with Genl Lee on the great question of religion. I visited him on duty. He was alone and introduced the subject. He is in earnest. Wept a good deal as we talked of Jackson. He is deeply concerned for the spiritual welfare of the soldiers." As demonstrated in the various letters written in May, Lee still mourned Stonewall's death while exhibiting enthusiasm for carrying on his religious campaign of spiritual revival in the army. Further, that the normally stoic Lee would allow himself to break down in the presence of a subordinate officer reveals much about that officer as well as the reason for the emotional exchange. Very few indeed would be the moments in the war in which an eyewitness would report Robert E. Lee in tears.[10]

Staff officers of famous generals during the war often wrote the most insightful commentaries and observations of their chiefs, but also tended to be protective of their reputations and, if they lived long enough, postwar legacies. No two groups of officers more faithfully and frequently chronicled their leaders than the staffs of Lee and Jackson, and considering the close personal and professional relationship of the two men, few staffs had such an opportunity to view firsthand the effects of personal loss on senior-level leadership. Henry Kyd Douglas approached General Lee the day after Stonewall died as a representative of the deceased's old brigade, asking on the soldiers' behalf if they might escort their commander's body to Richmond. Lee "received me kindly," he said, "listened patiently, and then in a voice gentle and sad replied, 'I am sure no one can feel the loss of General Jackson more deeply than I do, for no one has the same reason.'" But the commanding general could not release the Stonewall Brigade for such duty, "as those people over the river are again showing signs of movement." Sympathizing deeply with the men, Lee added, "I cannot leave my Headquarters long enough to ride to the depot and pay my dear friend the poor tribute of seeing his body placed upon the cars." Douglas, whose reputation as a Lost Cause and pro-Jackson acolyte is well-known, nonetheless carefully noted afterwards, "I have given these remarks of General Lee as spoken, for I wrote them out in my diary and they are verbatim."

That Lee referred to Stonewall as "my dear friend" while speaking with one of his former staff officers is a powerful testimony, even if the account came from Douglas.[11]

James Power Smith, whose candor is more highly regarded and who so eloquently recounted the events at Jackson's headquarters of the previous winter and spring, had been detailed to escort his fallen commander's widow and child to her father's home in North Carolina following Jackson's burial in Lexington. Fulfilling that mission, he was recalled to the Army and a staff position by Lieutenant General Richard S. Ewell, who had been named by Lee as Jackson's successor during the post-Chancellorsville reorganization. Smith had a lot of ground to cover as he made his way up the Shenandoah Valley, through Maryland, and at last into Pennsylvania, where he caught up with the Army of Northern Virginia the day before the Battle of Gettysburg. Finding General Lee in a woods near Chambersburg at daybreak, he wished to report on his journey and then continue on to join Ewell. Saluting, he was given a "kind greeting" by the army commander, who then immediately "inquired with much tenderness of Mrs. Jackson and her child." After satisfying his concerns for their well-being, the general freely "spoke with sadness and emotion of the loss he had experienced in the death of Jackson." Reflecting back many decades on this meeting, beset with old age and perhaps a foggy memory bent on enshrining the value of his long-dead chief, Smith's testimony could be dismissed as a fluke were it not for a similar statement written in December 1864 by Charles Venable, one of Lee's own staff officers. Responding to a query from former Jackson chief of staff, Rev. Robert Dabney, whose wartime biography of Jackson would appear that year, and benefitting from daily interactions with Lee during the year and a half since Stonewall's demise, Venable was in a good position to comment on how the loss affected the commanding general. "I know that he misses that great and good man every day and every hour," he wrote, "both in council and in action." By the time Venable put pen in hand and replied to Dabney, Lee had failed at Gettysburg, been frustrated in the Mine Run Campaign in the fall of 1863, endured the entire Overland Campaign and half of the siege of Petersburg, and found himself strategically and operationally stymied by Union General Ulysses S. Grant in a static defense of that city and Richmond. In the West, the war had been utterly lost, William T. Sherman's Federal army had devastated much of the Deep South, and the newly reelected Abraham Lincoln was not about to seek a compromise. For all but the patriotically blind, the end was near. How events may have evolved differently must have entered Lee's mind over the course of these momentous events. Doubtless, he thought of Jackson, as Venable's letter confirmed.[12]

The loss of Lee's partner Jackson was in and of itself a strategic-level blow to the Confederacy because of how it affected Lee, the nation's only successful army commander, both professionally and personally. "Of all who mourned his death, none felt more acutely the loss the country and the army had sustained than General Lee," wrote Rev. J. William Jones, missionary chaplain for A. P. Hill's new corps.[13] But Lee was far from the only Confederate who realized after Stonewall's death that the Southern war effort had been irrevocably damaged. As John Esten Cooke indicated, a great majority of rebels in and out of uniform, at all ranks of society and throughout the entire South came to believe that with his passing the road to independence—the chief policy objective—was now, at the very least, obscured and uncertain. Too often dismissed by recent writers as Lost Cause apologia, countless accounts written during the remainder of the war itself strongly support this argument, as do those written afterward from trustworthy sources. The hero of the Valley Campaign, who had sustained Southern morale during a dark period when defeat after defeat seemed to afflict the Confederacy, was suddenly and cruelly snatched away. The general who, up to the end of 1862, claimed the highest rank of esteem in rebel hearts, equal to or even above Lee, had inexplicably perished. To a religious people it appeared, as one astonished diarist wrote, that God was passing judgment. Taken together, these and other grief-ridden reactions represent a reality almost as strategically significant as the effect of Jackson's death on Lee and his army: they portray a *perception* held by most Confederates that the croak of doom could be heard, however faintly, reverberating from a small room at Guiney's Station, Virginia. Certainly, the victory at Chancellorsville raised morale in the ranks and on the home front about the Army of Northern Virginia's prospects vis-à-vis its adversary, the Army of the Potomac, even to the point of believing the former invincible against the latter. Many also shared the hope, as did Lee (and perhaps directly influenced by his public remarks, such as General Orders No. 61), that the Lord would raise up a worthy successor to Stonewall or that his Christian spirit would instill new strength into the army, but those statements of martial and spiritual confidence were frequently tempered with an ominous reckoning that God had judged the Confederacy and found it wanting, and that the terrible vacuum his loss created was unfillable.[14]

If Jefferson Davis turned to religion to salve the news about Jackson, there is no record of it. In early 1862, especially after the botched Romney Campaign but even as the Army of the Valley had marched from victory to victory, the president had been somewhat cool to Jackson's entreaties to change the strategic character of the war. As time passed, however, he grew to appreciate Jackson's inestimable value to the Confederate cause. Now, as the full flower of a beautiful tidewater spring began to grace Richmond, the chief executive of the Confederacy quickly gauged the strategic nature of the disaster occasioned by his accidental shooting and later death. He was also personally shocked, especially because the newspapers, as well as communications from Lee, had assured him in the first week of May that Old Jack was on the mend. By the 9th, it became clear that the general's condition was very grave, and Davis found himself "unable to think of anything but the impending calamity." Feeling utterly helpless and in deep despair, the president "sat silent" in his home in Richmond "until twelve or one o'clock" in the morning. He stationed men at the telegraph office and the railroad station to glean any information that might come in, yet the hours wore torturously on with no report. Anxious to do something—anything—but wait for the dreaded news, the president sent a solicitous telegram on the 10th to the dying Stonewall and his attendants enquiring about his health "and sending some exceedingly kind and courteous messages." Jackson reportedly received this note before he expired and asked Hunter McGuire to "tell Mr. Davis I thank him—he is very kind." Kind wishes could not save Stonewall, however, and Davis shortly found himself riding solemnly behind his coffin in the grand funeral procession in the capital. Bending over Jackson's corpse in its first repository, the reception room of the Governor's House, Davis supposedly became emotional, dropping a tear on the general's cold face. The president failed to regain his composure to conduct the rest of the day's business, an official visitor enduring an awkward moment of silence as the devastated executive sat quietly in his presence, unable to speak. "You must excuse me," Davis apologized, "I am still staggering from a dreadful blow. I cannot think." To Lee on May 11, the Confederacy's chief policymaker stated, "A great national calamity has befallen us, and I sympathize with the sorrow you feel. The announcement of the death of General Jackson followed frequent assurances that he was doing very well, and though the loss was one which would have been deeply felt under any circumstances, the shock was increased by its suddenness. There is sincere mourning here, and it will extend throughout the land as the intelligence is received." Years later, reflecting on the defeat of the nation he had led, the president wrote of Stonewall, "He was the complement of Lee; united, they had achieved such results that the public felt secure under their shield. To us, his place was never filled." For the normally reserved yet altruistic Davis, these were important words that revealed how acutely damaging he believed Jackson's loss was to the young Confederacy. [15]

Other high-ranking Confederates, from the policy level down to the tactical, agreed with their president that Jackson's passing was a turning point in the war that boded ill for the independence of the South. In his annual report for the year 1863, Secretary of War James A. Seddon devoted almost a full page to a eulogy for the fallen general, whose death "saddened [the] hearts of the people of the Confederacy, who mourn the death of their chosen champion, stricken, by 'an accursed chance,' in the hour when the prowess of a stroke of daring and generalship just accomplished had opened the way to crowning victory." Integral to "almost every important movement and brilliant victory in Virginia," and "without disparagement to others, it may be safely said he had become, in the estimation of the Confederacy, emphatically 'the hero of the war.' Around him clustered with peculiar warmth [the people's] gratitude, their affections, and their hopes." Echoing Lee's religious sentiments, Seddon declared that Stonewall had died a Christian "martyr," whose memory "and the spirit he inspired glow through the hearts of [the] armies," but, in the end, "his loss is felt to be . . . irreparable." Powerful words, these, from a man in Davis's inner circle who had an influence on the prosecution of the war. He and Jackson had had brief communications earlier in the conflict, but most of his impression of the dead leader must have come secondhand. If the routinely even-tempered Seddon called Jackson a "champion" and "the hero of the war" in an official report (that was filed with the Confederate Congress) it was reflective of others' thoughts and not just his own. The effect of Jackson's demise on the secretary is further alluded to in a letter to Dabney, just weeks after Stonewall was laid to rest in Lexington. In response to Dabney's request for information regarding what he should censor in his future biography, Seddon answered, "No one feels a deeper interest than myself in the portrayal of the character of the illustrious deceased in all its noble proportions." [16]

In the Army of Northern Virginia, generals and staff officers at all ranks, some of whom personally knew Jackson and had fought for him, mourned his death profoundly and despaired about the future. The ever-observant Jed Hotchkiss looked around Stonewall's old headquarters camp at Hamilton's Crossing on May 19 and moaned to his wife, "he is gone and sleeps in the Valley he loves so much—we miss him all the time and a void is made here which time can hardly fill." Hotchkiss suffered more than most because his friend, James Boswell, Jackson's official topographical engineer, had been a member of the general's party when it was fired upon the night of May 2, and fell dead off his horse, a bullet through his heart. "It seems not like our 'old Hd.Qrs' to any of us and least to me than to any one else, for my tent mate is gone as well as my General," the mapmaker added. Yet hope sprung eternal for the evangelical Hotchkiss, replying to his wife's report of widespread sadness at Stonewall's death: "I am sorry the people despond . . . lives have been sacrificed, but such is the price of liberty and without it there can be no redemption—all [original emphasis] will mourn, I doubt not, but the days must come when sorrow shall be turned into joy." Major Benjamin Leigh, who had assisted in carrying Stonewall from the scene of his wounding that night, wrote his wife a few days after the army learned of Jackson's death, refusing to go into the painful details but striking a similar tone. "I shall not attempt to describe the unusual and deep mourning of the Army for his loss. The country will participate in it as fully as we. . . . It has pleased God to take him from us. God's will be done!"

Jeb Stuart, on whom Lee relied greatly during this period, was kept perpetually busy watching and probing the defeated Yankees on the other side of the Rappahannock, but in quiet moments in his tent emotions overcame him. Like President Davis, he called Jackson's loss a "national calamity," and in a letter to his brother after the eventful Battle of Brandy Station on June 9, lamented, "the great and good Jackson was the dearest friend I had, and I feel that I possessed his full confidence and regard. His messages were always: 'give him my love.'" But as a professed Christian, Stuart joined Lee, Hotchkiss, Leigh, and countless others in seeking solace in his faith, declaring "his example, his Christian and soldierly virtue are a precious legacy to his countrymen and to the world." As with Lee and Seddon, Stuart hoped that Stonewall's spirit, in its evangelical and military manifestations, would pervade the army and help ameliorate his earthly departure, yet the grief the cavalry chief felt was terribly real and needed an additional outlet. Taking pen in hand one night, he wrote a sympathy note to Mary Anna Jackson that included a heartfelt "tribute of admiration" for her husband. How gratifying it must have been for Stuart to receive back from her a letter dated August 1, in which she wrote, "I need not assure you of that which you already know, that your friendship and admiration were cordially reciprocated by him. I have frequently heard him speak of Gen'l Stuart as one of his warm personal friends and also express admiration for your soldierly qualities." Another of Jackson's closest companions, William Nelson Pendleton, assuaged his grief, as befitted a man of the cloth, through his faith. "His end was perfect peace," he exclaimed to his wife. "A glorious Christian! A noble man! I thank God for intimate friendship with him. . . . Who will fill his place we do not yet know." [17]

Some officers had mixed reactions, coupling feelings of personal, organizational, or national loss with more equivocal statements. Artillery major William Pegram admitted on May 11, "there is quite a gloom over the army today, at the news of Jackson's death. We never knew how much we all loved him until he died." Yet, he added, "his death will not have the effect of making our troops fight any worse." A captain serving in the 60th Georgia exclaimed in a letter home, "General Lee is a far greater General than 'Old Stonewall' but he can never excite the enthusiasm which this old war horse did with his faded coat and cap and his sun burnt cheek." Hunter McGuire, who had been by the general's side to the very end, still mourned the loss of the great leader decades later but offered a contrary generalization: "After Jackson's death the troops were always in fine humor, always sanguine of success." Richard Ewell, Stonewall's former division commander and successor in command of the Second Corps, curiously left no written record of how he felt about the general's demise except for an official general order published on June 11. It reiterated two of Jackson's famous hallmarks, discipline and strict obedience to orders "as the means to secure success," and asked the troops "to join with him in asking that Divine Aid which was the reliance of our lamented and illustrious Chief." Ewell came to embrace his Christian faith while serving under Stonewall in 1862 and seemed to follow the course set by Lee: the best way to honor the deceased's memory was to uphold his evangelical legacy and beseech the Lord to instill His spirit in the army. The hot-tempered but gifted A. P. Hill, who had been wounded minutes after Jackson on May 2, kept to himself. Perhaps he still held a grudge against his old boss. "He behaved very coarsely to all the members of Jackson's staff" when he assumed temporary command of Jackson's Corps after Chancellorsville, one of them wrote, and Henry Kyd Douglas recalled that "Hill had not forgotten or forgiven." Yet such behavior is at odds with Hill's tender cradling of Jackson's head that fateful night in the Virginia woods. Hill probably had mixed feelings about it all, and in any case may have had little time to mourn, as he was promoted to Lieutenant General on May 24, coequal with Ewell and Longstreet. He would be the new commander of the newly created Third Corps. [18]

The day Jackson expired in his room at Guiney's Station, a large percentage of the rank and file of the Army of Northern Virginia attended outdoor church services "in the hot broiling sun" of an unusually warm and bright spring day. A few lucky soldiers found shade. The branches on the birch, poplar, and sycamore trees responded to the heat, transforming from the small young leaves present during the late battle to green, leafy bunches. The oaks and other late-blooming trees were in full bud and beginning to burst. Everywhere nature was regenerating itself with new life, and for a brief moment in time, peaceful normalcy reigned. "Some few ladies from the neighborhood were present, and softened by their appearance and voices the worship of [the] rough, dirty, and ragged soldiers." Thousands of them, inspired by their chaplains' preaching and the surrounding beauty, lifted their hearts in prayer to Heaven, many of them beseeching the Lord to spare their beloved leader. Lee and most of his lieutenants were with them, specifically attending Reverend Lacy's service at Jackson's headquarters as they had when Stonewall was alive and well. The chaplain preached from the Book of Romans, chapter 8, and Jackson's favorite verse: "And we know that all things work together for good to them that love God, to them who are called accordingly to *His* purpose." Another man of the cloth, seated among the congregation of almost 3,000, recorded, "I have never witnessed such thoughtfulness and seriousness depicted on the faces of men." A bird flying over the Confederate camps outside of Fredericksburg that Sunday morning would have beheld the partial realization of Stonewall's dream: a revived, Christian army kneeling humbly and thankfully before its creator for His many blessings. [19]

Their expressions of humility and heartfelt prayers of the morning notwithstanding, the soldiers learned later that day that their efforts had failed: Jackson was dead. "In a very short time everybody knew it," one of them noted. In the evening word spread from regimental camp to regimental camp, the peculiar character of the soldiers' gossip system working like a human telegraph. Men stood in clumps around their campfires, shocked, some openly weeping, others shaking their heads and refusing to believe the news. The more religious among them knelt in prayer individually and collectively. Many took pen in hand as a means of release. Letters home, written that night or in the following week, revealed a general progression of emotions, starting with disbelief, turning to intense grief, and then to despair for the future. Charles Minnigerode of Fitzhugh Lee's cavalry brigade was representative. "How deep must be the mourning of the whole Confederacy at the death of Jackson," he wrote his mother on May 12. "Nothing during the whole war has been so distressing to me and I know that almost every man in the Army feels his loss as much as I do." If, along with their own personal sense of loss, Lee and the officer corps came to intellectually comprehend the strategic nature of Jackson's passing and turned to their faith to salve the pain, the soldiers understood in their hearts what it meant and intrinsically perceived the significance of his death. That perception became reality, and despite the palliative effects of Christianity for some of them, impressed itself on their thoughts about the prospects for the Confederacy. Geographic origin, branch of service, or rank had little impact on the noticeable unanimity of feeling. As one enlisted man put it, "It is not extravagant to say that . . . more sorrow was expressed in tears than was ever known in the history of the world at the loss of one man."[20]

William Fulton Jr., a member of the Stonewall Brigade, remembered "we of his old command could not realize it. Our hearts were heavy and our eyes filled with bitter tears. . . . We could only exclaim in our deep sorrow, 'God's will be done.'" A fellow Virginian observed the battle-field impact, noting that "men who had fought without flinching up to this time became timid and fearful of success." An Alabaman who had marched under the general through the last several campaigns lamented to his cousin back home, "What a loss to the army and the country! The name of the laurel-crowned hero was never spoken in this Army but with adoration . . . But the star-crowned champion is gone and 'Earth may not look upon his like again.'" Another soldier from the Yellowhammer state was more directly pessimistic in his expectations: "Stonewall Jackson was kild [sic] . . . I think this will have a [great] deal to due [sic] with this war. I think the north will whip us soon." South Carolinian David Ballenger wrote his brother, "the Army of Northern Virginia, and especially the Second Army Corps, mourns the loss of Lieut. General T. J. Jackson. . . . The nation may truly mourn the loss of so great a man." He continued, "I do not think that the Confederacy afforded many such men as Gen. Jackson." William Wirt Gilmer of the 2nd Virginia Cavalry made some comparisons as he scribbled in his diary: "Our shield and buckler, the noblest man on record Thos. J. Jackson fell . . . [he] inspired his men; with 1 to 2 to 3 Yankees, he never failed to beat them; his equal can never be found for fighting; for planning, Genl Lee stands unsurpassed; for both, I place Genl Jackson at the head of any list." Another cavalryman, a member of Stuart's staff, recalled a "gloom [fell] over the whole command, and I felt as if I had lost a near and dear relative." More disconsolate was a soldier in the 26th Georgia, who mournfully predicted on May 15, "all hopes of Peace and Independence had forever vanished" with Stonewall's last breath. For him, the future looked especially dark. Echoing that melancholy was North Carolinian Ross Gaston, a member of Lane's brigade, the pitiable organization responsible for Jackson's accidental wounding, who recalled "we never got over Jackson's death, for all the men lost all hopes of success after he was gone."[21]

As William Fulton emphasized, the Stonewall Brigade was especially devastated with grief. This was not surprising, considering the tight bond that had developed between the organization and their old commander and the sense of élan evolved over many hard-fought, bloody fields and countless long marches. They were Jackson's first command, they were his "old guard," and they collectively required more to assist them through their pain than Chaplain Lacy's sermons (which they attended en masse) and Robert E. Lee's general orders. Gathering together as an entire brigade on May 16, they passed four resolutions to be submitted formally to the Secretary of War. One of them requested that their organization be officially recognized on the rolls as the "Stonewall Brigade" in memory of their departed chief. Another agreed to submit the other three resolutions to the Richmond authorities. The other two dealt exclusively with the command's sense of loss: "Resolved, first, that in the death of Lt. Gen'l Jackson the world has lost one of its best and purest men—our country and the church of God a bright and shining light; the army one of its boldest and most skillful leaders, and this brigade a firm and unwavering friend." The second declared, "that while we mourn for him, and feel that no other leader can be to us all that he has been, yet we are not cast down or dispirited, but even more determined to do our whole duty, and if need be give our lives for a cause made more sacred by the blood of our martyrs." These were brave words, ones expressing collective sadness as well as a determined sense of Christian hope, not unlike those of Lee, Seddon, Hotchkiss, and many others. Ted Barclay of the 4th Virginia, who was present at the meeting, reflected his comrades' thoughts in a letter to his sister: "A deep gloom is over our camp over the death of Gen. Jackson. He was taken away from us I believe because we made almost an idol of him. Though we mourn his loss still we do not feel that we are without a leader. God is our leader and protector. He can raise up many a Jackson and will yet deliver us from the power of the enemy." Certainly, Barclay mourned at a personal and organizational level and worried about the future. Yet like many of his brothers in arms, he placed his faith in the Almighty to create a new leader to compensate for the crushing loss of Jackson. The Stonewall

Brigade, the Army of Northern Virginia, and indeed the entire Confederacy *could* still prevail in the great struggle if they had enough faith in the Lord. Yet as time passed, no great successor to Jackson emerged, no more spectacular victories ensued like the one at Chancellorsville, and the tone in Barclay's letters changed. On October 21 he wrote his sister again, from a camp along the Rappahannock. "Oh how much this army has lost in the death of Jackson. I think Lee instead of losing his arm by his death has lost his head." It is unclear if Barclay intended this declaration to be meaningful on multiple levels, but it certainly appeared to be. As the months ground onward, the immediate pain of Jackson's death subsided, but was replaced in the minds of the more reflective by contemplative regret or foreboding. [22]

Soldiers and officers from commands other than the Army of Northern Virginia also responded to Jackson's death, indicating that the grief felt in Lee's army was shared universally across the Confederacy's military. One Kentucky staff officer, lamenting the disaster, added that God "will provide another whose arm he will strengthen to drive the invaders from our soil," and a chaplain in Braxton Bragg's army likewise despaired at first, but similarly realized, "God can remove the chief of workmen, and still carry on the cause of liberty." This sentiment mirrored the providential hope of Barclay and a minority of soldiers in the Virginia army, but other accounts from outside the Old Dominion betrayed more ominous chords about the future. Colonel Abram Fulkerson of the 63rd Tennessee wrote of his regiment's feelings on May 18, "We feel that his death is a national calamity," and, like most fighting men, "The poorest soldiers among us appreciated his worth—loved the man, and mourn his loss." A Georgia surgeon stationed at Vicksburg was shocked to learn from his wife that Stonewall was gone, joining her in thinking him "worth ten thousand men to our cause." D. H. Hill, Jackson's brother-in-law in charge of a department in North Carolina, composed a general order in late May deeply mourning his loss and declaring "his genius and courage have been the chief elements in Southern success." While literarily hyperbolic and to be expected from the biased Hill, such was not the case with Brigadier General Humphrey Marshall, whose command operated in the southwest Virginia/eastern Tennessee region. En route to Richmond by train Marshall unexpectedly found himself sitting across from Judge G. D. Camden, an old neighbor of the young Jackson from his pre–West Point days. The two struck up a cordial conversation as the beautiful green countryside rolled by outside their window. According to Camden, Marshall "expressed to me very emphatically that in his opinion [Jackson's] mind was superior to all others engaged in the war, and that his loss would be greatly felt on that account." Camden himself told R. L. Dabney that "the Genl was in fact regarded by the masses at least as the great man of the war . . . as the mastermind of the war."[23]

The public's outpouring of grief from across the Confederacy, both privately and in the press, vindicated Camden's observation. "Our idol has been taken from us. The man we delighted most to honor, the chieftain loved and trusted beyond all others, is no more. . . . Jackson leaves a void which no man can fill," one newspaper editor wailed. Another exclaimed, "The affections of every household in the nation were twined about this great and unselfish warrior. . . . He has fallen, and a nation weeps." If newspaper editorials reflected (and directed) the thoughts of the readership, then the catastrophe suffered by Robert E. Lee and his army in Stonewall's death was reenacted hundreds of thousands of times throughout the kitchens and parlors of the Confederacy. Private letters and diary entries, if anything, exhibited even deeper emotional distress. Jackson had become a national hero after his Valley Campaign—*the* great hero of the South before Lee's 1862 victories—and his luster only increased after he joined the Army of Northern Virginia. A preacher in Lexington, Virginia, eulogized, "The nation indulges a personal grief. . . . Never perhaps did such a throe of agony pierce a nation's heart." In North Carolina diarist Melinda Ray termed his death "a great and terrible stroke," deeming the general "necessary to us" and unsure how the army would carry on without him. Upon learning from the papers that Jackson was gone, a fellow Tarheel similarly wrote, "a chill went through my heart. . . . I have no heart to write more, tho [sic] the paper is full of news. I care for nothing but him." Another felt "miserable" for days and "nearly cried [her] eyes out . . . oh how we shall miss him," while a Mississippi woman penned a personal note of sympathy to Stonewall's widow, extolling his virtues and claiming, "the death of your beloved was felt keenly by every daughter of the South; we can form some idea of your agony when we, who never saw his face, loved him so much." Kate Stone, a young plantation mistress in Louisiana, vaulted quickly past the grieving stage and gravely intoned what the general's passing meant in a military sense: "In the death of Stonewall Jackson we have lost more than many battles. We have lost the conqueror on a dozen fields, the greatest general on our side." Civilian men and women thus endured feelings and patterns of loss similar to those that affected their kinsmen in the armies. Like Lee, the leaders of the government, and thousands of officers and soldiers, the people of the seceded states greeted the news of Jackson's death with surprise, intense sadness, dread for the future, hope that God would make good the loss (and instill the departed's spirit throughout the land), and a sense that the war effort would never be the same again. Some felt only a few of these emotions, but the historical evidence leaves no doubt the majority of the Southern people viewed Stonewall's demise as a turning point. As a democratic republic at war, what the people believed mattered in the Confederacy. As it was with the soldiers, *perception* of reality turned into reality. Stonewall Jackson's death became, at the time, a moment of strategic contingency.[24]

In Richmond, the first major city to receive the bad news, the response was visceral and very public. The *Enquirer* offered a poignant description worthy of a novel: "The morning press came forth with its columns shaded with long dark lines of mourning; and the people, of one accord, thronged the streets to give utterance with one another to the deep sorrow that enshrouded every heart. It seemed as if every man felt himself an orphan. . . . It would be impossible to measure the depth of love felt by the people for the great and good man whom they were now come forth to mourn. Many wept when they read the unhappy tidings . . ." Others "gazed at each other in dumb amazement," reported another paper, "wringing their hands and weeping as bitterly as if one near and dear to their hearts had been taken." Some of them had held vigil at the train depot on Broad and Eighth Streets, enduring the engines' clanking and whistling for hours on May 9 and 10, hoping for any optimistic scrap of information about the general's waning condition. Everyone, it seemed, had hung their hopes on Stonewall's recovery. A government bureaucrat mastered the art of understatement when he recorded in his diary on

May 6, "The country is deeply anxious for Jackson's fate," and then again on the 11th, "No man in the nation would be so universally regretted." When Jackson's flag-draped coffin passed through the streets of the city to tolling church bells that day, the boulevards were packed with reverent but dejected citizens, who knew not what else to do but come out and pay their respects. The gigantic crowd was a cross-section of Confederate society. Gruff dockworkers from Rocketts Landing rubbed elbows with invalided soldiers on crutches from Chimborazo Hospital, and well-dressed ladies wearing last year's fashions due to the shortage of fine clothes jostled politely with homespun farmers who had ridden in from the local suburbs. But few voices could be heard, "no noisy demonstration of any kind greeted the ear," an eyewitness reported, and a visitor to the city that day said, "I never saw human faces show such grief." Minutiae of the funeral procession and accounts of Jackson's life and military service were covered for weeks in most of the major newspapers, providing numerous proxy experiences for those prevented by distance from attending the real event. These were then reproduced in other papers throughout the Confederacy. In the words of one chronicler, it was for the Southern nation "the greatest personal loss it would ever know," and the capital city was its epicenter. The Richmond press eulogized Stonewall well into the beginning of the Gettysburg campaign, ensuring that Virginians—and thousands of their fellow citizens—would keep his death in the forefront of their minds. "Hannibal might have been proud of his campaigns in the Valley, and the shades of the mightiest warriors should rise to welcome his stern ghost," extolled the *Richmond Examiner*, whereas the *Enquirer* confessed that "Jackson alone is a dearer loss to us than Hooker and his whole hundred and fifty thousand would be to them." The *Richmond Whig* claimed that thousands of Confederates would have gladly traded their lives for Jackson's, and *The Record* lamented as late as June 18, "his is a picture draped in mourning in every heart." A mass funeral was held to succor the public's loss, "great numbers unable to find entrance to the church." Ewell and Stuart joined "the vast crowd" in "deep emotion in memory of a man whom they had followed in his greatest toils, whose honors they had shared in so many fields of splendid victory, and whom for his goodness and piety they had learned to love as a brother."[25]

In Lynchburg, Virginia, a eulogy was held on May 24 at the First Presbyterian Church. The Reverend James Ramsey held forth for hours to a packed sanctuary, agreeing with Lee, Davis, and many in the military and at home about the scope of the disaster and what now must be done about it. Yet he offered, perhaps more clearly than others, a troubling reason why God had chosen to take Jackson home. Admonishing his congregants and hundreds of visitors that "such an occasion occurs but once in any generation," he admitted Jackson's passing was a shock to the national body politic. "We are all bereaved . . . The inquiry is natural, why this terrible blow? Why raise up just the instrument we needed, and then remove him when we seemed to need him as much if not more than ever?" The answer was as terrifying as it was simple: the country had sinned and brought the tragedy upon itself. "If this nation had an idol it was Jackson. If there was any mere instrument to whom they were in danger of giving glory beyond what is man's due, it was he." Confederates, he insinuated, had ceased to trust in the Lord, as "men hardly ever felt the need of prayer" with Jackson in the field. But "God will not give his glory to another," Ramsey thundered. Jackson, he said, trembled at "the thought that men were praising *him*," [original emphasis] as he worried about "heavier judgments through God's displeasure." The heaviest judgment had now befallen the Confederacy, but even in its despair it could yet rise up "to triumph and perpetuity." The country could best honor Jackson now, the minister claimed, in two ways: "rally round the throne of grace as never before . . . and humble itself under the mighty hand of a holy God," and imbibe "the spirit of Jackson, in our rulers, our military leaders, and our people." Doing so would "save us and perpetuate us as a nation."[26]

The grief of the Deep South mirrored that displayed in Richmond and in Lynchburg. No funerary processions or public viewings of the dead general were possible there, nor did preachers so overtly remind their flocks of their collective sin and spiritual duty, but editors of prominent newspapers ensured their readers received almost the same emotional impact. "If not the head, he was at least the heart of the revolution," the *Savannah Republican* pronounced. Now that "heart" had been torn out of the body of the country, and no one knew what would result. Fear and uncertainty laced many commentaries. The Atlanta *Southern Confederacy* placed the news of Jackson's death at the very top of its masthead on May 11: "This is by far the most serious loss we have yet sustained in the death of an officer since the war commenced. He was one of the purest and best of men, the most unselfish and patriotic. His very name was a tower of strength and inspired more enthusiasm among our soldiers than any other General in the service. . . . Who will rise up to fill his place?" Several subsequent issues repeated that rhetorical question, as if desperately grasping for a way to plug the hole in military leadership and national inspiration created by Stonewall's demise. On the 20th, an editorial mirroring Ramsey's sermon wailed, "A nation bent in speechless agony over his body, and, when the first paroxysm of grief was over, anxiously inquired, 'on whom has his mantle fallen?'" Soon Georgians would find out that both Ewell and Hill had replaced him in an organizational sense, but only time would tell if they could recreate the deceased's much-acclaimed personal character as well as his battlefield victories. As one editor declared before Jackson died, he was "the expression of [the Confederacy's] faith in God and in itself, its terrible energy, its enthusiasm and daring, its unconquerable will, its contempt of danger and fatigue. . . . He came not by chance in this day and to this generation. He was born for a purpose." In other words, Jackson was a sterling representative of what was noble and virtuous in the Confederate cause, and with his removal the fabric of national character sustained a mighty rip; yet Southerners could simultaneously nurture hope that he had done what he was foreordained to do. What the editor of this and other papers could not answer for their readers, however, was whether that purpose had been entirely fulfilled. Doubt would steadily gnaw away at that question, transforming into dread.[27]

Although Georgians may not have overtly read of the crack of doom evinced by Jackson's death, uneasy questions lay behind many of the editorials printed in the state's leading papers. In the Carolinas more pessimistic certainty prevailed. Echoing President Davis, the *Charleston Courier* proclaimed on May 12 that "every one mourns his loss as a personal bereavement and a national calamity," and in another issue lamented, "The shadow of this terrible grief rests upon every heart. Every home and every heart is clothed in mourning. The country weeps." The *Charleston Mercury* agreed: "Seldom has a people manifested so deep and universal a sorrow as that which has spread over the land." In Raleigh, the *Spirit of the Age* was even more disconsolate in an earthly sense, but like many in the military, resigned itself to the Lord's will: "'Stonewall' Jackson is dead! . . . No event of the war has cast such universal gloom over the country—no one has fallen whose loss is mourned with such heartfelt sorrow and whose place is felt to be so entirely irreparable. The soldiers and his whole countrymen loved him as they loved no other. But God knows best. He has taken the Christian, Hero, and Patriot to Himself—for Gen. Jackson was a soldier of the Cross of Christ, as well as his country." Just across town, the rival *Semi-Weekly Standard* wholeheartedly agreed, opining that it was good for the general that he was now with his Creator, but unquestionably bad for the Confederacy. "The death of no other citizen of the Confederate States would have caused as deep grief. The loss which the cause has suffered by his removal from the world, cannot be overstated . . . he was absolutely invaluable to the cause. He was the foremost *fighting* [original emphasis] man of the continent. . . . No man possessed in fuller measure, or more deservedly, the confidence of the government, the army, and the people."28

Readers of Alabama papers joined their countrymen in the East in rueful contemplation of the significance of Jackson's passing, evincing in it the national scope of the disaster and, like Reverend Ramsey, God's divine judgment. In Montgomery, an editor exclaimed the general was "the favorite of the people and the idol of the army. . . . His name became a household world." Yet the grief was too intense to say more; "at the present moment we feel too much regret, too much sorrow, to express all we feel on this sad occasion." Another sheet in the former capital waxed even more dramatic a week later: like the Charleston paper, the editor termed Stonewall's death "a national calamity" that "will be received by the entire people of the Confederate States with the utmost grief. The outburst of sorrow will surpass anything which has been witnessed during the war as every man and woman will look upon it as a personal bereavement." The *Jacksonville Republican* believed that the general was "brought to an untimely end by an inscrutable Providence" that may have wished "to ween us from a tendency to idolize man, and teach us our utter dependence upon God," but "the deep grief and profound sense of loss which have settled upon all attest the unequaled hold he had obtained upon their confidence, admiration, and affection. . . . He is gone, and a nation's tears bedew his grave." The *Mobile Advertiser and Register* admitted the news of Stonewall's death "has thrown a gloom over the entire community. It is hard to imagine a more serious catastrophe that could have happened. . . . The whole country, from the Potomac to the Gulf of Mexico, will deeply mourn his loss." Almost as if she had read that very editorial, Mrs. Thomas J. Semmes, wife of one of Louisiana's senators, recalled, "The death of General Jackson cast a shadow on the fortunes of the Confederacy that reached to the catastrophe of the war. His death was not only a loss to his country; it was a calamity to the world."[29]

In Dallas, Texas, beyond the Mississippi and half a world away from the dark shadows of the Wilderness where Stonewall was shot, the tone was equally, if not more despondent. The readers of *The Herald* were greeted with the news on June 3: "Every household hears in silence and tears the afflicting recital; the manly hearts of our veterans throb with pain and the eyes of beauty are dimmed with the holy tears of genuine sorrow. The Army weeps, the sad wail is taken up by the people, and the remote hills and hamlets respond to the echoes. We all mourn his loss, and the great victory is almost obscured by its sad disaster." In Tennessee, where rebel citizens faced the constant threat of incursions and occupation from Union armies, the editorial reaction was almost exactly the same. The *Knoxville Register*, representing the readership of one of the last rebel-held cities in the Volunteer State, noted, "For the first time since the war began this whole nation weeps as one man. . . . Virginia shall not weep alone over the grave of her fallen son. A nation has appropriated him." The *Chattanooga Daily Rebel* seemingly kept the tears at bay on May 13 but struck a similar chord: "the fall of Stonewall Jackson—that great and gallant spirit—that rare knight errant, who turned the tide of defeat into a flood of triumph, at a time when hope flickered and grew dim within the sternest heart—who rose above the dismal gloom of the last year like a banner, and led us out of the red sea of disaster even as Moses did of old . . . transparent within with the fire of true genius . . . the loss of such a chieftain is to be lamented more, far more, than a dozen [Chancellorsvilles] are to be vaunted."[30]

As these examples reveal, all across the Confederacy editors and private citizens chose similar phrases, watchwords, and mental images to record the depth of grief and despair created by Jackson's death: "The entire nation mourns . . . Every household weeps . . . Who will replace the great and good hero . . . A national calamity . . . The catastrophe of the war." Such correlative statements were not simple coincidences or mere mimicry of the influential Richmond press. Nor were they all exaggerations created by newspapermen eager to sell copies. Instead, they represented true feelings of public loss and anxiety across the seceded states—a national tragedy had occurred with far-reaching implications. Nineteenth-century editorial prose could verge on the melodramatic, to be sure, but behind the flowery language lurked realities—hard realities that the Confederate people now had to confront. The late spring of 1863 was a witching time for the secessionist South, a period of strategic reckoning, and citizens along with soldiers and statesmen sensed it. As the *Memphis Daily Appeal* (published in Jackson, Miss.) astutely observed on May 11, "Such a loss at such a time, is indeed a national calamity," and the *Montgomery Weekly Advertiser* phrased it almost verbatim, claiming "the loss of such a man at the present time is a public calamity." The *Montgomery Daily Mail* agreed: "The death of Stonewall Jackson is the most unfortunate event which could have happened at the present time, except perhaps the defeat of Lee's army in the late battle."[31]

The *strategic timing* of Jackson's death was, actually, quite "unfortunate" for the South and shook the Confederate body politic to its core. Along with his demise, the telegraph was hot with messages about the burgeoning danger posed to Vicksburg by Grant's Union army, the death of another lieutenant general, Earl Van Dorn, and Lincoln's call for 500,000 more volunteers. The effects of the Northern naval blockade were becoming increasingly deleterious, the state capital of Mississippi fell to the enemy and was burned, and Arkansans fought Union army occupiers, Unionist militias, and each other in a downward spiral of guerrilla warfare. Covering most of these events in detail, the Raleigh *Semi-Weekly Standard* presciently warned on May 19, "The death of Stonewall Jackson and the loss of Vicksburg, taken together, would occasion serious fears among our people as to the result of the war." Ominous forebodings indeed, but certainly not all the news was negative: the Federal Army of the Cumberland, under William S. Rosecrans, remained more or less idle in central Tennessee, rumors of rampant Copperheadism in the North were encouraging, Hooker and the Army of the Potomac appeared uninterested in further ventures south of the Rappahannock, and Lee and his army showed signs of going on the offensive. But Stonewall Jackson's death loomed over all of it in May and early June 1863. As most recent historians have agreed, the aspirations of the Confederate people were primarily pinned on the continued success of the vaunted Army of Northern Virginia under Robert E. Lee. Now that Jackson was gone, would those successes continue? Could the Virginia army continue to shield the national capital of Richmond and parry the titanic thrusts of the Yankees, which were certain to begin anew? How would Lee himself manage without his trusted subordinate—would another indeed arise to succeed the fallen Stonewall, both in character and ability? Most troubling of all, was the Confederacy being punished by the Almighty for trusting too much in the deeds of men?[32]

These questions raced through the heads of Confederates as spring gently gave way to early summer and the third full year of the war began in earnest. Yet secessionists were not the only ones who pondered the strategic meaning of Jackson's death at this point in the conflict. His value to the Confederacy was broadly recognized beyond the Potomac and even across the Atlantic. Sympathetic friends in England joined American Southerners in grieving the dead Stonewall, and Northern newspaper editors and soldiers alike acknowledged his significance and saluted his accomplishments. The *London Times* reported on May 26, "Probably no disaster of the war will have carried such grief to Southern hearts as the death of Gen. Jackson. . . . [He] is one of the most consummate Gen'ls that this century has produced." The same day the *London Post*, a government organ, observed, "As a soldier he will hold probably the foremost place in the history of the great American civil war. His name is indelibly associated with the most brilliant achievements of the Confederate armies. . . . To follow Jackson . . . was to march to certain victory." The following day, the *London Telegraph* summed up the conviction held in the British press: "Assuredly the most fatal shot of the war to the Confederates, whether fired by friend or foe, was that which struck down the life of Stonewall Jackson." These editorials, like those published by Confederate newspapers, reflected the sentiments of the people who read them. A. Dudley Mann, one of Richmond's official emissaries in London until April 1863, kept abreast of the pulse of public opinion after he was reassigned across the Channel to Belgium. He and Secretary of State Judah P. Benjamin conducted a lively exchange of letters in May and June 1863 confirming, despite Mann's propensity for redundancy and gossip, that a large percentage of the British people realized what Jackson's death boded for the American Confederacy. Benjamin wrote on May 15, "Brilliant as have been our recent successes the President and the Nation feel that they have been dearly purchased at the price of the life of our hero patriot, Jackson. His death has spread a pall over the country." Responding on the 28th upon receipt of Benjamin's note, Mann reported, "The death of Jackson has elicited a feeling the depth and power, if not the very existence, of which had wholly escaped my observation before, a feeling altogether incommensurate to anything ever manifested on any previous event of the war." He included several excerpts from the British press as evidence, and continued, "the death of no foreigner has ever so moved the popular heart."[33]

So, too, did the event affect the hearts and minds of the Confederacy's northern enemies. Newspapermen, generals, and even President Lincoln himself evinced a sense of respect for their fallen foeman that stretched to the point of acclamation. Of course, these sentiments did not reflect the majority, who rejoiced at Jackson's death. But more reflective souls remembered that the fallen leader was both a gifted adversary and a man of faith. The Washington *Daily National Intelligencer* extolled Jackson as "a noble Christian and a pure man," and hoped that the Lord would consider these qualities "against the sins of the secessionist." Across town, the *Daily Morning Chronicle* recorded on May 13, "While we are only too glad to be rid, in any way, of so terrible a foe, our sense of relief is not unmingled with emotions of sorrow and sympathy at the death of so brave a man." The editor, Charles Forney, then listed Stonewall's attributes, including "sublime devotion" and "purity of character." Lincoln wrote Forney a note the same day, stating, "I wish to lose no time in thanking you for the excellent and manly article in the *Chronicle* on Stonewall Jackson." The influential *New York Herald* also offered praise and alluded to the damage done to the Confederate cause by Stonewall's demise: "[His death] is a serious and an irreparable loss to the rebel army; for it is agreed on all hands that Jackson was the most brilliant rebel general generated by this war. . . . He resembled Napoleon in his early career more than any other General of modern times. The victory at Chancellorsville was dearly bought! Jackson was a universal favorite in the rebel army and popular even in our own." The famous preacher Henry Ward Beecher called him "a rare and eminent Christian," and a New England chaplain serving in the army observed he had been "a man of prayer and Christian experience," adding, "I wish we had more generals like him." A Union engineer, visiting the grave of Jackson's amputated arm during the 1864 Wilderness Campaign, "could [not] leave the spot without having experienced those peculiar feelings of awe and respect for the memory of the genius, which, though that of an enemy, possessed the faculty which inspired his Soldiers with a religious enthusiasm, resulting in most wonderful victories and made his name a terror to ourselves." Just a few miles away and a couple weeks later, the mistress of the Chandler plantation conversed with that officer's commanding general, Ulysses S. Grant, who had just established his new headquarters following the bloodbath at Spotsylvania. "This house has witnessed some sad scenes," she mused, revealing that "Stonewall Jackson of blessed memory" had died there only a year ago. Grant remembered him from their West Point days together and observed, "He was a gallant soldier and a Christian gentleman and I can understand fully the admiration your people have for him." Oliver Otis Howard, whose corps received the brunt of Jackson's flank attack at Chancellorsville, probably tendered the highest Federal commendation, albeit years later. "Stonewall Jackson was victorious," he recalled of the May 2 assault, "but, providentially for us, it was the last battle he waged against the American Union. For, in bold planning, in energy of execution, which he had the power to diffuse, in indefatigable activity and moral ascendancy, he stood head and shoulders above his confrères, and after his death General Lee could not replace him."[34]

Howard struck at the key strategic issue surrounding the loss of Jackson: Lee's inability to furnish an equally talented successor at a momentous time in the war when the Army of Northern Virginia's military power was at its height, and when the morale of the Southern people, badly shaken by Stonewall's death but buoyed by victory, demanded it. Confederates across the South, in the field and at home, sensed that the scales of independence or subjugation were in the balance, that *now* was the time, perhaps the last time, the war could be won. They despaired the loss of Jackson at this juncture and rightly assessed it a national tragedy. Lee's command team had thus far wrought wondrous success against mighty odds on the battle-field (and certainly the men in the ranks deserved credit), but those great victories at Second Manassas, Fredericksburg, and especially Chancel-lorsville were primarily the result of a maturing professional relationship between Lee and his top lieutenants built on a foundation of personal trust, and, in Jackson's case, friendship undergirded by faith. The bul-lets that cruelly pierced the flesh of Stonewall's arm and hand could not have been better aimed had they hit Lee himself, for they smashed that great partnership that had been the cornerstone of Confederate strategic and operational triumph in the East. With the fall of Jackson, Lee was emotionally wounded, a fact borne out by his own words, and one that by itself was a contingency point in Southern fortunes. Just as damaging, those bullets fired in the dark woods also permanently shattered the deli-cate triad of subordinate leadership in Longstreet, Stuart, and Jackson, carefully forged in the crucible of experience, that had provided a win-ning balance of offensive and defensive, solidity and audacity, caution and opportunism. It was an imperfect team, to be sure, but it was superior to anything its opposite in the Army of the Potomac had yet produced, and that disparity mattered, especially in the late spring of 1863. Not only would Lee now be forced to reckon with the organizational challenges inherent in replacing Jackson as wing commander, but he would also have to endure the requisite period of seasoning his titular replacements, Ewell and Hill, would require as new corps commanders. The enemy would not lie idle and would learn from his mistakes. The Western Theater would likely continue to deteriorate, and the ruthless arithmetic of economics would march onward against the Confederacy. Most troubling to Lee, unknowable second- and third-order effects could ensue during the coming months that would, as many Confederates feared, make Jackson's death truly irreparable.

None of those calculations mattered to a little girl in Lexington, Virginia, where Stonewall was laid to rest in the Valley he had so loved and ardently defended. Using a child's humble reasoning laced with a basic understanding of her small world, she offered a heartfelt testimony that contained in its innocent simplicity the essence of what the loss of Stonewall Jackson meant for her country: "[it] was the first time it had dawned on us that God would let us be defeated."[35]

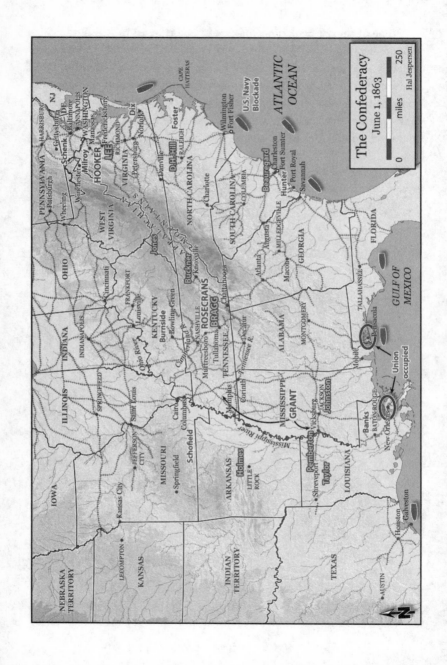

The Confederacy
June 1, 1863

0   miles   250

Hal Jespersen

*"If Jackson had been there
I would have succeeded."*

LEE, PENNSYLVANIA, AND
STRATEGIC CONTINGENCIES

Professor William Allan arrived at President Lee's office on a cold February morning in 1870 expecting to discuss a publication about a recent survey of Virginia's state border. The former general, his careworn face ringed with the same white hair and beard he had developed in the war, courteously greeted him at the door and asked Allan to sit down. Lee threw some coal into the small cast iron stove that heated the room, walked to the window for a moment as if checking the weather, and then sat down himself at his heavy oak desk, strewn with papers. Both men were busy with college duties, and it appeared as if this would be another perfunctory visit dealing with the topic at hand. Dispensing quickly with that, however, Lee changed the subject to the war, as he had done on previous visits, and Allan settled back in his chair. The president rarely wished to converse on his military career, but he had just received a letter from former Union general Fitz John Porter asking specific questions about Second Manassas, and as he began to discuss it the floodgates of memory opened up and he "talked nearly an hour about that and other battles." Something about Allan put Lee at ease, reassuring him it was safe to go back to the war and all its triumph, tragedy, and lost opportunities. Perhaps it was the fact that Allan had published, along with Jed Hotchkiss, a sympathetic history of the Chancellorsville Campaign and authored numerous, heartfelt articles about his experiences in the war. Perhaps it had to do with his status as a veteran officer in Lee's army, or, just possibly, it touched upon his previous service as one of Jackson's staff.[1]

Stonewall Jackson's former chief of ordnance had exchanged his old, gray lieutenant colonel's uniform in 1866 for the robes of an academician at the request of Lee, who had recently answered the call of small, struggling Washington College in Lexington, Virginia. The trustees' plea to the general about educating the young men of the South for the challenging future before them resonated in a way that none of the other job offers had, and feeling compelled by the same sense of duty that helped sustain him through the fall of the Confederacy, Lee became the institution's first postwar president. He realized that if the college were to survive, it was imperative to attract to the faculty scholars who could not only teach effectively in practical subjects, but also command the respect of the students, many of whom were former soldiers. Allan had prewar teaching experience, held an M.A. from the University of Virginia, and possessed sterling bona fides as one of Stonewall's associates. He was a natural choice, and happily accepted the invitation to become a professor of applied mathematics. Over the next three years he and Lee cultivated a cordial collegiality that echoed in its own intellectual manner the different but even stronger friendship Lee had enjoyed with his old corps commander. Allan felt privileged by the opportunities to fellowship with the president.[2]

Lee "spoke feelingly of Gettysburg" this day, admitting the operation had been a risk, but claiming "everything was risky in our war." True, the movement north was "a very bold game, but it was the only *possible* [original emphasis] one." To reinforce Pemberton at Vicksburg or Bragg in Tennessee in the late spring of 1863 would have taken too long to do much good, stripped Lee of his ability to accomplish anything productive in the Eastern Theater, and placed a percentage of the Army of Northern Virginia in the hands of generals who may not have utilized the reinforcements effectively. To remain on the defensive along the Rappahannock was out of the question for logistical and geographical reasons: the area had been picked clean of all forage, the railroads were inadequate to the task of supplying the army, and the position remained vulnerable to a repeat of Hooker's operational flanking maneuver. Lee knew it would therefore be but a matter of time until he was forced back closer to Richmond, and a potential siege that boded ill for the Confederacy's policy objective of independence. A return to the northern Virginia area was equally unsatisfactory: it had also been laid bare by two years of campaigning and the railroads were vulnerable to raids. Strategically, that left a thrust into Pennsylvania as the only viable option, one that both Lee and Jackson had previously believed could bear real fruit. "Mr. Davis did not like the movement northward," but the time to force a decision was then, and it had to be in the East. The Confederate president had been fearful for the safety of Richmond, but Lee knew that "by concealing his movements and managing well, he could get so far North as to threaten Washington before they could check him, and this once done . . . there was no need of further fears about their moving on Rich." Had Davis acted upon the promise to move P.G.T. Beauregard "with a few troops" to north-central Virginia "and threaten Washington in that quarter," Lee believed his chances for victory would have increased, implying the Federals might have detached a portion of the Army of the Potomac to contain Beauregard. That would have reduced the numerical odds against Lee and "produced a great diversion, a great moral effect." Despite this disappointment, Lee told Allan his army succeeded in getting into Pennsylvania "but failed at Gettysburg from a variety of causes," namely, "Stuart fail[ing] to give him information," which "deceived [Lee] into a general battle," and his subordinates' inability to deliver "a simultaneous attack on the enemy's position." Probably referring here to the disjointed nature of the assaults of corps commanders Richard Ewell, James Longstreet, and A. P. Hill on July 2,

Lee may have also been alluding to Hill's and Ewell's decisions to cease pursuit of the retreating Federals on the evening of July 1, resulting in Cemetery Hill's fortification by the enemy. Pausing, and looking out the window again, Lee took a deep breath and added one more reason for his reverse at the small, crossroads town: "If Jackson had been there [I] would have succeeded." A few, concluding remarks about college affairs likely brought the meeting to a close, and Allan rose from his chair, shook hands with the president, and hurried to his office. By the end of the day, the details still fresh in his mind, the professor had written out everything he could remember from that fateful conversation, preserving it for posterity. It was the last substantive historical conversation he had with Lee. Within eight months, the former general would be dead.[3]

Other accounts from personal conversations Lee held in the five years he lived after the war alluded to or directly cited his regret over the absence of Jackson in the Pennsylvania Campaign. With his cousin, Cassius Lee, a beloved friend in whom the general "had the greatest confidence," Lee discussed freely the events of the war over a span of several days in the summer of 1870. "It is believed that General Lee never talked about the war with as little reserve as on this occasion," according to Cassius's son, who witnessed the discussions. "He thought that if Jackson had been at Gettysburg they would have gained a victory," the son recorded, because he "would have held the heights" that Ewell failed to assault at the end of the first day. "A fine officer" overall, Lee stated that Ewell "would never take the responsibility of exceeding his orders, and having been ordered to Gettysburg, he would not go farther and hold the heights beyond the town." Lee had expressed some reticence about elevating Ewell to corps command for this very reason, and supposedly counseled him about taking his own initiative as a given situation dictated, but as one recent historian of the campaign has asserted, it may have been Lee's nearby presence on July 1 that squelched Ewell's burgeoning sense of independence. The bald-headed corps commander, scapegoated along with Stuart and Longstreet by Lee's ardent defenders after the war as the general who lost the battle, probably made a prudent—if not bold—decision to refrain from attacking Cemetery Hill that evening, but the commanding general remembered him as inferior to his former corps commander. Two years earlier, in a private conversation with William Preston Johnston, erstwhile aide to President Davis and chair of the history department at Washington College, Lee had expressed similar disappointment. At the Wilderness in 1864, Lee said, "Ewell showed vacillation that prevented him from getting all out of his troops he might." But "if Jackson had been alive and there, he would have crushed the enemy." To yet another professor in his faculty, William S. White, Lee confided while on a ride through the Rockbridge County countryside, "If I had had Stonewall Jackson with me, so far as man can see, I should have won the battle of Gettysburg." Pondering this last account, Douglas Southall Freeman declared, "it is certain that in the last years at Lexington, as Lee viewed the Gettysburg campaign in some perspective, he concluded that it was the absence of Jackson, not the presence of Ewell or of Longstreet" and their purported blunders, or those of Hill or Stuart, that most hindered Confederate fortunes. "The darkest scene in the great drama of Gettysburg," stated Lee's greatest biographer, "was enacted at Chancellorsville when Jackson fell."[4]

Many officers and soldiers who fought for Lee at Gettysburg agreed. William Seymour of the Louisiana Tigers wrote in his diary, "Here we all felt the loss of Gen. Jackson most sensibly; had he been alive and in command when we charged through the town, I am sure that he would have given his usual orders . . . 'push on the infantry.'" Another Louisiana officer who had marched under Old Jack overheard the men grumbling on the evening of July 1 and noted, "the troops realized there was something wanting somewhere. There was an evident feeling of dissatisfaction among our men [that] we were not doing [it] Stonewall Jackson's way." The stalwart John Casler of the Stonewall Brigade could not have agreed more, exclaiming in his postwar memoir, "I believed at the time, and believe now, and always shall believe, that if we had had Jackson with us at the battle of Gettysburg he would have flanked the enemy off those heights with his corps." More damning was the testimony of J. A. Strikeleather of the 4th North Carolina, who wrote a letter published in the Raleigh *Semi-Weekly Standard* claiming that only five hundred rebels were required to push the Yankees off Cemetery Hill on July 1. "The simplest soldier in the ranks felt it," he confessed, "but timidity in the commander that stepped into the shoes of the fearless Jackson, prompted delay, and all night long the busy axes . . . rang out clearly on the night air, and bespoke the preparation the enemy were making for the morrow." Admittedly, some Confederate commentators wrote their thoughts down years or decades later, and a percentage of them undoubtedly were tainted by Lost Cause motifs, motivated by attempts to exonerate Lee, or exalt the fallen Stonewall. John B. Gordon, who commanded a brigade under Jubal Early in Ewell's Corps, was among the worst of such offenders, his published memoirs speckled with half-truths and exaggerations. "No soldier in a great crisis ever wished more ardently for a deliverer's hand," he recalled of the evening of July 1, "than I wished for one hour of Jackson when I was ordered to halt. Had he been there, his quick eye would have caught at a glance the entire situation, and . . . he would have urged me forward." Henry Kyd Douglas, only portions of whose book memorializing Jackson are trustworthy, supposedly remembered hearing Sandie Pendleton remark under his breath about the same time, "Oh, for the presence and inspiration of Old Jack for just one hour!"[5]

Entangled as many of these recollections were with bitter criticisms of Longstreet's lethargy in launching the assault on the Union left on July 2, Ewell's reticence in finding it "practicable" to attack Cemetery Hill on the 1st, and Stuart's absence leaving the army blind at the outset of the battle, most modern chroniclers (excepting Freeman) have understandably dismissed them as wistful yearnings of defeated Southerners grasping at an explanation—any explanation, short of blaming Lee—for Confederate failure. That has been unfortunate for Lee, Jackson, and Civil War history in general, however. A closer look at the contextual reality of Jackson's absence in the Pennsylvania Campaign reveals that, Lost Cause influences notwithstanding, Lee and his army suffered serious lapses in strategic unity of purpose, operational and tactical command and control, and seasoned judgment at all three levels of war, not only during the battle itself but also while planning the campaign and in the week preceding the battle. These problems were primarily the result of the army-wide reorganization necessitated by Stonewall's death, the *timing* of the movement north shortly thereafter, and the real effects of Jackson's demise on Lee, Longstreet, and Stuart. In many ways, therefore, the great number of statesmen, soldiers, and civilians across the Confederacy who perceived the general's death in May as a strategic contingency point displayed uncanny prescience, although they had no idea what lay in store for their previously triumphant army in Pennsylvania.[6]

As Lee himself observed in postwar conversations, the Gettysburg Campaign *was*, in fact, a turning point in the war, but not because (when paired with the fall of Vicksburg, as it always is) it led inexorably to final Federal victory. Instead, it represented a unique moment in the timestream of the conflict in which a decisive rebel success would have opened strategic branches and sequels that could have only benefitted the Confederacy to the detriment of the Union. Northern civilian morale, so critical to Lincoln's continuance of the war, was waning in the aftermath of Lee's recent victories in Virginia. Peace Democrats in the lower North clamored for an end to the bloodletting and grew both in numbers and political influence. Irish and other immigrant workers chafed mightily under the perception of unfair draft laws, and German-Americans questioned their identity as northerners and Americans in the wake of the post-Chancellorsville wave of nativism. One more Southern victory, this time on northern soil, could have ignited any number of tinder piles and proven unmanageable for the beleaguered and weary Republican administration. Militarily and politically, the capture of the state capital of Harrisburg, one of Lee's operational targets, would have cut important railroads linking the East to the West, underscored symbolically the Union's inability to suppress the rebellion, and made Jackson's dream of burning out eastern Pennsylvania's coal mines within reach. If the Army of Northern Virginia could live off the fat of the Cumberland Valley for several months, the logistical pressure on Southern supply and transportation networks would have been substantially released, not to mention the encouragement given northern newspaper headlines lambasting Lincoln for failing to eject the rebels. And finally, if Lee could cripple the Army of the Potomac at this juncture of the war, before the northern draft laws came into full effect, after thousands of Yankee two-year volunteers had gone home, and while all these other contextual factors existed, anything might be possible. The impending loss of Vicksburg could be compensated, the pressure on

Bragg in Tennessee alleviated, the war elongated interminably, and Republican success in coming state and national elections put at serious risk. In sum, it was all those lost opportunities for the South, opportunities that would never again present themselves simultaneously, that made the days of late June and early July 1863 so pregnant with contingency, and it is in this historical context that we must consider the meaning of Stonewall's recent death on May 10. If Lee and a host of others present at Gettysburg believed, as Freeman insinuated, that Jackson's absence was a critical ingredient for rebel defeat, then it is worth investigating in light of the command relationships, geographical and logistical realities, and military and political imperatives that governed Confederate decision-making in the late spring of 1863. Essentially, from a theater-strategic and operational perspective, we must ask the question: what did the loss of Stonewall Jackson mean *at the time* for Lee, his army, and the military fortunes of the Confederate nation?[7]

From a planning standpoint, Jackson's passing deprived Lee of his primary partner in thinking about the campaign, its suitable objectives, and the theater strategy that would achieve those objectives. As early as 1861, and in multiple communications to Lee even before he marched his Valley Army to Richmond, Jackson had proposed raiding the North with an eye toward both shocking the northern people into accepting Confederate independence and depriving the Union of its means to wage war by destroying the major Pennsylvania coal mines. Lee, then military adviser to the president, had shown some interest, and as we have seen, generally accepted the strategic fitness of these ideas, but politely rebuffed Jackson at various times due to the paucity of Confederate manpower and logistical support and the political necessity of protecting the capital. But Stonewall never gave up on the correctness of his beliefs, and when he became one of Lee's principal lieutenants, and later a personal friend, found himself in a position to advise his chief and discuss freely with him prospects and proposals at all levels of war. An attempt to get into the North had been stillborn at Sharpsburg in September 1862, but both men kept the idea in their heads and had begun to plan what would become the Pennsylvania Campaign in March and April 1863. Unfortunately for the Confederacy, the process was interrupted by Lee's illness, unabated supply problems, the absence of Longstreet's two divisions, and finally Hooker's advance. The Chancellorsville Campaign ensued, after which Stonewall died. It had all happened so quickly, Lee must have thought, and in quiet moments in his tent or on rides along his lines the commanding general's sadness over his loss probably involved some despair about how best to think about the new movement north. It is impossible to know this for certain, as none of Lee's extant letters or those of his subordinates mention it overtly, but who else shared his vision for the coming campaign? Who else could be trusted to discuss it in detail? Davis and the cabinet in Richmond had to be persuaded it was the sagacious strategic choice, and in any event Lee, ever mindful of the line between his military prerogatives and those of his civilian masters, previously shared with them only what he deemed the necessary details. Division commanders, as proficient as some of them were, had not been consulted in operational planning since the Seven Days, when Lee was new to command. He knew it was not their place to be involved in such decisions. Once the major outline of the campaign plan was set, Stuart could be brought into the discussion, and should offer his valuable opinion at that point, but his was not a strategic mind. Who, then, could Lee turn to for sound advice and judgment?

James Longstreet wrote in his memoirs, published over forty years later, that he assumed that role for the commanding general. It was proper that he, as the surviving lieutenant general in Lee's command and a professional who had earned his trust through many hard-fought battles, would serve his chief in this manner. Unlike Jackson, however, who never personally met with a member of the national command authority independent of Lee, Longstreet saw fit to confer privately with Secretary of War Seddon at the famous Spotswood Hotel in Richmond on May 6. En route from Suffolk to Fredericksburg to rejoin Lee, the divisions of Hood and Pickett behind him, the general "called to report" to the Secretary. Who proposed the meeting is unknown, but Longstreet obviously believed it acceptable to speak to policymakers in Richmond *before* first discussing matters with his chief. For several long hours, Lee's remaining principal lieutenant talked national strategy with Seddon,

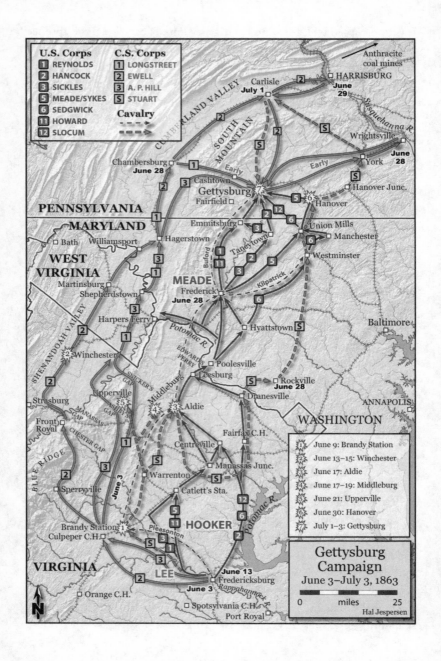

Hal Jespersen

U.S. Corps
1. REYNOLDS
2. HANCOCK
3. SICKLES
5. MEADE/SYKES
6. SEDGWICK
11. HOWARD
12. SLOCUM

C.S. Corps
1. LONGSTREET
2. EWELL
3. A. P. HILL
S. STUART

Cavalry

Anthracite coal mines

HARRISBURG
June 29
Carlisle
July 1
CUMBERLAND VALLEY
SOUTH MOUNTAIN
Susquehanna R.
Wrightsville
York
June 28
Hanover Junc.
Chambersburg
June 28
Cashtown
Gettysburg
Fairfield
Early
Early
Hanover
Union Mills
Manchester
PENNSYLVANIA
MARYLAND
Emmitsburg
Westminster
Bath
Williamsport
Hagerstown
Taneytown
WEST VIRGINIA
Buford
Kilpatrick
Martinsburg
Shepherdstown
MEADE
Frederick
June 28
Harpers Ferry
Potomac R.
Hyattstown
Baltimore
SHENANDOAH VALLEY
Winchester
EDWARDS FERRY
Poolesville
Leesburg
Rockville
June 28
Strasburg
Upperville
SNICKER'S GAP
ASHBY'S GAP
Middleburg
Aldie
Dranesville
ANNAPOLIS
Front Royal
MANASSAS GAP
CHESTER GAP
Fairfax C.H.
WASHINGTON
BLUE RIDGE
Centreville
Sperryville
June 3
Warrenton
Manassas Junc.
June 9: Brandy Station
June 13–15: Winchester
June 17: Aldie
June 17–19: Middleburg
June 21: Upperville
June 30: Hanover
July 1–3: Gettysburg
Brandy Station
Culpeper C.H.
Pleasonton
HOOKER
Potomac R.
LEE
Orange C.H.
June 13
Fredericksburg
June 3
Rappahannock R.
VIRGINIA
Spotsylvania C.H.
Port Royal

Gettysburg Campaign
June 3–July 3, 1863

0   miles   25

waiters coming and going from their private room with trays of food and drinks, quickly dismissed lest they overhear something sensitive. Seddon, a frail man who often had problems making decisions, asked for Longstreet's advice, unsure how he should himself advise the president at this moment in time. He, Davis, and Adjutant General Cooper had been receiving pressure since the early spring from governors, legislators, and generals in the Western Theater clamoring for reinforcements. Depending on the plaintiff, they would go to Pemberton at Vicksburg, Joseph Johnston at Jackson, Mississippi, or Bragg in Tennessee, despite Lee's frequent reassurances that the best elixir for the ailing Confederate state was a new northern offensive in the East. Longstreet, well aware of his commanding general's preferences through letters and telegrams, astonishingly advocated an opposite course, proposing that "the only prospect of relieving Vicksburg that occurred to me was to send General Johnston and his troops about Jackson to reinforce General Bragg's army; at the same time the two divisions of my command, then marching to join General Lee, to the same point; that the commands moving on converging lines could have rapid transit and be thrown in overwhelming numbers on Rosecrans before he could have help, break up his army, and march for Cincinnati and the Ohio River." Longstreet further suggested that, this miraculous feat accomplished, Grant would be forced to abandon his push on Vicksburg, as his "was the only army that could be drawn to meet this move." Their long meeting concluded, Seddon and Longstreet later talked with President Davis that evening, where they jointly argued for a concentration against Rosecrans in Tennessee.[8]

If indeed the corps commander voiced these ideas as he remembered them, it was tantamount to subversion of his chain of command and personally disloyal to Lee. But it was par for the course for the ambitious Longstreet, who had penned Joseph Johnston in October 1862 about leaving Lee and joining him, and who wrote Texas Senator Louis T. Wigfall in February 1863, "I have not consulted Gen Lee but I am quite satisfied that he will not object to my going anywhere where I can have a separate command." Lee almost certainly would have objected, as his correspondence with Richmond during that time reveals. Even though Civil War generals "understood the political nature of their positions," as one leading historian aptly put it, Old Pete was unusually political and had had a taste of independent command at Suffolk, an experience that probably fanned the flames of his ego and emboldened him to speak with Seddon and Davis. Other generals certainly engaged, as Jackson did himself, in direct communications with policymakers, but while on active duty this was done through telegrams and written dispatches, most of which dealt with matters of army administration, such as special requests for supplies, courts martial, or promotions. Jackson's correspondence with Congressman Boteler and Military Affairs Committee Chairman Miles regarding national conscription and northern raids were exceptions, but they displayed strategic thinking that generally paralleled Lee's, and some of them were written well before Stonewall joined the Army of Northern Virginia. Longstreet's flirtation—in person—with national military strategy in the May 6 meetings flouted his commander's known predilections and may have made Lee's task during the upcoming May 14–18 conference in Richmond, in which he laboriously won over Davis, Seddon, and most of the cabinet to his preferred strategic option, more onerous. Stonewall, then struggling for his life at Guiney's Station, would have been appalled at his colleague's behavior.[9]

Longstreet's difficulties as Lee's new primary adviser did not end with his private discussions in Richmond. On May 9 he arrived at Hamilton's Crossing and reestablished his corps headquarters, and two days later began three straight days of cloistered meetings with Lee, where he and the commanding general hammered out what both believed were the major parameters of the upcoming theater strategy. Based on "our close personal and official relations," Old Pete recounted, "I offered the suggestions made to Secretary Seddon," believing that "honor, interest, duty, and humanity called us" to do something about the deteriorating Western Theater. He even boldly asked Lee to incorporate "the aid of his counsels with the War Department," as if Longstreet's own counsel to Seddon was insufficient to assure the adoption of what the corps commander clearly believed to be the superior strategic option. The commanding general, apparently undisturbed by his subordinate's rogue behavior in Richmond, "recognized the suggestion as of good combination, and giving strong assurance of success, but he was averse to having a part of his army so far beyond his reach."

Longstreet's proposal must have carried great weight indeed with Lee, as he "reflected over the matter one or two days, and then fell upon the plan of invading the Northern soil." The tone in the memoirs now turned from self-adulatory to self-exonerative. "His plan or wishes announced," Longstreet claimed "it became useless and improper to offer suggestions leading to a different course. All that I could ask was that the policy of the campaign should be one of defensive tactics; that we should work so as to force the enemy to attack us, in such good position as we might find in his country. . . . To this he readily assented as an important and material adjunct to his general plan."[10]

Longstreet's recollections of the planning meetings in his memoirs have been picked apart by several generations of historians and biographers. Not only do they reveal an aged, embittered man despondent at becoming one of the main scapegoats for Confederate failure at Gettysburg, but also one who likely altered the historical reality to defend his sullied reputation and transfer blame for the defeat to Lee. The memoir account varies substantially from a wartime letter Old Pete sent to his friend and advocate, Louis Wigfall. Riding back to his own headquarters tent after he bade Lee farewell on the last day of their strategy sessions, Longstreet sat down on his camp chair, lit the candle on his traveling desk, and then ignited a cigar from its flame. A sheet of paper and a pen emerged from within a swirl of gray smoke, and the general began to write about what he and his chief had agreed. "There is a fair prospect of forward movement," he advised the senator. "That being the case we can spare nothing from this army to re-enforce in the West. On the contrary we should have use of our own and the balance of our Armies if we could get them." He continued, "If we could cross the Potomac with one hundred & fifty thousand men, I think we could demand Lincoln to declare his purpose." Pausing, he looked up from the paper for a moment and thoughtfully inserted, "When I agreed with the Secy & yourself about sending troops west I was under the impression that we would be obliged to remain on the defensive here. But the prospect of an advance changes the aspect of affairs to us entirely." Admitting that "Gen. Lee sent for me when he recd [sic] the Secy's letter," he defended his new line of reasoning: "I told [Lee] that I thought we could spare the troops unless there was a chance of a forward movement. If we could move of course we should want everything, that we had and all that we could get."[11]

The note to Wigfall demonstrates that Longstreet, in contradiction to his later claims, had come to see the sound logic behind the proposed northern movement. Three days of deliberations with Lee had convinced him, but damage had already been done; Seddon wrote to Lee on May 9 expressing his view, as promulgated by Longstreet earlier on the 6th, that the western concentration option was a better strategy. That letter unfortunately does not survive, but Lee quickly answered it in two dispatches to the secretary of War on May 10, and it may actually have been this missing letter to Lee from the secretary that prompted the three-day-long meeting with Old Pete, as the corps commander insinuated in his own missive to Wigfall. Longstreet needed to be corrected and realigned, Lee probably believed, and simultaneously the political threat from Richmond required immediate attention. The commanding general was direct in his replies to Seddon, declaring bluntly in the first—a telegram—that "the adoption of your proposition is hazardous, and it becomes a question between Virginia and the Mississippi." In a thinly veiled reference to the unreliability of Confederate transportation and generalship in the Western Theater, he added, "The distance and the uncertainty of the employment of the troops are unfavorable. But, if necessary, order Pickett at once." In the second communication, Lee specifically laid out most of the major reasons against shifting forces from his army to the West, reiterating "the uncertainty of [Pickett's Division's] arrival and the uncertainty of its application" caused "doubt" regarding "the policy of sending it." The climate in Mississippi also mitigated against any transfer of troops from Virginia, as they "would be greatly endangered by [it]" even as it "will force the enemy to retire" from his march on Vicksburg. Most importantly, reinforcements were needed in the East, not the West, lest "we may be obliged to withdraw into the defences around Richmond." That nightmare scenario, doubtless presented for argumentative effect since Lee was now contemplating a northern offensive, demonstrated his savvy in navigating the political vicissitudes of the Davis administration. No one wanted a siege of the city. The president wryly endorsed the general's first message, "The answer of General Lee was such as I should have anticipated, and in which I concur." Lee had therefore already won the first round in the impending Richmond conference. Davis, at the least, seemed open to the idea of a second raid beyond the Potomac.[12]

The enduring questions as they relate to the effect of Jackson's death on the Pennsylvania Campaign are whether Longstreet ever truly gave up on his initial strategic preference as voiced to Seddon, and if, as he stated in his memoirs, there had been an agreement between him and Lee to fight a tactically defensive battle in an offensively minded theater strategy. These questions are only significant, however, *because* Stonewall died. Had he survived, neither of those matters would have had much, if any bearing on the campaign. Jackson would have almost certainly retained primacy as Lee's preferred adviser, especially considering the recent consolidation of their friendship, the success of their joint design and Jackson's performance at Chancellorsville, and Longstreet's recalcitrance at Suffolk. Even had Stonewall been obliged to refrain from active duty to recover fully from the amputation, it is inconceivable he would not have frequently consulted and collaborated with Lee as the fair days of May waned into the heat of early June. Old Jack's untimely removal from Lee's side, just prior to the planning for the movement north and simultaneous with Longstreet's return to Fredericksburg, thus opened the door wide for that general's influence, which otherwise would have been present—and made itself felt—in a more muted fashion. Its effects on the campaign, although impossible to gauge in such a hypothetical scenario, should have therefore been reduced. What *is* possible to determine, based on the evidence in the historical record, is that Old Pete made it clear in his postwar memoirs and other publications what he thought about the efficacy of the Pennsylvania raid, and his peremptory discussions with Seddon and Davis in Richmond prior to meeting with Lee portray a subordinate who may have thought he knew better than his commanding general. Charles Marshall, who was in a unique position to observe Lee's interactions with others, believed this to be true: "Whenever Jackson disagreed with a plan of Lee's, he said so; but having stated his objection, he always deferred to Lee's decision and executed his orders with as much zeal and energy as if he had designed the plan himself. Longstreet, on the other hand, when he disagreed with Lee, always maintained that his own plan was best, and to the last moment of action endeavored to get his plan adopted." Certainly, Marshall's comment exhibits elements of Lost Cause–inspired "Longstreet denigration," but his description of Jackson's behavior matches numerous other accounts. Perhaps Old Pete's letter to Wigfall on May 13, 1863, reflected Longstreet's revised thinking directly after conferring with Lee, but he later changed his mind. Whether that change occurred *before* Gettysburg would be interesting to discover, and if it did happen between mid-May and early July 1863, then it would present a scenario in which Lee's chief subordinate disagreed with him about the strategic suitability of the campaign then underway. A situation unthinkable if Jackson had lived, as he and Lee were in strategic accord about the movement north and its potential benefits, this hypothesis, if true, would help explain Longstreet's long-pilloried "sulky" behavior on the second and third days of the battle. It cannot be proven one way or the other, however, mainly because Old Pete's early and later writings contradict each other, and it still leaves the second issue, regarding the supposed unity between Lee and Longstreet on potential battle tactics, as a major consideration. [13]

A topic of much analysis—and not a little hyperbole—by veterans and chroniclers after the guns fell silent, the question was directly addressed by the commanding general in one of Allan's postwar memoranda, in which Lee avowed he never made an agreement to fight only a defensive battle: "The Gen. said he did not believe this was ever said by Longstreet. That the idea was absurd. He had never made any such promise, and had never thought of doing any such thing." Longstreet supposedly spoke candidly with early war historian William Swinton, who proclaimed in his 1866 monograph that Lee had, actually, created an understanding with his corps commanders about inducing the Federals to attack them on ground of the rebels' choosing. Lee may have been referring to this account in his talk with Allan. If Swinton's early postwar assertion is true, it directly supports Longstreet's recollection in his memoirs and contradicts Lee's immediate memory of events. In such a case, it was Lee's word versus Longstreet's. Yet as he was wont to do, Old Pete further muddied the waters on the matter with another statement, an 1873 letter to Lafayette McLaws declaring that his objection to the Pennsylvania operation was "the delay that extensive preparations for a campaign in the enemys [sic] country would entail." Having conferred "almost every day from the 10th of May 63 until the Battle," Longstreet explained he and the commanding general nonetheless concurred on "the ruling idea of the campaign," which was to "exhaust our skill in trying to force the enemy to [attack] in a position of our own choosing. The 1st Corps to receive the attack and fight the battle. The other corps to then fall upon and try to destroy the Union Army of the Potomac." Half of this letter thus confirmed the "defensive tactics agreement" while the other half offered a completely different argument, and makes discerning Old Pete's true thoughts even more difficult. Did he really feel Lee broke a promise when he chose to repeatedly attack at Gettysburg rather than implementing another option (such as flanking the Union army to the south) that sought defensive battle? Lee went on record after the war claiming "he [Lee] did not want to fight, unless he could get a good opportunity to hit [the enemy] in detail," and preferred a campaign of maneuver that would allow him to remain until the Fall, collect ample supplies, relieve suffering Virginia, and create political woe for Lincoln and the Republicans. In his official report of the campaign, however, Lee echoed Longstreet's argument, stating, "It had not been intended to deliver a general battle so far from our base unless attacked," although the circumstances of how the armies came together at Gettysburg meant that "a battle had, therefore, become in a measure unavoidable."[14]

Longstreet's surviving enemies and biased Lee acolytes took the corps commander's accounts of the pre-campaign agreement with Lee as "proof" that Old Pete behaved obdurately in launching his July 2 assault against the Union left flank at Gettysburg and exhibited outright insubordination on July 3, dooming the famous charge that the commanding general ordered him to oversee. They argued that Longstreet was dead set against any offensive tactics and thus balked at following Lee's orders. This, some of them claimed and even more insinuated, was antithetical to Stonewall's creed, and had he survived his wounds and been present, Old Jack, not Old Pete, would have been in charge of the July 2 attack (if the battle had even lasted into a second day), thus "guaranteeing" victory for Lee. Jubal Early and William Nelson Pendleton, both of whom staunchly admired and defended Jackson and Lee, were among the most condemnatory critics,

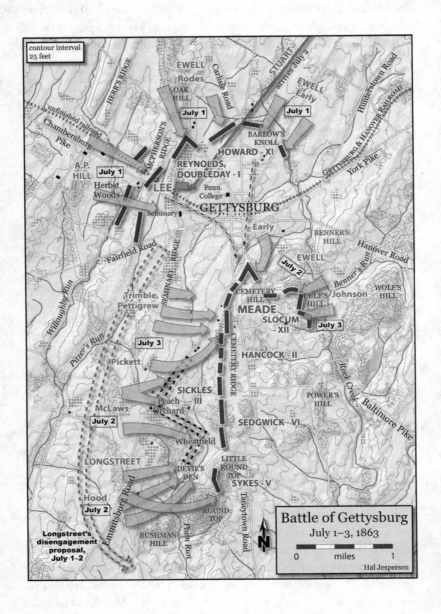

contour interval
25 feet

HERR'S RIDGE

EWELL
Rodes
OAK
HILL

Carlisle Road

STUART
arrives July 2

EWELL
Early

July 1

July 1

BARLOW'S
KNOLL

HOWARD - XI

GETTYSBURG & HANOVER RAILROAD

unfinished railroad

Chambersburg
Pike

McPHERSON'S RIDGE

A.P.
HILL

July 1

REYNOLDS,
DOUBLEDAY - I

Herbst
Woods

LEE

Penn.
College

GETTYSBURG

July 1

Seminary

York Pike

Early

BENNER'S
HILL

Hanover Road

Fairfield Road

EWELL

July 2

Benner's Run

Willoughby Run

SEMINARY RIDGE

Trimble,
Pettigrew

CEMETERY
HILL

CULP'S
HILL

Johnson

WOLF'S
HILL

MEADE
SLOCUM
- XII

July 3

Pitzer's Run

July 3

Pickett

CEMETERY RIDGE

HANCOCK - II

Rock Creek

Baltimore Pike

SICKLES
III

McLaws

Peach
Orchard

POWER'S
HILL

July 2

Wheatfield

SEDGWICK - VI

Emmitsburg Road

LONGSTREET

DEVIL'S
DEN

LITTLE
ROUND
TOP

SYKES - V

Taneytown Road

Hood

July 2

BUSHMAN
HILL

Plum Run

ROUND
TOP

Longstreet's
disengagement
proposal,
July 1–2

N

Battle of Gettysburg
July 1–3, 1863

0   miles   1

Hal Jespersen

but many others followed their lead. To his discredit, Longstreet lowered himself to his accusers' level and fought back with an obstinacy, over several decades, similar to that which they claimed he exhibited in Pennsylvania. It did not help that he became a Republican, advocated Southern submission to Reconstruction, and was publicly known as a friend of President Ulysses S. Grant. But most damaging to Longstreet's reputation was his forthright—perhaps overly skeptical—assessment of Lee's generalship, both at Gettysburg and throughout the war. Starting with some newspaper editorials and continuing with numerous articles and finally his memoirs, Old Pete hammered hard at his old chief. He claimed it was in self-defense against the Lee-Jackson crowd, but the intensity and cynicism of his remarks grew as he aged, alienating more and more former comrades. For his part, Lee told Professor Johnston in a conversation on May 7, 1868, that "Longstreet was often slow," and, like Ewell, underperformed at the Battle of the Wilderness because of that slowness. Was Lee generalizing about his former subordinate's overall reaction time during the war, including thereby the battle of Gettysburg? Perhaps, but regardless of his intent, Lee died long before Longstreet, an unfortunate event for both men. Had he lived longer, Lee might have been more charitable to his former lieutenant and could have urged others to follow his lead. Had Jackson survived his wounding in the Virginia woods and moved north with both Lee and Longstreet in June 1863, it is probable there would have been no prearrangement about tactics, if one ever existed historically; Gettysburg may well have not been the location of a great battle let alone a multi-day fight; and, if grievous Confederate mistakes were committed, the blame may not have fallen so heavily on Old Pete. In sum, the stream of time and events that actually evolved in early July 1863 would have been considerably altered, with leaders besides Longstreet playing key roles in the planning and execution of the campaign. [15]

Jackson's death before the Pennsylvania Campaign opened did not ensure James Longstreet did or did not do anything once the movement north commenced. What it *did* make certain was Lee's reliance on his senior corps commander as both chief adviser and primary operator. Thus it would naturally be to him that Lee would turn to execute the assaults that could win victory at Gettysburg. Ewell and A. P. Hill were new to their level of responsibility, and while Lee unquestionably believed them capable (at least when he appointed them in May) they were not yet trusted subordinates and friends, as Stonewall had been and Longstreet believed himself to be. The two junior corps commanders' actions on July 1 opened the battle favorably for the Confederates, but the enemy was not decisively defeated and it was up to Longstreet to finish the job. With Jackson gone, Lee depended strongly on him, heightening his relative significance in Pennsylvania, and potentially bringing every one of his actions under intense scrutiny. In a curious twist of fate, Stonewall's removal from the stage truly did not guarantee Longstreet would or would not do something, but it most certainly confirmed, in the eyes of thousands, that he was not Jackson.

By the end of the first day at Gettysburg, it was also apparent to many in the Army of Northern Virginia, including Lee himself, that neither Hill nor Ewell had magically transformed into their former corps commander. But there were good reasons why that was the case. Despite the unexpectedly stubborn resistance by John Buford's Union cavalry division in the morning, bloody fighting in the forenoon and casualty rates in some infantry brigades exceeding 30%, it had turned into a good day for Southern arms. The Yankee First and Eleventh Corps were soundly beaten in the early afternoon and driven from their positions west and north of town, retreating in some disarray, but by nightfall the Federals still held the high ground to the south, with reinforcements on the way. Ewell's failure to attack Cemetery Hill or occupy Culp's Hill—Lee's famous "if practicable" order (sent twice) notwithstanding—and Hill's sluggish response to the rapidly developing situation in the late afternoon were questioned almost immediately by certain officers and soldiers on the field, and by the end of the 19th century the two generals had joined Longstreet and Stuart in the garbage can of Lost Cause–inspired lamentation. Most of the disappointment over their performance, Ewell's in particular, was laden with unfair, poorly informed, and prejudicial comparisons with Stonewall's exploits earlier in the war, and few Confederate survivors—and almost as few scholars, at least up to the 1970s—were willing to place the bulk of the blame where it belonged: on Lee himself, for failing to force Ewell into action with a direct order and coordinating his actions with Hill. Had

Jackson only been present in the waning hours of daylight on the first day of the Battle of Gettysburg, the Ewell and Hill blamers averred, the Pennsylvania Campaign could not possibly have ended in Confederate defeat![16]

Careful modern historians of the battle have often laughed at the period and postwar recriminations against Ewell and Hill and rejected them out of hand as the cravings of Confederates and ex-Confederates looking for excuses. Most of them probably were just that. Yet the basic fact that Ewell and Hill both had been elevated to corps command a little over a week before the movement north commenced, *because Jackson died*, is of immense significance in the time-stream of what became the Gettysburg Campaign. Without his death, these two men would not have been in a position to affect the outcome of the battle, and with it the campaign and Confederate national fortunes, in such a profound manner. Certainly, they would have played important roles, but had Stonewall survived and been fit for duty he would have retained leadership of a corps. In that hypothetical reality, the reorganization of the army would have certainly been less drastic than it historically was. Possibly Lee would have kept the two-wing structure that had worked so well in 1862, Ewell and Hill each leading divisions, but he seemed to have realized by the spring of 1863 that that system had become somewhat unwieldy. "I have for the past year felt," he wrote Davis on May 20, "that the corps of this army were too large for one commander." Perhaps the commanding general still would have created a third corps just as he did historically, promoting either Hill or Ewell to lieutenant general. That he would have jumped from two large wings to four smaller corps, an arrangement he adopted in 1864, is less plausible. In his letter to the president he continued, "Nothing prevented my proposing to you to reduce [the corps'] size & increase their number, but my inability to recommend commanders," but "the loss of Jackson from the command of one half of the army seems to me a good opportunity to remedy this evil."[17]

In a few carefully worded lines, Lee then set forth Ewell and Hill as the leading candidates for command of two new corps, successors in name if not yet in deed to the lost Jackson. His words in describing them, although praiseful, were not effusive, indicating the commanding general may have harbored reservations. Lee claimed Ewell was "an honest, brave soldier, who has always done his duty well," while Hill was "the best soldier of his grade with me," the general confessing, "I do not know where to get better men than those I have named." In a letter to Stuart three days later, Lee thanked the cavalryman for his views "as to the successor of the great and good Jackson," and even more poignantly admitted, "Unless God in His mercy will raise us up one, I do not know what we shall do." These were not exactly ringing endorsements of the newly proposed candidates. Comparisons with how Lee earlier described "the great and good" Jackson, who had "indomitable courage and unshaken confidence in God" as well as "invincible determination," or Longstreet, "my old war-horse" who had become "the Staff of my right hand," are valuable and infer a sense of assurance and trust that neither Ewell nor Hill had yet attained in the general's mind. Obviously, Lee did not personally know either man as well as he did Jackson, Longstreet, or Stuart, but he had had opportunity to observe both over the past year, especially Hill, and knew Stonewall's opinion of them as combat leaders. Old Jack's comments about them, good and bad, doubtless joined Lee's own thoughts to uphold their names ahead of Anderson, Hood, or McLaws, but neither Ewell nor Hill had commanded more than a division prior to their advancement, whereas both Stonewall and Longstreet led multiple divisions before their de facto promotion to wing commanders in 1862. This fact was fraught with potential difficulty. While most Second Corps soldiers welcomed Ewell as a logical successor to the fallen Jackson, no one knew the effect the loss of his leg might have on his ability to lead large bodies of men, and the nine months he had been away from the army recuperating necessarily meant he missed opportunities for professional growth that Hill, his new colleague, had not. But Hill's elevation was greeted with more mixed reviews. Perhaps still shocked by Stonewall's recent death, one soldier wrote home, "Genl. Hill who now commands shows none of [the] striking characteristics of a great leader . . . If he can plan and execute I will be very agreeably surprised."[18]

For a brief moment in time, however, just after the two new corps commanders had risen to their new ranks, anxiety for the future was laid aside in the Confederate camps at Hamilton's Crossing. Celebrations were in order, for not only was one of Stonewall's best subordinates coming back to duty, he was returning a recently married man. Perhaps there was also a surge of hope, however tempered, that arrived with Richard Ewell, a belief that he would indeed embody the spirit of Jackson and that, even as the army mourned deeply for Old Jack, the horrific loss could be swept aside into the recesses of men's brains where it would linger but do no further noticeable harm. The one-legged Ewell reminded the old veterans of the Valley Campaign, especially, of halcyon days not so long ago when the war was young and aspirations buoyant; he was a physical emblem of victory over adversity. A Georgia colonel wrote, "the old confidence in Jackson has found a new birth in our faith in Ewell," and the circumspect Hotchkiss, so deeply affected by the death of his former chief, admitted to his wife, "as much of the ardor as could possibly be transferred to any man has been transferred by this Corps to Gen. Ewell." No wonder, then, as he stepped off the train with his new wife, three hearty cheers greeted Ewell's ears from the assembled troops, and by day's end he had established his head-quarters at Belvoir, the home of Thomas Yerby. [19]

The symbolism of the location was likely not lost on Jackson's erst-while staff, whom Ewell kept on as his own. There, behind its painted brick walls, Lee had recuperated from his spring illnesses, and there Jackson spent many happy hours with Mary Anna and Julia before being awakened that fateful April morning and called to his destiny. It was as if Belvoir and the fate of the Confederacy itself were mystically inter-twined. How fitting, therefore, that the mansion played host to one of the grandest balls in the history of the Army of Northern Virginia, thrown by the Yerby family in honor of the newlywed Ewells, in what many recalled as a last hurrah of genteel, old Virginia society. A female guest remembered it as a "handsome reception," where "the elegance of [the] entertainment was hard to associate with war. Plenty of music, beaux galore, luxuriant plants in the conservatory . . . and a delicious repast" enticed all to temporarily forget about recent tragedies and upcoming challenges. Out of thin air, it must have seemed to astonished soldiers and civilians alike, appeared tables groaning with "home-cured hams and home-raised turkeys," oysters, fried chicken, fresh fruit and biscuits, "little roasted pigs," and angel cake. How such a feast was assembled in a time of want no one could say. "Wine, mint-juleps, punch and coffee" whet the whistles of much of the army's high command as well as "the flower of Virginia aristocracy," some attendees "arriving in coaches even from the distant manor-houses of the Tide-water section." The younger guests drained the cup dry from the sparkling occasion, celebrating into the early morning hours and then enjoying a hearty breakfast. As the sun rose on a new day, everyone must have wondered when such lavish hospitality was likely to be repeated. For them, it was like the final burst of a brilliant fireworks display, soon to disappear. Little did "the graceful girls in their tight basques and full skirts curtsying low to the old Generals, gorgeous in gray and gold," realize the difficult strategic situation their country was then facing.[20]

With the great party ended, the hard work of reorganizing from two wings into three corps began. The process was an administrative nightmare, instigating a massive reshuffling and reassignment of units and positions throughout the army. New, less-experienced brigades marched in from North Carolina in exchange for Robert Ransom's veteran division, detached in the winter, and placed in a division under Harry Heth, whose battle record was acceptable but certainly not stellar. Coupled with Hill's own veteran "Light Division" and Richard Anderson's division, taken from Longstreet, A. P. Hill found himself in charge of a cobbled-together corps that had not yet fought in concert. To accommodate the three smaller infantry corps, Lee abolished the army artillery reserve and parceled out its batteries and officers, previously under William Nelson Pendleton, to the corps, which now would boast corps reserve battalions. Although not as momentous as the changes for the infantry, the loss of the army-wide reserve and creation of smaller corps reserves placed artillery units together that had not yet fought as a team and eliminated some old associations that had worked well, especially at Fredericksburg and Chancellorsville. The alterations for the cavalry, at first glance, appeared to be all positive and were independent of the elevation of Hill and Ewell: Stuart received *four* new brigades of horsemen from western Virginia and North Carolina, greatly augmenting the size of the mounted arm and giving Jackson's erstwhile friend the biggest command of his life. But here, too, possible troubles lurked. Two of those brigades, under Albert Jenkins and John Imboden, suffered from noticeable discipline issues and could almost be classified as irregulars. How reliable they would be in the coming campaign was an open question, as was how easily they, and the other two newly added brigades of William "Grumble" Jones and Beverly Robertson, would operate and integrate with the veteran brigades of Fitzhugh Lee, Wade Hampton, and John Chambliss. Stuart and Jones, for instance, did not get along, and Robertson's fighting reputation was checkered. The extra numbers were quite welcome and potentially very helpful in screening the army's northward advance, but they added to the complexity facing both Lee and Stuart, and for the latter, may have offered avenues of thought otherwise closed to him with a smaller command.[21]

These reorganizational changes, although undertaken in the spirit of necessity and constructive growth, were intrinsically understood by Lee and others at the time as potentially hazardous. Sandie Pendleton, representing Jackson's former staff, approached the commanding general about the propriety of submitting resignations to allow Ewell the freedom to select his own staff. Lee would hear none of it. "He disapproved entirely of any change in the staff, as officers have to become acquainted with the duties and with the command, and change almost necessarily produces confusion and injury in the service." If the staff was good enough for Jackson, it was certainly sufficient for the new corps commander, Lee continued, and the Army of Northern Virginia would persevere through this transition just as it had in earlier ones. The army had structurally realigned twice before, after the Seven Days with the removal of generals Lee perceived as subpar, and later in October 1862 with the formal creation of two wings under the new lieutenant generals Longstreet and Jackson. Yet those two prior shifts benefitted from a pool of more readily obtainable veteran leaders who, as subsequent events confirmed, could easily slide into the duties of their higher levels of responsibility. In the late spring of 1863 that supply was dwindling fast and would shortly cause knotty conundrums at the tactical and operational levels. The enemy had also been less adeptly led in 1862, but casualties, reappointments, and dismissals among the inept had allowed room for other, more competent Union leaders, such as George Meade and John Reynolds, to rise in the Army of the Potomac. In each successive campaign, the Federal generals grew more experienced and capable, and they had more men. Aware of the shrinking azimuth between his command team and Hooker's, Lee still felt confident about the level of experience of his divisional generals—excepting Heth, and despite the fact the majority had never led a full division—but further down the army's hierarchy the issue of command inexperience reared its ugly head in a foreboding manner. After the May reorganization over a third of all brigade-level officers were new to their positions, had had little time in combat, or both, and most of them were also concentrated in Hill's and Ewell's corps. Lee fully realized the weakness at this critical level of leadership in his army, but the battle casualties of the past year, D. H. Hill's stubbornness in not returning Ransom's five experienced brigades that had been loaned to his department, and the exigency of moving first, before the enemy, forced Lee to accept the unpleasant reality. He put his concern on record in his letter to Hood of May 21, the same one in which he lamented Stonewall's loss: "I agree with you in believing that our army would be invincible if it could be properly organized and officered," he wrote. The men could perform miracles if "properly led." But the difficulty lay there, he argued. "Proper commanders. Where can they be obtained?"[22]

As Lee surmised, attrition of Confederate strategic means in the form of dead, maimed, or captured general officers was now a chicken coming home to roost. Jefferson Davis sensed the problem, too, writing his brother on May 7. "A *General* [original emphasis] in the full acceptation of the word is a rare product, scarcely more than one can be expected in a generation," he mused. "But in this mighty war in which we are engaged there is need for half a dozen." The president was referring here to leaders of armies, but his statement also reflected the issue as it pertained to lower levels. By the late spring of 1863 the Confederacy was starting to feel the pinch of command quality deterioration. The loss of thousands of veteran enlisted men was alarming by itself, but officers, especially good, battle-hardened generals, were even more precious. Clausewitz notes in *On War* that superior leaders can offset other, obvious handicaps and help compensate for the strengths of the enemy, and to a large degree this had occurred in the Eastern Theater under Lee's direction. But the longer the war lasted, the fewer good generals the South could field vis-à-vis the North's growing number of capable equivalents. Jackson's own death was a case in point. And the war could not be won without victorious battles and campaigns that struck hard at northern political will while maintaining Southern home front support. Tactical and operational events, in other words, needed to build toward decisive strategic ends to justify and mitigate the unavoidable leader-ship attrition (let alone the enlisted casualties). Lee was unfamiliar with formal Clausewitzian theory but clearly understood the basic maxims behind the Prussian's strategic thinking. Chancellorsville had made the Southern people "wild with delight," Lee opined after the smoke cleared, but "I, on the contrary, was more depressed than after Fredericksburg; our loss was severe, and again we had gained not an inch of ground and the enemy could not be pursued." There was now no more time for hollow victories because, among other negative factors such as tepid recruitment, ramshackle transportation and supply networks, and declining territorial control, the Confederacy was running out of proficient generals. What was ironically required, then, to win Southern independence by this point in the conflict was exactly what Lee's army was growing deficient in.[23]

Time as a strategic factor possessed another troublesome aspect for Lee and his army in late May 1863, just as it still does for all armies at war. Not only did the passage of time inevitably cause attrition of officers at all ranks, but it also forced the commanding general to act promptly if he were to capitalize on the hard-won initiative his soldiers had wrested from the Federals at Chancellorsville. This characteristic of time, often referred to as *timing* for when judgments are made within a certain context, was then paramount in Confederate decision-making, from Jefferson Davis's and James Seddon's alarm over Vicksburg all the way down to the adjust-ments in the Virginia army at the brigade and battalion level after the reorganization. The logistical situation, although temporarily improved from the bleak winter months, was also time-dependent and, as he told Professor Allan after the war, weighed heavily in Lee's desire to get into Pennsylvania quickly, where he could easily forage his army. The enemy's timing also mattered and affected Lee's thinking. Hooker, Lincoln, and the northern public had been shocked by the recent defeat but would not remain quiescent for long. Grant continued his relentless quest for Vicksburg and Rosecrans was gearing up for another offensive in Tennessee. In sum, the timing of events now mattered a great deal for Confederate fortunes, and Lee the strategist knew it. He had won the cabinet over to his plan to strike northward, and now must execute it. On Sunday, May 31, he penned a letter to Mary, expressing concern that "Genl Hooker has been very busy the past week and equally active," portending a recrossing of the Rappahannock. Lee thus could not afford the luxury of allowing his army and its leaders time to settle in comfortably to their new configurations and positions.

But for Lee the Christian, all would be well in the end, because a providential God oversaw all things for good. He, Ewell, and "a large attendance" of other officers heard Reverend Lacy, who continued his mission after Jackson's death, preach that same Sunday "on the parable of the feast to which many were invited." (Luke 14) For Lee, the assurance that those who accepted Christ's invitation to the great banquet of heaven need fear nothing in this world was reinforced, and he shared his renewed conviction with Mary. The general prayed "our merciful Father in Heaven may protect and direct us. In that case I fear no odds & no numbers" and "hope we may be able to frustrate the [enemy's] plans in part if not in whole," an allusion to the campaign he was about to commence. Just a few days later, as the first part of his army broke camp at Fredericksburg and began the movement north, Lee wrote his wife again, declaring God "will watch over us, & notwithstanding our weakness & sins will yet give us a name & place among the nations of the earth." In Him Lee still drew great strength and confidence, but now was the time to act. For the commanding general, there was no other choice.[24]

All newly promoted leaders must endure a seasoning stage, a period of learning their new positions and flexing their mental, administrative, and charismatic muscles. It is not an easy period for most, as character flaws and intellectual shortcomings are inevitably exposed, and for all but a few, it is a vulnerable phase in which they undergo an apprenticeship while simultaneously performing the professional duties of a master. Subordinates look to them for wisdom, guidance, and inspiration whereas superiors expect loyalty, fast execution, and competence. Neither group is very tolerant of errors, allowing but a few before quickly passing judgment on the new leader. Time, therefore, is of the essence for the recently promoted, time to find their "sea legs" and learn their new trade, to listen to advice from those above and below, to accept mentorship, cut their teeth on smaller projects or campaigns and learn from them before tackling one at the strategic level with gigantic implications. Viewed through this theoretical lens, the impact of Jackson's demise on the Army of Northern Virginia in Pennsylvania is simple: his two successors, who rose to corps command quickly, and the new divisional and brigade commanders who served beneath them, had precious little time to adapt to their higher levels of responsibility. Hill reported to Lee in his tent at Hamilton's Crossing on May 24, 1863, and learned of his promotion in person. Ewell found out the next day via the Adjutant General's office in Richmond and arrived at Fredericksburg shortly thereafter. The movement north began on June 3. Neither man, and none of their newly shuffled subordinates, had much time at all to acclimatize themselves. Certainly, they were all professionals, nearly all had significant battle experience, and many would rise to the coming occasions that lay in store for them. Ewell, for instance, performed brilliantly at Second Winchester on June 13–15, bagging most of Union General Robert Milroy's much-reviled force and leading some to think he would, actually, be capable of filling Stonewall Jackson's place. Artillerist Major Robert Stiles termed the fight "one of the most perfect pieces of work the Army of Northern Virginia ever did," and another gunner crowed, "it equaled any movement made during the war." Yet there was no guarantee such success would continue, especially against the stronger and more hardened Army of the Potomac, fighting on northern soil. [25]

The flip side of the lack of leavening time for Lee's newly promoted officers was its effect on the commanding general himself. Much has been written about Lee's preferred method of issuing discretionary, intent-based orders to his lieutenants that left them a great deal of flexibility and oversight in achieving his intent. The size of the army and nature of the terrain it marched and fought over necessitated such an approach, Lee believed, and coupled with the inherent skills and qualities of his top generals, it made sense to him. "I plan and work with all my might to bring the troops to the right place at the right time; with that I have done my duty," he explained to a visiting Prussian staff officer. "As soon as I order the troops forward into battle, I lay the fate of my army at the hands of God," and it then is "my Generals' turn to perform their duty." Up through Chancellorsville, this leadership technique worked well for Lee with the triumvirate of Jackson, Longstreet, and Stuart as his immediate subordinates. With some occasional lapses, all three had demonstrated the ability to interpret clearly the commanding general's objectives, accomplish them more or less in a timely manner, and work together toward achieving army-wide goals.

The Second Manassas, Sharpsburg, Fredericksburg, and Chancellorsville Campaigns burnished the reputations both of Lee and his army thanks, in part, to these three generals' understanding, sometimes implicit, of Lee's command style. Jackson had a particular knack for it and flourished in the independence that it frequently mandated. The flamboyant Stuart did so as well, but seemed to require slightly more specific guidance, whereas Longstreet, though well-equipped to comprehend Lee's intent, sometimes allowed personal ambitions to mar his execution. His aptitude for independent command, as we have seen, presented an uneven record.[26]

Stonewall's elimination from Lee's immediate command team broke up its tried and tested synergy, destroyed the closest personal relationship Lee enjoyed within it, and removed the individual best suited to Lee's style of command. Indeed, as the general lamented to his brother, "who can fill his place I do not know." That admission, written under the duress of great grief, contained multiple layers, one of them Lee's realization that the man who most easily followed his orders to achieve stated objectives was gone forever. None other than Jefferson Davis noticed the peculiar professional bond Lee and Jackson shared when he spoke of "their mutual confidence in each other, and their prompt co-operation" in the war, where "they supplemented each other, and together, with any fair opportunity . . . were absolutely invincible." Perhaps exaggerated by twenty years of reflective hindsight, the former president's remarks highlighted a major dilemma facing Lee once he decided to begin the movement north: how to "build" another Jackson-type subordinate in Ewell and Hill within an extremely time-constrained and pressure-filled environment.[27]

The bottom line is that he could not. First, neither of the new corps commanders were similar enough to Jackson in that unique combination of personal and military traits—intrepid determination, religiously inspired conviction and confidence, aggressiveness, and an intuitive ability to understand Lee—that had gifted Stonewall. Part of the onus here might rightly fall on Old Jack, who had had opportunities to counsel and mentor both men under his command at different times, but instead chose not to, engaged in a litigious feud with Hill, and then lost Ewell to a battle wound. All of that was certainly not the fault of his erstwhile division commanders, and only time and experience could develop their own positive leadership qualities for corps command in a manner akin or equal to the dead Jackson's. Unfortunately for Lee and the Confederacy, that time did not exist. Second, overseeing the massive effort involved in shifting the Army of Northern Virginia northward, including the securing of food, fodder, and ammunition for the three corps, while simultaneously balancing communications with Richmond and analyzing the enemy's reactions, occupied Lee's every waking hour from the end of May until July 1. His small staff, efficient as they had become, were almost overwhelmed with work, and for their part, neither Ewell nor Hill had much time, if any, to sit down with Lee and engage in a few quality hours' worth of mentorship. As new corps commanders, in charge of new units and leaders and old ones artificially fused together, they too faced gargantuan administrative tasks. Lee probably did talk with Ewell about his propensity to wait for and expect direct, explicit orders—the kind he had gotten used to under Jackson—and admonished him to think more independently, but the evidence for this is scant. There is no mention anywhere of Lee speaking with Hill about the higher sphere of duties now required, perhaps because the Light Division's commander was more familiar to him and had saved the army at Sharpsburg by his timely arrival. But that is speculation. It is possible all three men simply trusted that, based on Ewell's and Hill's previous records, Lee's generalship, and the army's excellent fighting ability, success in the coming campaign against the repeatedly beaten Union army was highly likely and the new commanders would season soon enough. Lee was a demanding superior, however, and set a very high bar of expectation. Campbell Brown, one of Ewell's staff officers, wrote in 1864, "I have frequently noticed . . . that Gen. Lee's instructions to his Corps Comrs [sic] are of a very comprehensive & general description & frequently admit of several interpretations—in fact will allow them to do almost anything, provided only it be a *success* [original emphasis]. They caution them particularly against failure & very frequently wind up with the injunction to 'attack whenever or wherever it can be done to advantage.'"[28]

In the muted light of the early evening of July 1, 1863, Ewell, standing under a tree in the town square of Gettysburg along with members of his staff and other generals, interpreted Lee's orders to attack Cemetery Hill as giving him the discretion to make his own judgment. Although he may have wished to conduct the assault, he decided it would not be advantageous for his corps to undertake it alone, and, based on the condition of his troops and the intelligence he had at the time, not result in a success. Hill, standing next to Lee on Seminary Ridge around 4:30, may have believed it was not in his discretion to forward Richard Anderson's fresh division to the front, even though Anderson was only two miles distant. If Lee wanted the division ordered up, he would do it himself. And Lee, not yet fully acclimated to his new team and used to a command style honed under the old one, did not step into the breach. For about an hour's worth of time—a commodity so precious in war—the necessity of reorganizing the Army of Northern Virginia, an event caused by Jackson's death, was tested to the maximum. The timing of tactical decisions made now, or their absence, had strategic implications. History recorded the results. [29]

Arguably the most important of those consequences, the ensuing course of the Battle of Gettysburg, was not set in stone, and like any event in history, could have changed through alternate decisions made by either Union or Confederate leaders in the next two days. Hence, the choices of Lee and his subordinates in the early evening of July 1 *did not foreordain* how the campaign would conclude. They did, however, close off options and considerations Lee might have otherwise weighed, as well as those of his new Federal counterpart, George Meade, and caused others to emerge that would have been impossible had the rebels successfully assaulted Cemetery Hill or occupied Culp's Hill. Many of those possibilities, what are termed *branches and sequels* in policy and strategy circles, could have borne positive fruit for the Confederacy while others might have created a chain of events even worse for the Southerners than what historically happened. What is inescapably evident in these theoretical convolutions is the massive void in Lee's command and control system wrought by Jackson's death, the necessary changes shaped by that incident, and the branches and sequels that subsequently occurred as a result of both. From the perspective of last light on July 1, 1863, when Lee surveyed the Union troops fortifying the high ground south of town, Stonewall's loss was, as Freeman insinuated, a strategic contingency point for the Confederacy. An easy one-day victory, with its attendant political and military ramifications, was now out of the question. There would be no destruction of individual Federal corps, one at a time, as they came up from the south and stumbled into a united Army of Northern Virginia. There would be no gallant dash for Harrisburg, or other points east of the Susquehanna, at least not for some time, and wide-scale foraging in the enemy's country would have to cease until "those people" were pushed off their positions. The operational objectives of the campaign and Lee's theater strategy for the summer were now both in jeopardy. More fighting at Gettysburg would be required to determine if they were still feasible and suitable.[30]

Yet the removal of Jackson from Lee's hierarchy probably had already altered the course of the Pennsylvania Campaign well before the commanding general raised his binoculars to observe Cemetery Hill through the final rays of early evening sunshine. Indeed, it may have had an effect on the very location and timing of the battle itself. It is well-known that Lee's intention was to "avoid a general engagement" until his scattered corps and divisions could unite and, hopefully, attack a disunited enemy. Depending on the source consulted, he also desired to conduct a lengthy campaign of maneuver and avoid a major battle until southern Pennsylvania had been stripped clean of all portable supplies, which would have offered the beneficial side effect of heightening political pressure on Abraham Lincoln and depressing Northern civilian morale. All of this, however, was highly dependent on accurate, timely intelligence of the Union army's dispositions, routes of march, and numbers at any given time. No different in its basic essentiality from any of Lee's other campaigns, the role of good intelligence was instrumental to the success of the current operation, especially because it was being conducted in the enemy's country. Jeb Stuart's function as one of Lee's principal lieutenants was therefore as important as ever.[31]

According to Lee, Stuart failed to perform his primary function acceptably in Pennsylvania. Normally reserved about overtly censuring anyone in his official statements, the commanding general unleashed—for him—nothing less than a critical broadside at his cavalry chief in his report of the Gettysburg Campaign, dated January 20, 1864. Taylor wrote the words but Lee approved them. "The movements of the army preceding the battle of Gettysburg," the narrative began, "had been much embarrassed by the absence of the cavalry." When it became known that the

Federals had arrived in Maryland, "orders were sent to the brigades of Robertson and Jones . . . to rejoin the army without delay, and it was expected that General Stuart, with the remainder of his command, would soon arrive." But he did not, thanks to "the exercise of the discretion given him," and "determined to pass around the rear of the Federal Army with three brigades and cross the Potomac between it and Washington, believing that he would be able, by that route, to place himself on our right flank in time to keep us properly advised of the enemy's movements." A recounting of Stuart's ill-timed and circuitous ride around the enemy followed, in which Lee did admit that the Unionists played a role in the belated return of the cavalryman and his three brigades, often "interposing [themselves] between him and our forces." Yet the sting of the initial sentence and the tone of the next two were anything but exculpatory, and made clear Lee's dissatisfaction with Stuart himself and insinuated displeasure with the tardy Robertson and Jones, who did not initially heed the commanding general's order and arrived too late to assist rebel efforts at Gettysburg (Stuart being too far out of communication with them to send them any order). Lee's unhappiness with his subordinate in the campaign must have been significant for him to permit such reproving language, especially considering the cavalry chief's previous excellent service and the absence of such sharp verbiage regarding Longstreet, Ewell, and Hill in the rest of the report. After the war, Lee still harbored hard feelings, despite his known tender sentiments for the fallen cavalier. Allan recorded him stating on April 15, 1868, "He did not know the Federal army was at Gettysburg, *could not believe it*, [original emphasis] as Stuart had been specially ordered to cover his (Lee's) movement & keep him informed of the position of the enemy, & he (Stuart) had sent no word. He found himself engaged with the Federal army, therefore, unexpectedly, and had to fight."[32]

Lee did provide clear, unmistakable orders to Stuart on both June 22 and June 23, the second order carefully clarifying any possible misinterpretations in the first. As a detailed, modern analysis of these orders persuasively argues, it was unquestionable Lee did not intend for Stuart to take his three best brigades (Hampton's, Fitzhugh Lee's, and Chambliss's) and ride to the eastern side of the Union army, skirt Washington to the west, and then come north by a roundabout route that would obviously wear out his men and their mounts and create the possibility he would lose touch with the Confederate infantry corps. On the contrary, both orders gave Stuart the discretion only to choose whether he advanced north from his camps at Salem *through* the scattered Union infantry corps just to the east of the Bull Run Mountains or, if he could not do that "without hindrance," "*withdraw* this side of the [Blue Ridge] mountain tomorrow night, cross at Shepherdstown the next day," and advance on Frederick. There was no latitude given, as some Stuart defenders have claimed, that could be construed as allowing the cavalry to ride so far to the east. Lee did give Stuart a list of missions in these two orders, but he lucidly prioritized them with the statement, "In either case, after crossing the [Potomac] river, you must move on & *feel the right of Ewell's troops*, collecting information, provisions, etc." Whether or not the cavalry chief moved directly north through the Union army's camps or, finding that way blocked—which did happen because Winfield Scott Hancock's Second Corps had begun its march up the very road Stuart needed—had to return to the Valley first, his primary job was to reach Ewell's Corps, then in southern Pennsylvania, and shield it on the right, thus providing superb opportunities for gathering intelligence on the approaching enemy as well as fulfilling the secondary missions of gathering supplies and disrupting Federal communications and transportation networks. Had Stuart opted for either of Lee's suggested routes rather than the massive detour he historically took, it seems plausible he would have entered Pennsylvania much earlier than he actually did, posted himself on the right of Lee's advancing corps, and more or less done his job of screening the rebel army and discovering the whereabouts of the Federals. Lee probably would not have "found himself unexpectedly engaged" at Gettysburg, if indeed the first contact with a major element of the Union army had even occurred there. More possibly, the earlier presence of Stuart and his three brigades in the final days of June would have altered the course of the campaign, making a clash at Gettysburg on July 1, and in the manner it occurred, unlikely. Anything beyond that is gross speculation.[33]

Yet Stuart's belated arrival at Gettysburg on the afternoon of July 2, too late to do more than play a role in the combat on July 3 and later screen the army's retreat, bears further scrutiny. It is possible, although unproveable, that Jackson's death had some indirect effect on the cavalry leader's decision-making and actions that led to his delay. The friendship between Stuart and Jackson and their close professional working relationship, demonstrated as early as Harpers Ferry in 1861 and matured through the campaigns of 1862 and up to Chancellorsville, was valuable to the efficiency and efficacy of the Army of Northern Virginia. The two men greatly respected each other, enjoyed spending time together, and like the friendship between Lee and Jackson, were rooted in a common, evangelical-providential Christianity that cemented the personal and professional bond. But their rapport was different from the one between Stonewall and the commanding general. As lieutenants of the chief, they shared a joint duty (along with Longstreet) to serve him as proficiently as possible, both in their individual spheres of responsibility and as leaders of component parts of the army striving for uniformity of purpose tactically and operationally. Their ability to successfully fulfill these functions simultaneously had much to do with Lee's victories up to the Pennsylvania Campaign and the overall strategic success of the Confederacy's Eastern Theater. The Second Manassas and Chancellorsville Campaigns stand out as the shining examples of this partnership, but in virtually every campaign they participated in, with the exception of the Seven Days, the two subordinates achieved a remarkable symbiosis that was arguably one of the secrets of Lee's generalship. This does not diminish in any way the reputation of his leadership, but in fact demonstrates Lee's uncommon ability to take the measure of his generals and accurately forecast who would succeed in certain billets, who would not, and who would most likely enhance the workability of the command team. After chasing McClellan down the Peninsula, Lee accordingly jettisoned Holmes, Magruder, and Huger, while Longstreet, Jackson, Ewell, the two Hills, and Stuart were not only retained, but ultimately promoted to higher levels of responsibility. Unlike Ewell and A. P. Hill, however, Jackson, Stuart, and Longstreet were given the gift of time to grow into their higher positions and learn how to work together for the greater furtherance of Lee's objectives.

As they did so, Jackson discovered that in order to fulfill the missions Lee assigned him, such as the operational flanking maneuver around Pope or the tactical flank march around Hooker, he required Stuart more and more for real-time, up-to-date intelligence. Such bold actions were not achievable without it, and Lee realized this truism also, assigning Stuart to assist, escort, and screen Jackson not only in these campaigns but in most of the others as well (and not to the exclusion of assisting Longstreet). Jackson's death meant that the Stonewall-Stuart component of Lee's command team was broken, but not Stuart himself, who, Lee correctly believed, could continue his primary role as cavalry chief, performing the same function for the army's three smaller corps and their leaders that he had perfected for Jackson's. Indeed, that may well have still occurred in the last key week of June had not personal issues intruded into the mix. Stuart's surprise and near-defeat at Brandy Station on June 9 by an unnervingly aggressive and revamped Union cavalry force changed everything, and, as many scholars maintain, brought the cavalryman's strong sense of pride and powerful ego into play. Never before had the enemy horsemen caught him napping, and never before had they come so close to outfighting him. The back-and-forth saber charges and melees, some of which occurred just outside Stuart's own headquarters, almost resulted in disaster for the gray troopers. The Richmond press unforgivingly chided him on the close call, and when combined with the Federal cavalry's unrelenting and bellicose probes at Aldie, Upperville, and other hamlets in an attempt to uncover Lee's infantry, may have pushed Stuart over the edge. One author claims the constant screening actions required of Stuart began to wear him out intellectually and physically, impairing his otherwise sound judgment. Whatever the precise reasons, Stuart decided to shift himself and his three best brigades far to the east of Lee's intended routes for him, in an attempt once more to ride the entire way around the Union army and thereby restore what he perceived was a tarnished reputation. This ride, which encompassed many more miles than the previous ones and faced a reinvigorated enemy cavalry, would simply take too long to accomplish, leaving Lee and his infantry, according to Longstreet, "as a man might walk over a strange ground with his eyes shut." Walter Taylor put it even more pointedly, writing the army was like "a man deprived of his eyesight and beset by enemies."[34]

Jackson's death may have also influenced Stuart's behavior. It was a tragic personal loss to the cavalryman, who probably still mourned "the dearest friend I had" as the Pennsylvania Campaign commenced in early

June. If he was as affected as Lee was, the psychological damage was not yet healed by the time Brandy Station delivered yet another blow, and immediately thereafter he was required to begin screening the army's advance by blocking the passes through the Blue Ridge and parrying the enemy's scouting parties. In essence, there was little or no time to adjust to the reality of Stonewall's loss, either professionally or personally. Perhaps Stuart, therefore, underwent his own version of the malady suffered both by his chief and his two new corps commanders: not enough time to adapt to the new situation he now found himself in. Channing Price, his chief of staff, had died at Chancellorsville, depriving him of a steady administrative hand and close confidant. The earlier death in March of the "gallant" John Pelham, Stuart's beloved horse artillerist, had also deeply wounded the cavalryman. He wrote a letter to the young officer's mother not unlike the one he sent to Mary Anna Jackson, declaring "I loved him as a brother," and in an official report termed Pelham's loss "irreparable," later even naming his third child after him. Pelham was one of Stuart's protégés, but Jackson was his closest friend in the army, so if Stuart's reaction to Pelham's loss is any indication, it seems fair to conclude his response to Jackson's passing must have been even more emotional. Because of the scarcity of primary source materials, it is impossible to gauge exactly how much Old Jack's death affected Lee's cavalry chief, but that it did have something to do with Stuart's subsequent behavior in the movement north is a reasonable deduction. Stuart may have been in a heightened emotional state as a result of the sequence of events tracing back to Pelham's loss, Channing's death, the stressful Chancellorsville Campaign, Jackson's wounding and death, and Brandy Station, making it more likely (but certainly not definite) he would make an error or two in judgment.[35]

That possible emotional effect is interesting enough, but more significant for Lee, the fate of his army, and the Confederacy overall was the absence of Jackson as a colleague for Stuart as the actual campaign began. It is conjecture to theorize how a recovered Stonewall, still in command of his wing of the army or a corps, would have interacted with the cavalryman on the march north or with Lee vis-à-vis Stuart's role in the campaign, but again it seems plausible, based on what *is* unequivocally known about the command relationships in Lee's army *before* Old Jack left the scene, that

Stuart would not have engaged in his historical, roundabout ride around the Union army. That scenario, in fact, seems among the least probable sequels emanating from the contingency of Jackson's survival. Even had Stonewall not been well enough to participate himself in the campaign, he would have undoubtedly been involved in its planning, which by itself reduces the likelihood Stuart would have abandoned contact with the main Confederate infantry columns. And had Jackson recovered sufficiently to resume his leadership duties, it defies belief that, based on his previously successful collaborations with Stuart in earlier campaigns, he would have moved into Pennsylvania without Jeb Stuart and his cavalry brigades scouting the way. Lee would have ordered it, Jackson would have expected it, and Stuart would have wanted to do it, Brandy Station or no.[36]

From the cavalry leader to his commanding general, from citizens in Texas to the president in Richmond, the removal of Stonewall Jackson from the rebel war effort was mourned as a personal loss and contextually recognized as a strategic-level calamity. Lee's friend, primary adviser at all levels of war, and operational right arm was gone, handicapping his generalship at a momentously important time in the war. The Lord had called him home, leaving a spiritual legacy in the Army of Northern Virginia but a gaping hole in its command team that quickly and permanently bore ill fruit in the Pennsylvania Campaign. "Oh, for a Jackson!" yearned Walter Taylor in March 1864, as his army faced the prospect of another spring campaign in the very same wilderness that, ten months earlier, had witnessed the zenith of the Lee-Jackson partnership at Chancellorsville. This time, however, Old Jack would not be there, and instead of Joe Hooker the outnumbered Confederates would face the victor of Vicksburg, Ulysses S. Grant. Much had changed, and Taylor felt it intrinsically. "My chief is first rate in his sphere—that of a commanding general," he wrote, but "he must have good lieutenants, men to move quickly, men of nerve such as Jackson. With such to execute and the Genl to plan, we could accomplish anything within the scope of human powers." Unfortunately for Walter Taylor, his chief, and the Southern nation, such men were now a rare commodity.[37]

That conjures up an image of what *did not* happen. It is a warm, sunny day, perhaps June 22, 1863, as a one-armed Stonewall, the light of anticipated victory blazing from his bright blue eyes, rides Little Sorrel near the front of his column. He is leaning forward a bit in his saddle, anxious and impatient. Hotchkiss, his famous map of Pennsylvania handy in a satchel, Sandie Pendleton, Reverend Lacy, and J. P. Smith are with him, admiring from horseback the wondrously lush farmlands. Suddenly, a deep roar from thousands of throats behind them reaches their ears. It is faint at first, but grows to a deafening crescendo, joined now by the nearby pounding of horses' hooves. A turn to the left, and there is the familiar sight of Robert E. Lee in his gray coat and black boots, with Taylor, Venable, and Marshall close behind. Lee reins in Traveller next to Jackson, and the two friends exchange a nod of recognition, a courteous greeting. Lee poses a few questions, and Old Jack points to the front and right, in the direction of Harrisburg. Then both men notice a small cloud of dust on the road ahead. Taylor immediately raises his glass, says there is no danger, and smirks. His plumed hat and beard a bit dusty from his ride toward Chambersburg, Jeb Stuart and his staff pull up in a canter, and begin to report. The way is clear: nothing but Dutch farmers ahead, but Old Jack will impress them in his fine new uniform with gold lace. Lee laughs, Jackson stifles a snort, and off again gallops Stuart, back to his command. Lee turns to his partner and asks where the Mason-Dixon Line is—they must be close. Stonewall asks Hotchkiss for his map, examines it, then looks up into the sky, blinks, and raises his right hand for a moment. He replies, "By the grace of God, we have just crossed it."

APPENDIX

INSIGHTS ON LEADERSHIP DRAWN FROM THE LEE–JACKSON PARTNERSHIP

The death of Stonewall Jackson was a strategic blow to the Confederacy, an inflection point in the war that by itself did not foreordain rebel defeat but certainly made the policy goal of Southern independence more difficult to attain. It prompted a series of second- and third-order effects, such as Lee's reorganization of the Army of Northern Virginia and the operational and tactical decision-making that ensued in the fateful Pennsylvania Campaign. The timing of Jackson's loss was therefore paramount, especially in how it affected Lee personally and his command team's efficacy at a strategic juncture in the war. The South simply could not afford a major failure in the East simultaneous with the fall of Chattanooga and Vicksburg in the West, and the concurrent, long-term attrition of Confederate means in the form of dead and maimed soldiers and officers, escaped slaves, deteriorating transportation networks, and fragile civilian morale. Stonewall's unexpected demise hit the last of these hard, dampening enthusiasm over the victory at Chancellorsville and creating a sense of foreboding about the future that the defeats at Gettysburg and along the Mississippi seemed to confirm. The Confederate nation would survive these body blows and persevere through the bloody spring and summer of 1864, but Walter Taylor spoke for many when he noted that with Jackson's loss the decisive and energetic spirit of the army had noticeably dwindled. Opportunities to achieve rebel independence certainly lingered in the final year of the war, but they rested primarily on the now reduced chances of Lee's army scoring a spectacular battlefield victory—or series of victories—over the powerful Army of the Potomac. Grant, now general-in-chief of all Union forces and personally accompanying the Eastern Federal army, was unlike his predecessors and married an iron persistence with strong strategic and operational acumen. Lee, suffering from worsening health, a weaker command team (Longstreet fell badly wounded at the Wilderness in May 1864 and Stuart died later that month), and the exacerbated and continuing effects of failing means, was unable to deliver such successes that might have damaged Lincoln's chances for reelection in November. With that event, the doom of the Confederacy was all but sealed.

Although the cause for which Lee and Jackson fought failed in the end, their partnership—in all its aspects—offers modern leaders rich food for thought. Those who command, manage, and lead in their organizations, at any level, can benefit from a contextual understanding of the generals' multifaceted relationship, but individuals and executive teams at the strategic level may profit the most from pondering their successful collaboration. "Lessons learned," a phrase popular in certain government bureaucracies and business schools, is not, however, the best way to think about sucking the marrow from the proverbial historical bone in this case. Such a methodology, which by its nature tends to dwell at the tactical and operational levels, would have us chronicle the positive and negative record of the Lee-Jackson command team like a simple list of do's and don'ts, commenting superficially on what worked well and what did not with an eye toward avoiding their mistakes and inculcating positive takeaways immediately applicable to modern problems. It would probably brush too quickly past the complex historical context that served as the backdrop for their partnership and that so strongly influenced how and when they thought and acted. Most significantly, it would also likely devalue or overgeneralize the critical interactions of timing, chance, friction, and contingency, ageless elements of the nature of war that exerted especially profound effects in the course of the Confederate chieftains' joint career, but which could never again be duplicated in their specific combinations.

Instead, we ought to take an approach that is at once contemplative and pragmatic, historically accurate yet useful, one in which prominent figures do not hastily emerge as long-gone, overly heroic or tragically flawed icons but rather as once-living *people*, replete with foibles, personalities, and moments of excellence, who existed in a world that was vividly real to them. To do this for Lee and Jackson we need to think hard about the *distinctive attributes* of their relationship that, within the context of the first half of the Civil War in the East and Confederate strategic imperatives, placed them in an inimitable position to influence the fate of their country and the outcome of the conflict. We should consider what it was, exactly, that made Lee and Jackson the formidable force that almost shattered the Union. What made this duo so special? What were the ingredients to their dual leadership that made the Army of Northern Virginia, for a moment in time, the preeminent army of the war? And why was Jackson's death so debilitating, both to Lee and his army? We have already answered these and other questions in the preceding chapters, but an efficient encapsulation here might consolidate the essence of their collaboration's attributes in an easily accessible manner. Hopefully, future leaders, after reading the book, will turn to this summary with benefit as they scratch their heads about how best to utilize its information. As they do so, they should remember that the Lee-Jackson team was not the only successful one that emerged in the Civil War. The strategic relationships that were instrumental to Northern victory—Grant and Sherman, Grant and Lincoln, and Lincoln and the war governors, to name just a few—parallel in noticeable ways the bond between the two rebel chieftains. Those similarities, however, do not diminish the powerful insights to be gleaned from understanding how Robert E. Lee and Stonewall Jackson worked together. If anything, they underline the strengths of that great partnership, highlight its unique qualities, and accentuate its criticality for the fate of the Confederacy.

- *The delicate but critical team of the strategic adviser and the strategic leader.* As adviser to Jefferson Davis, theater commander, and army commander, Lee wore many strategic-level hats. Although fully capable of conceiving, designing, and executing strategy himself, Lee benefitted from Jackson's strategic and operational counsel from the Seven Days onward and later shared with him a vision for defeating the Army of the Potomac and winning the war. The commanding general could and did turn to his lieutenant whenever necessary to elicit his views; Jackson, in turn, respected the boundary of rank that separated him from Lee and proffered suggestions only when appropriate. Both men felt secure expressing their thoughts openly and candidly, and sometimes vigorously, indicating ideas moved freely in both directions. Such an exchange of views is a hallmark of a strong leader/adviser team. But truly excellent strategic leaders are hard to find, regardless of the historical era, and good strategic advisers are even scarcer. A combination like that enjoyed by Lee and Jackson is therefore rare but nonetheless attainable. At the strategic level, with so much at stake, it is imperative for the leader to have an adviser he respects and trusts implicitly, and who in turn feels free to offer unvarnished opinions without fear of recrimination. Moreover, decisions of great magnitude cannot be made in isolation and ideally should be debated among the leader and several chief advisers, a situation Lee enjoyed for a time with Jackson and Longstreet.

• *The value of friendship within command teams in creating trust to facilitate success.* Professional collegiality and competence are only the first steps in building successful command teams. More is needed to solidify senior leader relationships and create the flexibility necessary to react to an ever-changing environment. It may not always be possible, but if the leader of a given team can form friendships with his chief advisers and immediate subordinates without compromising his authority, as Lee did with Jackson and to a lesser degree with Longstreet and even the junior Stuart, a stronger personal understanding will be introduced that should allow for easier flow of command and control from the senior-most leader. The subordinate members of the team should be able to better execute intent-based or "mission command" style instructions because they have a deeper personal knowledge of the intellectual, emotional, and operational preferences of their principal. Ideally, they should also not require as much direct supervision in the performance of their duties nor should the team leader be apprehensive about whether or not the members understood their orders. Through friendship, a greater sense of professional ease and trust ought to develop that will only strengthen as success follows success. Such an evolutionary pattern characterized the Lee-Jackson relationship.

- *A deeper bond can reinforce senior leader friendships in command teams.* Underpinning leader teams by something more profound than simple friendships might be challenging in the 21st century, an era in which personal privacy and beliefs have become political and legal issues for governments and businesses alike. Yet the strategic-level team that can achieve a deeper bond among its members, whether that be through shared, transformative hardships and triumphs, familial ties, or religious commonalities—such as that enjoyed by Lee, Jackson, Stuart, and their staffs—possesses a gigantic bonus. The quality of communication, understanding, and execution should be enriched, intensifying and improving the friendships among team members and thus deepening the level of empathy and trust among them. This in no way refutes the significance of the previous point, but the example of the Lee-Jackson relationship stands as a reminder that, for example, a shared religious faith could augment leader friendships and thus command-team efficacy. Importantly, however, the personal and professional effects of Jackson's death on Lee and his team were severe and especially debilitating at a sensitive juncture in the war. That deeper connection Lee shared with his chief lieutenant may have therefore caused him (and Stuart) more pain and anguish than they otherwise would have experienced had it not existed. Thus, the damage done to a modern leader team that develops such a strong bond and experiences a similar event (current parallels might also include permanent relocation or retirement of members) could be likewise significant.
- *How to build the winning command team and its likely characteristics.* Lee realized after the Seven Days Campaign that he needed to reorganize his army under leaders who, in his judgment, possessed

the necessary abilities to command large, multidivisional parts of his army. He removed and sent away incompetent general officers who might have stood in the way of Longstreet's and Jackson's elevation and realized the competence of Stuart, creating among these three a triumvirate of gifted, effective subordinates on which he could rely. However, he was disappointed in Jackson's performance on the Peninsula and initially delegated a smaller fraction of the army to him than to Longstreet, waiting to see if Stonewall would improve. At Cedar Mountain and in subsequent campaigns, Jackson justified Lee's confidence and rebuilt his reputation, ultimately surpassing Longstreet in Lee's professional estimation by the time of the Chancellorsville Campaign. Yet in each of his three immediate lieutenants, Lee possessed complementary skill sets. Stuart fulfilled the all-critical role of intelligence gatherer and processor, a senior position required in all organizations. Longstreet evolved into the solid, dependable operator who, with enough guidance and time, could prepare both thunderous offensives and impervious defenses. And Jackson became Lee's "number one," an audacious flanker and attacker who could both fix the enemy and slash him after long marches that other generals could not attempt. One might argue that Longstreet was Lee's hammer and shield while Jackson served as his sword and Stuart his proverbial eyes and ears. Each depended on the others to accomplish their given missions; each understood the others' merits and capabilities. Most importantly, Lee knew he had built a winning team and could depend on its synergy to triumph. But when Jackson died, the team suffered, with no successor seasoned enough to replace him in time. The problem Lee faced with Jackson's death is one too easily duplicated today: the loss of one key member of the command team irrevocably damages not only the commander's ability to succeed, but also the ability of the remaining members to achieve their objectives. The only remedy is to mentor and groom sub-leaders beneath the chief subordinates who have the ability to rise to the occasion and take their places in emergencies, but doing so is no guarantee they will actually accomplish what is expected of them. In the case of Hill and Ewell, Stonewall failed to mentor them and Lee had no time to do it before the fateful Pennsylvania Campaign. Although other factors also influenced the final result, Gettysburg was a defeat with strategic implications.

• *Adjusting the strategic vision or adapting a leadership style to account for risk.* After the failure to trap Pope between the Rappahannock and the Rapidan rivers in August 1862, Lee was forced to adjust his vision for the Virginia Theater and embarked on what became the Second Manassas Campaign. Mauling Pope's army was still the objective, but the operational ways employed to achieve this end had to change, and therefore Lee and his command team considered other options. Jackson was entrusted with the bold flanking maneuver that positioned his wing behind Pope and astride his communications with Washington while Lee and Longstreet deceived the enemy with demonstrations along the river and then closed in for the ostensible kill. Realizing that detailed, specific orders and timelines such as he had issued during the Seven Days would no longer suffice, Lee switched his command method to the famous intent-based style that would serve him well through the ensuing campaigns. The latitude he therefore afforded Jackson allowed his subordinate the freedom of maneuver to take opportunities and risks as he saw fit. Likewise, in the Sharpsburg and Chancellorsville Campaigns, Lee gave Stonewall similar liberties in devising operational and tactical remedies to pressing problems, resulting in two of the Confederacy's most impressive victories: the fall of Harpers Ferry and the flank attack at Chancellorsville. Of course, the flip side of intent-based instructions is that they do offer great freedom to subordinates to make decisions, some of which, if poorly conceived or executed, might result in serious harm to the organization. The "enemy gets a vote" as well, and it certainly benefitted Jackson and Lee that they faced adversaries in Pope, McClellan, and Hooker, who failed to make the right decisions themselves during these risky rebel endeavors. Such may not be the case in modern scenarios and relying on the enemy to do nothing while one moves against him is, frankly, dangerous.

During the Pennsylvania Campaign, moreover, Lee failed to adapt his command style enough to account for the green nature of newly elevated corps commanders Ewell and Hill, both of whom probably required more direct supervision and specific orders. Whether or not the commanding general should have or could have adjusted his strategic vision for the campaign after Jackson's death is highly debatable, but he risked much on the abilities of the two new subalterns at the same time his relationship with Longstreet changed, with Old Pete asserting himself more forcefully.

- *Recognizing a nexus point and clinching the coup d'oeil.* Clausewitz's famous observation about the most gifted military commanders inherently grasping the correct instant within a given campaign or battle to decisively strike the opponent is as true today as it was during the Civil War. These moments and places in time where the tactical, operational, and strategic levels of war converge are precious and must be exploited. At Glendale on the Peninsula and at Clark's Mountain in the summer of 1862, and again at Chancellorsville on May 2 and at Gettysburg on July 1, 1863, Lee saw his opportunity and seized it. Decisive defeat of the enemy eluded him in the first two instances but graced his efforts in the latter two, although strategic-level effects were not ultimately achieved. Jackson was less gifted at identifying nexus points himself and even contributed to Lee's failure to cripple McClellan at Glendale, but was well-equipped as Lee's chief operator to implement his friend's plans. Without competent operators to execute, strategic leaders who comprehend when a nexus point arrives are powerless to take advantage of it.

- *Recognizing a strategic contingency point.* Jackson was gifted with an ability to notice, at different points in his career before and after he joined Lee, fleeting periods when the Confederacy could clench the strategic initiative and possibly win the war. His proposals on a national draft, desire to move northward to Pennsylvania after Cross Keys and Port Republic, plea at Clarks Mountain to move immediately against Pope, and likely influence on Lee's decision-making to undertake both of the northern raids demonstrated an uncanny aptitude to assess the strategic environment, think hard about Confederate national ends, ways, and means, and consider risks versus possible rewards. If some of his ideas, such as those proposed to brother-in-law Rufus Barringer, exhibited some naïveté about available rebel means versus attainable strategic ends, they still indicated a mind at once creative and critical in how it thought about the strategic disproportionalities facing the Confederacy and the need for decisive, even ruthless campaigns to shock the North into accepting Southern independence. Lee also clearly understood the concept of strategic contingency, as exhibited in nearly all his campaign plans from the Seven Days through Gettysburg. In each case, he developed operational strategies and tactics designed to strike the Union Army of the Potomac heavy, if not deadly blows with an eye toward influencing northern political conditions and home front morale. Only by making the war for reunion too costly (in blood and treasure) to wage, he reasoned, could the Federals be brought to the bargaining table. From the moment he took command of the Army of Northern Virginia in June 1862 until Lincoln's reelection in November 1864, Lee embraced a theater strategy of exhaustion and pounced on opportunities, such as those afforded at Second Manassas and Chancellorsville, to capitalize upon mistakes made by his opponent with the hope of achieving political effects through smashing battlefield victories. He truly epitomized Clausewitz's maxim that "war is policy by other means." Lee also recognized the strategic contingency presented by Jackson's death for all that it was worth, joining President Davis, Secretary of War Seddon, and the people of the Confederacy in assessing it a "national calamity." Today, it is just as important for senior leaders to identify strategic-level inflection points, whether they be positive or negative. Failure to recognize and assess them can, at the least, cause stunning opportunities to go unexploited and at the worst set conditions for the ultimate downfall of the organization.

BIBLIOGRAPHIC NOTE
AND ACKNOWLEDGMENTS

The number of published works written since 1865 focusing on the wartime careers of Robert E. Lee and Stonewall Jackson individually would fill most of a moderately sized public library. Very few authors have attempted dual biographies or conducted an analysis of their relationship, however, a fact highlighted in the notes, and none have examined them together as strategic-level leaders working as a team. Readers interested in the various historiographic debates and major works on Lee, Jackson, the Army of Northern Virginia, Confederate strategy, and the Civil War in the East should carefully read through the notes, where I have spilled considerable ink discussing the vagaries of other writers' contributions to the historical literature. A full bibliography of all the secondary works consulted, including those not specifically cited, would amount to dozens of pages and serve little purpose here but use up more space. That said, it is important to mention the most significant archives where primary source materials on the two generals, their staffs, and eyewitness accounts are stored.

Any researcher seriously delving into a study of Lee, Jackson, or the Army of Northern Virginia (ANV) high command necessarily must explore the holdings of the Southern Historical Society at the Wilson Special

Collections Library at the University of North Carolina, Chapel Hill (cited in the notes as UNC); The David M. Rubenstein Rare Book and Manuscript Library at Duke University, Durham (cited as Duke); The Albert and Shirley Small Special Collections Library at the University of Virginia, Charlottesville (UVA); the manuscript and archival records of the Library of Virginia in Richmond (LOV); the records of the Lee family at Washington and Lee University Special Collections and Archives, Lexington (WLU); the Jackson letters preserved at the Virginia Military Institute's Preston Library Archives, also in Lexington (VMI); the Lee and Jackson letters held in the Museum of the Confederacy Collection of the American Civil War Museum, available at the Virginia Historical Society, Richmond (MOC); the extensive and rich archival collections of many of the ANV's prominent figures, also at the Virginia Historical Society (VHS); the Robert L. Dabney letters located in the archives of Union Presbyterian Seminary, Richmond (UPS); the Jedediah Hotchkiss Collection at the Library of Congress, Washington, D.C. (LOC); and the bound volumes of copies of primary sources drawn from around the country at the archives of Fredericksburg-Spotsylvania National Military Park, Fredericksburg (FSNMP). These libraries, archives, and special collections were positively essential for the research required to write this book. It should be noted that some, but not all, of the principal primary source files available at most of these repositories can be accessed in digital format online.

Other locations, perhaps not as obvious as those above, possess collections or copies of original period letters written by or about Lee, Jackson, and prominent ANV figures. The Lee Family Digital Archive, maintained by Stratford Hall, grows by the month and is accessible online. The Manuscripts Collection at the Huntington Library, San Marino, California, contains an extensive number of letters written by Jeb Stuart, Jackson, Joseph E. Johnston, and others. The New York Historical Society in New York City (NYHS) and the associated Gilder Lehrman Institute Collection, housed in the Society's lower level, are troves filled with much more Confederate and ANV primary source material than one might expect, and the Military History Institute at the United States Army Heritage and Education Center in Carlisle, Pennsylvania (USAMHI), holds extensive files of Confederate soldiers' and staff officers' letters and reminiscences, some of which reference Lee and Jackson. All these archives also proved helpful during my research and are heartily recommended to future scholars and writers.

To all the archivists in each of these aforementioned locations, some of whom I never met but who assisted me through their tireless efforts to place materials online, I owe a debt of thanks. Historians cannot research nor write books without these brave souls, who spend their days making the past accessible to the present. Without them, we would never find that key document or rare book containing just the right quote or the necessary evidence to prove a point. John Coski at the Museum of the Confederacy, Tammy Kiter at the New York Historical Society, and Tom Camden at Washington and Lee especially exemplified the spirit and practice of the archivist's art in their prompt and generous replies to my queries.

Other scholars of the American Civil War read the manuscript in its entirety or portions thereof, or graciously answered emails about research methodologies, or obligingly provided their thoughts on aspects of the Lee-Jackson relationship both esoteric and important. Gary Gallagher, Bud Robertson, Bobby Krick, Peter Carmichael, Mark Neely, Aaron Sheehan-Dean, Dick Sommers, Peter Cozzens, and Christopher Stowe, among others, freely gave of their time and wisdom. To each of them I offer a literary bow and a gentle nod of gratitude. My department chair, Mark Duckenfield, and dean of the School of Strategic Landpower, Richard Lacquement, enthusiastically supported my application for a sabbatical in the 2017–18 academic year, during which I wrote the bulk of the book and without which I could not have completed it, and my colleagues at the War College, especially Tami Biddle, Paul Jussel, and Mike Neiberg, superb historians all, listened patiently and obligingly over the better part of a decade as I conceptualized, researched, and then wrote the manuscript. One could not ask for better people to work with.

The team at Pegasus Books made that key part of the publication process—revisions—as painless as possible and exhibited a flexibility and friendly professionalism that are rare in the industry, while my agent, Greg Johnson, displayed a steadfast faith in me, literally and figuratively, that was nothing short of inspirational. Hal Jespersen created outstanding maps and reminded me just how important geography is to good military history. Without these individuals, this book may never have transitioned from manuscript to bound volume.

Finally, friends and family inevitably carry the heaviest burden while historians ply their trade, and to them I must offer my deepest thanks. Michael and Cindy Mayer, Joseph Walker, Ted Sahlin, Ryan McCann, Andy Ulsamer, Scott Reno, Sam Floca, and Holt Merchant all boosted, encouraged, and happily distracted me at the appropriate times over many years. My stalwart research assistant, John Ackerman, who indefatigably supported me during many archival visits, introduced me to useful new technologies, and spent countless hours checking through online sources, became a close friend as we jointly journeyed through Confederate history. My aunt and uncle, Bev and Tom Phillips, and my mother, Patricia, learned far more about Robert E. Lee and Stonewall Jackson than they thought possible and smiled as they did so, while my long-suffering and steadfast wife, Kelley—my sounding board in love, life, and history—kept me sane, alive, and present in the correct century. God bless you all.

—Christian B. Keller, Fall 2018
Carlisle, Pennsylvania

ENDNOTES

INTRODUCTION

1   Robert E. Lee to James A. Seddon, May 10, 1863, reprinted in U.S. War Department, *The War of the Rebellion: A Compilation of the Official Records of the Union and Confederate Armies*, 127 vols., index, and atlas (Washington, D.C.: Government Printing Office, 1880–1901), Series 1, vol. 25, part 1, 791 (hereafter *O.R.*).

2   James I. Robertson, *Stonewall Jackson: The Man, the Soldier, the Legend* (New York: Macmillan, 1997), 750; Rev. B. T. Lacy's Narrative, Jackson-Dabney Papers, Series II, Box 2, Folder 4, Item 210, LOV (duplicate in Charles William Dabney Papers, UNC, hereafter Lacy Narrative).

3   "Address of Gen. R. E. Colston Before the Ladies' Memorial Association, at Wilmington, N.C., May 10, 1870," reprinted in *Southern Historical Society Papers* 21 (1893), 45–46 (hereafter *SHSP*); Henry Kyd Douglas, *I Rode With Stonewall* (1940; reprint St. Simons Island, GA: Mockingbird Books, 1983), 221; Lee to Seddon, May 10, 1863, op. cit.; General Orders No. 61 reprinted in *O.R.*, Series 1, 25, part 2, 793; J. William Jones, *Life and Letters of Robert Edward Lee, Soldier and Man* (1906; reprint Harrisonburg, Va.: Sprinkle Publications, 1986), 242; Lee to George W. Custis Lee, May 11, 1863, reprinted in Clifford Dowdey and Louis H. Manarin, eds., *The Wartime Papers of R. E. Lee* (Boston: Little, Brown and Company, 1961), 484, (hereafter *Wartime Papers*); Davis to Lee, May 11, 1863, *O.R.*, Series 1, vol. 25, pt. 2, 791. The exact time Lee received word of Jackson's death is unknown, but this estimate is based on the distance between Guiney's Station and Hamilton's Crossing, the location of the commanding general's headquarters, and the average speed of a healthy horse at a fast trot on a good road of the period.

4   Stephen J. Gerras, ed., *Strategic Leadership Primer*, 3rd ed. (Carlisle, Penn.: U.S. Army War College, Department of Command, Leadership, and Management, 2010), 1–2, 6.

5   The idea of military contingency or inflection points will be analyzed throughout the book. A good start to understanding military contingency overall may be found in United States Department of Defense, *Joint Publication 5-0: Joint Planning* (June 2017), chapter 3, 3–4. Used interchangeably with "contingency point" is the term "inflection point," which is ably described by Tyrone L. Groh and Richard J. Bailey, Jr., "Fighting More Fires with Less Water: Phase Zero and Modified Operational Design," *Joint Force Quarterly* 77 (2nd Quarter 2015), 107.

6   For military and strategic definitions of a nexus or nexus point, see Stuart Kinross, *Clausewitz and America: Strategic Thought and Practice from Vietnam to Iraq* (New York: Routledge, 2008), 205, and Christian B. Keller and Ethan S. Rafuse, "The Civil War Battlefield Staff Ride in the Twenty-first Century," *Civil War History* 62, No. 2 (June 2016), 203.

7   These definitions of the levels of war as applicable to the Confederate war effort are drawn from the author's thirteen years of experience teaching at the operational and strategic level of professional military education. A basic discussion of them drawn from the Department of Defense may be found in Keller and Rafuse, 203–204.

8   Multiple scholars over the years have debated the strategic suitability of an irregular or guerrilla-centric national military strategy for the Confederacy. The consensus is clearly on the side that such an approach would have failed spectacularly. Notable authors who have evaluated this idea include Michael Fellman, *Inside War: The Guerrilla Conflict in Missouri During the American Civil War* (New York: Oxford University Press, 1989); Robert R. Mackey, *The Uncivil War: Irregular Warfare in the Upper South, 1861–1865* (Norman: University of Oklahoma Press, 2005); Clay Mountcastle, *Punitive War: Confederate Guerrillas and Union Reprisals* (Lawrence: University Press of Kansas, 2009); Daniel E. Sutherland, *A Savage Conflict: The Decisive Role of Guerrillas in the American Civil War* (Chapel Hill: University of North Carolina Press, 2009); Gary W. Gallagher, *The Confederate War: How Will, Nationalism, and Military Strategy Could Not Stave Off Defeat* (Cambridge, Mass.: Harvard University Press, 1997), and William B. Feis, "Jefferson Davis and the 'Guerrilla Option': A Reexamination," in Mark Grimsley and Brooks D. Simpson, eds., *The Collapse of the Confederacy* (Lincoln: University of Nebraska Press, 2002), 104–128.

9   Davis's perimeter defense strategy has been well documented in the secondary literature on Confederate strategy. Authors who have spilled considerable ink on it include Richard E. Beringer, Herman Hattaway, Archer Jones, and William N. Still Jr., *Why the South Lost the Civil War* (Athens: University of Georgia Press, 1986); Thomas Lawrence Connelly and Archer Jones, *The Politics of Command: Factions and Ideas in Confederate Strategy* (Baton Rouge: Louisiana State University Press, 1973); Emory Thomas, *The Confederate Nation, 1861–1865* (New York: HarperCollins, 1981); Gallagher, op. cit.; Joseph L. Harsh, *Confederate Tide Rising: Robert E. Lee and the Making of Southern Strategy* (Kent, Ohio: Kent State University Press, 1998); Steven E. Woodworth, *Davis and Lee at War* (Lawrence: University Press of Kansas, 1995); James M. McPherson, in both *Battle Cry of Freedom: The Civil War Era* (New York: Oxford University Press, 1988) and *Embattled Rebel: Jefferson Davis and the Confederate*

Civil War (New York: Penguin, 2014); and Donald Stoker, *The Grand Design: Strategy and the U.S. Civil War* (New York: Oxford University Press, 2010).

10   Most historians now agree that the Union principally won and the Confederacy lost the war in the Western Theater. See the works listed in the previous note as well as Herman Hattaway and Archer Jones, *How the North Won: A Military History of the Civil War* (Urbana: University of Illinois Press, 1983). Harsh, Gallagher, Stoker, Woodworth, Thomas (in other works), and McPherson also contend that only in the Eastern Theater, thanks to Robert E. Lee's military leadership, did the Confederacy have a fighting chance to secure its independence after the late spring of 1862. Also see Joseph T. Glatthaar, *General Lee's Army: From Victory to Collapse* (New York: The Free Press, 2008), xv, who maintains that "General Lee's army came far closer to winning the war than any other Confederate field command." Ethan Rafuse, in *Robert E. Lee and the Fall of the Confederacy, 1863–1865* (New York: Rowman & Littlefield, 2008), argues that after mid-1863 the prowess of the Union Army had grown to the point that such a possibility was remote.

11   The Lost Cause has been the subject of numerous fine studies over the past forty years. Few historians dispute its existence or deny its influences on source materials. David W. Blight's *Race and Reunion: The Civil War in American Memory* (Cambridge, Mass.: Harvard University Press, 2001) remains the best comprehensive modern treatment. He drew extensively from, among other secondary sources, Gaines M. Foster, *Ghosts of the Confederacy: Defeat, the Lost Cause, and the Emergence of the New South* (New York: Oxford University Press, 1987) and Thomas L. Connelly, *The Marble Man: Robert E. Lee and His Image in American Society* (Baton Rouge: Louisiana State University Press, 1977). Gary W. Gallagher has also spilled considerable ink on the subject. His *Lee and His Generals in War and Memory* (Baton Rouge: Louisiana State University Press, 1998) contained several fine essays on how the Lost Cause influenced popular conceptions of the army commander and his subordinates (including Jackson) over time, and, with Alan T. Nolan, he also edited *The Myth of the Lost Cause and Civil War History* (Bloomington: Indiana University Press, 2000). The subject of southern women's roles in the phenomenon is ably presented by Karen L. Cox, *Dixie's Daughters: The United Daughters of the Confederacy and the Preservation of Confederate Culture* (Gainesville: University Press of Florida, 2003) and Caroline E. Janney, *Burying the Dead but Not the Past: Ladies' Memorial Associations and the Lost Cause* (Chapel Hill: University of North Carolina Press, 2008). A book instrumental to understanding the Lost Cause's influence on the chroniclers of Jackson is Wallace Hettle's *Inventing Stonewall Jackson: A Civil War Hero in History and Memory* (Baton Rouge: Louisiana State University Press, 2011).

ONE

1   Daniel H. Hill, "Lee's Attacks North of the Chickahominy," in Robert U. Johnson and Clarence C. Buel, eds., *Battles and Leaders of the Civil War: Being for the Most Part Contributions by Union and Confederate Officers* (New York: Century Co., 1887),

vol. 2, 347 (hereafter *Battles and Leaders*); Robertson, *Stonewall Jackson*, 461; Robert K. Krick, *Civil War Weather in Virginia* (Tuscaloosa: University of Alabama Press, 2007), 60.

2   Joseph T. Glatthaar, *Partners in Command: The Relationship Between Leaders in the Civil War* (New York: The Free Press, 1994), 8; Paul D. Casdorph, *Lee and Jackson: Confederate Chieftains* (New York: Paragon House, 1992), 8, 73–74, 100.

3   A. Wilson Greene, *Whatever You Resolve to Be: Essays on Stonewall Jackson* (Knoxville: University of Tennessee Press, 2005), 26; Glatthaar, ibid., 8–11. It is not the purpose of this chapter or this book to delve deeply into the political or ideological convictions of Lee and Jackson, subjects that have been well covered by other authors over many generations. Readers interested in more analysis of Lee and these topics should see, among others, Elizabeth Brown Pryor, *Reading the Man: A Portrait of Robert E. Lee Through His Private Letters* (New York: Viking, 2007), especially chapters 16–18; Emory M. Thomas, *Robert E. Lee: A Biography* (New York: W.W. Norton, 1995), chapters 14–15; and Douglas Southall Freeman's magisterial biography, *R. E. Lee: A Biography*, 3 vols. (New York: Charles Scribner's Sons, 1934), vol. 1. For Jackson, see Robertson, op. cit., especially chapter 8; Frank E. Vandiver, *Mighty Stonewall* (New York: McGraw-Hill, 1957), chapter 7; and Hettle, *Inventing Stonewall Jackson: A Civil War Hero in History and Memory*, especially chapters 5 and 7.

4   Vandiver, 161, 185–195; Pryor, 302–303, 319–320; Glatthaar, 11–12, 22–23, 27. Peter Cozzens's *Shenandoah 1862: Stonewall Jackson's Valley Campaign* (Chapel Hill: University of North Carolina Press, 2008), offers a corrective to previous Lost Cause–influenced works and argues that Jackson's record in the campaign was a mixed bag, comprising hard-fought victories in which he threw in his units piecemeal and harsh marches for the men, often ordered without apparent concern for the elements or human physical limitations. His Federal opponents emerge not as complete bunglers but as generals hampered by logistical, political, and intelligence issues. See especially pp. 508–509. William Allan, one of Jackson's erstwhile staff officers and a professor at Washington College, the institution that Lee led as president for five years after the war, wrote careful notes of several conversations he held with Lee in his office. In one of those "memoranda," dated December 17, 1868, and speaking of the Valley Campaign, Lee told him, "All of Jackson's movements were in accordance with letters from [me]." See Gary W. Gallagher, ed., *Lee the Soldier* (Lincoln: University of Nebraska Press, 1996), 15.

5   Hill, "Lee's Attacks North of the Chickahominy," 347; Robertson, *Stonewall Jackson*, 462; Freeman, *R. E. Lee*, vol. 2, 108–109.

6   Inspiration for the interior furnishings of Lee's office drawn from a modern photo in Dabbs House Museum, available at: https://henrico.us/rec/places/dabbs-house/; Hill, ibid.; Carol Reardon, "From 'King of Spades' to 'First Captain of the Confederacy': R. E. Lee's First Six Weeks With the Army of Northern Virginia," in Gary W. Gallagher, ed., *Lee the Soldier*, 309–312; Donald C. Pfanz, *Richard S. Ewell: A Soldier's Life* (Chapel Hill: University of North Carolina Press, 1998), 237; Glatthaar, *Partners in Command*, 8–9.

7   Hill, "Lee Attacks North of the Chickahominy," 347; Pryor, *Reading the Man*, 65, 182–3, 193–4; Hunter H. McGuire, "General Thomas J. Jackson: Reminiscences of the Famous Leader," *SHSP* 19 (1891), 298–318; Robert E. Lee to E.B.D. Julio, January 15, 1869, R. E. Lee Family Collection, Box 2, Museum of the Confederacy (hereafter MOC); G.F.R. Henderson, *Stonewall Jackson and the American Civil War* (New York: Grosset & Dunlap, 1936), 125, 634; Greene, *Whatever You Resolve to Be*, 14, 36.

8   Hettle, *Inventing Stonewall Jackson*, 16; *Richmond Dispatch* May 29, 1862; Archer Jones, "Military Means, Political Ends: Strategy," in Gabor S. Boritt, ed., *Why the Confederacy Lost* (New York: Oxford University Press, 1992), 55–58; Thomas, *Robert E. Lee*, 214, 218. In addition to these military fiascos, the Confederate diplomatic initiative to achieve early foreign recognition of its statehood was foundering. "King Cotton Diplomacy," a diplomatic-economic policy that featured a self-imposed embargo of cotton exports to cajole England and France into officially acknowledging Confederate sovereignty, was a failure. Only the short-lived naval victory of the CSS *Virginia* over portions of the Union fleet anchored at Hampton Roads, Virginia, on March 8 provided Confederates with any substantive good news in the winter-spring of 1862.

9   Freeman, *R. E. Lee*. Vol. 2, 4–7; Charles P. Roland, "The Generalship of Robert E. Lee," in Gallagher, ed., *Lee the Soldier*, 162–163; Steven E. Woodworth, *Davis and Lee at War* (Lawrence: University Press of Kansas, 1995), 59–60, 147–148; Glatthaar, *Partners in Command*, 8. The Jackson quote on following Lee blindfolded is well-known and has been reprinted in many biographies and histories, but one of the earliest references comes from Dr. Hunter H. McGuire, his personal surgeon and later corps medical director, in a speech delivered on July 9, 1897. It is reprinted in McGuire, "An Address by Hunter McGuire, M.D., Medical Director Jackson's Corps, at the Dedication of Jackson Memorial Hall, Virginia Military Institute, and Repeated Before R. E. Lee Camp, No. 1, C.V., Richmond, Va., July 9, 1897" (Richmond: R.E. Lee Camp, No. 1., C.V., 1897), 21.

10   Hill, "Lee's Attacks North of the Chickahominy," 347; Walter H. Taylor, *General Lee: His Campaigns in Virginia, 1861–1865, With Personal Reminiscences* (1906; reprint: Dayton, Ohio: Morningside Bookshop, 1975), 60; Jeffry D. Wert, *General James Longstreet: The Confederacy's Most Controversial Soldier* (New York: Simon and Schuster, 1993), 76–77; 84–85, 107, 134; Allen C. Guelzo, *Gettysburg: The Last Invasion* (New York: Alfred A. Knopf, 2013), 21; Robertson, *Stonewall Jackson*, 463.

11   Hill, ibid., 347–348; A. L. Long, *Memoirs of Robert E. Lee: His Military and Personal History* (New York: J.M. Stoddart & Company, 1886), 170; James Longstreet, *From Manassas to Appomattox* (Philadelphia: J.B. Lippincott Company, 1896), 120–121; Vandiver, *Mighty Stonewall*, 295–296; Harsh, *Confederate Tide Rising: Robert E. Lee and the Making of Southern Strategy*, 88.

12   Lee to Jackson, April 25, April 29, May 1, May 16, and June 8, 1862, and Lee to Davis, June 5, 1862, all reprinted in Clifford Dowdey and Louis H. Manarin, eds., *Wartime Papers*, 156–157, 160–163, 174–175, 183–184, 187; Henderson, *Stonewall*

Jackson, 302–303; Roland, "The Generalship of Robert E. Lee," 163–164; Harsh, ibid., 77–81. Jackson's proposals about raiding Pennsylvania were first publicly revealed by his earliest wartime biographers, John Esten Cooke and Robert Lewis Dabney, but those close to him during the war, including his staff, Jeb Stuart, and Robert E. Lee, were quite aware of his desire to take the war to the enemy, some of them documenting the fact during and after the war in private writings. Henderson and Freeman reiterated what was printed in the earlier works and augmented them with a few quotes from primary sources recently uncovered, and more modern Jackson biographers Vandiver and Robertson mention the general's known offensive tendencies toward the North, but do not emphasize them or develop a meaningful analysis of what they represented. Among the few authors who have seriously contemplated Jackson's dream to attack the North are James A. Kegel, *North with Lee and Jackson: The Lost Story of Gettysburg* (Mechanicsburg, Penn.: Stackpole Books, 1996), especially elements of chapters 5, 9, and 12, and Charles Royster, *The Destructive War: William Tecumseh Sherman, Stonewall Jackson, and the Americans* (New York: Alfred A. Knopf, 1991), 40–41. Kegel's work builds on an idea briefly presented by Royster, namely, that Jackson intended to bring "destruction" into the North as a way to achieve southern independence, but his argumentation is not supported by enough evidence and he fails to meaningfully connect Jackson's proposals to Lee's thinking and decision-making. That evidence and connection, although not unequivocally ironclad, does exist and will be presented in the next several chapters. Bevin Alexander, in *Lost Victories: The Military Genius of Stonewall Jackson* (New York: Henry Holt & Co., 1992), makes a dubious case, also based on very thin evidence, that Jackson's aggressive theater strategy (including proposals to invade Pennsylvania) at the beginning of the war was the real impetus behind Lee's own offensive thinking and that the commanding general, in the end, rejected Jackson's more aggressive advice to the discomfiture of the Confederacy. One of the theses of this book takes an opposite view: Lee and Jackson were actually more unified than opposed in their views regarding offensive campaigns in the North, and that the partnership the two created was a powerful combination of two strategically aligned minds that was never given the opportunity to operate north of the Mason-Dixon Line.

13 Royster, 40–41; John Esten Cooke, *Stonewall Jackson: A Military Biography* (New York: D. Appleton and Company, 1866), 76; G.F.R. Henderson to Hunter H. McGuire, November 2, 1896, Hunter Holmes McGuire file, Mss2M1793a1, Virginia Historical Society (hereafter VHS); G. W. Smith to G.F.R. Henderson, n.d., reprinted in Henderson, 132–133. Cooke published several editions of his famous biography, which must be read with care. The 1863 edition quoted later in this study contains different material from the 1865 and 1866 versions. In the 1866 publication, Cooke describes the parameters of another Pennsylvania raid Jackson had in mind at the outset of the ill-fated Romney Expedition, December 1861–February 1862. Instead of Philadelphia as a principal target it envisioned Pittsburgh and its Federal arsenal (pp. 86–88).

14   Carl von Clausewitz, *On War*, ed. and trans. Michael Howard and Peter Paret (Princeton, N.J.: Princeton University Press, 1989), 89; Christopher Bassford and Edward J. Villacres, "Reclaiming the Clauswitzian Trinity," *Parameters* (Autumn 1995), 9–19; Lenoir Chambers, *Stonewall Jackson*, 2 vols. (New York: William Morrow, 1959), vol. 1: 103, 263–265; Henderson, ibid. For an exhaustive historiographical analysis of whether or not the Confederacy had a generally defensive or offensive-defensive national military strategy, see the series of articles and rejoinders published as a forum in volume 73, no. 2 (4, 2009) in *The Journal of Military History*: Donald Stoker, "There Was No Offensive-Defensive Confederate Strategy," 571–590; Joseph G. Dawson, "Jefferson Davis and the Confederacy's 'Offensive-Defensive' Strategy in the U.S. Civil War," 591–607; Donald Stoker, "Dr. Stoker's Rejoinder: The Case Stands: Davis Did Not Author an Offensive-Defensive Confederate Strategy," 608–610; and Joseph G. Dawson, "Dr. Dawson's Rejoinder: Yes, Virginia, There Was a Confederate Offensive-Defensive Strategy," 611–613. In the end, Stoker, in this series and in his *The Grand Design*, is technically correct that historians have misunderstood the term "offensive-defensive" in its Civil War context because most have conflated the levels of war, whereas Dawson convincingly argues that the national military approach of the Confederacy actually did approximate the "cumbersome term." The debate was reopened just a few volumes later in Stephen Badsey, Donald Stoker, and Joseph G. Dawson, "Confederate Military Strategy in the U.S. Civil War Revisited," *Journal of Military History* 73, no. 4 (10, 2009): 1273–1287. This book accepts the premise that the Confederate national command authority in Richmond generally approached the national war effort from a militarily defensive standpoint, but frequently advocated for and supported field commanders' theater and operational offensives when practicable.

15   A. R. Boteler, "Stonewall Jackson in Campaign of 1862," *SHSP* 40 (September 1915), 164–166, 172; Lee to Jackson, telegraphic dispatch May 28,1862, item# ViHMss3L515a, VHS; Davis to Jackson, June 4, 1862, in *O.R.*, Series 1, vol. 12, part 3, 905 (all references are to Series 1 unless otherwise noted); Lee to Davis, June 5, 1862, op. cit.; Lee to Randolph, June 5, 1862, *O.R.*, vol. 11, part 3, 575; Woodworth, *Lee and Davis at War*, 156–158. Boteler died in 1892, long before this article on Jackson in the Valley Campaign was published. When he actually wrote it is unknown.

16   Lee to Jackson, June 8, 1862, reprinted in Dowdey and Manarin, *Wartime Papers*, 187; "Narrative of A. R. Boteler," (notes taken by Robert L. Dabney in preparation for writing his wartime biography of Jackson), Jackson-Dabney Papers, Series II, Box, 2, Folder 3, Library of Virginia (hereafter LOV); Boteler, ibid., 172–175; Allan "Memoranda," December 17, 1868, reprinted in Gallagher, ed., *Lee the Soldier*, 15; Jackson to Lee, June 13, 1862 and Lee to Jackson June 16, *Wartime Papers*, 193–194. In the midst of all this, Lee received word of the death of his grandson in early June. His response, reflecting both earthly sadness and evangelical joy, was emblematic of his religious beliefs. He wrote his wife, "I cannot help grieving at his loss. . . . But when I reflect upon his great gain by his merciful transition from earth to Heaven, I

think we ought to rejoice. God grant that we may all join him around the throne of our Maker to unite in praise and adoration of the Most High forever." Lee to Mary Lee, June 10, 1862, *Wartime Papers*, 189.

17　Jackson to William Porcher Miles, December 28, 1861 and March 15, 1862, William Porcher Miles Papers, Box 4, Folder 47, Southern Historical Collection, Wilson Library, University of North Carolina (hereafter UNC); *Journal of the Congress of the Confederate States of America, 1861–1865* (Washington, D.C.: Government Printing Office, 1905), vol. 5, 67; Jackson to Boteler, March 3, 1862, AMHC, New York Historical Society (hereafter NYHS); "Proceedings of the Committee on Military Affairs of the House of Representatives of the Permanent Congress, February 26, 1862–February 26, 1865," bound volume, AHMC, NYHS, especially minutes for 13, 14, 21, 24, 27 March 1862.

18　Longstreet, *From Manassas to Appomattox*, 121–122; Hill, "Lee's Attacks," 347–348; Douglas Southall Freeman, *Lee's Lieutenants: A Study in Command*, 3 vols. (New York: Charles Scribner's Sons, 1942), vol. 1, 496–498; Wert, *General James Longstreet*, 134; Robertson, *Stonewall Jackson*, 464–466. There is still conjecture whether Jackson answered Longstreet's query with the 25th or the 26th of June. Hill, an in-law by marriage to Jackson, wrote in his account it was the 26th, whereas Longstreet, who came to feel some rivalry with Jackson later, claimed it was the 25th, Stonewall only agreeing to the following day after Longstreet queried him further. I have chosen to accept Longstreet's version, and added the likelihood that the question about the date was discussed with Lee when he returned to the office, which is supported by a conversation William Allan held with Lee after the war on December 17, 1868. Allan notes, "Jackson appointed a certain day to be up, and then Lee was to meet him with the mass of the army before Richmond. Lee told Jackson that he had not given himself time enough, and *insisted* [original emphasis] that he should be allowed 24 hours more." See "Memoranda of Conversations with General Robert E. Lee," reprinted in Gallagher, ed., *Lee the Soldier*, 15.

19　Krick, *Civil War Weather in Virginia*, 60; Hunter McGuire to Jedediah Hotchkiss, March 30, 1896, Jedediah Hotchkiss Papers, "Warbook" files, Library of Congress (hereafter LOC); Freeman, ibid., 498; Robert K. Krick, "Sleepless in the Saddle: Stonewall Jackson in the Seven Days," in Gary W. Gallagher, ed., *The Richmond Campaign of 1862: The Peninsula and the Seven Days* (Chapel Hill: University of North Carolina Press, 2000), 69; Vandiver, *Mighty Stonewall*, 299.

20　McGuire to Hotchkiss, ibid.; Vandiver, 300–301; Freeman, *Lee's Lieutenants*, vol. 1, 502–503; Greene, *Whatever You Resolve to Be*, 42–44; Robertson, *Stonewall Jackson*, 468–470; Stephen Sears, *To the Gates of Richmond: The Peninsula Campaign* (New York, Houghton Mifflin Company, 1992), 197.

21　Mary Anna Jackson, *Memoirs of Stonewall Jackson* (Louisville, Kent.: Prentice Press, 1895), 291–292; Krick, "Sleepless in the Saddle," 71; Robert L. Dabney, *Life and Campaigns of Lieut.-Gen. Thomas J. Jackson* (1865; reprint, New York: Blelock & Co, 1866), 440; Pfanz, *Richard S. Ewell*, 267. Carl von Clausewitz, *On War* (Book 1, chapter 5), available at https://www.clausewitz.com/readings

/OnWar1873/BK1ch05.html#a. According to Clausewitz, "friction" is defined as the "only concept that more or less corresponds to the factors that distinguish real war from war on paper." Physical danger and exhaustion, mental strain, errors in decision-making, unclear, incomplete, or purposefully misconstrued information ("fog"), and unexpected enemy actions all constitute friction. See Book 1, chapter 7, available at https://www.clausewitz.com/readings/OnWar1873/BK1ch07.html. Interestingly, the Prussian argues that "Perseverance in the chosen course is the essential counter-weight. . . . only great strength of will can lead to the objective. It is steadfastness that will earn the admiration of the world and of posterity." How well this definition of leadership applies to both Lee and Jackson is obvious and requires no further elaboration. Krick is a major proponent of the "Jackson exhaustion thesis" as a primary reason Lee's plans for June 26 and subsequent days went awry, but adds that poor staff work (or nonexistent staff, for that matter), subpar communication between Lee and Jackson and other generals, and the overall inexperience of the army's new command team also played roles. This is at odds with Stephen Sears, who argues that "Stonewall Jackson's puzzling behavior on June 26 suggests that he did not really understand what Lee expected him to accomplish that day. He seemed unaware that time was the critical factor in the plan," or that his army's movements were the key to entire plan (pp. 197–199). That Jackson failed to comprehend Lee's intent or his own tardiness appears, based on the evidence available, indefensible. Another modern scholar of the campaign, Joseph P. Cullen, believes that Jackson's and other generals' (including Lee's) mistakes were to be expected because the Seven Days Campaign was "a shake-down cruise" in which the army's leadership had to find its footing and learn to fight together. On a basic level, that contention makes sense, but it implies that the command team was more or less perfected by mid-July, which is untrue. See Cullen, *The Peninsula Campaign, 1862* (Harrisburg, Penn.: Stackpole Books, 1973), especially 165–169. As in most military blunders, one or two easy, crisp explanations are never sufficient; rather, multiple reasons tend to converge to paint a complex picture of event causation.

22 Krick, 74–75; Sears, *To the Gates of Richmond*, 197–200; Dabney, 441; Vandiver, *Mighty Stonewall*, 301; Robertson, *Stonewall Jackson*, 472–473; Jeffry D. Wert, *Cavalryman of the Lost Cause: A Biography of J.E.B. Stuart* (New York: Simon and Schuster, 2008), 48–49. Wallace Hettle offers a convincing critique of Dabney's trustworthiness as a source on Jackson in chapter 2 of *Inventing Stonewall Jackson*. "Dabney's brief and frustrating tenure as Jackson's chief of staff seems to have transformed him intellectually, as the once-ambivalent Confederate devoted himself to vindicating the cause and character of the general he so admired." (p. 38). Yet, Hettle continues, "subsequent military historians, including the recent Jackson biographers James I. Robertson Jr. and Charles Royster, have viewed Dabney as a sometimes unreliable but still indispensable source." (p. 40). This assessment hits the mark, as Dabney's work was far and away the most comprehensive wartime biography and contains details on Jackson only close proximity and familiarity with the general could have generated. Some are definitely "indispensable," as Hettle notes, but others

must be circumspectly evaluated in light of Dabney's agenda. His postwar writings were strongly influenced by other Lost Cause motifs and must likewise be used with caution. I have used Dabney sparingly, and only when the probability of historical truth was, in my judgment, high.

23   Allan, "Memoranda," December 17, 1868, reprinted in Gallagher, *Lee the Soldier*, 16; James I. Robertson, *General A. P. Hill: The Story of a Confederate Warrior* (New York: Random House, 1987), 69–71; Emory Thomas, *Robert E. Lee*, 236–237; Freeman, *R. E. Lee*, vol. 2, 133–135; Gary W. Gallagher, ed., *Fighting for the Confederacy: The Personal Recollections of General Edward Porter Alexander* (Chapel Hill: University of North Carolina Press, 1989), 100; Walter Clark, ed., *Histories of the Several Regiments and Battalions From North Carolina in the Great War, 1861–'65*, 5 vols. (Raleigh, N.C.: E.M. Uzzell, 1901), vol. 1, 756.

24   Sears, *To the Gates*, 210–212; Robertson, *Stonewall Jackson*, 474–476; Freeman, ibid., 138.

25   Hunter McGuire to Jedediah Hotchkiss, June 15, 1896, Hotchkiss Papers, "War Book," LOC; Freeman, 141; Krick, "Sleepless in the Saddle," 75; Greene, *Whatever You Resolve to Be*, 49–50.

26   Sears, *To the Gates*, 213–214; Dabney, *Life and Campaigns*, 443–445; Krick, 76–77; Hotchkiss to S.J.C. Moore, June 6, 1896, Hotchkiss Papers, "War Book," LOC; Allan "Memoranda," December 17, 1869, op. cit.; Charles S. Venable, "Personal Reminiscences of the Confederate War," handwritten manuscript, p. 43, UVA; Lee quoted in Reardon, "'From King of Spades' to 'First Captain,'" 321.

27   Greene, *Whatever You Resolve to Be*, 62–66; William Allan, *The Army of Northern Virginia in 1862* (1892; reprint: New York: Da Capo Press, 1995), 106–108, 120–121; Jackson to Mary Anna Jackson, July 7, 1862, partially reprinted in Mary Anna Jackson, *Life and Letters of General Thomas J. Jackson (Stonewall Jackson)* (New York: Harper and Brothers, 1892), 302; McGuire, "General Thomas J. Jackson," 305–306; Krick, 80–82; G. Moxley Sorrel, *Recollections of a Confederate Staff Officer* (1905; reprint: Dayton, Ohio: Morningside Bookshop, 1978), 81; Gallagher, ed., *Fighting for the Confederacy*, 108–109.

28   *O.R.*, vol. 11, part 2, 495; Jackson quoted in Henderson, *Stonewall Jackson*, 382; Robertson, 497; Greene, 62; Freeman, *R. E. Lee*, 235–236; Jim Stempel, *The Battle of Glendale: The Day the South Nearly Won the Civil War* (Jefferson, N.C.: McFarland, 2011), 155. Another recent, fine work on Glendale that agrees with Stempel on the overall thesis that Lee could have nearly destroyed the Army of the Potomac with better coordination and communication among his subordinates is Douglas Crenshaw, *The Battle of Glendale: Robert E. Lee's Lost Opportunity* (Charleston, S.C.: The History Press, 2017).

29   Frederick Maurice, ed., *An Aide-de-Camp of Lee: Being the Papers of Colonel Charles Marshall, Sometime Aide-de-Camp, Military Secretary, and Assistant Adjutant General on the Staff of Robert E. Lee, 1862–1865* (Boston: Little, Brown and Co., 1927), 109. Marshall, quoted here by Maurice, states, "But for Jackson's delay at White Oak Swamp, General Lee would have this day inflicted on General McClellan the signal

defeat at which his plans aimed." Marshall was in a good position at Glendale and throughout the campaign to observe Lee's undertakings. What he calls a "signal defeat" can be viewed as equivalent to a decisive, strategic-level victory. Although the term "contingency point" has been already defined in the introduction, "inflection point," which is an interchangeable expression in this book, may be defined as "a moment in time when the normal progression of a particular phenomenon significantly changes," a "period of such intense change that the actor experiencing the change has not had time to adjust to it." See Tyrone L. Groh and Richard J. Bailey Jr., "Fighting More Fires with Less Water: Phase Zero and Modified Operational Design," 107. Different authors offer different explanations of these terms, and not all contingency/inflection points need witness the converging of the three levels of war, although that is often the case in military operations and seemed especially true in the Civil War. Contingency points in a war can also theoretically occur when a policymaker or a diplomat makes a key decision that alters the course of the conflict, such as Lincoln's issuance of the Emancipation Proclamation after the Battle of Antietam, or when he ordered Secretary of State William Seward to back down following the Trent Affair in early 1862, which had strongly inflamed tensions with the British Empire and threatened war with England.

30 McGuire to Jedediah Hotchkiss, May 28, 1896, Papers of Jedediah Hotchkiss, Mss2822, Box 1, "Correspondence—Dr. Hunter McGuire, Small Special Collections Library, University of Virginia (hereafter UVA); R. L. Dabney to Jedediah Hotchkiss, month and day missing, 1896, in Hotchkiss Papers, "War Book," LOC; McGuire, "General Thomas J. Jackson," 303–305; Woodworth, *Lee and Davis at War*, 87–90, 171–172. McGuire's and Dabney's recollections of the actual words of the conversations are remarkably similar.

31 R. L. Dabney to Jedediah Hotchkiss, ibid.; McGuire, "General Thomas J. Jackson," ibid.; Woodworth, 172. Other authors, including Dabney himself in his early biography, Henderson, Freeman, and Robertson, have all referenced the Poindexter meeting and all of them reconstruct it from Dabney's and McGuire's accounts, claiming in various degrees of forcefulness that Jackson's aggressive pursuit idea was a missed opportunity. The general, temporarily recovered from his sleepless stupor of the past days, appreciated the war-winning possibility that existed in theory in the fleeting hours after Malvern Hill, but was probably unaware of the realities besetting Lee's army that prevented such an action. If Dabney's and McGuire's accounts are to be believed, it is possible Jackson was willing to risk poor local intelligence and forge ahead regardless, much as he had after the Battle of Winchester. But the contextual differences between the Valley in late May and the Peninsula in early July were severe, and Jackson was not in sole command of the Confederate forces in question.

32 "Narrative of A. R. Boteler," op. cit.; A. R. Boteler, "Stonewall Jackson in Campaign of 1862," 180–181; Robertson, *Stonewall Jackson*, 508–509. Boteler's postwar account of this meeting is partially corroborated by a wartime interview conducted by Dabney in preparation for his biography. In 1864 there was little reason for Boteler to

prevaricate, and most Jackson scholars have accepted Boteler's more comprehensive postwar source as reasonably accurate.

33 Sears, *To the Gates of Richmond*, 349; *Southern Literary Messenger* 34, no. 8 (August 1862), 504; Richmond *Dispatch* July 12 and 14, 1862; Krick, 85–86; Freeman, *Lee's Lieutenants*, vol. 1, 656–657. Writing after the war in 1905, Walter Taylor, probably the best-functioning of Lee's staff officers during this campaign and one who delivered messages to Jackson several times during the Seven Days, wrote to a friend, "Jackson's wonderful achievements elsewhere is the reason that so little is said of his failure in the seven days battle." (Taylor to William Henry Palmer, July 24, 1905, Manuscript Collection, M2009.486, Jessie Ball duPont Memorial Library, Stratford Hall, Va.). Freeman writes that Brigadier Robert Toombs, who commanded a brigade in Magruder's Division, unleashed venom at virtually all higher-ranking officers, including Jackson. "Stonewall Jackson and his troops did little or nothing in these battles of the Chickahominy," he wrote in a contemporary letter, "and Lee was far below the occasion." Longstreet may have also whispered loudly in his headquarters what he later wrote in an essay in *Battles and Leaders of the Civil War*: "Jackson was a very skillful man against such men as Shields, Banks, and Frémont, but when pitted against the best of the Federal commanders he did not appear so well." See Freeman, ibid., 628, 657.

34 Freeman, *R. E. Lee*, vol. 2, 232–243; Harsh, *Confederate Tide Rising*, 90–97; Glatthaar, *General Lee's Army*, 145–147; Sears, 343–345; Gary W. Gallagher, "The 1862 Richmond Campaign in Perspective," in Gallagher, ed., *The Richmond Campaign of 1862*, 20–22; Reardon, "From 'King of Spades' to 'First Captain of the Confederacy,'" 314–324; *O.R.*, 1, vol. 12, part 3, 915. Harsh makes the excellent point that even after the Seven Days, McClellan still posed a deadly risk to Richmond, and was geographically in a stronger position with his base on the James and with complete support of the Union Navy. Thus, he claims, Lee did not "share in the euphoria that swept Richmond after the retreat of McClellan's army. . . . Lee and the Confederacy had simply emerged into a lighter shade of darkness." (p. 99) The question troubling Lee was whether the Union commanding general perceived he was defeated and would retreat even as Pope and his army moved south, and until that unknown was clarified, the Confederacy had to hedge its bets and split its outnumbered forces defending Richmond. In that light, moving Jackson and two divisions northward was a wise precaution and prevented an early overcommitment.

35 *O.R.*, vol. 11, part 2, 497; Lee to Mary Lee, July 9, 1862, and General Orders No. 75, July 7, 1862, reprinted in Dowdey and Manarin, *Wartime Papers*, 229–230 and 210–211; R. David Cox, *The Religious Life of Robert E. Lee* (Grand Rapids, Mich.: William B. Eerdmans Publishing Company, 2017), 132–133; David Winn, 4th Georgia, quoted in Sears, *To the Gates of Richmond*, 344; Freeman, *Lee's Lieutenants*, 658; Gary W. Gallagher, ed., *Fighting for the Confederacy: The Personal Recollections of General Edward Porter Alexander* (Chapel Hill: University of North Carolina Press, 1989), 96; Baron de Jomini, *Summary of the Art of War, or a New Analytical Compend of the Principal Combinations of Strategy, of Grand Tactics and of Military Policy*, O. F. Winship and E. E. McLean, eds. and trans. (New York: Putnam, 1854), 201.

TWO

1   Jedediah Hotchkiss journal entry, August 17, 1862, reprinted in Archie P. McDonald, ed., *Make Me a Map of the Valley: The Civil War Journal of Stonewall Jackson's Topographer, Jedediah Hotchkiss* (Dallas, Tx.: Southern Methodist University Press, 1973); Dabney, *Life and Campaigns of Lieut.-General Jackson*, 510. Hotchkiss's journal is a goldmine of detailed information on Jackson's whereabouts, thoughts, and actions, as well as those of Robert E. Lee and Jeb Stuart, with whom he would also share close relationships. His skill as an accurate mapmaker made him almost unique in the army's command circles.

2   Freeman, *R. E. Lee*, vol. 2, 279; Lee to Jackson, July 23, 25, 26, and 27, and August 4, 7, and 12, 1862, most containing references to letters from Jackson and all reprinted in *Wartime Papers*, 235–236, 238–240, 245, 247–248, 251; Lee to Jackson, August 8, 1862, *O.R.* vol. 12, part 3, 926; the famous "miscreant" quote is in Lee to George W. Randolph, July 28, 1862, in *Wartime Papers*, 240–241; on Lee's damaged opinion of Jackson see Hotchkiss journal entry, March 6, 1863, Jedediah Hotchkiss Papers, Diaries, 1845–1899, LOC; Robertson, *Stonewall Jackson*, 518, 540; Jackson on sending an army north cited in Jackson to R. L. Dabney, July 24,1862, typescript, R. L. Dabney Papers, Box 3-8, Union Presbyterian Seminary Archives, Richmond (hereafter UPS); Jackson to Samuel Cooper, August 10, 1862, Stonewall Jackson Papers, Eleanor S. Brockenbrough Library, Museum of the Confederacy (hereafter MOC). The best secondary source on the Battle of Cedar Mountain remains Robert K. Krick's authoritative *Stonewall Jackson at Cedar Mountain* (Chapel Hill: University of North Carolina Press, 1990).

3   Krick, ibid., 27–30; 260–261, 351, 376–377; Jackson to Mary Anna Jackson, August 11, 1862, partially reprinted in Mary Anna Jackson, *Memoirs of Stonewall Jackson*, 312; Jackson on whipping Banks quoted in McGuire, "General Thomas J. Jackson," 311.

4   Lee to Jefferson Davis, August 16,1862, in *Wartime Papers*, 256–257; Harsh, *Confederate Tide Rising*, 122–125; Allan, *The Army of Northern Virginia in 1862*, 181–182; Benjamin Franklin Cooling, *Counter-Thrust: From the Peninsula to the Antietam* (Lincoln: University of Nebraska Press, 2007), 67–70.

5   Roland, "The Generalship of Robert E. Lee," 164–166; Gary W. Gallagher, "Another Look at the Generalship of Robert E. Lee," in *Lee the Soldier*, 278–279; Gallagher, *The Confederate War*, 133–134, 138; Pryor, *Reading the Man*, 389–390; Harsh, 124–125; John J. Hennessy, *Return to Bull Run: The Campaign and Battle of Second Manassas* (New York: Simon and Schuster, 1993), 35.

6   Harsh, 126; Cooling, *Counter-Thrust*, 70; Freeman, *R. E. Lee*, vol. 2, 280; Hennessy, 38–41.

7   Vandiver, *Mighty Stonewall*, 335; Hunter McGuire to Hotchkiss, June 27, 1896, Hotchkiss Papers, "War Book," LOC; Wert, *Cavalryman of the Lost Cause*, 121; Jackson to Stuart, July 31, 1863, Thomas Jonathan Jackson Papers, Mss1St923a16, VHS; Lee to Jackson, August 8, 1862, op. cit.; Lee to James Longstreet, August 14, 1862, in *Wartime Papers*, 252–253; Hennessy, 43.

8   A. G. Grinnan, "General Lee's Movement Against Pope, August 1862," enclosure with letter from R. L. Dabney to Hotchkiss, May 21, 1896, Hotchkiss Papers, "War Book," LOC; Hennessy, 43–44; Harsh, *Confederate Tide Rising*, 127; Pryor, *Reading the Man*, 386–388. The Clark's Mountain meeting is recounted in only a very few histories. That it occurred at all would be unknown were it not for Grinnan's account, which is itself based on a detailed conversation he had weeks later with an eyewitness to the meeting. Both Dr. Grinnan and the eyewitness, Jeremiah Morton, were men of considerable stature in Culpeper County and not likely to fabricate an event for their own purposes, which gives this source the ring of truth. It should be reiterated, however, that Dabney definitely had an agenda both in the various editions of his Jackson biography and after the war, including a bias against Longstreet. All of the quotations used here are from the Grinnan account.

9   Grinnan account, ibid.; A. L. Long, *Memoirs of Robert E. Lee*, 186–187; Allan, *The Army of Northern Virginia in 1862*, 183; Cooling, *Counter-Thrust*, 71–72; John W. Thomason, Jr., *Jeb Stuart* (1929; reprint Lincoln, Neb.: Bison Books, 1994), 221–227; Lee to Davis, August 23, 1862, in *Wartime Papers*, 261–262.

10   Hennessy, *Return to Bull Run*, 76–80; Thomason, 225, 228, 235; Stuart to wife, August 19 and 25, 1862, Mss1St923c, JEB Stuart Papers, VHS; Harsh, *Confederate Tide Rising*, 129–131. About war, Clausewitz notes: "No other human activity is so continuously or universally bound up with chance. And through the element of chance, guesswork and luck come to play a great part in war." (Clausewitz, *On War*, Paret translation, 85). One of the best modern explanations of Clausewitz's understanding of chance (or uncertainty, as it is sometimes called) as it relates to war may be found in Katherine L. Herbig, "Chance and Uncertainty in *On War*," in Michael I. Handel, ed., *Clausewitz and Modern Strategy* (Abingdon, U.K.: Frank Cass, 1986), 95–108.

11   Jackson-Stuart exchange recorded in Wert, *Cavalryman of the Lost Cause*, 131. Wert is skeptical of the historical veracity of the story. Stuart may have shown Jackson the note to Pope proposing the exchange, which stimulated a laugh.

12   Hotchkiss journal entry, August 24, 1862, reprinted in McDonald, ed., *Make Me a Map of the Valley*, 70; Susan Leigh Blackford, comp., *Letters From Lee's Army: Or Memoirs of Life In and Out of the Army in Virginia During the War Between the States* (New York: Charles Scribner's Sons, 1947), 124–127; Robertson, *Stonewall Jackson*, 545–546; Hennessy, *Return to Bull Run*, 88–89.

13   Henry Kyd Douglas, *I Rode With Stonewall*, 135; Harsh, *Confederate Tide Rising*, 137; 193. Harsh erroneously states that Douglas's book, which must be read cautiously as a reputable source, was the only primary source referencing the Jeffersonton council. Hunter McGuire wrote a letter to Jackson's biographer Henderson discussing the meeting. See Henderson, *Stonewall Jackson*, 432. Freeman, despite the corroboration of Douglas's account with McGuire, chooses to dismiss the meeting (see *Lee's Lieutenants*, vol. 2, 82). Hennessy consulted both McGuire and Douglas in constructing his narrative (see Hennessy, 93), whereas Cooling cited Harsh, Hennessy, and another scholar but not the original sources (see Cooling, 83). Thomas, Vandiver, and Robertson

mention the meeting quite briefly in their biographies, but Thomas cites Vandiver and Freeman, Vandiver cites Freeman and Douglas only, and Robertson offers no documentation. Jeffry D. Wert, in *A Glorious Army: Robert E. Lee's Triumph, 1862–1863* (New York: Simon and Schuster, 2011), offers another brief, but better documented overview on p. 78–79. The most comprehensive narrative is the most recent, in S. C. Gwynne, *Rebel Yell: The Violence, Passion, and Redemption of Stonewall Jackson* (New York: Simon and Schuster, 2014), 413, although Gwynne only uses Douglas as his source. None of the authors cited here, with the possible exception of Harsh, have analyzed the greater strategic significance of the Jeffersonton conference for the development of Lee's command style and the command team that would henceforth govern Confederate fortunes in the Eastern Theater. Harsh notes on p. 137 that Lee issued complicated written orders in the Seven Days and along the Rapidan a week earlier that had failed to achieve his goals; the "new approach would permit flexibility and adaptability in new situations as they might arise." Then he proceeds to note the downside of such flexibility: subordinates overstepping their authority and committing "his army to actions contrary to Lee's overall strategy."

14   Douglas, ibid.; Hunter McGuire to G.F.R. Henderson, n.d., cited in *Stonewall Jackson*, 432; Hotchkiss journal entries August 12, 13, and 14, 1862, and March 4, 1863, reprinted in McDonald, ed., *Make Me a Map of the Valley*, 68. Kegel especially believes what became the Sharpsburg Campaign was first contemplated with Jackson's turning movement against Pope, but offers no concrete evidence. See Kegel, *North with Lee and Jackson*, 149.

15   Robertson, *Stonewall Jackson*, 548; *O.R.*, vol. 12, part 2, 643, 650; Lee to Davis, August 23 and 24, 1862, and Lee to Mary Lee, August 25, 1862, all in *Wartime Papers*, 261–264; Harsh, *Confederate Tide Rising*, 138. A good example of the failure of civil-military relations in the Confederate leadership may be found in Glatthaar, *Partners in Command*, 118–122, which describes the poor relationship between Johnston and Davis in mid-1863. Archer Jones also addresses this topic in numerous chapters in *Civil War Command and Strategy: The Process of Victory and Defeat* (New York: The Free Press, 1992), especially 220–222.

16   Wert, *A Glorious Army*, 79–80; Henderson, *Stonewall Jackson*, 434–435; Dabney, *Life and Campaigns of Lieut.-General Jackson*, 517; McGuire, "General Thomas J. Jackson," 305; *O.R.*, vol. 12, part 2, 643. My description of the "Jackson on the rock" scene is a fusion of Henderson, Dabney, and McGuire's accounts.

17   A wartime, Confederate-published edition of *The Officer's Manual: Napoleon's Maxims of War* (Richmond, Va.: West and Johnston, 1862) may be found at: http://www.gutenberg.org/files/50750/50750-h/50750-h.htm; Wert, ibid., 80–82; G. Moxley Sorrel, *Recollections of Confederate Staff Officer*, 90; Allen C. Redwood, "With Stonewall Jackson," *Scribner's Magazine* 18 (1879), 228–229; Pender to wife, September 2, 1862, reprinted in William Woods Hassler, ed., *One of Lee's Best Men: The Civil War Letters of General William Dorsey Pender* (Chapel Hill: University of North Carolina Press, 1965), 171; Captain Hugh White, 4th Virginia, quoted in Robertson, *Stonewall Jackson*, 553.

18 Cooling, *Counter-Thrust*, 84–85; Wert, *General James Longstreet*, 163–164; Hennessy, *Return to Bull Run*, 103–104, 107–109, 116–117; McDowell to Pope, August 26, 1862, 3:30 P.M. in *O.R.*, vol. 12, part 2, 350; Halleck to Pope, August 26, 1862, 11:45 A.M. in ibid., part 3, 66.

19 W. W. Blackford, *War Years with Jeb Stuart* (New York: Charles Scribner's Sons, 1945), 116–117; Hennessy, 136–137, 144–145, 166–168, 490, 498; Cooling, 103; James Longstreet, *From Manassas to Appomattox*, 176.

20 The Jackson-Barringer conversation is recorded in a long letter from Rufus Barringer to his sister, Mary Anna Jackson, n.d., in chapter 16 of Mary Anna Jackson, *Life and Letters*, 310–317. Henderson and Vandiver do not mention it, Robertson accords it a couple small paragraphs, and Gwynne quotes only a few lines from it. The value of the discussion, which admittedly may have been altered to some degree by Barringer, is the insight it offers into the consistency and growth of Jackson's strategic thinking. Jomini, a French general on Marshal Ney's staff under Napoleon, intrepid publisher, and self-promoter partially contemporaneous with Clausewitz (the Prussian died long before Jomini, giving the latter the ability to freely criticize without fear of reprisal), has traditionally been touted as the military theorist most influential on the operational and strategic thinking of Civil War leaders. See Baron Antoine-Henri de Jomini, *The Art of War* (Philadelphia: Lippincott, 1862), 212. According to Jomini, enemy civilians should be left out of war as much as possible, and when interactions with them are impossible, soldiers should "display courtesy, gentleness, and severity united, and, particularly, deal justly." What he called "absolute war" was to be waged only against enemy combatants, lest the horror of the Spanish insurgency against Napoleonic rule in 1809–1814 be repeated. Carol Reardon has explained, however, that most northern military leaders understood Jomini's theorems only superficially, and combined them with a multitude of other would-be strategic writers as they wrestled with how to think about prosecuting the war. See Reardon, *With a Sword in One Hand and Jomini in the Other: The Problem of Military Thought in the Civil War North* (Chapel Hill: University of North Carolina Press, 2012), especially the introduction and chapter 1.

21 Mary Anna Jackson, ibid., 313–314; Woodworth, *Davis and Lee at War*, 68–69, 156–159; Robertson, *Stonewall Jackson*, 515.

22 Mary Anna Jackson, 314–315.

23 Jomini's four determining principles, which coalesce all his other maxims, are mass, maneuver, concentration, and decisive points. Often hawked as the defining characteristics of Jominian warfare, "interior and exterior lines" of approach fall under the rubric of maneuver. One of the best short synopses of Jomini's theories as they related to the Civil War—and compared with Clausewitz's, which no general North or South had yet read—may be found in Donald Stoker's fine book, *The Grand Design: Strategy and the U.S. Civil War* (New York: Oxford University Press, 2010), 3–10.

24 Mary Anna Jackson, *Life and Letters*, 316–317. Jackson's reference to the possibility of McClellan retaining command over Pope probably meant that he comprehended McClellan was politically conservative and waged war according to the understood

principles of the day, unlike Pope. McClellan had protected slaveholder's property and upheld their Constitutional rights on the Peninsula, a fact not lost on Confederates. That the Union general was so anti-Lincoln was probably not as well-known in the South yet, but a Union war effort with McClellan still at the head of the principal Federal army in the East would have removed Jackson's excuse to make hard war on the North.

25 Lee on Arlington House and "affections" available at: https://www.arlingtonhouse .org/about/history; Pryor, *Reading the Man*, 306–307; Mary Lee to Mrs. William Henry Stiles, March 8, 1862, and Lee to Mary Lee, December 25, 1861, both cited in ibid., 307.

26 Jonathan Horn, "White House on the Pamunkey," *New York Times*, June 29, 2012; Mary Lee note reprinted in Pryor, ibid., 307; Stuart quote cited in Horn; Pryor, 308, 327, 364.

27 Hennessy, *Return to Bull Run*, 209–223; 245–266; 271–286; 311–313; Cooling, *Counter-Thrust*, 112–133; Wert, *Cavalryman of the Lost Cause*, 135; Gallagher, ed., *Fighting for the Confederacy*, 133–134; Longstreet, *From Manassas to Appomattox*, 183–185. Pope was enraged with Porter's "failure" to advance on August 29. In November, long after Pope's removal from command, a court-martial was convened and Porter found guilty of misconduct and disobedience; he was thrown out of the Union army and was only exonerated of wrongdoing in 1878.

28 McGuire to Hotchkiss, April 23, 1896, Mss2822, Hotchkiss Papers, UVA; W. W. Blackford, *War Years with Jeb Stuart*, 118; McGuire, "General Thomas J. Jackson," 311. The "slow Longstreet" debate is covered in detail in chapter 6. Hotchkiss and McGuire seemed to take particular glee in attacking Longstreet whenever possible after the war, so the elephant analogy, although amusing, should be weighed against other accounts. Most historians now agree that Longstreet executed both his march to Manassas and his tactical movements in the battle with skill and as much timeliness as contextual circumstances permitted. A good summation of the historical evidence supporting this conclusion may be found in Gary W. Gallagher, "Scapegoat in Victory: James Longstreet and the Battle of Second Manassas," in Gallagher, *Lee and His Generals in War and Memory*, 139–157.

29 Lee to Davis, telegraphic dispatch, 10:00 P.M., August 30, 1862, in *Wartime Papers*, 268; Robertson, *Stonewall Jackson*, 135–136; Jackson quoted in Hunter McGuire Narrative (notes taken down by R. L. Dabney in 1863–64 in preparation of his wartime biography), Charles William Dabney Papers, file 1412, UNC; J. William Jones, *Christ in the Camp: or Religion in Lee's Army* (Richmond, Va.: B.F. Johnson & Co., 1887), 83; Dabney, *Life of Lieut.-General Jackson*, 98–99; cadet cited in Robertson, 137.

30 Lee to Mary Lee, April 19, 1857, Lee Family Papers, Mss1L51c201, VHS; Thomas, *Robert E. Lee*, 160; Cox, *The Religious Life of Robert E. Lee*, xvi, 129.

31 Daniel B. Ewing to R. L. Dabney, September 8, 1863, Dabney-Jackson Papers, Box 1, Folder 24, Series II, item #178, LOV; Thomas, ibid., 397; Pryor, *Reading the Man*, 193–194; J. William Jones, *Life and Letters of Robert Edward Lee, Soldier and*

Man, 466–467, 469–471. Verbally, both Lee and Jackson could be harsh if events did not unfold as they had planned. On several rare occasions Jackson almost lost his temper, but Lee did lose his temper several times during the war, such as after the indecisive, piecemeal Confederate attacks at Salem Church on May 4, 1863. His staff privately wrote about how hard he was on them even as they admired his leadership. See Pryor, 407.

32 Harrison Family Memoirs, Loudoun County Museum, 1–2, cited in Joseph L. Harsh, *Taken at the Flood: Robert E. Lee and Confederate Strategy in the Maryland Campaign of 1862* (Kent, Ohio: Kent State University Press, 1999), 86; Heros von Borcke, *Memoirs of the Confederate War for Independence*, 2 vols. (Edinburgh: William Blackwood and Sons, 1866), vol. 1, 183; Keith S. Bohannon, "Dirty, Ragged, and Ill-Provided For: Confederate Logistical Problems in the 1862 Maryland Campaign and Their Solutions," in Gary W. Gallagher, ed., *The Antietam Campaign* (Chapel Hill: University of North Carolina Press, 1999), 106–112; Lee to Davis, September 3, 1862, in *Wartime Papers*, 292–294; Gary W. Gallagher, "The Autumn of 1862: A Season of Opportunity," in Gallagher, ed., *Antietam: Essays on the 1862 Maryland Campaign* (Kent, Ohio: Kent State University Press, 1989), 1–13. There are now a multitude of excellent studies focusing on the Maryland Campaign (also variously denoted as the Sharpsburg or Antietam Campaign). I am citing only those directly consulted in writing this section.

33 Joseph L. Harsh, *Sounding the Shallows: A Confederate Companion for the Maryland Campaign of 1862* (Kent, Ohio: Kent State University Press, 2000), 149–150; Pelham to parents, September 4, 1862, partially reprinted in William Woods Hassler, *Colonel John Pelham: Lee's Boy Artillerist* (Chapel Hill: University of North Carolina Press, 1960), 77; Lee to Davis, September 4, 1862, in *Wartime Papers*, 194–195.

34 Harsh, *Taken at the Flood*, 51, 78–79, 81–83, 123–127; "To the People of Maryland" proclamation in *Wartime Papers*, 299–300; Davis to Lee, September 7, 1862, *O.R.*, vol. 19, part 2, 598–599; Lee to Davis, September 8, 1862, *Wartime Papers*, 301. Also very illuminating on Lee's dispatches to Davis at time and his dabbling in Confederate policy is Ezra A. Carman and Thomas Clemens (ed.), *The Maryland Campaign of September 1862, Vol. I: South Mountain* (El Dorado Hills, Calif.: Savas Beatie, 2010), 79–82, 102–108; and D. Scott Hartwig's magisterial, *To Antietam Creek: The Maryland Campaign of September 1862* (Baltimore: Johns Hopkins University Press, 2012), 52–53.

35 Harsh, 51, 82, 85–86; Longstreet, *From Manassas to Appomattox*, 200–201; Bradley T. Johnson, "Address on the First Maryland Campaign," *SHSP* 11 (1883), 503–506; Hartwig, ibid., 50–52; Allan, "Memoranda" February 15, 1868, reprinted in Gallagher, ed., *Lee the Soldier*, 7; Lee to Davis, September 3, 1862, op. cit. Lee was also aware of General Kirby Smith's prong of the Confederate advance into Kentucky, as illustrated by a victory message he distributed to his army on September 6 in General Orders No. 103. See *O.R.*, vol. 19, part 2, 596.

36 Lee to Davis, September 8, 1862, op. cit.; Hartwig, 53; Palmerston quoted in Stephen Sears, *Landscape Turned Red: The Battle of Antietam* (New York: Houghton Mifflin

Company, 1983), 47. One of the best recent treatments of England's diplomatic and economic involvement in the American Civil War is Amanda Foreman, *A World on Fire: Britain's Crucial Role in the American Civil War* (New York: Random House, 2011). Chapters 12 and 13 are the most relevant to the state of diplomacy among the British Empire and the Union and Confederacy in the critical summer-fall period of 1862. Another valuable study (that Foreman often cites) is Howard Jones, *Union in Peril: The Crisis Over British Intervention in the Civil War* (Chapel Hill: University of North Carolina Press, 1992), especially chapters 7 and 8. It should be noted that formal diplomatic *recognition* of Confederate independence was not necessarily a prerequisite to a mediation offer, and neither action was equivalent in any way to actual military *intervention*, which would have been a very extreme, and—as Foreman, Jones, and other scholars have argued—internationally dangerous move for the British Empire to make. Once the Union announced emancipation, it would be almost impossible for England to ally itself formally in any way with the Confederacy. Napoleon III's France was more of a diplomatic wildcard, but the Emperor, already embroiled in a war in Mexico, looked to England for support before making a move himself.

37   Allan, *The Army of Northern Virginia in 1862*, 326–328; Hartwig, 99–100, John Riley quoted on p. 100; Wert, *A Glorious Army*, 113; Lee to Davis, September 9, 1862, *O.R.*, vol. 19, part 2, 602–603; Taylor, *Four Years with General Lee*, 66.

38   Henderson, *Stonewall Jackson*, 500–502; Hartwig, 118, 120–121; Jackson quoted in D. H. Hill to R. L. Dabney, July 21, 1864, Robert L. Dabney Collection, UPS; Jedediah Hotchkiss, *Confederate Military History, Extended Edition: Vol. IV: Virginia* (1899: reprint Wilmington, N.C.: Broadfoot Publishing Company, 1987), 337–339.

39   Longstreet, *From Manassas to Appomattox*, 201–203; Harsh, *Taken at the Flood*, 166; Special Orders No. 191, reprinted in *Wartime Papers*, 301–303. In a rare moment of 20/20 hindsight, Harsh argues vehemently that "Lee made a critical mistake in issuing S.O. 191 and dividing his army. . . . He was wrong in believing the enemy garrisons would flee to safety and wrong in assuming the movement could be completed in three days. More importantly, he misjudged the Federal advance from Washington. Either Lee misinterpreted the information he was receiving from his cavalry chief, or Stuart was supplying faulty intelligence." Doubtless, Harsh would have felt differently if a copy of the order had not fallen into McClellan's hands, but he was correct that Stuart was not providing his normal level of information to Lee. A bigger problem for Lee was straggling, which was severe by this point in the campaign and would only get worse. E. Porter Alexander later wrote, "stragglers were lining the roads," and along with the casualties in the recent battles, "divisions had sunk to little more than brigades, & brigades nearly to regiments." See Gallagher, ed., *Fighting for the Confederacy*, 139. Bohannon paints a more analytically complete but equally dire portrait in his essay in Gallagher, ed., *The Antietam Campaign*.

40   Carman and Clemens, 200–202; Philip Leigh, *Lee's Lost Dispatch and Other Civil War Controversies* (Yardley, Penn.: Westholme Publishing, 2015), 137–139; Harsh, 237–238; Taylor, *Four Years with General Lee*, 66–67; Allan, "Memoranda," February 15, 1868, reprinted in Gallagher, ed., *Lee the Soldier*, 8.

41 McClellan quoted in Sears, *Landscape Turned Red*, 115; Harsh, 237–241, 243–245; Jackson to Lee, September 14, 1862, *O.R.*, vol. 19, part 1, 951. Although Sears, Hartwig, Carman and Clemens, and most of the other histories of the Antietam Campaign include sections on South Mountain, two recent works focusing on that battle commend themselves: John David Hoptak, *The Battle of South Mountain* (Charleston, S.C.: The History Press, 2011) and Brian Matthew Jordan, *Unholy Sabbath: The Battle of South Mountain in History and Memory* (El Dorado Hills, Calif.: Savas Beatie, 2012).

42 Hartwig, 480–484; Sears, 161–162; Harsh, 302–303; Carman and Clemens, 391–395.

43 James M. McPherson, *Crossroads of Freedom: Antietam* (New York: Oxford University Press, 2002), 112–114; Jomini, *The Art of War*, 268; Clausewitz, *On War*, 141; Michael I. Handel, *Masters of War: Classical Strategic Thought* (London: Frank Cass, 1992), 3rd ed., 190–191; William Duggan, "Coup D'oeil: Strategic Intuition in Army Planning" (Carlisle, Penn.: Strategic Studies Institute, 2005), 2–3, available at: http://publications.armywarcollege.edu/pubs/1734.pdf.

44 Robertson, *Stonewall Jackson*, 604–605; New York soldier quoted in ibid., 604; *O.R.*, vol. 19, part 1, 528, 743; Edward A. Moore, *The Story of a Cannoneer Under Stonewall Jackson* (New York: Neale Publishing Company, 1907), 139; Jackson to Lee, "Near 8 AM," September 15, 1862, *O.R.*, vol. 19, part 1, 951.

45 Lee quoted in William M. Owen, *In Camp and Battle with the Washington Artillery of New Orleans: A Narrative of Events during the Late Civil War* (Boston: Ticknor and Company, 1885), 139; Longstreet, *From Manassas to Appomattox*, 228; Lee to Davis, September 16,1862, *O.R.*, vol. 19, part 1, 140–141. Owen is the only source for Lee's quote, but a detachment of the Washington Artillery was posted on Cemetery Hill, where Lee established his headquarters, at the time the commanding general received Jackson's dispatch.

46 Douglas, *I Rode with Stonewall*, 166, is the source for the generals' September 16 morning meeting at Lee's headquarters. As in other episodes, he should be read with care, but here offers enough specific detail about the meeting to inspire confidence. Harsh believes the conference took place based on the common-sense deduction that upon his arrival in Sharpsburg, Jackson would have naturally reported first to Lee. Lee quoted in Lee to Mary Anna Jackson, January25, 1866, typescript located in Hotchkiss Papers, General Correspondence, 1846–1899, LOC.

47 Stoker, *The Grand Design*, 189–190; Ezra A. Carman and Thomas G. Clemens (ed.), *The Maryland Campaign of 1862: Vol. II: Antietam* (El Dorado Hills, Calif.: Savas Beatie, 2012), especially chapters 17, 18, 19, 20, 21–1, and 21–2; Longstreet, *From Manassas to Appomattox*, 252–254; *O.R.*, vol. 19, part 1, 885–890; 1024–1025; Lee quoted in Harsh, *Taken at the Flood*, 419.

48 The original source for this remarkable post-battle council is a letter from Stephen D. Lee to Hotchkiss on July 31, 1896 (Hotchkiss Papers, "War Book," LOC). Elements of it were cited in older secondary sources, such as Henry Alexander White, *Robert E. Lee and the Southern Confederacy* (1897; reprint New York: Haskell House

Publishers, 1968), 224–225. Henderson, Chambers, Vandiver, Robertson, Gwynne, Thomas, Harsh, Hartwig, and others all refer to it. The generals' quotes are restructured as closely in syntax and tense as possible to Lee's quotations of them, utilizing the same wording.

49   Lee to Hotchkiss, ibid.; McPherson, *Crossroads of Freedom*, 154–157; Brooks Simpson, "General McClellan's Bodyguard: The Army of the Potomac After Antietam," in Gallagher, ed., *The Antietam Campaign*, 53–56, 58, 61–66.

50   Hunter McGuire to Hotchkiss, May 28, 1896, Hotchkiss Papers, "War Book," LOC; Gallagher, ed., *Fighting for the Confederacy*, 154–156; White, *Robert E. Lee and the Southern Confederacy*, 233; Lee to Davis, October 2, 1862, *O.R.*, vol. 19, part 2, 633; Blackford to wife, n.d. (but between August 5 and 21, 1862), quoted in Susan Leigh Blackford, comp., *Letters from Lee's Army*, 116. Lee suffered a heavy personal blow during the fall, coming on the heels of the loss of his grandson, with the death of his daughter, Annie, on October 20. When he received the news by letter, he was "overcome with grief," and wrote his wife, "To know that I shall never see her again on earth . . . is agonizing in the extreme." See Pryor, *Reading the Man*, 365. Lee's increased interest in chaplains and army religious services, which was noticed at this time and corresponded with Jackson's, may have been related to the deaths. According to staffer A. L. Long, "General Lee attend[ed] services whenever circumstances permitted." See A. L. Long, *Memoirs of Robert E. Lee*, 230.

51   Jackson to Mary Anna Jackson, October 20, 1862, reprinted in Mary Anna Jackson, *Memoirs of Stonewall Jackson*, 349; for descriptions of Jackson's duties, pleasant camp, and adulation of Jackson see ibid., 347; Dabney, *Life and Campaigns of Lieut.-Gen. Stonewall Jackson*, 584–587, 589–590; Wert, *Cavalryman of the Lost Cause*, 164–165; Hotchkiss diary entry, October 7, 1862, in McDonald, ed., *Make Me a Map of the Valley*, 87: "Gen. R. E. Lee came up to our Hd. Qrs this morning and he and Gen. Jackson are having a long conversation aided [by] my maps of Maryland and Pennsylvania. No doubt another expedition is on foot." For Smith, see James Power Smith, *With Stonewall Jackson in the Army of Northern Virginia* (1920; reprint Gaithersburg, Md.: Zullo and Van Sickle Books, 1982), 20–21. Stuart presented Jackson with a brand-new uniform during October, which Jackson would temporarily stow away, only to wear it again with pride at Fredericksburg.

52   Lee to Jackson, November 23, 1862, in *Wartime Papers*, 343–344.

THREE

1   Details on Jackson's headquarters camp drawn from W. G. Bean, *Stonewall's Man: Sandie Pendleton* (Chapel Hill: University of North Carolina Press, 1959), 102–104, and Rev. J. P. Smith, public address, "Stonewall Jackson in Winter Quarters at Moss Neck," delivered in Winchester, Va., January 19, 1898 (typescript in FSNMP), 3; details on Christmas Day 1862 weather drawn from Krick, *Civil War Weather*, 79. Jed Hotchkiss, who had received a leave of absence for the holiday and was home

at Staunton, recorded in his journal that the day was "warm and pleasant." See McDonald, ed., *Make Me a Map of the Valley*, 103.

2   Smith, ibid.

3   Ibid.; Hunter McGuire "Narrative," file #1412, UNC; Dabney, *Life of Lieut.-General Stonewall Jackson*, 638; Robertson, *Stonewall Jackson*, 669.

4   Freeman, *Lee's Lieutenants* vol. 2, 497–8; Smith, ibid.; Dabney, ibid. The best, most-detailed account of the dinner is in Smith's 1898 address, which was reprinted almost entirely in *The Southern Historical Society Papers*, vol. 5 (August 1920), 35–43. Although written from memory decades after the event, Smith was in charge of the occasion at the time and witnessed it all. John Esten Cooke also attended, but the first (1863) edition of his *Life of Stonewall Jackson* does not cover the event, although Freeman claims a later edition did. Frank Vandiver failed to mention the memorable feast in his biography, and Dabney, Henderson, Freeman, Robertson, and Gwynne all conflate the Christmas dinner with Stuart's first visit to Jackson's "office," a small outbuilding on the Corbin estate grounds. Smith made it clear in his address that these were two distinct events separated by a period of time. "About a week later," he wrote, "Gen. Jackson had earache, and Dr. McGuire said he had taken cold, and must go to a room in the house. And the general consented to occupy an office building in the grounds." It is likely that the later chroniclers drew their narrative from Dabney and the second and third editions of Cooke and failed to notice the nuanced chronological progression in Smith's accounts.

5   Lee to Mary Lee, December 25, 1862, in *Wartime Papers*, 379–380; J. B. Jones, diary entry for December 25, reprinted in *A Rebel War Clerk's Diary*, 141.

6   In recent years several good studies of the Fredericksburg Campaign have emerged. Among the best are George C. Rable, *Fredericksburg! Fredericksburg!* (Chapel Hill: University of North Carolina Press, 2002); Francis A. O'Reilly, *The Fredericksburg Campaign: Winter War on the Rappahannock* (Baton Rouge: Louisiana State University Press, 2003); Gary W. Gallagher, ed., *The Fredericksburg Campaign: Decision on the Rappahannock* (Chapel Hill: University of North Carolina Press, 1995), especially Alan T. Nolan, "Confederate Leadership at Fredericksburg" and Gallagher's own essay, "The Yanks Have Had a Terrible Whipping: Confederates Evaluate the Battle of Fredericksburg"; and Daniel E. Sutherland, *Fredericksburg and Chancellorsville: The Dare Mark Campaign* (Lincoln: University of Nebraska Press, 1998). As these authors explain, Jackson was responsible for the flawed disposition of his troops in the forest behind the railroad in his sector of the rebel line, inexplicably creating a gap where none need to have existed. Federals under Major General George G. Meade found the gap and temporarily exploited it, creating unnecessary casualties for the Confederates. Stonewall discovered the breakthrough, however, and quickly plugged the hole with reserves.

7   See Freeman, *Robert E. Lee*, vol. 2, 476–477, for a good analysis of Lee's thoughts about these strategic issues and an assessment of the army's morale; also see Gallagher, "Another Look at the Generalship of R. E. Lee," in *Lee the Soldier*, 278–280.

8   Lee to Agnes Lee, February 6, 1863, in *Wartime Papers*, 400; Jackson to Anna Jackson, December 25, 1862, Dabney-Jackson Collection, LOV; Lee to Mary Lee, op. cit.

9   Smith, "Stonewall Jackson in Winter Quarters at Moss Neck," 3; Shaw, *Stonewall Jackson's Surgeon*, 27; A. L. Long, *Memoirs of Robert E. Lee*, 240; Freeman, *Lee's Lieutenants*, vol. 2, 497; Freeman, *Robert E. Lee*, vol. 2, 484–485; Vandiver, *Mighty Stonewall*, 436.

10   Glatthaar, *General Lee's Army*, 212–215; Lee to Davis, February 16, 1863, in *Wartime Papers*, 404; Vandiver, op. cit.; Freeman, *Robert E. Lee*, 477–478; Henderson, *Stonewall Jackson*, 632.

11   Roberta Cary Corbin Kinsolving Reminiscences, quoted in Robertson, *Stonewall Jackson*, 669–670; Thomason, *Jeb Stuart*, 347–349.

12   Smith, "Stonewall Jackson in Winter Quarters," 4; "Proceedings of the Committee on Military Affairs of the House of Representatives of the Permanent Congress, February 26, 1862–February 26, 1865," minutes for January 20 and February 2, 1863, NYHS. Douglas noted, "As the General corresponded regularly with Colonel Porcher Miles of South Carolina, Chairman of the Congressional Committee on Military Affairs, it is not doubtful that he gave him the benefit of many suggestions. Indeed, I am informed that Colonel Miles frequently acknowledged his indebtedness to General Jackson for valuable suggestions, and that the General framed one or two bills passed by that body." (Douglas, *I Rode with Stonewall*, 39) Here is another example in which Douglas's veracity may be confirmed by a different primary source.

13   Gwynne, *Rebel Yell*, 514–515; Robertson, *Stonewall Jackson*, 670, 672–675, 684; Jackson's "converted army" quote cited in Rev. B. T. Lacy Narrative, Dabney Papers, UNC; Hotchkiss quoted in Robertson, 672. Jackson was scrupulous about inviting candidates for the chaplaincy and guest ministers who were nondenominational. As he succinctly put it in a letter to a clergyman, "As a general rule, I do not think that a chaplain who would preach denominational sermons should be in the army." He also donated $300 of his own money to pay for Bibles and tracts and gave Big Sorrel, one of his personal horses, for Lacy's official use. The feud with Hill about his earlier arrest would continue all winter. Hill pressed for a formal court-martial, and Lee, sensing the potential damage such an event would cause in his command team, refused, writing Hill on January 12 in a manner that could be construed as defending Jackson: "I do not think that in every case where an officer is arrested there is a necessity for a trial by Court-Martial, and I consider yours one in which such a proceeding is unnecessary. . . . In the present instance, Genl. Jackson exerted the authority for what he thought at the time, good and sufficient reasons. He exercised a discretion which you, or any other commanding officer must use. . . . Upon examining the charges in question, I am of [the] opinion that the interests of the service do not require they should be tried." (Lee to A. P. Hill, January 12, 1863, *O.R.*, Series 1, vol. 19, part 2, 732.) Hill kept fuming, writing a letter to Lee describing Jackson as a "slumbering volcano," and Stonewall and his staff amassed a great deal of paperwork in support of a court-martial, should one occur. Hill also opened up

another fight with his superior over Jackson's occasional habit of skipping over him and directly issuing orders to Hill's subordinates and staff officers. Jackson, weary of the administrative hassle and unwilling to give one inch, finally wrote Lee to recommend Hill be transferred from his command. Neither the court-martial nor the transfer ever happened, as Lee essentially tabled the escalating feud until the Chancellorsville Campaign intervened. The Jackson-Hill controversy was seemingly laid to rest with Jackson's wounding on May 2, 1863.

14   Jed Hotchkiss diary entries, March 5, 6, and 7, 1863, reprinted in McDonald, ed., *Make Me a Map of the Valley*, 118–119; Freeman, *Robert E. Lee*, vol. 2, 488–489; Lee to Mildred Lee, December 25, 1862, in *Wartime Papers*, 381. Jackson and Lee also played host to a multitude of official and unofficial visitors, from Congressmen to foreign newspaper correspondents and military observers. Biographers Freeman, Thomas, Henderson, and Robertson, and the earlier chroniclers who served with both men, such as Dabney, Smith, Hotchkiss, Pendleton, Marshall, Long, and Taylor, all refer to multiple visits by various individuals to both headquarters. Some of the more interesting character portraits of the generals emerged from accounts of these visits. Lee also had a regular visitor during these winter months, who stayed with him up through the Gettysburg Campaign: a little hen, which he allowed to come and go from his tent. For his indulgence he was rewarded each morning with a freshly laid egg for breakfast. (Long, *Memoirs of Robert E. Lee*, 241)

15   Lee to Seddon, January 10, 1863, in *Wartime Papers*, 388–390. For other official letters to Davis or Seddon during the January–February 1863 period, many of which dealt with the manpower issue, see Lee to Seddon, January 5 and 29, and February 4, 1863; Lee to Davis January 6, 13, 19, and 23, and February 5, 16, 18, and 26, 1863. All reprinted in Dowdey and Manaran, *Wartime Papers*. Lee also sent numerous messages to Adjutant General Samuel Cooper, Chief of Ordnance Josiah Gorgas, and Commissary General Lucius Northrup. Northrup was particularly troublesome to Lee as he held the reins of power regarding food and forage and their transportation to the army, and disingenuously claimed he had foreseen all the problems but was powerless to stop them. Stephen W. Sears called him a "Jeremiah-like prophet of doom" and "the bane of every general in the field." See Sears, *Chancellorsville* (New York: Houghton Mifflin, 1996), 32.

16   Stoker, *The Grand Design*, 149–150; Dowdey and Manarin, 375–376; Freeman, *Lee's Lieutenants*, vol. 2, 467; Lee to Seddon, January 5, 1863, reprinted in *Wartime Papers*, 385–387; *O.R.*, Series 1, vol. 14, 762–763.

17   Freeman, *Robert E. Lee*, vol. 2, 483; Freeman, *Lee's Lieutenants*, vol. 2, 468–9; Woodworth, *Davis and Lee at War*, 218; Jeffrey D. Wert, *General James Longstreet*, 228–229; Lee to Longstreet February 18, 1863, in *Wartime Papers*, 405–406. Wert claims that Longstreet had recently suggested to Lee (just weeks before his and his divisions' departure for Richmond) the idea of detaching his corps and sending it west, under his command, to assist Bragg against Rosecrans in Tennessee. Jackson's corps would be sufficient to hold the Rappahannock line, Longstreet argued. How much this discussion may have influenced Lee in sending off Longstreet is impossible to tell.

Woodworth, citing Wert and other Longstreet biographers, states that "Longstreet welcomed the change. He had been growing restless within the Army of Northern Virginia for a number of months. Seeming to resent Lee's authority and desiring a chance to demonstrate his abilities in independent command, he had recently been angling to get Braxton Bragg's job out in Tennessee. The present assignment was not quite as prestigious but still represented the opportunity for operations on his own." See p. 218. How much Lee noticed this "restlessness" on Longstreet's part is unknown, but it seems unlikely, considering Lee's superb political situational awareness, that the commanding general was unaware of his subordinate's political intrigues with Texas Senator and rabid Davis denouncer Louis T. Wigfall, who openly argued for the return of Joseph E. Johnston to command of the Virginia army and privately supported Longstreet's ambitions.

18 Freeman, *Lee's Lieutenants*, vol. 2, 469–476; Wert, op. cit., 229–232.

19 Wert, op. cit., 232–233; Lee to Longstreet, March 19, 1863, in *Wartime Papers*, 414; Longstreet to Lee, March 19, 1863, *O.R.* Series 1, vol. 18, 926–927.

20 Lee to Longstreet, March 21 and 27, 1863; Lee to Mary Lee, March 21, 1863; Lee to Seddon, March 27, 1863, all in *Wartime Papers*, 415–419.

21 Smith, "Stonewall Jackson in Winter Quarters," 4; Robertson, *Stonewall Jackson*, 671.

22 Jackson to Boteler, December 31, 1862, reprinted in full in Douglas, *I Rode with Stonewall*, 40–41, original in Gilder Lehrman Collection, New York, #GLC07080; John Esten Cooke diary entry, January 31, 1863, quoted in Jay B. Hubbell, ed., "The War Diary of John Esten Cooke," *Journal of Southern History* 7, no. 4 (November 1941), 537.

23 Smith, "Stonewall Jackson in Winter Quarters," 5–6; Freeman, *R. E. Lee*, vol. 2, 486–487; Robertson, 682; description of the house gleaned from text and photos of restored mansion, available at: http://www.aggregate.com/documents/brochures /aboutus-history-hayfield.pdf/.

24 Smith, ibid., 5; Freeman, ibid., 69; Heros von Borcke, *Memoirs of the Confederate War for Independence* (Philadelphia: J.B. Lippincott and Co., 1867), 334–335. According to Smith, Colonel Leslie, the Chair of the Military Affairs Committee, told him at the end of the visit that "Jackson was the best informed military man he met in America, and as perfect a gentleman as he had ever seen." Various chroniclers have recounted the dinner episode, but the original source is Von Borcke's account, that states Lee "laughingly" received his tardy foreign guests. Likewise, the original source for the snowstorm account comes from Smith, both his 1898 Winchester address and the almost verbatim reprinting of the speech in 1920 in the Southern Historical Society Papers. All Jackson biographers mention it.

25 Mary Anna Jackson, *Life and Letters*, 427–428; Robertson, op. cit., 696; Lee to Mary Lee, May 11, 1863, Lee Family Papers, Mss1L51c450, VHS; Donald A. Hopkins, *Robert E. Lee in War and Peace: The Photographic History of a Confederate and American Icon* (El Dorado Hills, Calif.: Savas Beatie, 2013), 35–37. Hopkins cites Robertson (who cited Mrs. Jackson's and Douglas's accounts) as well as Douglas, who claims

that Cowell resorted to a ploy to get Jackson to sit for the photograph, stating that Lee would not sit for his own unless Jackson did so first. He also correctly identifies the studio as Minnis and Cowell, not "Minnis and Crowell" as inaccurately spelled by Robertson. Hopkins speculates that Lee may have still been recovering from his spring illnesses and thus could not initially sit for his photo or photos, but the May 11 letter to Mary indicates Lee was likely well enough, and very willing. Further, two famous wartime photos of Lee which are reputed to have been taken just prior to Chancellorsville, Hopkins argues, match in style, formatting, and identification stamps to the known Jackson "Chancellorsville photo," suggesting they likely came from the same studio and were taken almost at the same time. Probably remorseful at having missed the joint sitting with Jackson (which may or may not have produced a truly joint portrait), Lee must have made an effort to sit for Cowell later, but before the battle of Chancellorsville opened. That would place the timing of the likely Lee "Chancellorsville" photos to the very last days of April, 1863. For her part, Anna Jackson thought the photo of her husband gave "a sternness to his countenance that was not natural." Not surprisingly, Jackson's soldiers and surviving veterans loved it for that very reason.

26　McGuire, "Narrative," op. cit.; John Esten Cooke, quoted in Wert, *Cavalryman of the Lost Cause*, 198; Smith, op. cit., 3; discussion of Virginia plantation offices drawn from Freeman, *Lee's Lieutenants*, vol. 2, 497, footnote 3. Both Freeman and Robertson conflate the famous Christmas Dinner with Stuart's first visit, which is at odds with Smith's firsthand account. Stuart's autograph book, in the archives of the Virginia Historical Society, includes Jackson's signature with the appendage, "Your much-attached friend." (Autograph Book, JEB Stuart Papers, VHS).

27　One of the earliest and best chroniclers of the Chancellorsville Campaign (and a Union veteran of the Eleventh Corps), Augustus C. Hamlin, wrote of Lee and Stonewall, "Between Jackson and his illustrious commander, General Lee, there was much of that steady friendship, that sincere and mutual regard, that admirable adjustment and harmony, which threw an immortal lustre around the names and the actions of the great Marlborough and the Prince Eugene, less than two centuries ago." Written in 1895 for inclusion in Mary Anna's Jackson's *Memoirs* in a section of reminiscences near the end of the book, these words might be dismissed as maudlin reconciliationist verbiage, but they nonetheless convey the spirit of the personal relationship the two generals shared. See p. 559.

28　R. David Cox, *The Religious Life of Robert E. Lee*, xviii, 23–25, 132–135; Robertson, *Stonewall Jackson*, x, xii, xv; Robert E. Lee, General Orders No. 46, March 23, 1863, *O.R.*, series 1, vol. 25, part 2, 683; Lee to Mary Lee, March 27, 1863, in *Wartime Papers*, 419; Jackson to Mary Anna Jackson, April 10, 1863, reprinted in Mary Anna Jackson, *Memoirs of Stonewall Jackson*, 405. Many wartime letters written by Lee, both private and official, and practically all penned by Jackson, give thanks to God, demonstrate acceptance of God's will, and/or commend the fortunes of the army or object in question to the Lord's care. See *Wartime Papers*, especially chapters 6–13 and Dabney, *Life of Jackson*, op. cit., especially 583–592 and 635–659. A good summary of Jackson's petitions and references to the Almighty may be found in Warren J. Richards, *God Blessed Our Arms with Victory: The Religious Life of Stonewall Jackson* (New York: Vantage Press, 1986), 73–81. In an 1897 address at VMI, James Power Smith, who probably understood Jackson's religious character as well as any man, recalled "two notable things" about his chief's faith: "his belief in the providence of a present God, ruling and directing in wisdom, power and goodness in all the affairs of men; and his consequent belief in the right and power of prayer to Him whose ears are always open to the cry of His children, and who is ready to hear and answer above all that His children can ask or think." Smith, "Jackson's Religious Character: An Address at Lexington, Va.," June 23, 1897, reprinted in *Southern Historical Society Papers* 43 (September 1920), 67–75.

29   Cox, 130–132, 183–184; George C. Rable, "Stonewall Jackson: The Christian Soldier in Life, Death, and Defeat," 188–189; Pryor, *Reading the Man*, 235–236; Robertson, ibid., 134–136; Jackson quoted in Mary Anna Jackson, ibid., 394; 445; "Introduction," in Randall M. Miller, Harry S. Stout, and Charles Reagan Wilson, eds., *Religion and the American Civil War* (New York: Oxford University Press, 1998), 4–5; George C. Rable, *God's Almost Chosen Peoples: A Religious History of the American Civil War* (Chapel Hill: University of North Carolina Press, 2010), 1–3, 194; Mark A. Noll, *The Civil War as a Theological Crisis* (Chapel Hill: University of North Carolina Press, 2006), 5–7, 17–19, 84–86; Steven E. Woodworth, *While God is Marching On: The Religious Life of Civil War Soldiers* (Lawrence: The University Press of Kansas, 2001), 8–11, 52–54, 66, 76; Allen C. Guelzo, in *Gettysburg: The Last Invasion* (New York: Vintage Books, 2013), 125, notes, "Howard was, in fact, a sign of how thoroughly evangelical religion had permeated Anglo-American society in the nineteenth-century, and even begun to acquire a grudging respect in the profane culture of the military profession."

30   Gary W. Gallagher argues convincingly that Lee and his army (led also by his command team, it is implied) were the principal buoy of Confederate home front morale by mid-1863. It is a central argument of his *The Confederate War* and is succinctly expressed in "Another Look at the Generalship of Robert E. Lee," in Gallagher, ed., *Lee the Soldier*, 278–279. Of course, this team included the currently absent Longstreet and Jeb Stuart, but Jackson's previously won fame in the Valley Campaign—as Gallagher concedes—coupled with his exploits after attachment to Lee's army had elevated his reputation to a close second behind his chief in the opinion of most Southerners, both in and out of the army. As we have seen, before Lee took over command of the main Virginia army in June 1862, Stonewall's reputation probably exceeded Lee's.

31   Rable, "Stonewall Jackson," 188; Rev. B. T. Lacy's Narrative, pp. 2, 6–7, op. cit.; Emory Thomas, *Robert E. Lee*, 277–278; Lee to Mary Lee, April 5, 1863, in *Wartime Papers*, 428–429; William C. Davis, *Crucible of Command: Ulysses S. Grant and Robert E. Lee: The War They Fought, the Peace They Forged* (Boston: Da Capo Press, 2014), 285. See Lee to Mary Lee, March 9 and April 19, 1863, for references to his receipt of the *Southern Churchman*, and the March 20 issue of the newspaper for

a thinly veiled Jackson letter appealing for chaplains, asking that "each Christian denomination send one of its great lights into the army." The *Southern Churchman* was founded in Alexandria in 1835 as an organ of the Episcopal Church but moved to Richmond during the war and evolved into a more ecumenical evangelical Protestant publication. It was strongly pro-Confederate.

32   Lacy Narrative, pp. 1–5; Smith, "Stonewall Jackson in Winter Quarters," 6; W. G. Bean, "Beverly Tucker Lacy, Stonewall's Jolly Chaplain," *West Virginia History* 29, No. 2 (January 1968), 80, 87, 95; Samuel A. Firebaugh Diary entry, March 8, 1863, Civil War Documents Collection, Box 39, Folder 3, USAHEC; Rev. John W. Jones, *Christ in the Camp or Religion in Lee's Army*, 518–519.

33   Smith, ibid.; Lacy Narrative, p. 5; H. Rondel Rumburg, *"Stonewall" Jackson's Chaplain: Beverly Tucker Lacy* (Spout Spring, Va.: SBSS, 2012), 193; Lacy to editor, *Central Presbyterian*, April 7, 1863; Hotchkiss Diary entry, April 5, 1863, reprinted in McDonald, ed., *Make me a Map of the Valley*, 126. The original Lacy quote, taken from the newspaper, included General Lee among the April 5 attendees, but careful cross-referencing with Lee's correspondence indicates that Lee, still ill at this point, was not likely present. To Mary, Lee wrote in the April 5 letter, "I am suffering with a bad cold as I told you, and was threatened the doctors thought with some malady which must be dreadful if it resembles its name, but which I have forgotten. So they bundled me up on Monday last and brought me over to Mr. Y[erb]y's where I have a comfortable room with Perry to attend to me." (Reprinted in *Wartime Papers*, 428–429.) It is *possible* Lee still attended the April 5 service, which, if true, only lends credence to the argument that Lee was an ardent supporter of the chaplain. Sandie Pendleton wrote his mother on April 8, "Lacy . . . has stirred up the chaplains and infused some of his energy into them, and is doing a great work. He preaches well and is a charming companion." (Quoted in Bean, ibid., 92.) Lacy also preached sermons to individual regiments and brigades throughout his tenure, which would last well into 1864. After Jackson's death, he continued to serve as Second Corps "Chaplain General" under Richard Ewell and later Jubal Early.

34   Lacy Narrative, p. 5; Jones, *Christ in the Camp*, 95–96; Thomason, *Jeb Stuart*, 347; Lee to Mary Lee, April 12, 1863, in *Wartime Papers*, 432–433; *Richmond Enquirer* April 28, 1863 quoted in Robertson, *Stonewall Jackson*, 694. Hotchkiss noted in his diary at least one visit by Jackson to the ailing Lee, on March 29: "Gen. Lee is sick and Gen J. went over to see him in the P.M." See McDonald, ed., *Make Me a Map of the Valley*, 124; in a letter to his wife, Hotchkiss also wrote that Jackson prayed hard for Lee's recovery. See Vandiver, *Mighty Stonewall*, 451.

35   George W. Leyburn to J. William Jones, February 14, 1867, reprinted in Jones, 488–489; Smith, "Stonewall Jackson in Winter Quarters," 6; Hotchkiss diary entry, April 26, 1863, reprinted in McDonald, ed., *Make Me a Map of the Valley*, 134; Lacy Narrative, ibid.; Mary Anna Jackson, *Memoirs of Stonewall Jackson*, 411–412; Freeman, *Lee's Lieutenants*, vol. 2, 521. Freeman places Lee's visit to Mrs. Jackson at the Yerby House before the April 26 church service, which seems out of chronological order according to her narrative.

36   Jones, 245–246; Bean, "Beverly Tucker Lacy," 92–93; Lee to Hood, May 21, 1863,
      in *Wartime Papers*, 447; Lacy Narrative, p. 8. A fine narrative of Jackson's interac-
      tions with all chaplains and missionaries that also offers a good overview of their
      individual and collective effects on the army's spirituality may be found in John W.
      Schildt, *Jackson and the Preachers* (Parsons, W.V.: McClain Printing Company, 1982).

37   Freeman, *Robert E. Lee*, vol. 2, 499–500; Vandiver, *Mighty Stonewall*, 440–445 (Lee
      quote on p. 445); Jackson to Mary Anna Jackson, March 14, 1863, reprinted in
      Dabney, *Stonewall Jackson*, 655–656; Jackson to Boteler, March 7, 1863, Stonewall
      Jackson Correspondence, Coll. #0041, Washington and Lee University Special Col-
      lections; Hunter McGuire quoted in Freeman, *Lee's Lieutenants*, vol. 2, 519; Kegel,
      North with Lee and Jackson, 191; Freeman, ed., *Lee's Dispatches*, 74–75.

38   Jedediah Hotchkiss diary entries, February 23 (for original order from Jackson to
      create the map), 24–28 February, 2–6, and March 10, 12, 13, and 16, 1863 reprinted
      in McDonald, ed., *Make Me a Map of the Valley*, 116–121. For evidence of Lee's pres-
      ence in Richmond at the conference, see Hotchkiss's March 16 entry and Lee to
      Jeb Stuart, March 12, 1863, *O.R.*, Series 1, vol. 25, part 2, 664, and Lee to Davis,
      March 19, 1863, in ibid., 675.

39   McDonald, ibid., 294, footnote 25; John H. Reagan, *Memoirs: With Special Reference
      to Secession and the Civil War* (New York: Pemberton Press, 1968), 150–151; Lee to
      Longstreet, March 21, 1863, in *Wartime Papers*, 415–416: "I had hoped that you
      would have . . . accomplished the object proposed in my letter of the 17th . . ."; Davis
      to J. E. Johnston, March 20, 1863, *O.R.*, Series 1, vol. 23, part 2, 712.

40   Jedediah Hotchkiss, *Confederate Military History, Extended Edition: Vol. IV: Virginia*
      (1899: reprint Wilmington, N.C.: Broadfoot Publishing Company, 1987), 375–376;
      Lee to G.W.C. Lee, February 28, 1863, in *Wartime Papers*, 411. Hotchkiss also noted
      on p. 375 that "while tented in his winter quarters back of Fredericksburg, Lee was
      considering a plan of campaign for the coming spring, having frequent consultations
      with Jackson and Stuart." This work was published the year of Hotchkiss's death,
      thirty-six years after the events he describes, but that time lapse and his pro-Jackson
      bias aside the mapmaker's memory for detail and historical accuracy have been well-
      regarded by numerous historians over the years. Freeman, Vandiver, Robertson, and
      Gallagher, among others, have all cited him.

41   Lee to Mary Lee, April 3, 1863, in *Wartime Papers*, 416–417; *O.R.*, Series 1, vol.
      25, part 2, 681–682; Seddon to Lee, March 31, 1863, in *O.R.* ibid., 693–694;
      Lee to Davis, April 2, 1863, *O.R.*, ibid., 700–701. Besides an actual advance into
      the North, Seddon also may have been referring to plans that Lee, General John
      Imboden, and General Sam Jones, the latter two commanding minor forces in the
      Valley, had concocted earlier to liberate the northern half of the Shenandoah, eject
      the pillaging forces of Milroy (whom Lee and Jackson both seemed to place in a
      special class of cretin), and procure supplies. Lee had even promised elements of Jeb
      Stuart's cavalry to the scheme, but that idea was stillborn with the Union descent
      on Hampton Roads and Suffolk in February. The Valley commanders were left to
      their own devices with their meager means, but planning between them and Lee

continued, as is demonstrated by dozens of letters and dispatches in the late March–early April timeframe in the *Official Records*. Lee clearly believed attacking Milroy and making an effort in the Valley would have a positive effect on any offensive operations he would conduct against Hooker, and, according to David G. Smith in "'Clear the Valley': The Shenandoah Valley and the Genesis of the Gettysburg Campaign," *Journal of Military History* 74 (October 2010), 1069–1096, the "situation in the Shenandoah Valley was a key part of Lee's conceptualization" of the next northern campaign, whenever it would occur.

42 Freeman, *Robert E. Lee*, vol. 2, 502–3; Thomas, *Robert E. Lee*, 277–28; Lee to Mary Lee, April 5, 1863, in *Wartime Papers*, 427–428; see *O.R.*, Series 1, vol. 25, 685–710, for letters from Lee during the height of his sickness to various other officers and elected officials, signed by Taylor or Chilton; Dabney, *Life and Campaigns of Lieut.-Gen. Stonewall Jackson*, 654–655; Lee to Agnes Lee, April 11, 1863, 431–432.

43 Lee to Seddon, April 9, 1863, in *Wartime Papers*, 429–430; Lee to Jeremy F. Gilmer, April 11, 1863, *O.R.*, Series 1, vol. 25, part 2, 715; Gilmer to Lee, April 19, 1863, in ibid., 735; Lee to Cooper, April 16, 1863, in *Wartime Papers*, 433–434; Lee to Davis, April 16, 1863, Robert E. Lee Papers, Box 3, Rubenstein Library, Duke University; Freeman, *Robert E. Lee*, ibid., 503–504. A careful reading of all these letters and others in the Official Records and the *Wartime Papers* makes it clear that the chances for launching the offensive in time, before the Federals started theirs, depended on the timely dispatch of food and forage to the Army of Northern Virginia (from Longstreet's efforts or otherwise), Longstreet's return with his two divisions, and the continuation of the good weather that was drying out the roads, in descending order of significance. In these letters Lee accentuated his longstanding belief that sending any troops to the West would do little good: they would likely arrive too late to influence the course of a campaign there, and their absence from the East would concomitantly endanger the ability of the Virginia army to deflect the blows of the enemy, let alone progress toward realization of the goal of southern independence.

44 Jackson to Mary Anna Jackson, April 10, 1863, reprinted in Mary Anna Jackson, *Memoirs of Stonewall Jackson*, 405; *O.R.*, Series 1, vol. 25, part 2, 719–720; Freeman, *Lee's Lieutenants*, vol. 2, 519; Lee to Mary Lee, April 19, 1863, Lee Family Papers, Mss1L51c445, VHS; John Hampden Chamberlayne to mother, April 16, 1863, reprinted in C. G. Chamberlayne, ed., *Ham Chamberlayne—Virginian: Letters and Papers of an Artillery Officer* (Richmond, Va.: Press of the Dietz Printing Co., 1932), 168; Pender to wife, April 19, 1863, reprinted in Hassler, ed., *One of Lee's Best Men*, 225–226.

FOUR

1 Smith, "With Stonewall Jackson," 44; Hotchkiss diary entry, April 29, 1863, reprinted in McDonald, ed., *Make Me a Map of the Valley*, 136; Freeman, *Lee's Lieutenants*, vol. 2, 524; Robertson, *Stonewall Jackson*, 697–8.

2 Freeman, ibid., 524–5; Robertson, ibid., 698; Lacy Narrative, 8; Mary Anna Jackson, *Memoirs of Stonewall Jackson*, 415–417.

3   Hotchkiss diary entry, April 29, 1863, ibid.; Robertson, ibid.; Lee telegrams to
     Samuel Cooper, April 29, 1863 (twice) and Lee to Davis April 29, 1863 (twice),
     all reprinted in *Wartime Papers*, 441–443; *O.R.*, Series 1, vol. 25, part 2, 756–757,
     765; Sears, *Chancellorsville*, 163, 168; In response to Lee's communications, Davis,
     Cooper, and Seddon all sent telegrams of their own to various recipients, including
     D. H. Hill and Longstreet.

4   *O.R.*, ibid., 757–758; Lee to Davis April 29, 1863, ibid., 756; Lee to Davis, April
     30, 1863, ibid., 761; Hooker quoted in Sears, ibid., 120.

5   *O.R.*, ibid., Lee to Anderson, 6:45 P.M., April 29, 1863, and 2:30 P.M. April 30,
     1863; Lee to McLaws, 6:30 P.M., April 29, 1863, all 759–762.

6   Hotchkiss diary entry, April 30, 1863, reprinted in McDonald, 137; Robertson,
     Stonewall Jackson, 702; Freeman, *Robert E. Lee*, vol. 2, 512–513; Allan, "Memoranda
     of Conversations with General Robert E. Lee," February 15, 1868 and February 19,
     1870, reprinted in Gallagher, *Lee the Soldier*, 9, 18; "Address of General Fitzhugh
     Lee," Ninth Annual Reunion of the Association of the Army of Northern Virginia,
     October 29, 1879, reprinted in J. William Jones, comp., *Army of Northern Virginia
     Memorial Volume* (Richmond, Va.: J.W. Randolph and English, 1880), 310. A. L.
     Long, in his *Memoirs of Robert E. Lee*, claims it was a 2nd Corps artillery position
     that provided the perch for Lee and Jackson, but it appears he conflates events
     from this joint reconnaissance of the generals with another one the next day, so his
     information is somewhat suspect.

7   Hotchkiss diary entry, April 30, 1863, ibid.; Robertson, ibid., 703; Allan, ibid, 9.

8   "Address of General Fitzhugh Lee," 310–311; Freeman, *Lee's Lieutenants*, vol. 2, 527;
     "Special Orders No. 121," *O.R.*, Series 1, vol. 25, part 2, 762; Sears, *Chancellorsville*,
     181, 187–189.

9   Lacy Narrative, 9–10; Robertson, *Stonewall Jackson*, 704; William Allan Memoir,
     p. 175, Allan Papers, coll.#02764, UNC. Lacy documented in precise language
     the entirety of the conversation between him and Jackson on their way back from the
     Yerby Farm.

10   Lacy Narrative, 10; Allan Memoir, 176; Hotchkiss diary entry, May 1, 1863,
     reprinted in McDonald, 137; Sears, *Chancellorsville*, 198, 201; Daniel Butterfield
     to Joseph Hooker, *O.R.*, Series 1, vol. 25, part 2, 322.

11   Joseph Hooker, General Order, April 30, 1863, *O.R.*, Series 1, vol. 25, part 1, 171.

12   *Southern Historical Society* Papers, vol. 11 (1883), 137–138; Stuart to Jackson, 12:00
     P.M. May 1, 1863, and Jackson to Stuart, 12:30 P.M. May 1, 1863, both reprinted
     in same. The dispatches were part of the papers of Major R. Channing Price, Stu-
     art's adjutant general, who was killed at Chancellorsville. The account of Jackson
     praying in his tent on April 30 before the commencement of the movement was first
     related by Dabney in the 1864 edition of his biography, *The Life and Campaigns of
     Lieut.-General Jackson*, and has been recounted by most later biographers.

13   Sears, *Chancellorsville*, 202–203; William M. Dame to mother, May 2, 1863, copy of
     letter in FSNMP; Alexander quoted in Gallagher, ed., *Fighting for the Confederacy*,
     196; Allan, "Memoranda of Conversations with General Robert E. Lee (1868),"

9; Allan Memoir, 176; Freeman, *Robert E. Lee*, vol. 2, 517. In a frequently quoted passage, Alexander claims that Lee and Jackson rode together on the Plank Road from Fredericksburg: "Up the road from Fredericksburg comes marching a dense and swarming column of our shabby gray ranks, and at the head of them rode both General Lee and Stonewall Jackson. . . . And the conjunction of Lee and Jackson at head of the column meant that it was to be a supreme effort, a union of audacity and desperation." (p. 196). This account, written by Alexander from memory, contradicts that of Allan (both his 1868 notes from a conversation with Lee and his memoir), Dame (written the next day), Hotchkiss (written from recent and later memory) and others who claim Jackson rode alone and was later joined by Lee. Freeman agrees with Allan and the others.

14   *O.R.*, Series 1, vol. 25, part 1, 525, 825; Westwood Todd quoted in Sears, ibid., 205.

15   Sears, ibid., 208, 210; Hooker to Butterfield, May 1, 1863, *O.R.*, Series 1, vol. 25, part 1, 199; Butterfield to Hooker, May 1, 1863, ibid., part 2, 325–326. Sears correctly notes that a plethora of communications between Hooker and Butterfield litter the *Official Records* and the records of the Joint Committee on the Conduct of the War, which summoned Hooker before it, demanding explanations for the defeat at Chancellorsville. This summary of Hooker's informational and communicative problems is based partly on Sears and partly on the author's personal familiarity with these sources.

16   Hooker to Butterfield, May 1, 1863, 2:00 P.M., *O.R.*, ibid., 326; Hooker to Samuel P. Bates, April 2, 1877, quoted in Sears, ibid., 210, 212. Hooker's decision to withdraw his advancing corps has been a major topic of every history of the battle, and many historians over the years have opted for the oft-quoted canard, supposedly uttered by the commanding general himself, that "[he] just lost faith in Joe Hooker," meaning that he lost his nerve when confronted with the aggression of Lee and Jackson. See for instance, John Bigelow Jr., *The Campaign of Chancellorsville: A Strategic and Tactical Study* (New Haven, Conn.: Yale University Press, 1910), 254–255. Sears and other more recent historians, gifted by access to primary sources some of the earlier chroniclers did not possess, have not necessarily refuted that argument, but also contend that a lack of intelligence about the enemy combined with communications breakdowns were more likely the reasons behind the decision. Histories written by former Confederates, such as Hotchkiss and Allan, *The Battlefields of Virginia* (1867), op. cit., unsurprisingly credit the rebel leadership for so shocking Hooker by meeting him head-on that he was "compelled" to retreat to an unfavorable defensive position. Realistically, as this study argues, the historical truth likely lay in a combination of these explanations, and in the quick, adaptive flexibility displayed by the Confederate command team versus Hooker's more rigid and cautious reactions to the disruption of his campaign plan for May 1.

17   Bigelow, ibid., 252–253; Jackson to McLaws, 2:30 P.M., *O.R.*, Series 1, vol. 25, part 2, 764; Robert F. Beckham, official report, *O.R.*, Series 1, vol. 25, part 1, 1049; von Borcke, *Memoirs of the Confederate War for Independence*, 371–372; Furgurson, *Chancellorsville*, 133.

18   Allan, "Memoranda of Conversations with General Robert E. Lee (1868)," 9; Long,
      Memoirs of Robert E. Lee, 252, 254; Freeman, *Robert E. Lee*, vol. 2, 517–518.

19   T.M.R. Talcott to A. L. Long, July 19, 1886, Mss1T1434, VHS; Talcott, "General
      Lee's Strategy at the Battle of Chancellorsville," *Southern Historical Society Papers* 34
      (1906), 15–18; Chris Mackowski and Kristopher D. White, *That Furious Struggle:
      Chancellorsville and the High Tide of the Confederacy, May 1–4, 1863* (El Dorado Hills,
      Calif.: Savas Beatie, 2014), 43; Alpheus S. Williams to daughter, May 18, 1863,
      reprinted in Milo M. Quaife ed., *From the Cannon's Mouth: The Civil War Letters of
      General Alpheus S. Williams* (Detroit: Wayne State University Press, 1959), 187.

20   Talcott, "General Lee's Strategy," 14, 18; Fitzhugh Lee, "Address of General
      Fitzhugh Lee," 314–315; "A Reunion of Confederate Officers and their Ladies at
      a Dinner Party Given 24 February 1887, as Described by Col. David G. McIntosh
      CSA Very Soon After the Occasion," typescript, Mss7:1L515:13, David Gregg
      McIntosh Papers, VHS; Sears, *Chancellorsville*, 231.

21   Talcott to Long, July 19, 1886; Talcott, personal account, "General Lee's Strategy,"
      17, 20–21; Freeman, *Lee's Lieutenants*, vol. 2, 539–540; William Allan, "Memoranda"
      (1868), 9; Thomason, *Jeb Stuart*, 376. There is no solid firsthand account of the facial
      expressions of the generals involved (at this point in their planning process). The
      dramatization here is based on likely reactions of the men drawn from documented
      character portraits written down at other times during the war. Stuart's involvement
      in the Lee-Jackson meetings drops out of the historical record at this point; he may
      have spoken with Lacy in pursuit of the promised follow-up information and brought
      him to Lee later that night, but the evidence for this is limited.

22   Fitzhugh Lee, "Address of General Fitzhugh Lee," 315–317; R. E. Lee to A. T.
      Bledsoe, October 28, 1867, reprinted in same, 316; Lee to Mary Anna Jackson,
      January 25, 1866, reprinted in Henderson, *Stonewall Jackson*, 694–695; Talcott to
      Long, ibid; Talcott, "General Lee's Strategy," 17–18; A. L. Long, *Memoirs of Robert
      E. Lee*, 254–255; "A Reunion of Confederate Officers," op. cit.; Walter H. Taylor,
      Four Years with General Lee (New York: D. Appleton and Company, 1878), 84–85.
      As James I. Robertson aptly puts it, despite the arguments of Jackson's surviving
      staff officers—notably Dabney (who, of course, was not present at Chancellorsville),
      Morrison, and Hotchkiss—and Henderson, whose biography relied heavily on their
      correspondence, Stonewall did not first conceive of the idea to attack the Union right
      flank. "The evidence as a whole points to a different conclusion," Robertson wryly
      states (p. 711). Freeman devoted an entire appendix to the origination question,
      carefully sifting through the historical evidence then extant, and arrived at a similar
      result: "it is difficult to see how the controversy could have lasted so long or could
      have confused so many students of the campaign. . . . Lee originated the plan to turn
      Hooker's flank and to get in his rear; Jackson elaborated it by proposing to use his
      entire corps, and then executed the plan with assured genius." (Freeman, *Robert E.
      Lee*, vol. 2, 589) The facts do strongly point in this direction. Charles Marshall was
      very likely within earshot for most of this first segment of what would later become
      known as "The Last Meeting," and Talcott was close by for at least some of it. They

shared what they knew with Long and Taylor. No account survives indicating any of Jackson's staff officers were present for this first, pre-midnight conference. Most were asleep, Boswell was still out on his reconnaissance, and J. P. Smith was afield, serving as a courier for Lee. But Jackson himself left an account that bears on this still-flickering controversy. On May 3, while recovering from the amputation of his left arm, he told Chaplain Lacy, "Our movement of yesterday was a great success. I think, the most successful military movement of my life: but I expect to receive far more credit for it than I deserve. Most men will think that I had planned it all from the first, but it was not so." (Lacy Narrative, 15) Still, the 1863 edition of John Esten Cooke's *Life of Stonewall Jackson* claims that "General Jackson's suggestion that he should move well to the left and assail the enemy's right and rear near the Wilderness was speedily assented to by General Lee." (p. 249) Hotchkiss's personal copy of this wartime edition, copiously annotated with handwritten notes by himself, Sandie Pendleton (who was still alive at the first publication), and Hunter McGuire, unsurprisingly allows this assertion to stand without comment. (Hotchkiss's personal copy is preserved at UVA.) Hunter McGuire, writing to Hotchkiss in 1896, revealingly states, "I have always believed too, that Jackson suggested the detour around Hooker's Army, and the attack on Hooker's rear at Chancellorsville, but I have no positive proof of it; it was the common belief of our staff that he did it. I remember, Pendleton, Crutchfield, and myself often discussed it, and we all simply accepted it as a move proposed by Jackson." (McGuire to Hotchkiss, May 19, 1896, in Hotchkiss Papers, "War Book," LOC.) In an 1864 letter from D. H. Hill to Dabney, written in response to Dabney's request for personal information on Jackson for his forthcoming biography, Hill writes that J. G. Morrison told him of "an interesting incident" he experienced at Chancellorsville. "The night before the flank movement," Hill claims, Morrison said "he was lying down on the ground when he was awakened by an earnest conversation between Genl Lee and Jackson. The latter was earnestly advising a flank movement to which Genl Lee objected. Genl J then renewed his reasons & Genl Lee was silent for more than a quarter of an hour. At length he said in a hesitating, undecided manner, 'Well General, you may try it.' Genl Lee was for a front attack, which would have resulted most disastrously." (Hill to Dabney, July 21, 1864, Robert L. Dabney Collection, UPS.) Hotchkiss seems to have sullenly relented in the 1890s in his insistence that Stonewall first suggested the flank march to Lee, when he went to great lengths in some correspondence with Smith, McGuire, and Henry A. White to argue that he never meant to claim primacy for Jackson in his earlier *The Battlefields of Virginia*, published in 1867. His argumentation, although arcane, is essential because it reveals important details about both phases of the Last Meeting, such as the lack of light during the first conference and the words used by the generals in the second. See especially Hotchkiss to J. P. Smith, April 15, 1897 and Hotchkiss to White, April 18, 1897 (both in Hotchkiss Papers, "War Book," LOC).

23 Fitzhugh Lee, ibid., 316; Lee to Davis, May 2, 1863, *O.R.*, Series 1, vol. 25, part 2, 765.

24   The debate surrounding the wisdom of Lee's decision to dispatch Jackson on a march to attack the Federals right at Chancellorsville is almost as old as the decision itself, and a detailed analysis of it would require many pages. Most historians now agree that the decision was, as early Unionist chronicler William Swinton bluntly wrote, "full of risk" [Swinton, *Campaigns of the Army of the Potomac* (New York: Charles Scribner's Sons, 1882), 283], but that it was truly only a risk, not a bona fide "gamble," in which the result, if unfortunate for the Confederates, would equate with the destruction of the army. Lee's message to Davis, written on May 1, in between his meetings with Jackson and sent the next day, points strongly to that conclusion. The risk was mitigated by Lee's personal and professional trust in Stonewall and their joint faith in God, outlined in the previous chapter.

25   Dabney, *Life and Campaigns of Lieut.-General Jackson*, 675; Freeman, *Lee's Lieutenants*, vol. 2, 542; Robertson, *Stonewall Jackson*, 712; Hotchkiss to J. P. Smith, April 15, 1897, op. cit. The "cape incident" has become the stuff of legend over the years. What appears here is an amalgamation of accounts.

26   Vandiver, *Mighty Stonewall*, 465–466; Robertson, ibid.; Mary Anna Jackson, *Memoirs of Stonewall Jackson*, 420.

27   Long, *Memoirs of Robert E. Lee*, 252; the words and actions of Jackson and Lacy are taken verbatim from Lacy, Narrative, 11.

28   Hotchkiss diary entry May 2, 1863, reprinted in McDonald, *Make Me a Map of the Valley*, 137; Hotchkiss and William Allan, *The Battlefields of Virginia: Chancellorsville* (New York: D. Van Nostrand, 1867), 41–42; Lacy Narrative, ibid.; Hotchkiss to J. P. Smith, April 15, 1897, op. cit.; information on Wellford and Catharine Furnace found in Mackowski and White, *That Furious Struggle*, 53. None of Hotchkiss's accounts indicate that Lacy rode back with him to the headquarters crossroads, and Lacy's wartime narrative states simply, "Lacy went, found Ch. Bev. Welford [sic]. Hotchkiss returned." Most modern historians of the Chancellorsville Campaign and Jackson and Lee biographers claim both men rode back to the encampment. See, for instance, Sears, 234; Robertson, 713; and Freeman, *Robert E. Lee*. Vol. 2, 523. Interestingly, and more attuned to what the sparse historical record reveals, Freeman in *Lee's Lieutenants* credits Hotchkiss only with riding back to headquarters that night (vol. 2, p. 545).

29   Hotchkiss to J. P. Smith, ibid.; Hotchkiss to Hunter McGuire, October 8, 1898, Hotchkiss Papers, "War Book," LOC; J. P. Smith, *With Stonewall Jackson*, 46.

30   Long, *Memoirs of Robert E. Lee*, 258; Hotchkiss diary entry, May 2, 1863, reprinted in McDonald, 137.

31   Hotchkiss to J. P. Smith, April 15, 1897, op. cit. The imagery and description of Hotchkiss's directions are inspired by Vandiver, *Mighty Stonewall*, 467.

32   Hotchkiss and Allan, *Battlefields of Virginia*, 41–42; Hotchkiss to J. P. Smith, ibid.; Talcott, "General Lee's Strategy," 4–5; D. H. Hill to Robert L. Dabney, July 21, 1864, op. cit. The descriptions of the generals' thoughts during this discussion are, of course, conjecture, but combine the narratives of Henderson, Freeman, Vandiver, and Robertson, also taking into consideration likely questions and thought processes both

men may have wrestled with. Most of these accounts state that Lee said, "Well, go on," or "Well, go ahead." Hill's wartime quotation, drawn from a conversation with J. G. Morrison, who may have overheard some of the meeting (or its predecessor the night before), is another possibility. The exact wording of Lee's assent to Jackson's proposal to take his entire corps is unknown.

33   *O.R.*, Series 1, vol. 25, part 2, 719; Henderson, *Stonewall Jackson*, 665; Fitzhugh Lee, "Address of General Fitzhugh Lee," 317; E. P. Alexander's comment on cheering is in Gallagher, ed., *Fighting for the Confederacy*, 201; J. P. Smith, *With Stonewall Jackson*, 46.

34   Fitzhugh Lee, ibid., 317–318; Henderson, 666; Susan P. Lee, ed., *Memoirs of William Nelson Pendleton*, 259, 261; Sears, *Chancellorsville*, 239–240.

35   E. P. Alexander, *Military Memoirs of a Confederate* (New York: Charles Scribner's Sons, 1907), 330; Jackson quoted in Hunter McGuire, "Career and Character of General T. J. Jackson," *Southern Historical Society Papers* 25 (1897), 110; Alexander cited in Gallagher, ed., *Fighting for the Confederacy*, 201; George W. Slifer to uncle, May 9, 1863, FSNMP; Robertson, *Stonewall Jackson*, 717–718; B. B. Carr, "Sketch of the Battle of Chancellorsville," original in Civil War Collection, North Carolina State Archives, copy in FSNMP.

36   *O.R.*, Series 1, vol. 25, part 1, 385–386, 408; ibid., part 2, 361; Sears, *Chancellorsville*, 219, 245; James H. Van Alen (Hooker's aide-de-camp) to O. O. Howard, 9:30 A.M., cited in Christian B. Keller, *Chancellorsville and the Germans: Nativism, Ethnicity, and Civil War Memory* (New York: Fordham University Press, 2007), 53; Keller, ibid., 55; Furgurson, *Chancellorsville*, 148. Howard was tired on the morning of May 2, having stayed up late the night before, and after Hooker's morning inspection, had actually closed his eyes for a nap at his headquarters. One of his division commanders, Carl Schurz, awakened him with the 9:30 order and remonstrated that better precautions needed to be taken, but to no avail. After the war, Howard's memory of the events that morning and afternoon were notoriously foggy and imprecise. See Keller, 53–55.

37   *O.R.*, Series 1, vol. 25, part 1, 385, 979; Alexander, *Military Memoirs*, 331–332; William Allan Memoir, 177–178; Bigelow, *Chancellorsville* 280–81; Sears, ibid., 256; Keller, *Chancellorsville and the Germans*, 55. Hooker also ultimately ordered part of Slocum's Twelfth Corps to move south to the furnace. According to many recent authors, Sickles's preemptive conclusion that the Confederates were retreating, and the concomitant effect it had on Hooker and Howard, represented yet another inflection point in the campaign.

38   Fitzhugh Lee, "Address of General Fitzhugh Lee," 320; E. P. Alexander on Jackson's demeanor cited in Gallagher, ed., *Fighting for the Confederacy*, 201–202; J. P. Smith, *With Stonewall Jackson*, 47–48; Jackson to Lee, "Near 3 P.M." May 2, 1863, reprinted in same (original in Stonewall Jackson Collection, LOV); Vandiver, *Mighty Stonewall*, 470; Sears, ibid. Chancellor's, as Jackson called it, was another local name for Dowdall's Tavern, which, from his earlier vantage point on the hill with Fitzhugh Lee, Jackson viewed as the strongest point in the enemy line.

39   E. P. Alexander, cited in Gallagher, ibid., 201; Keller, *Chancellorsville and the Germans*, 55–56, 59–60; von Borcke, *Memoirs of the Confederate War for Independence*, 374.

40 Von Borcke, ibid., 375; Robertson, *Stonewall Jackson*, 721; *O.R.*, Series 1, vol. 25, part 1, 798, 941; J. P. Smith, *With Stonewall Jackson*, 48. Many participants wrote of the warmth and pleasantness of that late afternoon. Thomas Munford, a recent VMI graduate whose cavalry regiment had been in the lead of Fitzhugh Lee's brigade, claimed he was also present for Jackson's order to go forward, stating that Jackson had just uttered a few words about how many VMI graduates were present before giving Rodes the order. Jackson's famous statement, "The Institute will be heard from today," can be traced to Munford's (somewhat questionable) reminiscence of the event. See Munford quoted in *Lynchburg Advance*, April 20, 1923, cited in Robertson, ibid.

41 J. P. Smith, ibid., 49.

42 Eugene Blackford Memoir, Civil War Misc. Collection, 3rd Series, USAMHI; A. B. Searles, "On Picket at Chancellorsville," *Boston Journal*, n.d., copy in FSNMP; David Ackerman, 153rd PA, to Jacob H. Ackerman, May 11, 1863 (Ackerman Letters, 153rd Pennsylvania, P5-3, Cumberland County Historical Society, Carlisle, Penn.); Keller, *Chancellorsville and the Germans*, 57–58; North Carolinian quoted in Robertson, *Stonewall Jackson*, 722; *Southern Historical Society Papers* 40 (1915), 76–77.

43 Carl Schurz, "Reminiscences of a Long Life: The Eleventh Corps at Chancellorsville," *McClure's Magazine* (June 1907), 175; *Southern Historical Society Papers*, ibid., Keller, ibid., 63–68; Hecker quoted in *Pittsburgher Freiheitsfreund* May 22, 1863. When precisely Howard returned from his adventure with Sickles into the chaos of Jackson's attack is unknown. Sears and Furgurson disagree on the timing. It is probable it occurred after the Wilderness Church line broke but before the formation of the "Buschbeck Line," the second of the two Eleventh Corps stands near the Tavern. See Sears, *Chancellorsville*, 277, and Furgurson, *Chancellorsville*, 181. Howard's behavior upon his return was much debated by Eleventh Corps survivors after the war.

44 Augustus C. Hamlin, *The Battle of Chancellorsville* (Bangor, Me.: privately published, 1896), 68–69; Vandiver, *Mighty Stonewall*, 475; Robert E. Wilbourn to Charles J. Faulkner, May 1863 (precise date unknown), Charles J. Faulkner Papers, Mss1 F2735a FA2 (Box 37), VHS, available at: http://www.vahistorical.org/collections -and-resources/virginia-history-explorer/general-orders-no-61/eyewitness-account; Robert E. Wilbourn to Robert L. Dabney, December 12, 1863, Dabney Papers, Box 19, UNC. Most scholars of the campaign now agree that, contrary to Lost Cause accounts of the battle (such as that portrayed by Dabney), the chances of Jackson overcoming the numerical, temporal, and terrain difficulties facing him to achieve the destruction or near-destruction of Hooker's army were quite low. The Union First and Fifth Corps barred the way to U.S. Ford by the late evening, when Stonewall was trying to reconstitute his assault, and the tangled forest in front of them was especially challenging, even in daylight. A student of Napoleon, who argued that "the moral is to the physical as three is to one," Jackson probably perceived that he had achieved an immense advantage with the element of surprise and the momentum of his flank attack, and wished to see it inflict as much damage on the Federals as

possible. If he could somehow cut off the enemy from U.S. Ford and sustain that position, he likely believed he could achieve the magnitude of victory he and Lee had hoped for, but it is unfair to assume that he would have blindly and rashly adhered to a tactical course of action in defiance of realities, as modern detractors argue. Doing so would have flown in the face of most his battle record so far in the war. For an early, evenhanded assessment of Jackson's decisions and position after nightfall but before his wounding, see H. B. McClellan, *The Life and Campaigns of Major-General J.E.B. Stuart: Commander of the Cavalry of the Army of Northern Virginia* (1885: reprint, Secaucus, N.J.: The Blue and Grey Press, 1993), 251–255. Another objective assessment, which has influenced Furgurson, Sears, and other modern chroniclers, is in Bigelow, *Chancellorsville*, 337–338.

45   Sears, 290–291; James I. Robertson, *General A. P. Hill: The Story of a Confederate Warrior* (New York: Vintage Books, 1987), 184–185; Jackson quoted in Bean, *Stonewall's Man*, 115.

46   J. G. Morrison to E. P. Alexander, July 2, 1869, E. P. Alexander Papers, Box 3, Folder 25a, UNC; David J. Kyle reminiscence, 1895, volume 207, FSNMP; J. G. Morrison to Robert L. Dabney, October 29, 1863, Dabney Collection, UNC.; Krick, *The Smoothbore Volley that That Doomed the Confederacy*, 5–11 and 13–22. Krick pioneered the modern research into where, how, and when Jackson was wounded, piecing together his analysis from dozens of firsthand and secondhand accounts. His essay, first appearing in Gary W. Gallagher, ed., *Chancellorsville: The Battle and its Aftermath* (Chapel Hill: University of North Carolina Press, 1996), was reprinted in the aforementioned anthology by Krick. A recent work that adds to Krick's superb foundation and continues the narrative up to Jackson's death is Chris Mackowski and Kristopher D. White, *The Last Days of Stonewall Jackson: The Mortal Wounding of the Confederacy's Greatest Icon* (El Dorado Hills, Calif.: Savas Beatie, 2013).

47   Jackson on wounds by his own men quoted in Cooke, *The Life of Stonewall Jackson* (1863 ed.), 254; Krick, *Smoothbore Volley*, 31–33, 35–38; Jackson quoted in Lacy Narrative, 15–16; Robertson, *Stonewall Jackson*, 731, 739. Exactly when the general dictated the note is unknown. The two most likely time periods are directly before or after the amputation or early the next morning. I have chosen the former option based on impressions gleaned from other sources that mention the note to Lee. Chaplain Lacy fetched the amputated arm and buried it on the grounds of his brother's nearby estate, Ellwood, where it remains to this day.

48   Wilbourn to Faulkner, May 1863, op. cit.; Hotchkiss diary entry, May 2, 1863, reprinted in McDonald, ed., *Make Me a Map of the Valley*, 138; Hotchkiss to G.F.R. Henderson, March 6, 1897, Hotchkiss Papers, "War Book," LOC; White, *Robert E. Lee and the Southern Confederacy*, 269–270; John Esten Cooke, undated diary entry (but probably May 10, 1863), reprinted in Hubbell, ed., "The War Diary of John Esten Cooke," 537; Lee to Stuart, May 3, 1863, 3:00 A.M. and 3:30 A.M., both reprinted in Dowdey and Manarin, *Wartime Papers*, 451; E. P. Alexander quoted in *Military Memoirs of a Confederate*, 345; E. P. Alexander to H. B. McClellan, May

16, 1885, reprinted in H. B. McClellan, *The Life and Campaigns of Major-General J.E.B. Stuart*, 255–256.

49   Marshall quoted in Maurice, ed., *An Aide-de-Camp of Lee*, 173; Lee to Jackson, May 3, 1863, George H. and Katherine M. Davis Collection, Tulane University Manuscripts Division (copy at VHS); Jackson quoted in J. P. Smith, *With Stonewall Jackson*, 54. On the afternoon of May 3, Lee dispatched McLaws eastward down the Orange Turnpike to reinforce the brigade of Cadmus Wilcox, the only viable Confederate force between Sedgwick's oncoming VI Corps and Lee's rear at Chancellorsville. That evening McLaws and Wilcox stopped Sedgwick cold at Salem Church, and, along with Anderson and a reconstituted Early, launched a strong assault against the Unionists the next day. With no corps-level leader to direct them, however, Lee's division commanders failed to coordinate their attacks and Sedgwick, battered but intact, withdrew to safety across the river. This was the first instance when Jackson's absence handicapped Lee's ability to achieve his objective, and the commanding general publicly lost his temper with his subordinates, whom he had hoped would work matters out while he remained at Chancellorsville. There he watched a chastened but numerically superior Hooker, who had recovered from his accident of the previous day and withdrawn his army to a tight, defensive "apex" line hugging the Rappahannock. With Sedgwick's retreat, Hooker lost hope his campaign could be resurrected and slipped across to the northern bank shortly thereafter. There was little Lee could do to prevent his escape.

50   Robert E. Lee, General Orders No. 59, May 7, 1863, in *O.R.*, Series 1, vol. 25, part 1, 805; Shaw, *Stonewall Jackson's Surgeon*, 36; Pendleton-Jackson exchange recorded in Bean, *Stonewall's Man*, 118; Just before arriving at Guiney's Station, Jackson asked if he could cover his chest with cold, wet towels to help alleviate the pain developing in his side (not his stump arm) and provide relief from the rising temperature. An example of one of Stonewall's idiosyncratic homeopathies, the "wet towel controversy" rages to this day as a possible reason the general contracted pneumonia and died. One of the doctors attending him, Harvey Black, wrote his wife on May 10, the very morning Jackson passed, stating "it is supposed this caused the attack" of pneumonia, and the observant William Dorsey Pender claimed in a May 9 letter that Jackson "has pneumonia contracted by wrapping himself in wet towels after he was wounded." Harvey Black to wife, May 10, 1863, Black Letters, Special Collections, Virginia Polytechnical University (copy at FSNMP) and Pender to wife, May 9, 1863, reprinted in Hassler, ed., *One of Lee's Best Men*, 236. William Nelson Pendleton, mutual friend of both Lee and Jackson agreed with these assessments. In a letter to his wife on May 9, he wrote "General Jackson is extremely ill from pneumonia, taken by wrapping himself, all wounded and sore as he was, in a wet sheet." Pendleton to wife, May 9, 1863, partially reprinted in Susan Lee, ed., *Memoirs of William Nelson Pendleton*, 269.

51   James Power Smith telegram to sister, May 10, 1863, Stonewall Jackson Collection, MOC; Walter Taylor, *Four Years With General Lee*, 86; David Lloyd George quoted in Mackowski and White, *That Furious Struggle*, 129. The Confederates

suffered almost 13,000 casualties in the Chancellorsville Campaign, which also included the battles of Second Fredericksburg and Salem Church. In that number were nine general officers and 64 of 130 regimental commanders, losses in smaller unit leadership the South could not afford nor easily replace. (See Mackowski and White, 128.) Federal casualties amounted to nearly 17,000. The greatest blow to the Union as a result of the failed campaign was political, not military, however. Yet another northern offensive in the East had come to naught. Lincoln despairingly asked, "My God, my God, what will the people say?" Northern home front morale plummeted and the advocates for peace gained popular strength throughout many voting districts, especially in the lower Midwest and rural Pennsylvania. Morale in the Army of the Potomac initially suffered but rebounded by scapegoating Hooker and the German soldiery of the Eleventh Corps.

FIVE

1   Cooke, *The Life of Stonewall Jackson*, 1863, 271.

2   "Dreadful blow" quote cited in Wert, *A Glorious Army*, 209.

3   Cooke, 271. Cooke's biography, like Dabney's slightly later one, is valuable if read carefully, with an eye toward who wrote it and why, and with an understanding of the context in which it was written (literally in camp in between missions). Both biographies underwent numerous rewrites and editions over the years, and both subsequently edited out sections that evinced strong feeling against the North and anything that could be construed as critical of Jackson. The earliest editions of both are historically the most trustworthy; later ones drip with Lost Cause clichés. Cooke's depictions of how Confederates reacted to Jackson's death should therefore be taken—when considered alongside the plethora of similar primary accounts—as the distillation of impressions gathered by an eyewitness at the time. See Wallace Hettle, *Inventing Stonewall Jackson*, chapter 3 (pp. 53–68) for a critical appraisal of Cooke.

4   Lee to Mary Custis Lee, May 11, 1863, DeButts-Ely Papers, LOC (now in possession of VHS); Lee to Stuart, May 11, 1863, *O.R.*, Series 1, vol. 25, part 2, 792. Just after Jackson's death, the heartbroken Pendleton tearfully told the general's widow, Anna, "God knows I would have died for him." See Pendleton Reminiscences, FSNMP.

5   Robert E. Lee, *Recollections and Letters of General Robert E. Lee: By His Son Captain Robert E. Lee* (New York: Doubleday, Page, and Company, 1904), 94; the "executive officer" quote has been repeated by various chroniclers almost since 1865, but is most conspicuous in Freeman, *Lee's Lieutenants*, vol. 2, 687; Lee to Charles Carter Lee, May 24, 1863, transcription in Robert E. Lee Collection, Box 1, Small Special Collections Library, UVA. Regarding Lee's inner circle: Lee certainly trusted Longstreet professionally, despite his disappointment with the latter's performance in the recent Suffolk Campaign, and had enjoyed his company in camp from time to time in previous campaigns. There is little evidence, however, that he viewed him

as a personal friend by the spring of 1863. The same could be said of Jeb Stuart, whom Lee trusted and admired implicitly, but whom he regarded more paternally than on an equal personal footing. Age differences probably played a role in both instances. A. P. Hill and Richard Ewell, who would soon rise to corps command, were division commanders whom Lee strongly respected and relied upon, but they, too, were significantly younger than Lee and had been part of Jackson's command team. John B. Hood, one of Longstreet's division chiefs and also much younger than Lee, curiously appears to have enjoyed more of his personal esteem to some degree, but the evidence for this is spotty at best. (See Lee to Hood, May 21, 1863, cited below, for instance, in which Lee signs off, "I am, now and always, your friend.") Lee also believed Hood a "bold fighter" but a weaker administrator and thinker, as evidenced when Davis asked his opinion of the general prior to giving him command of the Army of Tennessee in 1864. Only in the similarly aged chief of artillery, William Nelson Pendleton (Sandie Pendleton's father and an Episcopal minister), did Lee find a true friend and confidant. According to Joseph Glatthaar, "he could speak freely and reveal his emotions with Pendleton." See Glatthaar, *General Lee's Army*, 340.

6   Lee to J. B. Hood, May 21, 1863, reprinted in *The Lost Papers of Confederate General John Bell Hood* (Eldorado Hills, Calif.: Savas Beatie, 2015), letter 11.3; for incomplete transcriptions of this letter see Rev. J. William Jones, D.D., *Life and Letters of Robert Edward Lee: Soldier and Man* (1906, reprint Harrisonburg, Va.: Sprinkle Publications, 1986), 247; and Dowdey and Manarin, *Wartime Papers*, 490; Lee to William C. Rives, May 21, 1863, Lee Collection, Van Dyke McBride File, MOC; Lee to Charles Carter Lee, op. cit.; Lee to General Samuel Cooper, Adjutant and Inspector General, "Battle Report of Chancellorsville Campaign," September 23, 1863, reprinted in *Wartime Papers*, 469.

7   General Orders No. 61 is reprinted in numerous publications, including the *O.R.*, Series 1, 25, part 2, 793, and *Wartime Papers*, 485. Elizabeth Brown Pryor, in her magisterial work, *Reading the Man*, offers a concise history of Lee's faith journey from childhood to old age in chapter 14 (pp. 223–240), yet mentions nothing about Jackson's influence in the maturation of Lee's Christianity and is somewhat skeptical of the genuineness of his evangelicalism. She does admit that "something changed in his outlook" during the war, and that "he struggled to trust that [God's] merciful providence would order all things for the benefit of the Confederacy." (p. 235) Her work builds upon that of Freeman, who also spilled considerable ink on Lee's religiosity in his classic three-volume biography, as well as subsequent biographers such as Dowdey and Emory Thomas. None of them, however, have identified or even hypothesized that the wartime relationship with Jackson, peaking in the winter of 1862–1863, may have made a difference, probably because there are no extant "smoking gun" letters that overtly mention this or even allude to it. Cox comes the closest in his recent and persuasively argued book, *The Religious Life of Robert E. Lee* (op. cit.), but even Cox has very little to say about the Jackson connection except that Lee joined Jackson as a believing, providential evangelical. The eyewitness

accounts of Lacy, Jones, Leyburn, Dabney and others during the war, cited previously, offer much evidence, however, that a shared providential-evangelical Christian faith served as a glue for the two generals' friendship, and that Jackson's personal oversight of chaplains and religious services during the post-Fredericksburg months was approved and appreciated by Lee. It is clear that only a few months after Jackson's death, following Gettysburg, a committee consisting of many of Jackson's old chaplains, including Lacy, approached Lee about keeping Sundays sacred, spreading the ongoing revival, and supporting chaplains' work in general. After they explained their reasons for coming to him, "we saw his eye brighten and his whole countenance glow with pleasure; and as, in his simple feeling words, he expressed his delight, we forgot the great warrior, and only remembered that we were communing with a humble, earnest Christian." When Lacy then told Lee how the chaplains prayed for him personally, "tears started in his eyes, as he replied, 'I sincerely thank you for that, and I can only say that I am a poor sinner, trusting in Christ alone for salvation.'" See Jones, *Life and Letters*, 466–467.

8   William Preston Johnston, "Reminiscences of General Robert E. Lee," *Belford's Magazine* 5, no. 25 (June 1890). Lee had served under (then) Colonel Albert Sydney Johnston as Lieutenant Colonel of the Second Cavalry in the mid-1850s, and had first met the younger Johnston in Louisville as he made his way west to report for duty to his father. Ironically, A. S. Johnston was considered, at the beginning of the war, to be the Confederacy's best general and was a close friend of President Davis, but his untimely death at the Battle of Shiloh in April 1862 opened an opportunity for Lee to become the president's most influential general. Over the years, W. P. Johnston had countless opportunities to observe and talk with Lee, and later served as one of his faculty at Washington College after Lee accepted the presidency of the institution. His recollections here are not likely to be inflated.

9   Longstreet, *From Manassas to Appomattox*, 328, 332. Longstreet clearly believed he and Lee had jointly planned the coming Pennsylvania campaign and that Lee relied strongly on his counsel in it. Yet nowhere in his published or unpublished writings did he mention Jackson's influence on the decision to strike north in 1863. See Wert, *General James Longstreet*, 242–247. Longstreet's published memoirs and several other postwar publications cannot be taken 100% at face value, tainted as they were by his attempts to vindicate his fallen reputation, and, perhaps, inflate his role in the war. In a private postwar letter, he stated, "That Jackson was clever there is no doubt, but that he was superhuman as the Virginians who have written about him would have the world believe there is room for grave doubts." See Wallace Hettle, *Inventing Stonewall Jackson*, 101.

10   William Nelson Pendleton to wife, June 1, 1863, William Nelson Pendleton Papers, Box 3, Folder 33b, UNC. On May 17, 1864, Pendleton wrote his wife about the death of Jeb Stuart, claiming "he is indeed a great loss to us, next to Jackson." Pendleton's postwar writings and his postwar memoirs—highly edited by his daughter and published in 1893—must be read with an eye toward Lost Cause influences, but his unedited wartime letters offer candid, detailed accounts of the relationships,

thoughts, and actions of the Army of Northern Virginia's most senior officers, especially Lee and Jackson.

11   Douglas, *I Rode With Stonewall*, 221–222.

12   James Power Smith, *With Stonewall Jackson*, 55; Charles Venable to R. L. Dabney, December 21, 1864, R. L. Dabney Papers, Box 2-4b, UPS. Venable's letter also lamented "our late disasters" but closed with hope that "your work will soon be published and that it may accomplish much good in holding up that great Christian patriot as a bright exemplar to his countrymen."

13   Rev. J. William Jones, D.D., *Personal Reminiscences of General Robert E. Lee* (New York: D. Appleton and Company, 1874), 29. As a leading chaplain in the army, Jones had opportunity to observe firsthand Lee's reactions to Jackson's passing. This, his first book, is considered a fairly reputable source on Lee's thoughts and actions during the war and especially afterward, when he spent countless hours with him in Lexington. Jones was a Baptist minister in the town when Lee was president of Washington College. Some scholars caution citation of direct quotes, however, and his later publications were often tainted with Lost Cause motifs.

14   Charles Royster, in *The Destructive War*, claims that "many Southerners' private writings in May and June of 1863, like their public exhortations," took the optimistic view that Jackson's death would be made good by God, but ironically cites far more evidence that they simultaneously realized a dreadful turning point had been reached (see pp. 227–228 especially). The historical record of 1863–1865, along with trustworthy postwar accounts, points more convincingly to the latter, with the former used more as a balm to ameliorate the tragic sense of loss. Appreciation and recognition that Jackson had gone to his own reward for being such a Christian exemplar—"he is happy and at peace," as Lee told Hood—is mentioned in wartime sources as frequently if not more often than the hope of holy compensation for the dead leader. Another noticeable theme in religious reactions to Jackson's death was, as George C. Rable explains, a belief that "the Southern people had relied excessively on 'an arm of flesh,'" that "the general's death proved the folly of placing too much faith in even the most upright human being" instead of in the Lord, and that God had therefore chastised the Confederacy for the collective sin. Each of these religious themes, well examined by Royster and Rable, helped grieving Confederates cope with their loss, and "turned the general's life into an evangelical object lesson." See Rable, "Stonewall Jackson: the Christian Soldier in Life, Death, and Defeat," in Lawrence Lee Hewitt and Thomas E. Schott, eds., *Lee and His Generals: Essays in Honor of T. Harry Williams* (Knoxville: University of Tennessee Press, 2012), 181–200, and especially 190–193. For a similar argument, see also Daniel W. Stowell's fine essay, "Stonewall Jackson and the Providence of God" in Randall M. Miller, Harry S. Stout, and Charles Reagan Wilson, eds., *Religion and the American Civil War*, 187–207.

15   Most of Davis's reactions to Jackson's passing are found in his wife's postwar memoir of his presidency. Certain sections of this work are considered historically questionable by scholars, but others, including the one from which these quotations were

drawn, are more reliable. Varina Davis, *Jefferson Davis, Ex-President of the Confederate States of America: A Memoir*, vol. 2 (New York: Belford Co., 1890), 382–383; Hunter McGuire, "General Thomas J. Jackson: Reminiscences of the Famous Leader," 305; Jones, *A Rebel War Clerk's Diary*, 205; O.R., Series 1, vol. 25, pt. 2, 791; Davis, *Rise and Fall*, vol. 2, 365.

16 O.R., series 4, vol. 2, 994; Seddon to R. L. Dabney, May 30, 1863, Charles William Dabney Papers, Subseries 3.1, folder 251, UNC. Freeman quoted just a few lines from Seddon's telling report, but emphatically stated it was "in correct presentation of the public's judgment." See Freeman, *Lee's Lieutenants*, vol. 2, 689.

17 Hotchkiss to wife, May 19, 1863, Hotchkiss Papers, Family Correspondence 1863, Box 9, Reel 5, LOC; Benjamin Leigh to wife, May 12, 1863, transcribed by R. L. Dabney in Charles William Dabney Papers, op. cit.; Stuart to William Alexander Stuart, n.d., reprinted in part in John W. Thomason, Jr., *Jeb Stuart* (New York: Charles Scribner's Sons, 1929), 412; Wert, *A Glorious Army*, 209; Mary Anna Jackson to Stuart, August 1, 1863, J.E.B. Stuart Papers, Mss1St923c3-26, VHS; William Nelson Pendleton to wife, May 14, 1863, reprinted in Susan P. Lee, ed., *Memoirs of William Nelson Pendleton*, 271–272. Reverend B. T. Lacy wrote to J. P. Smith in early June, "We hope soon to have you with us—our little military family, which was so sadly dispersed by the death of our great leader and dear friend, is again gathering together. You and Lieut. Morrison are all who are now away." Lacy to Smith, June 2, 1863, Beverly Tucker Lacy Papers, Mss2l1196a1, VHS.

18 Pegram quoted in James I. Robertson, Jr., *General A. P. Hill*, 192; William J. Reese to unknown recipient, May 15, 1863, quoted in Glatthaar, *General Lee's Army*, 255; Hunter McGuire to Jedediah Hotchkiss, December 23, 1897, Hotchkiss Papers, General Correspondence 1897, LOC; Ewell General Order transcribed by Hotchkiss as General Order #43, June 11, 1863, in Hotchkiss Papers, Writings File: War Papers Digest of General Orders and Letters of General T. J. Jackson, 1861–1863, Reel #49, LOC; speculations on Hill's possible grudge and staff officer quoted in Robertson, *A. P. Hill*, op. cit.; Henry Kyd Douglas, *I Rode With Stonewall*, 196. Another General who may have had reason to think ill of Jackson was Brigadier General Richard Garnett, whom Jackson had tried to court-martial for retreating the Stonewall Brigade at Kernstown in March 1862. Lee defused the situation by reassigning Garnett to Pickett's Division (a brigade of which Garnett would lead in Pickett's Charge at Gettysburg), but Garnett felt poorly handled. His brigade encamped near Richmond when Jackson's body arrived, Garnett attended the first viewing at the Governor's Mansion and broke into tears. Taking Sandie Pendleton and Henry Kyd Douglas to a nearby window, he exclaimed, "I wish here to assure you that no man can lament his death more sincerely than I do. I believe he did me great injustice, but I believe also he acted from the purest motives. He is dead. Who can fill his place!" (Quoted in Freeman, *Lee's Lieutenants*, vol. 2, 685.)

19 Depiction of the services, scene in the camps, and the weather drawn from Daniel Lyon, Medical Director's Office, Army of Northern Virginia, to his wife, May 14, 1863, transcription at FSNMP (from original at VHS); Bean, "Stonewall Jackson's

Jolly Chaplain," 89–90; Jones, *Christ in the Camp*, 484. It was before and after this particular church service that Lee approached Lacy inquiring about Jackson's condition, as narrated in the introduction to this book. It should also be noted that thousands of soldiers chose not to participate in morning worship that day.

20 "Everyone knew it" quote cited in Krick, *The Smoothbore Volley*, 39; Charles Minnigerode to his mother, May 12, 1863, reprinted in Marietta Minnigerode Andrews, *Scraps of Paper* (New York: E.P. Dutton & Co., 1929), 113–116; "It is not extravagant to say" quote is cited in Robertson, *Stonewall Jackson*, 755. Also see Casler, *Four Years in the Stonewall Brigade*, 155, for a good synopsis of the reaction in the camps when the soldiers first heard that Jackson was dead.

21 Fulton quote drawn from his 1919 reminiscence, transcribed and available at http://history-sites.com/civilwar/units/5albn/Chapter%2010.htm; Samuel D. Buck, 13th Virginia, quoted in Royster, *The Destructive War*, 227; R. F. Crenshaw to cousin Sallie, May 12, 1863, Lewis Leigh Collection, Book 50, Letter 44, USAMHI; Joshua Howell to his wife, May 14, 1863, FSNMP; David Ballenger to his brother, May 19, 1863, FSNMP; William Wirt Gilmer, "Notes on the War of 1861–1865" derived from wartime diary entries, Mss8461, UVA; Joseph Hilton to his cousin, May 15, 1863; Blackford, *War Years with Jeb Stuart*, 206; and Ross Gaston reminiscence quoted in Krick, *The Smoothbore Volley*, 40. A very few of the soldiers' letters reviewed revealed no concern for the future. One of these was written by A. C. Cooper of Cabell's Artillery Battalion (McLaws Division): "The loss is heavy to the South, but is not [an] irreparable one. We have Genl's here far superior to him. Lee and Longstreet are more popular and competent leaders than he. Others will soon be his equal. The South places her defense in no man. Leaders will spring up as fast as others are killed. . . . This is all nonsense and toadyism." A. C. Cooper to his mother, May 18, 1863, FSNMP.

22 "The Death of Stonewall Jackson—Action of the Stonewall Brigade," transcription in Dabney-Jackson Collection, #24816, Series II, Box 23, item 173, LOV, reprint in James Power Smith, *With Stonewall Jackson*, 100–102; Ted Barclay to his sister, May 12, 1863 and October 21, 1863. The entire set of these remarkably detailed and poignant letters are available from Washington and Lee Special Collections online at https://repository.wlu.edu/handle/11021/23994. Barclay was likely very influenced in his October letter by the anticlimactic denouement of the Bristoe Station Campaign. Officers and soldiers alike, including Lee, had held high hopes of striking a telling blow against George Meade and the Army of the Potomac, but Meade carefully evaded and parried every trap and flanking maneuver. A. P. Hill performed particularly below par in this campaign. See Bill Backus and Robert Orrison, *A Want of Vigilance: The Bristoe Station Campaign, October 9–19 1863* (El Dorado Hills, Calif.: Savas Beatie, 2015) for a good overview of what became Lee's last theater offensive.

23 William C. Davis and Meredith L. Swentor, eds., *Bluegrass Confederate: The Headquarters Diary of Edward O. Guerrant* (Baton Rouge: Louisiana State University Press, 1999), 276; Thomas W. Cutrer, ed., *Our Trust is in the God of Battles: The*

Civil War Letters of Robert Franklin Bunting, Chaplain, Terry's Texas Rangers, C.S.A. (Knoxville: University of Tennessee Press, 2006), 162; Abram Fulkerson to his wife, May 18, 1863, cited in Chris Mackowski and Kristopher D. White, *The Last Days of Stonewall Jackson: The Mortal Wounding of the Confederacy's Greatest Icon* (El Dorado Hills, Calif.: Savas Beatie, 2013), 90; Kate Peddy to George W. Peddy, May 12, 1863, reprinted in George Peddy Cuttino, ed., *Saddlebag and Spinning Wheel, Being the Civil War Letters of George W. Peddy, M.D., and his Wife Kate Featherston Peddy* (Macon, Ga.: Mercer University Press, 1981); D. H. Hill, General Orders No. 20, May 26, 1863, D. H. Hill Papers, Box 6, LOV; Marshall quoted in G. D. Camden to R. L. Dabney, November 25, 1863, Dabney Papers, UNC, op. cit.

24   *Southern Literary Messenger* 37, Issue 6 (June 1863), 374–375; *Richmond Daily Dispatch* May 12, 1863; Rev. James Ramsey, eulogy delivered at Jackson's funeral, Lexington, Va., May 15, 1863, cited in Mackowski and White, *The Last Days of Stonewall* Jackson, 89; Melinda Ray diary entry, May 13, 1863, Civil War Collection, Box 78, Folder 32, State Archives of North Carolina, Raleigh, available at http://digital.ncdcr.gov/cdm/ref/collection/p15012coll8/id/13079; Catherine Ann Devereux Edmonston diary entry, May 11, 1863, reprinted in Beth G. Crabtree and James W. Patton, eds., *Journal of a Secesh Lady* (Raleigh: North Carolina Department of Archives and History, 1979), 392; Kate S. Sperry, Winchester, Va., diary entry May 13, 1863, quoted in Robertson, *Stonewall Jackson*, 755; Louise Fellowes to Mrs. Stonewall Jackson, August 14, 1863, in Thomas J. Jackson Papers, VMI Archives; Kate Stone diary quote reprinted in John Q. Anderson, ed., *Brokenburn: The Journal of Kate Stone, 1861–1868* (Baton Rouge: Louisiana State University Press, 1972), 211. Drew Gilpin Faust, in her award-winning *This Republic of Suffering: Death and the American Civil War* (New York: Vintage Books, 2008) offers the intriguing thesis that Jackson's death served as a national representation of thousands of previously unmourned deaths, that as "the ideal embodiment of the Christian soldier," the Confederacy could both symbolically mourn for all those who had died while simultaneously "assert[ing] its claims to religious superiority." See 154–155. Faust also correctly posits that Jackson's passing joined Lincoln's death as one of the two great moments of mourning in the Civil War. In other words, Jackson's loss to the Confederacy equated for the people of the South what the assassination of Lincoln meant for the North (158–159).

25   Richmond *Enquirer* May 12 and 15, 1863; *Richmond Daily Dispatch* May 12, 1863; Robert Garlick Hill Kean, diary entries May 6 and 11, 1863, reprinted in Edward Younger, ed., *Inside the Confederate Government: The Diary of Robert Garlick Hill Kean* (New York: Oxford University Press, 1957), 57, 60; Varina Davis, *Jefferson Davis*, 382; "noisy demonstration," "human faces," and "greatest personal loss" quotes cited in Robertson, 755–756 and 758; *Richmond Examiner* May 11, 1863; *Richmond Whig* May 12, 1863; Richmond *Record* June 18, 1863; *Southern Churchman* May 22, 1863. For other interesting accounts of Richmonders' reactions to Jackson's death, see the *Southern Illustrated News* May 23 and August 29, 1863, and the (German language) *Richmonder Anzeiger* May 16, 1863. Faust, ibid, offers a vignette of the

funeral procession and the crowds, approximating 20,000, who filed past Jackson's coffin in the Confederate House of Representatives. See p. 155.

26   James B. Ramsey, "True Eminence Founded on Holiness: A Discourse Occasioned by the Death of Lieut. Gen. T. J. Jackson. Preached in the First Presbyterian Church of Lynchburg, May 24, 1863," 18–20, available at: http://docsouth.unc.edu/imls /ramsey1/ramsey.html. Apparently, Ramsey made a circuit throughout Virginia preaching the same sermon, which was also delivered in Lexington at Jackson's funeral on May 15.

27   *Savannah Republican* May 11, 1863, quoted in Royster, *Destructive War*, 228; Atlanta *Southern Confederacy* May 11 and 20, 1863; see also May 12 and 19 for repetition of the "successor to Jackson" theme; John Esten Cooke quoting contemporary newspaper editorial, possibly Richmond *Enquirer* or *Southern Illustrated News*, in Cooke, *Life of Stonewall Jackson* (1863 ed.), 8. The themes of Jackson as the spotless representative of Confederate character and as one who lived for a specific purpose reinforced each other in numerous editorials in the *Southern Confederacy*. See May 11, 19, 20, and 21 issues. Private citizens reiterated the morally pure character theme in letters and diaries throughout the South. Mary Jones of Georgia wrote her husband, "The death of our pious, brave, and noble General Stonewall Jackson is a great blow to our cause! May God raise up friends and helpers to our bleeding country!" Mary Jones to Charles C. Jones Jr., May 19, 1863, reprinted in Robert Manson Myers, ed., *The Children of Pride: A True Story of Georgia and the Civil War* (New Haven, Conn.: Yale University Press, 1972), 1063. See also Royster, 226–227.

28   *Charleston Courier* May 12 and 15, 1863, editorial from the 12th quoted in Royster, 221; *Charleston Mercury* quoted in Mackowski and White, *The Last Days of Stonewall Jackson*; Raleigh, N.C., *Spirit of the Age*, May 18, 1863; Raleigh *Semi-Weekly Standard* May 12, 1863. Also see the Salem, N.C., *People's Press* July 31, 1863, for an example of the ongoing lamentation associated with Jackson's death well into the summer of 1863 and Carolinian attempts to place him properly in collective national memory.

29   *Montgomery Daily Mail* May 13, 1863; *Montgomery Weekly Advertiser* May 20, 1863; *Mobile Advertiser and Register* May 17, 1863; *Jacksonville (Ala.) Republican* May 16, 1863; Mrs. Thomas J. Semmes quoted in A. Wilson Greene, *Whatever You Resolve to Be*, 118.

30   Dallas, *Herald* June 3, 1863; Richmond *Daily Dispatch* citing Knoxville *Register*, May 15, 1863; *Chattanooga Daily Rebel*, May 13, 1863. For another Texas paper expressing noticeable sadness over Jackson's demise, see the Houston *Tri-Weekly Telegraph* May 27, 1863.

31   *Memphis Daily Appeal*, May 11, 1863; *Montgomery Weekly Advertiser*, op. cit.; *Montgomery Daily Mail* op. cit.

32   Raleigh *Semi-Weekly Standard*, May 19, 1863. Regardless of location, several issues of the newspapers surveyed made invidious comparisons between Jackson and Van Dorn, with the latter portrayed as an immoral philanderer (albeit a good general) and the former, unsurprisingly, as an exemplar of Christian values and an even better general. Van Dorn was reportedly shot at his Spring Hill, Tennessee, headquarters

by a jealous husband who claimed that the general had carried on an affair with his wife. Regarding Jackson's value to Lee, the Army of Northern Virginia, and the Confederate people, Gary W. Gallagher notes, "His exploits helped convey an aura of success to the Army of Northern Virginia that lasted until very near the end of the war. That aura bolstered Confederate civilian morale when only bad news emanated from every other theater of the conflict. In this sense, Jackson's influence on Confederate fortunes reverberated well beyond the specific battlefields on which he fought and continued past his death." Gary W. Gallagher, *Lee and His Generals in War and Memory*, 108–109.

33   *London Times* May 26, 1863; *London Post* May 26, 1863; *London Telegraph* May 27, 1863; Judah P. Benjamin to A. Dudley Mann May 15, 1863, and Mann to Benjamin May 28, 1863, both reprinted in *O.R.*, series 2, vol. 3, 769–784. Also see the *London Herald* May 27, 1863 for another editorial eulogizing Jackson and comparing him to the "bragging imbeciles in the field" leading Union armies. A July 2, 1863, letter from Confederate envoy James Mason in London to Benjamin confirmed that the British public remained interested in eulogizing Jackson, including a "committee of gentlemen" committed to raising GBP 1500.00 for a statue of the dead general. See *O.R.*, series 2, vol. 3, 824–827.

34   *Washington Daily National Intelligencer* May 16, 1863; Washington *Daily Morning Chronicle*, May 13, 1863; Abraham Lincoln to John W. Forney, May 13, 1863, reprinted in Roy P. Basler et al., eds., *The Collected Works of Abraham Lincoln*, 9 vols. (New Brunswick, N.J.: Rutgers University Press, 1953), vol. 6, 214; *New York Herald* May 14, 1863; Henry Ward Beecher and Chaplain Alonzo Quint quoted in Rable, "Stonewall Jackson: the Christian Soldier," 190–191; Wesley Brainerd, journal entry May 7, 1864, cited in Mackowski and White, *The Last Days of Stonewall Jackson*, 70–71; Grant and Mary Chandler exchange reprinted in same, 76; Oliver O. Howard, "The XI Corps at Chancellorsville," in Johnson and Buel, eds., *Battles and Leaders of the Civil War*, vol. 3, 202.

35   Elizabeth Preston Allan, *A March Past* (Richmond, Va.: Dietz Press, 1938), 152.

SIX

1   Allan, "Memoranda of Conversations with General Robert E. Lee," February 19, 1870, reprinted in Gallagher, ed., *Lee the Soldier*, 16–17. Information about the objects in and layout of Lee's office, located on the first floor of what would later become known at Lee Chapel, Washington and Lee University, drawn from personal visits and photographs available at https://www.wlu.edu/lee-chapel-and-museum /photography.

2   Donald W. Gunter and the *Dictionary of Virginia Biography* (Richmond: Library of Virginia, 2006), "Allan, William" entry in *Encyclopedia Virginia*, available at https://www.encyclopediavirginia.org/Allan_William_1837-1889#start_entry. The best narrative of Lee's post–Civil War years remains Charles Bracelen Flood, *Lee: The Last Years* (New York: Houghton Mifflin, 1981).

3   Lee's quoted remarks recorded in Allan, "Memoranda of Conversations," February 19, 1870; see "Memoranda" April 15, 1868 for supplemental remarks on his theater-strategic reasons for the Pennsylvania Campaign. Also see Lee to James A. Seddon, May 10, 1863, and Lee to Jefferson Davis, May 11, 1863, reprinted in Dowdey and Manarin, *Wartime Papers of Robert E. Lee*, 482–484, for the general's reasoning about moving his army northward at that particular juncture in the war. There are countless secondary sources that chronicle Lee's motivations for embarking on what would become the Gettysburg Campaign. Among the best recent publications are Scott Bowden and Bill Ward, *Last Chance for Victory: Robert E. Lee and the Gettysburg Campaign* (Cambridge, Mass.: Da Capo Press, 2001), 29–35; Donald Stoker, *The Grand Design*, 277–281; and Allen Guelzo, *Gettysburg: The Last Invasion*, 19–20, 33. One of the ablest summaries of Lee's arguments and the responses of the Davis administration may be found in Steven E. Woodworth, *Lee and Davis at War*, 241–245. Woodworth maintains that Davis halfheartedly supported Lee's theater strategy, hedging too many bets at once and not giving Lee the full numerical support he requested (such as his failure to move Beauregard north and demand the release of Lee's "missing brigades," jealously retained by D. H. Hill in North Carolina). Lee, for his part, "modestly understat[ed] what he hoped to accomplish, along with his manipulating of the president by telling him only what he wanted to hear." (p. 242) There are some slight variances between what Lee told the Richmond authorities in May and June 1863 and what he told Allan and other interviewers after the war but the major points, outlined here, remained the same.

4   Robert E. Lee-Cassius Lee conversation recounted in Robert E. Lee Jr., *Recollections and Letters of General Robert E. Lee*, 415–416; Allen Guelzo, *Gettysburg: The Last Invasion*, 219; William Preston Johnston, "General Robert E. Lee, Memoranda of Conversation, May 7, 1868," reprinted in Gallagher, ed., *Lee the Soldier*, 29; Lee-White exchange recorded in Freeman, *Robert E. Lee*, vol. 3, 161. Freeman notes that Lee's statement about Jackson was originally published in Henry M. Field, *Bright Skies and Dark Shadows* (New York: Charles Scribner's Sons, 1890), 303–304, and was subsequently embellished by later writers into more flowery language. Freeman also commenced the third volume of *Robert E. Lee* with a chapter entitled "The 'Might-Have-Beens' of Chancellorsville." In this chapter, which is a sort of preamble to the volume, he makes a case for Lee's failure to insist on bringing up Longstreet and his two divisions from Suffolk in time as the greatest lost opportunity.

5   William J. Seymour, diary entry, July 1–2, 1863, reprinted in Terry L. Jones, ed., *The Civil War Memoirs of Captain William J. Seymour: Reminiscences of a Louisiana Tiger* (Baton Rouge: Louisiana State University Press, 1991), 72; Colonel David Zable, 14th LA, quoted in Terry Jones, *Lee's Tigers: The Louisiana Infantry in the Army of Northern Virginia* (Baton Rouge: Louisiana State University Press, 1987), 169; John O. Casler, *Four Years in the Stonewall Brigade*, 153–154; J. A. Strikeleather to mother, published in Raleigh, N.C., *Semi-Weekly Standard* August 4, 1863, quoted in Gallagher, *Lee and His Generals in War and Memory*, 163; John B. Gordon, *Reminiscences of the Civil War* (New York: Charles Scribner's Sons, 1903), 154–155; Douglas, *I Rode*

With Stonewall, 247. Peter Carmichael entitled a scholarly essay with Pendleton's alleged quote exploring how Lost Cause apologists such as Jubal Early and Henry Kyd Douglas used Jackson's absence at Gettysburg as a springboard for invidious comparative analyses of Ewell's battlefield performance, in particular. Their goal was the exoneration of Lee from any wrongdoing in the Pennsylvania Campaign. See Peter S. Carmichael, "Oh, For the Presence and Inspiration of Old Jack: A Lost Cause Plea for Stonewall Jackson at Gettysburg," *Civil War History* 41, no. 2 (June 1995): 161–167.

6   Freeman believed strongly that the reorganization of the army had much to do with how the Confederates fought in Pennsylvania, entitling the second chapter in volume three of *Robert E. Lee*, "The Reorganization That Explains Gettysburg." Despite chronicling *what* happened in the reorganization in painstaking detail, Freeman only devotes the final paragraph of the chapter to *how* the reorganization likely affected the army, Lee, and rebel fortunes in the ensuing campaign, writing in ominous generalizations.

7   The idea of thinking about historical time as a "stream" in which the character of early events directly influences later ones, precluding others all together, and in which certain branches (or rivulets) are created that lead to different outcomes, is currently a major emphasis of professional military education. It provides much room for thinking about the role of human agency and/or chance in moments of contingency, when key decisions were made or unexpected events intruded that promulgated long-term (sometimes strategic) consequences. The leading work on this subject remains Richard E. Neustadt and Ernest R. May, *Thinking in Time: The Uses of History for Decision Makers* (New York: The Free Press, 1988), especially the preface and chapters 13 and 14.

8   Longstreet, *From Manassas to Appomattox*, 327; John B. Jones, diary entry May 6, 1863, reprinted in Miers, ed., *A Rebel War Clerk's Diary*; Archer Jones, *Civil War Command and Strategy: The Process of Victory and Defeat* (New York: The Free Press, 1992), 122–125; Connelly and Jones, *The Politics of Command*, 123–127; Wert, *General James Longstreet*, 239–241.

9   Longstreet to Johnston, October 5, 1862, James Longstreet Papers, Duke University Special Collections; Longstreet to Wigfall, February 4, 1863, quoted in Glatthaar, *General Lee's Army*, 347; Glatthaar, ibid., 353–354. Again, it was not uncommon for generals north and south to ignore the chain of command, but in the Army of Northern Virginia this behavior was rare. Glatthaar notes that a factor mitigating against the politicization of generals in the Virginia army was Davis's respect for Lee, which ensured the commanding general was left to make most of his own personnel decisions and recommendations. But Longstreet sought—and received— such political patronage independently, as did John B. Hood later, who successfully befriended Davis with an eye toward independent command (which he received, to the detriment of Confederate fortunes). Jackson's careful and well-considered correspondence with politicians stands in noticeable contrast to Longstreet's more overt and ambitious examples.

10 Wert, *General James Longstreet*, 242–243; Longstreet, *From Manassas to Appomattox*, 331. In an earlier postwar published account, Longstreet's description of the three-day meeting was even more self-serving. In "Lee's Invasion of Pennsylvania," a chapter in the famous *Battles and Leaders of the Civil War*, vol. 3, 246, Longstreet claimed he "found [Lee's] mind made up not to allow any of his troops to go west. I then accepted his proposition to make a campaign in Pennsylvania, provided it should be offensive in strategy but defensive in tactics." Longstreet, as Lee's junior in rank, was in no position to "accept" anything, but was duty-bound to follow orders without question once the commanding general made a decision. Edwin Coddington, in his magisterial *The Gettysburg Campaign: A Study in Command* (New York: Charles Scribner's Sons, 1984), 10–11, diminished Longstreet's initial strategic disagreement with Lee as well as his self-edifying verbiage in various postwar accounts, arguing that Lee and Longstreet were in agreement about the theater strategy.

11 Longstreet to Wigfall, May 13, 1863, partially reprinted in Wert, ibid, 244. Freeman was among the first scholars to question Longstreet's overall veracity in his postwar memoirs, followed by, among others, Connelly and Jones, Gallagher, Wert, and, most pointedly, Robert K. Krick in "'If Longstreet . . . Says So, it is Most Likely Not True': James Longstreet and the Second Day at Gettysburg," in Krick, *The Smoothbore Volley that Doomed the Confederacy*, 63–64, 72–73. William Garrett Piston, *Lee's Tarnished Lieutenant: James Longstreet and His Place in Southern History* (Athens: University of Georgia Press, 1987), takes a generally positive view of Longstreet's Confederate career, defending his actions in the Gettysburg Campaign and elsewhere, but questions the truthfulness of many of his postwar historical writings. Most earlier postwar publications by Longstreet matched the tenor and argument of his later memoirs, such as his aforementioned entry in *Battles and Leaders*; an article in the Philadelphia *Weekly Times* November 3, 1877; and his essay, "Lee in Pennsylvania," in A. K. McClure, ed., *The Annals of the War, Written by Leading Participants North and South* (Philadelphia: The Times Publishing Company, 1879), 414–417.

12 Lee to Seddon, May 10, 1863, telegraphic dispatch with Davis endorsement; Lee to Seddon, May 10, 1863, both in *O.R.*, Series 1, vol. 25, part 2, 790. Lee's comments on the climate as a factor against dispatching troops from his army to the West should not be viewed as a weak excuse, but rather as a statement of commonly held assumptions among both the Union and Confederate high commands throughout the Civil War. Richard M. McMurry makes a strong case for this in "Marse Robert and the Fevers: A Note on the General Strategist and on Medical Ideas as a Factor in Civil War Decision Making," *Civil War History* 35, No. 3 (Fall 1989), reprinted in John T. Hubbell, ed., *Conflict and Command*, 255–265.

13 Charles Marshall, cited in Maurice, ed., *An Aide-de-Camp of Lee*, 170; see Allen Guelzo, *Gettysburg: The Last Invasion*, 21, for Lee's reliance on Longstreet on the eve of the campaign. Longstreet wrote a curious letter to his uncle Augustus B. Longstreet on July 24, 1863 that boldly proclaimed his dissatisfaction with Confederate tactical and operational conduct in the Pennsylvania Campaign but also elicited a strong loyalty to Lee, willingness to follow his orders, and, unlike postwar writings,

a desire to accept some blame for the failure: "The battle was not made as I would have made it. My idea was to throw ourselves between the enemy and Washington, select a strong position, and force the enemy to attack us." Victory would have most certainly ensued, he continued, "had we drawn the enemy into attack upon our carefully chosen position in its rear." But "General Lee chose the plans adopted; and he is the person appointed to choose and to order. I consider it a part of my duty to express my views to the commanding general. If he approves and adopts them, it is well; if he does not, it is my duty to adopt his views, and to execute his orders as faithfully as if they were my own . . . yet I am much inclined to accept the present condition as for the best. I hope and trust that it is so . . . As we failed, I must take my share of the responsibility. In fact, I would prefer that all the blame should rest upon me. As General Lee is our commander, he should have the support and influence we can give him. If the blame, if there is any, can be shifted from him to me, I shall help him and our cause by taking it . . . The truth will be known in time, and I leave that to show much of the responsibility of Gettysburg rests on my shoulders." Letter reprinted in McClure, ed., *The Annals of the War*, 414–415.

14   Allan, "Memoranda," April 15, 1868, reprinted in Gallagher, ed., *Lee the Soldier*, 14–15; William Swinton, *Campaigns of the Army of the Potomac: A Critical History of Operations in Virginia, Maryland, and Pennsylvania, from the Commencement to the Close of the War, 1861–1865* (1866; revised ed., New York: Charles Scribner's Sons, 1882), 340–341; Longstreet to Lafayette McLaws, July 25, 1873, Folder 19, Lafayette McLaws Papers, UNC; *O.R.*, Series 1, vol. 27, part 2, 318.

15   It is not the intent of this book, nor of this paragraph, to wade deeply into the postwar Lee-Longstreet controversy. That ground has been amply plowed by numerous historians over the years and the finer points of the debate are well-known. Piston's book, op. cit., is probably the best book-length analysis of the controversy to date, although it favors Longstreet. Gary W. Gallagher, "'If the Enemy is There, We Must Attack Him': Lee and the Second Day at Gettysburg," in Gary W. Gallagher, ed., *The Second Day at Gettysburg: Essays on Confederate and Union Leadership* (Kent, Ohio: Kent State University Press, 1993), 1–32 offers a concise, eminently readable overview, as does William L. Richter, "'The Road to Hell is Paved With Good Intentions': James Longstreet in War and Peace," in Lawrence Lee Hewitt and Thomas E. Schott, eds., *Lee and His Generals*, 203–227. A decidedly anti-Longstreet interpretation, albeit well-supported with primary source evidence, is Krick's essay, "'If Longstreet . . . Says So, it is Most Likely Not True,'" op. cit. Krick makes an interesting comparison at the end of his essay between Jackson's flank attack at Chancellorsville and Longstreet's assault on the Union left on July 2 at Gettysburg. "When he ostentatiously announced to all listeners, then and later, that Lee's bad plan must be followed," Krick asserts, Longstreet was delineating as starkly as any critic ever could the chasm that separated his attitude from that of Stonewall Jackson." (pp. 75–76) Of course, there is no way to know if a hypothetical Jackson who had survived the amputation of his left arm would be fit for active campaigning so soon after the operation.

16   Bowden and Ward, *Last Chance for Victory*, 185–209, and Gary W. Gallagher, "Confederate Corps Leadership on the First Day at Gettysburg: A. P. Hill and Richard S. Ewell in a Difficult Debut," in Gallagher, ed., *The First Day at Gettysburg: Essays on Confederate and Union Leadership* (Kent, Ohio: Kent State University Press, 1992), 30–56, both provide cogent, comprehensive analyses of Ewell's, Hill's, and Lee's generalship on July 1, 1863, as well as contemporary accounts documenting the dissatisfaction of officers and soldiers with Hill's and Ewell's actions. Bowden and Ward find more fault with Ewell and Hill than does Gallagher. Also see Carmichael, "Oh, For the Presence and Inspiration of Old Jack," op. cit., and Harry W. Pfanz, "'Old Jack' Is Not Here," in Gabor S. Boritt, ed., *The Gettysburg Nobody Knows* (New York: Oxford University Press, 1997), 63–64 and 67–74 for analyses of eyewitnesses', Confederate veterans', and early historians' accounts. Pfanz, in this essay as well as in his monumental *Gettysburg: The First Day* (Chapel Hill: University of North Carolina Press, 2001), finds only minor faults with Ewell's decision-making and offers a more favorable appraisal than, for instance, E. P. Alexander, Freeman, Bowden and Ward, and others. Wert, in *A Glorious Army*, 243–246 and Guelzo, *Gettysburg*, 214–221 also fault Ewell but slightly and argue that the final decision not to attack the hills lay with Lee.

17   Lee to Davis, May 20, 1863, *O.R.*, series 1, vol. 25, part 2, 810. The hypothetical arguments presented here are offered with an eye toward explaining the criticality of Jackson's death as the primary motive for Ewell's and Hill's promotions. These arguments, in turn, are based on a careful consideration of the professional and personal relationship Lee and Jackson had forged, as explained in earlier chapters.

18   Lee to Davis, ibid.; Lee to Stuart, ibid., 820–821; Thomas, *Robert E. Lee*, 289–290; Robertson, *General A. P. Hill*, 192–193; Pryor, *Reading the Man*, 332–334; Freeman, *Lee's Lieutenants*, vol. 2, 694–697; Pfanz, *Richard S. Ewell: A Soldier's Life*, 273–274, 276; Guelzo, *Gettysburg*, 22–23; Charlie "MF" to wife, May 15, 1863, cited in Glatthaar, *General Lee's Army*, 341. Pryor quotes Lee describing the ideal general as "attentive, industrious & brave;" "prompt, quick and bold"; and "cheerful under all circumstances." (p. 332) These qualities could be easily ascribed to the dead Jackson, although there is no evidence Lee was thinking of him when he supposedly made these remarks.

19   Pfanz, 276–277; Hotchkiss diary entry, May 29, 1863, reprinted in McDonald, *Make Me a Map of the Valley*, 146; Hotchkiss to wife, May 31, 1863, Hotchkiss Papers, Family Correspondence 1863, Box 9, Reel 5, LOC.

20   Pfanz, ibid.; Marietta Minnigerode Andrews, *Scraps of Paper* (New York: E.P. Dutton & Co., 1929), 110–112; John Hennessy, "Belvoir Today—the Yerby Place and Stonewall Jackson," available at https://npsfrsp.wordpress.com/2010/06/17/belvoir-today-the-yerby-place-and-stonewall-jackson/. Today Belvoir is only a ruin in the woods on private property, but as Hennessy states, "the site of Belvoir is a magnificent place."

21   Freeman, ibid., 699–701, 705–713; Coddington, *The Gettysburg Campaign*, 12–16; Wert, *A Glorious Army*, 214–216; Bowden and Ward, *Last Chance for Victory*, 44–45.

As it turned out, Jenkins delivered a good performance considering the heavy burdens placed on his command by the absence of Stuart and his three best brigades. Robertson and Jones lingered too long in their roles as guards of the Blue Ridge mountain passes, and Imboden left Ewell's flank and ventured into Maryland just days before contact with the Federals at Gettysburg. He performed better during the Confederate retreat.

22 Sandie Pendleton to mother, May 24, 1863, William Nelson Pendleton Papers, UNC; Wert, ibid., 217; Bowden and Ward, ibid., 44, 46; Lee to Hood, May 21, 1863, reprinted in *Wartime Papers*, 490.

23 Very few scholars have specifically analyzed the loss of Confederate general officers before Gettysburg. See Alan T. Nolan, "General Lee," in Gallagher, ed., *Lee the Soldier*, 246, and especially his citation of Robert K. Krick's assessment. More general indictments of Lee's generalship creating irreplaceable casualties include Grady McWhiney and Perry D. Jamieson, *Attack and Die: Civil War Military Tactics and the Southern Heritage* (Tuscaloosa: University of Alabama Press, 1982), especially the introduction and chapter 1; George A. Bruce, "Lee and the Strategy of the Civil War," in Gallagher, ed., *Lee the Soldier*; Thomas L. Connelly, *The Marble Man*; and J.F.C. Fuller, *Grant and Lee: A Study in Personality and Generalship* (1933; reprint, Bloomington: Indiana University Press, 1957). Davis to Joseph Davis, May 7, 1863, reprinted in Crist and others, eds., *The Papers of Jefferson Davis*, vol. 9, 166–167. See Clausewitz, *On War*, especially Book 1, Chapter 3, "The Genius for War" on the qualities of successful military leaders and how they can mitigate the army's challenges. Available at: https://www.clausewitz.com/readings/OnWar1873/BK1ch03 .html#a. Lee on post-Chancellorsville despondency quoted in Carmichael, "Lee's Search for the Battle of Annihilation," 14.

24 A crisp historical summary of the role of and theory of timing in war may be found in Phillip S. Meilinger, "Time in War," *Joint Force Quarterly* 87 (October 2017), 93–100; Neustadt and May, *Thinking in Time*, 246, 251, 254–255, also comment on time and timing as they relate to historical event sequencing and time streams; Jed Hotchkiss diary entry, May 31, 1863, reprinted in McDonald, ed., *Make Me a Map of the Valley*, 146; Lee to Mary Lee, May 31, 1863, and June 3, 1863, reprinted in *Wartime Papers*, 498–500; Davis, *Crucible of Command*, 313.

25 This theory of new leader acclimation is based on fourteen years of personal experience teaching field grade and senior military leaders. For historical studies that comment on the topic, see Eliot Cohen, *Supreme Command: Soldiers, Statesmen, and Leadership in Wartime* (New York: The Free Press, 2002), especially chapter 2 on Abraham Lincoln, and John Keegan, *The Mask of Command* (New York: Viking, 1987), 213–214, 219–221; Bowden and Ward, *Last Chance for Victory*, 41; Coddington, *The Gettysburg Campaign*, 86–89; Robert Stiles, *Four Years Under Marse Robert* (New York: The Neale Publishing Company, 1904), 192; William S. White, war "diary," quoted in Pfanz, *Richard S. Ewell*, 290.

26 Taylor, *Four Years with General Lee*, 95–96; Charles P. Roland, "The Generalship of Robert E. Lee," 43; Joseph T. Glatthaar, *Partners in Command*, 27–28, 31–32;

Joseph G. Dawson III, "JEB Stuart, R. E. Lee, and Confederate Defeat at Gettysburg," in Hewitt and Schott, eds., *Lee and His Generals*, 117–120; Justus Scheibert, *Seven Months in the Rebel States During the North American War, 1863* (Tuscaloosa, Ala.: Confederate Publishing Company, 1958), 75n. Lee's reference to God in this statement once again confirms his providential belief in the Lord's omniscience and the general's acceptance of His will in deciding military outcomes, in which human agency plays a secondary and subservient role.

27 Lee to Charles Carter Lee, May 24, 1863, op. cit.; J. William Jones, "A Visit to Beauvoir—President Davis and Family at Home," *Southern Historical Society Papers* 14 (1886), 451.

28 Glatthaar, *General Lee's Army*, 338–339; Terry L. Jones, ed., *Campbell Brown's Civil War: With Ewell and the Army of Northern Virginia* (Baton Rouge: Louisiana State University Press, 2001), 188–190; Pfanz, *Richard S. Ewell*, 279; Allan, in "Memoranda of Conversations with Lee," February 15, 1868, wrote "Gen. Lee had feared the old habit of E. when he assigned him to the Corps, but had hoped he had gotten over it, & talked long and earnestly with him when he assumed command." The "old habit" referred to was "his quick alterations from elation to despondency his want of decision &c." This is the only evidence indicating that Lee attempted to mentor and counsel his new corps commanders. Campbell Brown quoted in Carmichael, "Lee's Search for the Battle of Annihilation," 15–16.

29 Pfanz, ibid., 308–310; Smith, "With Stonewall Jackson," 56–57; Coddington, *The Gettysburg Campaign*, 315–317; Gallagher, "Confederate Corps Leadership on the First Day," 174–180. The debate about Ewell and Hill using their discretion on the late afternoon and early evening of July 1 rages to this day in countless publications, some of them already cited in this chapter. Scholars still disagree about the intelligence available to Ewell and the capabilities of his brigades to undertake an attack on Cemetery Hill, as well as the failure to occupy Culp's Hill. They also still debate the veracity of the few, extant sources on Hill's decision-making that late afternoon, and how Lee's nearby presence may or may not have stifled him. Coddington and Gallagher both concisely and effectively engage these persistent questions, as does Donald Pfanz in his biography of Ewell and Harry Pfanz in his book on the First Day. Gallagher offers a pithy recapitulation of the overriding issue at hand on July 1 near the end of his essay: "At Gettysburg, Lee applied the same loose rein with Ewell and Hill that had worked so well with Longstreet and Jackson during the previous year. He as yet had no concrete evidence that his new lieutenants would prove unequal to the task of directing a corps (that evidence would accumulate rapidly from July 1863 onward), and it made sense to give them latitude." (p. 180–181)

30 A good, basic definition of branches and sequels on a theoretical level may be found in the current Department of Defense Joint Publication 3-0. This definition might apply just as well to the Civil War era as it does to modern warfare: "Branches and sequels directly relate to the concept of phasing [in military operations]. Their proper use can add flexibility to a campaign or major operation plan. Branches are

options built into the basic plan. They may include shifting priorities, changing unit organization and command relationships, or changing the very nature of the joint operation itself. Branches add flexibility to plans by anticipating situations that could alter the basic plan. Sequels are subsequent operations based on the possible outcomes of the current operation; victory, defeat, or stalemate. At the campaign level, phases can be viewed as sequels to the basic plan." (JP 3-0, Chapter III, para 5i) Available at: http://www.au.af.mil/au/awc/awcgate/opart/opart-jrm.htm.

31 *O.R.*, series 1, vol. 27, part 2, 321; Long, *Memoirs of Robert E. Lee*, 268–269; Taylor, *Four Years with General Lee*, 90–91; Stephen Sears, *Gettysburg* (New York: Houghton Mifflin, 2003), 501–502.

32 *O.R.*, ibid.; Sears, ibid., 501; Allan, "Memoranda," April 15, 1868, reprinted in Gallagher, ed., *Lee the Soldier*, 13–14. As previously mentioned, in the same conversation Allan noted that Lee said, "Stuart's failure to carry out his instructions *forced the battle of Gettysburg* [original emphasis]." (p. 14) That Lee would castigate Stuart twice in the same conversation about the same issue indicates the strength of his feeling about it.

33 Bowden and Ward, *Last Chance for Victory*, 103–114, offers a highly convincing analysis of the two Lee orders to Stuart, specifically investigating words and phrases from the perspectives of Lee and Stuart and in the context of geographical features and the positions of the two armies' corps. The dispatches and writings of Longstreet and John S. Mosby (who actually scouted the intended route through the Union army corps that Stuart subsequently found blocked) are also considered, and the authors' maps of the various intended routes versus Stuart's historical route north clarify a great deal. Joseph G. Dawson, "Jeb Stuart, R. E. Lee, and Confederate Defeat at Gettysburg," 122–128, is also useful, as is Emory Thomas, "Eggs, Aldie, Sheperdstown, and J.E.B. Stuart," in Boritt, ed., *The Gettysburg Nobody Knows*, 101–121. Excellent overall studies of Stuart and the Confederate cavalry in the campaign may be found in Warren C. Robinson, *Jeb Stuart and the Confederate Defeat at Gettysburg* (Lincoln: University of Nebraska Press, 2007) and Eric J. Wittenberg and J. David Petruzzi, *Plenty of Blame to Go Around: Jeb Stuart's Controversial Ride to Gettysburg* (El Dorado Hills, Calif.: Savas Beatie, 2006). Freeman, Coddington, Sears, Guelzo, and Wert, in his *Cavalryman of the Lost Cause*, also examine the overall subject of Stuart's role in the campaign. As in the Lee-Longstreet debate earlier, it is not the intention here to delve too deeply into the Stuart-Lee controversy, but it is important to know the major parameters of Lee's intent and Stuart's execution in order to theorize the possible significance of Jackson's loss in Stuart's performance.

34 Brandy Station is covered in many histories of the greater Gettysburg Campaign, but two books specifically on the battle commend themselves: Eric J. Wittenberg, *The Battle of Brandy Station: North America's Largest Cavalry Battle* (Charleston, S.C.: The History Press, 2010), which was superseded by Eric J. Wittenberg and Daniel T. Davis, *Out Flew the Sabres: The Battle of Brandy Station, June 9, 1863* (El Dorado Hills, Calif.: Savas Beatie, 2016). See Bowden and Ward, 94–95; Dawson,

ibid., 124; and Emory Thomas, ibid., 102–103, for Stuart's reactions to the battle and a discussion of his probable exhaustion level. Longstreet quoted in Dawson 128; Taylor, *Four Years with General Lee*, 281.

35   William Woods Hassler, *Colonel John Pelham: Lee's Boy Artillerist* (Chapel Hill: University of North Carolina Press, 1995), 167.

36   The assertions made in this paragraph are, of course, unproveable, but they are based on the historical realities of the Jackson-Stuart relationship as it actually existed and the probabilities, based on familiarity with both leaders' previous records and predilections, of what would have most likely occurred. It is in no way an assured pronouncement of what would have certainly happened, an error made by Bevin Alexander in *Lost Victories* (p. 130). Clausewitzian chance, fog, and friction, the actions of the Union army, and weather phenomena all would have also influenced outcomes.

37   Walter Taylor to wife, March 4, 1864, reprinted in R. Lockwood Tower and John S. Belmont, eds., *Lee's Adjutant: The Wartime Letters of Colonel Walter Herron Taylor, 1862–1865* (Columbia: University of South Carolina Press, 1995), 131. Taylor wrote several times about the absence of Jackson in the months after his death. In this same letter, he laments "those distressingly long conferences between those high in authority which too often result in the utter discomfiture of all our plans, because they but consume time and give the enemy an opportunity to get out of the way. I don't like to witness these long talks." In a possible reference to the Last Meeting at Chancellorsville, he added, "It was not so in Jackson's time." Then on July 10, 1864, writing of Jubal Early's early success in the Valley, he declared, "Oh! if Jackson was only where he is!" That Lee's adjutant would so openly pine for the dead Stonewall is another indication of the impact he had upon Lee, his staff, the army, and the Confederacy. Charles Minor Blackford, another staff officer who had so carefully described Lee and Jackson in the fall of 1862, agreed. He wrote his wife on January 7, 1864, from Longstreet's headquarters in East Tennessee, lamenting Longstreet's poor management of his second independent command. "Lee and Jackson are the only men who seem to rise to the height of our occasion." (Charles Minor Blackford III, ed., *Letters from Lee's Army*, 231.)

INDEX